CONCEPTS OF ORDER AND GENTILITY IN WALES 1540-1640

Bardic Imagery and Interpretations

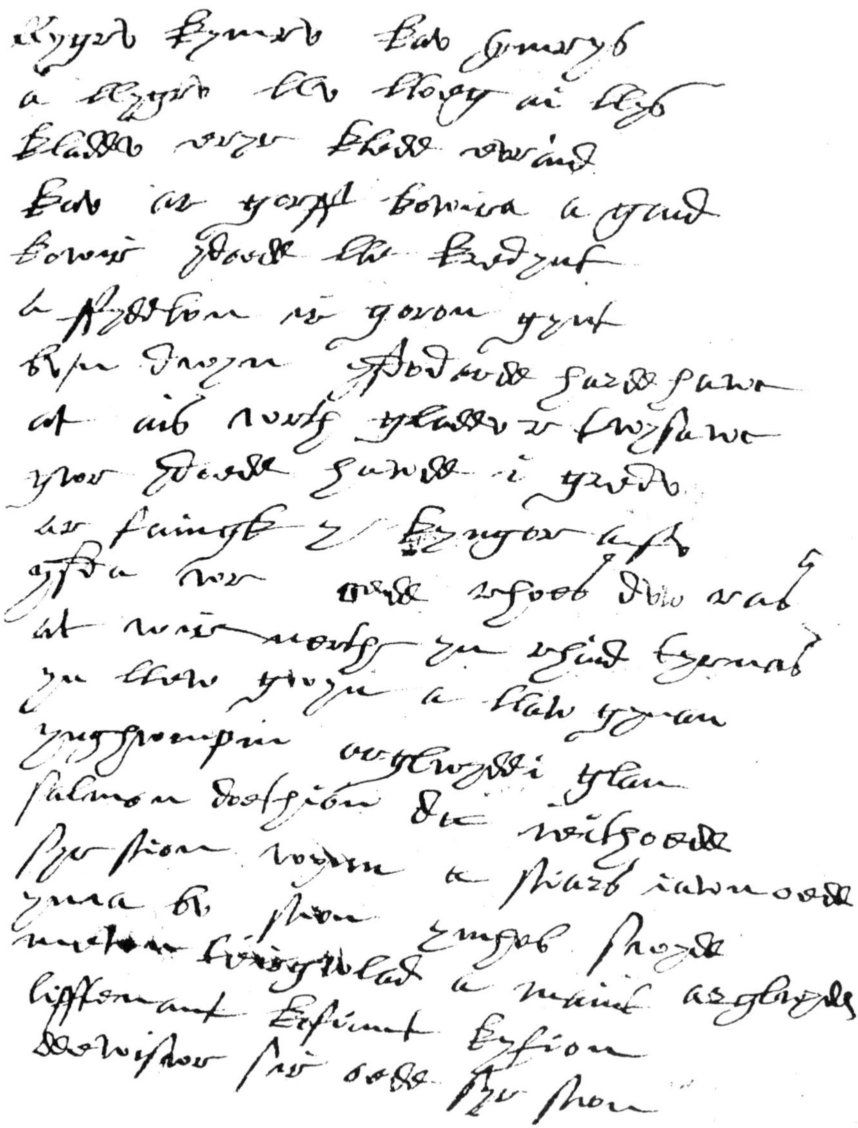

An extract from Rhisiart Cynwal's elegy for Sir John Wynn of Gwydir (UCNW Mostyn MS. 8, 10v). It is written in Huw Machno's hand and describes the patron's qualities as a public figure in north Wales in the late sixteenth and early seventeenth centuries.

(By courtesy of Lord Mostyn and UCNW, Bangor)

Concepts of Order and Gentility in Wales 1540-1640

J. GWYNFOR JONES

Gomer Press
1992

First Impression—1992

ISBN 0 86383 772 7

This volume is published with the support of the Welsh Arts Council.

Printed by J. D. Lewis and Sons Ltd., Gomer Press, Llandysul, Dyfed

Cyflwynaf y gyfrol hon i'r Athro Emeritws Gwynedd O. Pierce, cyn-Bennaeth Adran Hanes Cymru yng Ngholeg y Brifysgol, Caerdydd, gan ddiolch iddo am ei gyfeillgarwch, ei garedigrwydd a'i gyfraniad i ysgolheictod yng Nghymru.

gwnaf dy lywodraethwyr yn wŷr heddychol
a'th feistradoedd yn gyfiawn . . .
Ni chlywir mwyach am drais yn dy wlad,
nac am ddistryw na dinistr o fewn dy derfynau . . .
Bydd dy bobl i gyd yn gyfiawn,
yn gwreiddio yn y tir am byth.
(Eseia 60 17-18,21)

Acknowledgements

I am indebted to several for their assistance and support during the period when this volume was in preparation. I wish to thank Mr Bryn Jones of the South Glamorgan County Library, Cardiff, and Mr Peter Keelan, Keeper of the Salisbury Library, University of Wales College of Cardiff, as well as the staffs at Glamorgan Archives, the National Library of Wales, Aberystwyth and the library of University College of North Wales, Bangor—especially the Archivist Mr Tomos Roberts—for many kindnesses. Mr Brian Ll. James read the proofs thoroughly and I thank him most sincerely for this painstaking task which he undertook so willingly and conscientiously. The support and guidance given by Emeritus Professor Glanmor Williams has been a source of inspiration to me over many years and I wish to thank him for the interest he has taken in the work and for the valuable suggestions he made at the earlier stages of writing. Mr Arwyn Lloyd Hughes, Archivist at the Welsh Folk Museum, St Ffagan, allowed me to use freely on a long-term basis his own personal copy of his dissertation on the Merioneth patrons and I appreciate his kindness and forbearance. It is appropriate also that I record my thanks to Emeritus Professor D. J. Bowen—a leading authority on the Welsh bardic order—for his published scholarship in this field of study which I found to be indispensable. Likewise, I am greatly indebted to his strong band of postgraduate researchers from whose dissertations on individual poets and regional patronage I have benefited immensely as the bibliography to this volume amply testifies. Lord Mostyn willingly gave me permission to reproduce an extract from Bangor (Mostyn) MS. 8 for illustrative purposes and I wish to thank him for his kindness. Mr Philip Riden, Lecturer in the Extra-Mural department at University College, Cardiff, assisted me in compiling the index, Dr Dyfed Elis-Gruffydd of Gomer Press, Llandysul, in his polite manner gave me expert guidance at each stage of publication, and the printing staff produced the volume with their customary courtesy, patience and efficiency. I also wish to thank my wife for her unfailing support and interest which made the completion of this work possible.

Contents

Preface

This volume is designed to examine some of the fundamental features of the doctrine of gentility in Wales in the period spanning the Acts of Union (1536-43) and the decades preceding the outbreak of Civil War in 1642. It presents new aspects on an old theme since concepts of order and deference have not seriously occupied literary historians in Wales to the same extent as have the structure, form and technique of poetic composition. While it must be conceded that the study of bardic tradition in the 'century of crisis', in relation to the protracted course of the 'anglicization' of the Welsh gentry has, in the past, been given sufficient attention, the fundamental ideas which governed the poetic craft have largely been taken for granted and discussed invariably against a background of cultural decay and changing social habits. Bardic artistry, nevertheless, when applied to the active career of the Welsh gentleman *par excellence* in his regional community, assumed an entirely different and more positive rôle. It was functional, and fulfilled a specific purpose as well as exposing the manner in which *uchelwriaeth* was defined and applied to practicalities in the social structure of Tudor and early Stuart Wales.

The principal source for this study is the inordinately large *corpus* of poetry composed in strict metres (cynghanedd) by the Poets of the Uchelwyr, a group of professional practitioners of formal verse who, in the age following the Tudor settlement of Wales, continued to maintain rigid medieval conventions associated with the bardic schools. The most prominent among them, in the middle and later decades of the sixteenth century, were disciples of Gruffudd Hiraethog, widely acclaimed as the most renowned Chief of Song and herald poet of his day. He was a lexicographer, a collector of Welsh proverbs in manuscript and also a prolific poet whose impact on the bardic order was remarkable. His wide cultural interests, which were highly applauded by William Salesbury, Edmwnd Prys and others, made him the most typical Renaissance poet in Wales of his generation. Among the poets who were taught by him were Wiliam Llŷn, Wiliam Cynwal and Siôn Tudur whose compositions contain a rich variety of poetic attitudes to social conventions and developments. This study aims to examine also the works of a large group of declaimers, some more conspicuous than others, which represented the crucial period in the declining fortunes of the Welsh bardic order down to the outbreak of the Civil War in 1642—poets such as Morus Dwyfech, Siôn Mawddwy, Lewys Morgannwg, Llywelyn Siôn, Dafydd Benwyn, Siôn Brwynog, Simwnt Fychan, Siôn Phylip, Huw Machno and Siôn Cain. Most of the bardic evidence in that period came from north and west Wales, chiefly because of the survival of strong native cultural forces in those regions compared to the more anglicized areas of the borders and south-east Wales. In spite of increasing extraneous influences it was in those conservative regions that the traditional Welsh *uchelwr* is portrayed most richly and abundantly in strict-metre composition. Nevertheless, the central problems which occupied the poets were as acute in Glamorgan and Gwent as they were in Gwynedd but the intrusive elements which sadly affected their livelihood had made themselves felt more potently in those parts of Wales historically subject to foreign invasion and settlement.

In a century when significant legal,political and economic changes had occurred these poets, most of whom stemmed from gentle stock, as percipient observers of social trends projected a view of a deferential society as the centrepiece of community life. The qualities which created the ideal gentleman emerged as the microcosmic equivalent of those virtues which constituted the organic unity of the national sovereign state or polity. The highest was justice which manifested, not only public integrity but also, more significantly, an inherent code of discipline and order, the essence of which was rank and status.

In this period, when the Welsh gentry families were attaining the ascendancy in politics and legal administration, the bardic fraternity clung firmly to an ultra-conservative brand of *uchelwriaeth*. They also focused, at an increasing level, on more advanced images of gentility which were gradually gaining favour in Welsh polite society. In a formative era, when Renaissance ideals were gradually flowing from the continent into English intellectual and social circles, the political order in Wales was significantly assuming a different perspective; it was to have lasting ramifications for society at large leading, among the upper ranks, to a gradual recession in the practice of benign hospitality. The positive evidence for such a remarkable phenomenon, however,is more blurred than historians generally are prepared to accept. Social reorientation there certainly was, but it was not pre-ordained or pre-conceived but rather subtle, sporadic and often ill-defined. Regardless of social reorganization the poets delivered their encomiums with gusto, their odes incorporating the substance of the *gravità riposata* of the perfect gentleman.This constituted the prime feature of the deferential society, and the poets, in a peculiarly Welsh fashion, displayed the attributes of the native *brëyr* or free clansman in his new rôle and environment in the emergent national sovereign state.

The moral code of the Welsh Tudor gentleman exposed three vital components. In the first instance,the strict-metre and highly formal *awdl* and *cywydd* were engaged to project the essence of gentility. The poetry of Wiliam Llŷn, in particular, provides a worthy example of the manner in which a resourceful master of the poetic craft portrays the innate qualities of individual *uchelwyr* renowned for their *grazia*. The *bonheddig cynhwynawl* (innate gentility) assumes pride of place in this revered and well-tested tradition. The *uchelwyr* emerged as functional guardians appointed by the state, and were considered to be the barometers of public morality in their respective communities. In character and demeanour they matched the Aristotelian concept of the ruler recognized by his integrity and munificence. Each individual composition, in fact, overtly displayed the corporate entity of the Renaissance gentleman. His *mores*—customs and habits—were identified with strict legitimacy and the *vita activa*, a courtly culture spawned by Neoplatonism. He exemplified true justice exercised for the common good. Welsh *uchelwriaeth* stemmed from ancient *virtù* designed to develop and perpetuate the human capacity to reflect and propagate goodness. Such concepts exposed the merits of the individual as well as the basic skills of poetic declaimers who portrayed those qualities universally acclaimed in the character of the public governor. It was the symbolic correlation between these inbuilt resources and forces that earned for the Tudor *uchelwr* his esteemed station in refined society. He was, in fact, the heir to a more cultivated, more dynamic and urbane type of gentility fostered by the Renaissance spirit and applied to the peculiar features of the Welsh social scene.

Furthermore,the virtues of gentility were reflected primarily in the gentleman's public demeanour, private morals and rôle in law and administration. The purpose of bardic eulogy was to identify the humanistic ideal of the polished and gracious man of affairs destined to serve higher authority in the state with skilful elegance.In this context, the portrait of idealized leaders stemmed from the medieval image of the *gwrda* or *arglwydd* as laid down in the bardic grammar, and it was this concept, adapted to meet the needs of a Tudor version of gentility, which emerges in poetic composition. The ethos of the Tudor and early Stuart periods is artistically woven into the fabric of bardic eulogy and highlighted in the various strands of public activity.The structure of the landed *élite* in that age rested principally on hierarchy, patriarchalism and patrilineal descent. By exercising *virtù* the *uchelwr*, in his native region (gwlad; tiriogaeth), preserved the organism of the state or *imperium*.

Gentility often eludes strict definition. Like the cosmic order it was composed of many parts, each sufficiently varied so that it creates the image of the classical governing *élite* applied to the new humanism. Social commentators had endeavoured, in the spirit of the age, to establish the philosophical foundations of courtly etiquette which behoved the perfect *homme du monde*. On the continent the pattern of the *cortegiano*, which had emerged since Petrarch in the fourteenth century, achieved its *locus classicus* in Castiglione's masterpiece. The emphasis on *virtù* and the accomplishments of education introduced new and exciting elements. The courtier, in Castiglione's view, resembled Plato's guardians, the able, ambitious and loyal protectors of the state.Sir Thomas Elyot introduced into England a sound but less spectacular version, but the courtly tradition still prevailed, and eventually found its way into Welsh panegyrics with significant repercussions. *Gentilitas* (derived from *gens*), the well-born refined in manners, assumed a Welsh image in prose and poetry and represented a subtle fusion of two traditions in the concept of gentility. Regardless of receding patronage and declining standards it is essentially in this context that the work of Wiliam Cynwal,Siôn Tudur, Siôn Phylip; Huw Machno and their colleagues need to be interpreted and revalued.

Certain features of the alleged 'anglicization' of Wales in the sixteenth and early seventeenth centuries defy clarity and definition.It is undeniable that the force of the Tudor settlement did gradually change attitudes, undermine confidences and create a yawning gulf between the *uchelwr* and the native community. Furthermore,the bardic order doubtless was often retrogressive and inert when challenged by newer modes of literary expression, and disillusioned by changing gentry habits and attitudes. Nevertheless, this traditional craft, particularly in the late sixteenth century, consisted of features which betrayed well-defined Renaissance influences. It can, therefore, be suggested that the surviving bardic eulogy in this period, aided by social and intellectual influences in rural mansion houses, the towns and the regional institutions of government, did attempt to portray the Welsh *uchelwr* in broader, more exciting and meaningful dimensions.

Abbreviations

BBCS	*Bulletin of the Board of Celtic Studies*
BGHM	D.L.James, 'Bywyd a Gwaith Huw Machno' (unpublished M.A. dissertation, University of Wales, 1960)
BWLl	J.C.Morrice (ed.), *Barddoniaeth Wiliam Llŷn* (Bangor, 1908)
CCM	J.Fisher (ed.), *The Cefn Coch MSS* (Bangor, 1899)
CLl	J.Jones (ed.), *Cynfeirdd Lleyn, 1500-1800* (Pwllheli,1905)
CSB	R.M.Kerr, 'Cywyddau Siôn Brwynog' (unpublished M.A. dissertation, University of Wales, 1960)
CSPFD	*Calendar of State Papers Foreign and Domestic, Henry VIII, 1509-1547* (London, 1862-1932)
DWB	J.E.Lloyd and R.T.Jenkins (ed.), *Dictionary of Welsh Biography down to 1940* (London, 1959)
EDDN	J.Rhys, 'Bywyd a Gwaith Edward Dafydd a Dafydd o'r Nant, a Hanes Dirywiad y Gyfundrefn Farddol ym Morgannwg' (unpublished M.A. dissertation, University of Wales, 1953)
EP	J.W.Roberts, 'Edmwnd Prys: ei Fywyd a Chasgliad o'i Weithiau' (unpublished M.A. dissertation, University of Wales, 1938)
GCH	Glanmor Williams (ed.), *Glamorgan County History, IV, Early Modern Glamorgan* (Cardiff, 1974)
GEUGH	T.T.Jones, 'Testun Beirniadol o Farddoniaeth Edward Urien a Gruffudd Hafren, gyda Rhagymadrodd, Nodiadau a Geirfa' (unpublished M.A. dissertation, University of Wales, 1966)
GGH	D.J.Bowen, *Gwaith Gruffudd Hiraethog* (Cardiff, 1990)
GMD	O. Owens, 'Gweithiau Barddonol Morus Dwyfech' (unpublished M.A. dissertation, University of Wales, 1944)
GOG	D.R.Saer, 'Testun Beirniadol o Waith Owain Gwynedd ynghyd â Rhagymadrodd, Nodiadau a Geirfa' (unpublished M.A. dissertation, University of Wales, 1961)
GSM	J.D.Davies, 'Astudiaeth Destunol o Waith Siôn Mawddwy' (unpublished M.A. dissertation, University of Wales, 1965)

GST	E.Roberts (ed.), *Gwaith Siôn Tudur* (Bangor, 1978)
GWC(1)	R.L.Jones, 'Astudiaeth Destunol o Awdlau, Cywyddau ac Englynion gan Wiliam Cynwal' (unpublished M.A. dissertation, University of Wales, 1969)
GWC (Mostyn III)	S.Rh. Williams, 'Testun Beirniadol o Gasgliad Llawysgrif Mostyn III o Waith Wiliam Cynwal ynghyd â Rhagymadrodd, Nodiadau a Geirfa' (unpublished M.A. dissertation, University of Wales, 1965)
HGF	John Wynn, *The History of the Gwydir Family,* ed. J.Ballinger (Cardiff,1927)
LlC	*Llên Cymru*
MDLlS	T.O.Phillips, 'Bywyd a Gwaith Meurig Dafydd (Llanisien) a Llywelyn Siôn (Llangewydd)' (unpublished M.A. dissertation, University of Wales, 1937)
NBM	G.Davies, *Noddwyr Beirdd ym Meirion* (Dolgellau, 1974)
NBSD	R.L.Roberts, 'Noddwyr y Beirdd yn Sir Drefaldwyn' (unpublished M.A. dissertation, University of Wales, 1980)
NBSF	A.Ll. Hughes, 'Noddwyr y Beirdd yn Sir Feirionnydd. Casgliad o'r Cerddi i Deuluoedd Corsygedol,Dolau-gwyn, Llwyn, Nannau, Y Rug, Rhiwedog, Rhiw-goch, Rhiwlas ac Ynysmaengwyn' (unpublished M.A. dissertation, University of Wales, 1969)
NBSG	E.R.Ll. Davies, 'Noddwyr y Beirdd yn Sir Gaerfyrddin' (unpublished M.A. dissertation, University of Wales, 1977)
NLW	National Library of Wales
NLWJ	*National Library of Wales Journal*
SLl	J.Rowlands, 'A Critical Edition and Study of the Welsh Poems written in Praise of the Salusburies of Lleweni' (unpublished D.Phil. dissertation, University of Oxford, 1967-8)
Trans. Cymmr.	*Transactions of the Honourable Society of Cymmrodorion*
UCNW	University College of North Wales.
WHR	*Welsh History Review*

Introduction

George Owen, the celebrated Pembrokeshire historian, extravagantly applauded the Tudor achievement in Wales. Writing in the last decade of the sixteenth century he described the country in an advanced state of prosperity compared to the situation that had existed in the earlier years of the century: 'No country in England so flourished in one hundred years as Wales hath done sithence the government of Henry VIII to this time', he maintained,' in so much that if our fathers were now living they would think it some strange country inhabited with a foreign nation, so altered is the country and countrymen, the people changed in heart within and the land altered in hue without, from evil to good and from bad to better.'[1] His views of Wales were doubtless exaggerated and represented the opinions of a man who had himself benefited immensely from the Tudor settlement of Wales. His effusive responses to the 'blessings' bestowed by Tudor administration and the impact of law and sound government on the Welsh people had created a feeling of complete satisfaction with a monarchy which, in view of its Welsh ancestral connections, had commanded the full support of the people of Wales.

The most prominent element in Welsh society in the fifteenth century was the class of *brehyrion, gwyrda,* or *uchelwyr* (freemen who had inherited their patrimonies), the descendants of individual free clansmen (*priodorion*) who, in the wake of social and economic change and reorganization, emerged gradually and triumphantly to become the leaders in Wales and the Marches in the Tudor age.[2] Their reputation as natural governors in native communities had been well established in the later centuries of the Middle Ages, and bardic eulogy had developed by that time to become a significant symbol of their status and public function in their regions. They had also become noteworthy military leaders in the royal campaigns overseas and in the wars and rebellions at home.[3] Significant individuals, such as Owain Glyndŵr, Sir William Herbert and Jasper Tudor, had been regarded, in an age of mounting social and political tension, as potential 'sons of prophecy' destined to lead the nation from bondage and oppression. They had contributed extensively as leaders of men into battle, as had others of their rank in Wales and the Marches in the wars of England at home and abroad, and their military careers had shown how highly respected they were in official circles.

The Glyndŵr rebellion had left a legacy of bitterness and hatred, and the dark and obscure vaticinatory tradition in poetic composition heightened a sense of vengeance and expectation that a military type national leader would emerge from among existing gentry, armed with the qualities of an Arthur or a Cadwaladr, to emancipate the Welsh nation.[4] Regardless of the emotional desires, economic reverses, social upheaval, the impact of wars, plague and rebellion as well as the continual dynastic strife and disorder—all of which affected the *uchelwyr* in diverse ways—the fifteenth century saw the emergence of a virile and tenacious group of landed proprietors. It was they who successfully manipulated English methods of landholding as well as regional and local offices in the Principality and the Marches. They were men who were consciously aware of their power and authority based on reputable ancestry and innate skills as well as the esteem which they enjoyed among their people.[5] Their services to the Crown—both Lancastrian and Yorkist—and community were far-reaching and continuous and were diligently recounted in an impressively large *corpus* of bardic compositions. They were also conscious of their obligations to a community structure and to the organic unity of a broader political entity which depended largely on dedicated leadership and protection. The observance of these duties, whether in law and administration or on the field of battle, enhanced the prestige of the *uchelwyr* and made them, by the accession of Henry Tudor to the throne of England in 1485, men of power and renown in their localities, eager to serve the Crown, preserve their own landed and official interests and govern firmly within their spheres of jurisdiction. Regardless of the degree of turbulence which occurred in the political world of Wales and the Marches in the course of the fifteenth century it is a well-established fact that the consequences of the Glyndŵr rebellion were not as devastating in all parts of Wales and among all ranks in society as has in the past been generally assumed, that the gentry were not permanently oppressed by the anti-Welsh laws of Henry IV throughout the fifteenth century and that their activities were not all aimed at prolonging disruption and instability in the countryside.[6] The economic *malaise*, so often alluded to when referring to the condition of Wales following the

Glyndŵr rebellion, was not as totally devastating in the growth-period of the gentry families as older generations of historians thought since a large number of them were confidently on the up-grade and had made ample use of whatever assets they possessed—lands, kindred affinities, military leadership, patronage and offices—to fortify their cherished rights and privileges in public affairs.

The gradual recovery which occurred in Welsh society during the course of the fifteenth century—which varied in extent in different parts of the country—symbolized the permanent arrival of a group of *uchelwyr* who were busily occupied in building their *plastai*, strengthening local and regional political contacts, consolidating their landed properties and maintaining firm bonds of affinity with kindred and, in political and administrative affairs, with the Crown and Marcher lords. In the absence of many of these lords from their possessions individual members of this tenacious group assumed positions as deputies and obtained experience of government at grass-root level.[7] In such a context Guto'r Glyn, that most exuberant of professional poets in the mid-fifteenth century, hailed William Gruffudd of Penrhyn, the direct descendant of the illustrious Ednyfed Fychan, the founder of the Tudors of Penmynydd, Anglesey and Llywelyn ab Iorwerth's chief counsellor, as a powerful and dignified *uchelwr* in the ascendant in the middle years of the Lancastrian and Yorkist era.

> Ector o frig y tir fry
> Yw dy henw wedi hynny . . .
> Dy blas ni welwyd heb wledd,
> Dy blaid llonaid holl Wynedd.[8]

According to the poet, this patron's position in a society dominated by faction and internecine jealousies between kindreds, stood supreme and unchallenged. 'You are Hector', he remarked, 'elevated in your land; your mansion is never without its feast and your supporters occupy the whole of Gwynedd.' This grandiose presentation to the scion of a rising family in north Wales doubtless confirmed him further in his rôle as regional protector and custodian. By means of his status, persistent ambition, natural skills and tenacity this prime *uchelwr* was in the process of establishing for himself and his family a status high above others, including his own kinsmen who stemmed, by descent, from the same social order. This was achieved principally by his defiant attitude towards his kindred and others who dared thwart his designs, oppose him or disregard his authority. His lineage and other personal qualities, in the poet's estimation, had enhanced his reputation and that of his family at Penrhyn, as the prime leaders in the public life of Gwynedd.

About fifty years later, in the early sixteenth century, Tudur Aled, arguably the greatest of the later medieval Welsh poets whose achievements in verse represented the bardic order at its most proficient, addressed Dafydd ap Maredudd ap Hywel, a gentleman from Llanycil in Merioneth, in splendid terms. His portrayal of this modest but staunch supporter of the Tudors is striking in that he combines in his ode references to the qualities of military prowess, moral rectitude and beneficent housekeeping as well as to his firm protective powers in his native community. He was the 'very soul' or essence of gentility among his men and possessed courage, tenacity and strength of purpose in all his dealings.

> Un gwayw ydych yn geidwad,
> Un gwalch glew yn gwylio'ch gwlad.[9]

The *uchelwr*, in this context, is described formally in purely military terms as a 'protecting spear' and a 'strong hawk' concerned primarily with defending the community in his charge. The couplet succinctly exposes the grandeur and awesome appearance of a person who was regarded as a protector of his province primarily because of his virtuous descent. The attributes of the *uchelwr*, as they appealed to the poets, became gradually associated with recognizably permanent features which characterized the native nobleman during the following century and a half. One major medieval feature passed on to subsequent generations was the rôle of the *perchentywr* (housekeeper), described admirably by Dafydd Nanmor in one of his famous poems to Rhys ap Maredudd of Tywyn in south Cardiganshire.[10] The *tai cyfrifol* (responsible houses) emerged as residences which symbolized power, public responsibility and cultural unity where the itinerant professional poets were genuinely and lavishly sustained. In these houses the bonds of *uchelwriaeth* (nobility)were combined to form a coherent and organic communal entity based essentially on a common heritage. This concept was amply manifested in *awdlau* and *cywyddau*—the chief poetic metres—which expressed in formal terms the qualities of gentle status and authority. The essence was aptly captured again by Dafydd Nanmor in the following couplet from a memorable *cywydd* for Rhys ap Rhydderch ap Rhys of Tywyn.

A dyfo o bendefig
A dyf o'i wraidd hyd ei frig.[11]

'He who springs from noble stock:, the poet explained, 'grows from its roots to its apex' in the sense that he is a confident, enterprising and resourceful gentleman. It is during the course of the fifteenth century that such a concept became recognizably a convention to which all poets adhered since they could identify it more positively with persons and families associated with particular regions. It was this social phenomenon that was inherited and developed further in the compositions of the sixteenth-century professional poets who endeavoured to emulate their predecessors, emphasizing the essential qualities of family pedigree, public function and private virtue. Gradually there emerged the image of the *gwladwr* (statesman) superimposing his authority, in the King's name, over his region and symbolizing the magnitude of the Tudor monarchy as well as the Renaissance ideal of the perfect gentleman.[12] The Welsh nobility, who were essentially a different breed from the English aristocracy, were given their most extravagant publicity in the odes of the poets who considered the order of *uchelwyr*, as well as their *plastai*, as the mainstays of civilized life and public duty. The rise of the gentry in Wales had established strong bonds of cultural kinship with the bardic fraternity since, in exchange for patronage, the *uchelwyr* enjoyed added prestige and publicity which enhanced their reputation and elevated them as patterns of excellence. This laudatory exercise served to entertain and remind patrons of the ways by which they could excel in their rôle as protectors of their communities.

Da'n ei wlad annwyl ydoedd
A da iawn yn ei dai oedd . . .
Llaw gadarn yw'n holl geidwad
Llew biau'r tir lle bu'r tad.[13]

These lines by Wilam Llŷn to Edward Almor of Almor and Pantiocyn, Denbighshire, relate the close affinity which had developed between the poet and the *uchelwr* through the hospitality that was granted to the bardic fraternity during the periodic visits of professional declaimers in the provinces of Wales. 'He was good and endeared in his locality', it was said, 'an exemplary person in his houses, a protector with a powerful hand and a lion who owns the land after his father.' The couplets uncover the strength of purpose and magnitude of such a patron's authority and influence.

* * *

What can be said of the bardic order itself in this age of transition? Its origins can be traced to the early medieval *bardd teulu* (family bard) resident in the royal courts of Wales, and his prime function was to praise the virtues of Welsh nobility of regal stock. The *Gogynfeirdd*, or Poets of the Princes, had developed advanced techniques in composition so that they might eulogize their Welsh rulers in the most grandiloquent and sophisticated manner.[14] This artistry had been refined in the bardic schools, about which more information becomes available from the mid-fourteenth century onwards. The patronage of the poets, in a critical period following the Edwardian conquest and settlement of Wales (1282-4), was gradually entrusted to the emerging *uchelwyr*, thus inaugurating a new and dynamic period in the development of the Welsh cultural tradition down to the seventeenth century. The Poets of the Nobility became the worthy custodians of the bardic conventions handed down from one generation of poets to another, and that body of social custom was jealously guarded and kept secret. The earliest known bardic grammar (Dwned) which contained the formal code of education which the poets required, is ascribed to Einion Offeiriad and was compiled c.1322-7 or possibly later. This compilation, according to Sir Thomas Wiliems of Trefriw, the famous lexicographer and genealogist, was dedicated to Sir Rhys ap Gruffudd of Cantref Mawr in Carmarthenshire, one of the most opulent *uchelwyr* of his day and a descendant of Ednyfed Fychan. He was a patron of poets, and Einion Offeiriad composed an *awdl* in his honour. His status and official functions demanded that he should be esteemed, in this context, as the highest in rank among the native gentry of his generation.[15]

The bardic traditions are exclusively associated with the emerging *uchelwr* class in the fourteenth century, the chief purpose of the elaborate strict-metre *awdl* and more concise *cywydd deuair hirion* being to entertain the nobility in their houses during the feasts of Christmas, Easter and Whitsuntide and on other special occasions, such as the elevation of a squire to public office or the celebration of a wedding feast (neithior).[16] The poets would itinerate and follow the customary *cwrs clera* (bardic itinerary). In their schools poets were instructed by a Chief of Song (Pencerdd) in the technical details relating to their expert knowledge and mastery of genealogy, heraldry and other aspects of bardic lore. They were required to learn the bardic grammar, which was a Welsh version of a formal Latin text designed to acquire basic skills in understanding fundamental intellectual disciplines. In Einion Offeiriad's version further information is given relating to the twenty-four feats or masteries, poetic metres and regulations concerning those considered to be worthy of eulogy and the attributes which should be accorded to them. Bardic learning was eventually recorded in writing and appeared in the manuscripts of Gwilym Tew and Gutun Owain in the fifteenth century and c.1570 in *Pum Llyfr Cerddwriaeth* by Simwnt Fychan, works which were formal renditions of a variety of aspects, originally transmitted orally, of the teaching imparted in the schools. The *eisteddfodau* or bardic assemblies that were periodically organized—the most famous of which were held at Carmarthen(1451) and Caerwys(1523 and 1567)—graded poets and revised bardic conventions and standards.[17] The grading of poets also occurred at wedding feasts, the highest position being granted to the Chief of Song. Many of the poets were themselves members of the *uchelwr* class and composed their odes without having to rely exclusively on the financial support of others. At the lower end of the bardic hierarchy stood the *clêr*, itinerant minstrels of inferior status who were often regarded as vagabonds. They did not compose poetry of the quality expected and sang chiefly on 'wasteful metres' ('ofer fesurau'), confining their verse to 'entreating, satirizing and defaming' ('ymbil a goganu a gwarthuso') individuals.

It is this tradition which survived into the sixteenth century and which continued to maintain a high standard of verse during the opening decades until the death of Tudur Aled in 1525. He was doubtless the chief exponent of the bardic craft at a time when patronage in Wales was at its most flourishing.[18] In the ensuing generations, especially following the Acts of Union (1536-43), the standards began gradually to decline although the tradition did reach a peak of excellence in the works of Gruffudd Hiraethog (*ob.*1564)—teacher and Chief of Song—and his disciples Wiliam Llŷn, Simwnt Fychan, Wiliam Cynwal and Siôn Tudur, all of whom graduated at the second Caerwys *eisteddfod* in 1567. Gruffudd Hiraethog was himself an influential figure in cultural spheres in Wales of his day; he was associated with William Salesbury, the famous Protestant humanist scholar, and attracted poets to practice the craft under his instruction. He was also appointed a deputy herald for Wales in the College of Arms and enjoyed a distinguished reputation as a herald-poet which enabled him to compile numerous pedigrees and arms preserved in manuscript.[19] It is the work of poets of his calibre which reflects the triumphs and shortcomings of surviving traditions in the latter half of the sixteenth century. It is their *awdlau* and *cywyddau* which reveal the aspirations and anguish of the bardic fraternity in its period of decline. It is in their compositions also that social and economic trends are given publicity in the manner in which they affected the eulogistic tradition in Wales. They composed in an unsettled age when strains and tensions were revealed in a social structure subject to change and reorganization. At a crucial moment in the survival of patronage it was envisaged by a handful of humanist scholars that far-reaching reforms were urgently needed to improve the standards of the literary tradition and to create a new school of amateur gentlemen poets. Their ideas, it was conceived, would form an essential part of an ambitious design to adapt the Welsh language as an acceptably fit vehicle of Renaissance thought and ideals. The change envisaged, however, did not materialize because the ancient traditions of the bardic schools had proved to be too resilient and conservative to allow for any significant structural reform in this critical period. The traditions had been the subject of vigorous comment and criticism by humanist scholars, such as Siôn Dafydd Rhys who, in his preface to *Cymraecaeve Linguae Institutiones Rudimenta* (1592), urgently exhorted the professional poets to modify their canons. Scholars endeavoured to enliven and improve the quality of poetry as a medium by initiating a code of reform which recommended four major modifications. Firstly, the poets should cease to flatter their patrons for personal gain and be prepared to satirize as well as acclaim. Secondly, they should widen their horizons by acquiring knowledge of the liberal arts and incorporating that knowledge in their verse. Thirdly, they should improve the quality of their craft by refining their rhetorical techniques, and lastly they should cast aside the traditionally mystical features of the bardic craft by making their conventions more accessible to others[20]. Three years later, in his preface to *Deffynniad Ffydd Eglwys Loegr,* Maurice Kyffin, who had been instructed by Wiliam Llŷn, harshly criticized the unlearned and unskilled practitioners and emphasized the futility of traditional bardic verse.

From the poets' point of view, however, the glory of the bardic convention lay chiefly in its ultra-conservatism; its long-established connections with the traditions derived from Taliesin, traditions that were best suited to an earlier heroic age less materialistic and more inclined to appreciate ideals of distinguished valour. It was in that very context also that the bardic order was doomed since it had precariously survived into an age of changing social habits and lifestyles. The most poignant observations on social trends and etiquette often appear in the elegant eulogies and elegies composed by the more skilful practitioners of their craft. Their analysis of *uchelwriaeth* and its most valued qualities throws into high relief the extent to which it had faded and lost its purport by the latter half of the sixteenth century in certain sections of Welsh community life where new ideas and modes of living were well advanced. Not all patrons, however, had become totally oblivious of their responsibilities to their dependants in this cultural context, even in the earlier decades of the seventeenth century. In 1618, for example, Siôn Phylip was able to applaud William Wynn of Glyn Cywarch, Talsarnau, one Merioneth patron of modest means, for defying the adverse economic conditions of his generation and maintaining a good house which he had rebuilt.

Da gennym, ein digoni,
Dy weled yn dy le di . . .
Gweriaist ti—oes gŵr sad ail?—
Gisteidiau ar gost adail.[21]

Siôn Phylip came from a remarkable family of Ardudwy poets in Merioneth who, between them, had experienced the painful transformation which occurred in the cultural life of the Welsh gentry. In his odes Siôn Phylip reflected the significant breaches which had weakened the traditional bardic order in the period between the Elizabethan age and the Civil Wars. In this poem the poet expresses his joy because a renowned patron had remained resident at his country seat. 'It is good for us, for our sustenance', he observed, 'to see you in your place where you do expend chests [of gold] on buildings.' He continued by enquiring whether there was, in reality, an equal in the country for lavish hospitality.

Numerous other examples indicate how well bardic conventions, which described *perchentyaeth* and virtuous living, had survived into the seventeenth century, albeit in trite and uninspired verse. The evidence, however, points overwhelmingly in the other direction towards a gloomy decline in patronage whereby a large group of poets was sustained composing verse on antiquated themes in a flattering manner and employing outmoded symbolism. The poetic craft had revealed clear signs of decline, and even the most noteworthy of late sixteenth-century practitioners found it almost impossible to avoid using uninspiring and repetitive images and interpolations. The most ebullient among them, nevertheless, clinging firmly to the best that eulogy could provide, lamented the decay, usually in worthy and memorable couplets;it was among the lesser grades of poets, who struggled to keep up appearances, that the degeneracy reached its lowest ebb.[22] By the end of the sixteenth century, at a time when free verse was gaining in popularity at the expense of the more conventional metres, poetic content and style became more pedestrian.

In the early seventeenth century the change in attitudes among an increasing number of Welsh gentry became more apparent, even among some prominent heads of families as well as less well-endowed younger sons. The *eisteddfod* at Caerwys in 1567 was not followed by any significant attempt to reform the bardic order;indeed, a petition submitted to the Council in the Marches by a number of leading north Wales gentry, requesting that another *eisteddfod* might be held in 1594, came to nothing.[23] It was a period of harsh economic conditions, and the danger remained that the status and professionalism of the poets might be undermined. The deep-felt effects of financial inflation and the consequent rise in prices sorely affected the efficiency and achievement of the poets, principally because an increasing number of prospective patrons had gradually withdrawn their support and hospitality.[24] In addition, the impact of growing social relations between a larger section of the *uchelwr* class and families and institutions elsewhere had significant and equally devastating consequences on the ability and inclinations of *uchelwyr* to discharge their traditional responsibilities. The gentry of the period had channelled much of their energies and resources into consolidating their relations, in an economic and social context, with their English neighbours and had failed to devote the attention needed to foster traditional modes of cultural life. They too, even in the remotest areas of Wales, wished to integrate themselves with their English counterparts over Offa's Dyke who became a source of wealth, reputation and prestige through marriage, landownership and other economic ties.

Although rigid constraints were placed upon the professional poets it was often the case that increased attempts were made to present a realistic portrait of the gentleman in his natural environment. It appeared as if the poets were prepared to break with convention where they considered it appropriate in order to expose aspects of life and activity which characterized particular individuals. This feature was not unknown among poets in previous generations but it seemed to suggest that they were becoming increasingly eager to depict the less elegant and more unpleasant aspects of *uchelwriaeth*. Regardless of their strict training they considered it essential, in a period of social readaptation, to identify less worthy traits usually by comparing the patron's exemplary character to the inadequacies of other unnamed men of status.

The rise of new families, the *nouveaux riches*, who participated actively in the economic life of urban and rural communities, added yet another significant dimension to the modification of the traditional social order. The more conservative elements among the *uchelwyr* resented the emergence of 'gent and upstarts of the first head', chiefly because they had exploited the situation to their own advantage, thus acquiring status and challenging the rôle traditionally reserved for well-established families.[25] It was the appearance of these new social factors which entailed the growth of new sources of economic prosperity, that inspired Edmwnd Prys, Edwart ap Raff, Siôn Tudur and other poets of their *milieu* to scorn the adventurous and covetous.

> Aeth y byd diffaith heb wedd
> Ar olwyn afreoledd;
> Bonedd a fwrian' benyd
> Ar bawb o wrengwyr y byd.[26]

Edmwnd Prys was clearly in a despondent mood, surveying the world about him, principally as an ardent churchman, and perceiving how wretchedly uncaring men in authority were of the welfare of the common people. 'The world is desolate and has lost its direction in the wheel of disorder', he maintained, 'and those of gentle stock exact a penalty from all the under-privileged.' 'The world has declined into bondage', the poet maintained further on an ominous note, 'and greed has created hardship and unease.' Such utterances highlight the grievances of the poets who, in this context, identified themselves with the lower orders subject to oppressive behaviour and extortion in less well-endowed communities. It is a world, Edmwnd Prys declared, deprived of learning and sympathy for the ancient bardic craft; there is no respect for its practitioners and they have lost their dignity. It is a world of misery, he continued, where the traditional leaders in Welsh society had forsaken their essential duties in their respective regions.

What, in fact, had accounted for such adverse social and cultural conditions? There is no doubt that the Tudor political settlement had left a deep imprint on the *uchelwyr* and had shaped their responses to the new and exciting challenge of a broader political community of which they now formed an essential part. Gradually, from the 1530s onwards, with the imposition of a common legal and administrative system in the Principality extended to cover the old Marcher lordships, the horizons of powerful gentry were extended.[27] They became *de jure* the rulers of specific areas of jurisdiction and, like their forbears, became involved increasingly in local government and administration. What they had accomplished *de facto* in those regions was now given the force of statute law, and gradually the territorial authority traditionally exerted over ancient provinces was narrowed to extend over the shire community. In addition to the creation of the courts of Great Sessions and the establishment of the Council in the Marches at Ludlow on a statutory basis as the chief executive organ of the central government supervising the public affairs of Wales, there was also imposed a common language in matters relating to law and administration.

The *uchelwyr* were constantly occupied with managing the affairs of Tudor government, principally in the courts of Quarter Sessions and other lower courts, as justices of the peace and sheriffs.[28] Those individuals representing more modest families and possessing the offices of escheator, bailiff and coroner, were also eulogized since, in their administrative capacities, they were identified with the concept of the all-embracing and all-powerful state as it emerged in Tudor England. George Owen exaggeratedly praised the Acts of Union in the most lavish manner. In less emotional terms Rhys Meurig of Y Cotrel, in Glamorgan, in 1578 expressed his adulation stating that 'this alteration of government is worthy of remembrance as well for the singular commodity the inhabitants of Wales receive thereby as the commonwealth universally'. Such views, however, although they reflected contemporary thought on the matter, were expressed at a time when these commentators were confidently enjoying the benefits of Tudor rule.[29]

The aims and long-term impact of the Acts of Union have doubtless been exaggerated. While they did introduce significant legal and administrative elements, which unified England and Wales, they also maintained the *status quo* in matters regarding the structure and organization of local government. Their full consequences, however, were hardly felt in their own day and age, but the so-called 'anglicizing' trends, which existed previously, were given further impetus, and the changing attitudes of the gentry to their distinctive rôle in the Welsh countryside did seriously affect cultural relations and affinities.[30] Nevertheless, with or without the Tudor settlement, social and economic forces in the late medieval and early modern periods doubtless would have had a significant influence on the lifestyle of the Welsh *uchelwyr*. As things were in the 1530s these forces were accelerated although the consequences were not as traumatic as historians in the past have reckoned. Far from establishing an entirely new environment based on radical policies the legislation rather heightened a feeling of Welsh consciousness stemming from ancient traditions, which the Crown, politically, had it in mind to exploit in the new territorially extended Principality. Furthermore, the Welsh gentry in the sixteenth century did not entirely abandon their Welsh interests or totally discard their rôle in preserving their cultural heritage. In fact, many of them contributed significantly to maintaining the surviving literary tradition by continuing to perform benevolent duties, grant hospitality and engage themselves in various cultural pursuits.[31]

The emergence of the Protestant faith and the creation of the sovereign state demanded that a new and dynamic concept of national solidarity should serve to combat the political threats of Counter-Reformation forces. Ideologically, concepts of ancient British history, in a secular and religious context—particularly those associated with the writings of Geoffrey of Monmouth—were revived to recreate a common bond of unity in the realm.[32] The Tudor settlement served to fortify that affinity and, in time, to ease the anxieties of Welsh humanist scholars who desired a revival of learning and antiquity in the vernacular. It is reasonable to suggest that the national cultural entity in Wales survived because of rather than despite the annexation with England. The poets, in fact, paid very little attention to the terms of the legislation in 1536-43, but they could not ignore its consequences. In their eulogies they appeared to support the spirit of the policies initiated by Thomas Cromwell and his advisers. Existing trends in public life adopted by the *uchelwyr* were encouraged in *awdlau* and *cywyddau moliant* alike. The forces of financial inflation and the periodic waves of bad harvests and plagues, to which the poets often referred despondently in their verse, were not, after all, the direct consequences of any Tudor legislation relating to Wales. They caused concern in Wales, as they did in other parts of the realm, but the backward economy and its impact on a conservative social structure did create further distress and hardship in the remoter shires of the Principality. The lack of a national focus and the scarcity of wealthy urban centres where economic and new cultural trends could be fostered constituted a major setback in any attempt to preserve Welsh cultural institutions and maintain the allegiance of traditional *uchelwyr* to their native heritage.[33] This is a fundamental factor in any understanding of the often arduous task faced by the professional poets while they grappled with the reality of the situation.

> Y brud oedd i brydyddion
> Yn wir sydd yn yr oes hon;
> Aethant lle'r haeddynt gynt ged
> Is gil yn gas eu gweled . . .
> Maent wŷr ifanc mewn trefi
> Yn gwatwar gwaith ein iaith ni.[34]

The opening couplets of this *cywydd* by Simwnt Fychan to Sir John Wynn of Gwydir ominously refer to the tragic impact on the bardic order of non-residence and gradual changes in attitudes towards the cultural heritage of Wales among an increasing band of young Welsh gentry . 'The prophecy relating to the poets', Simwnt Fychan states, 'can be applied appropriately to this age.' 'Whereas in the past', he continues, 'they were worthy of their honour, now they are derided, and young men in the towns scorn the products of our craft.' Together with an increasing number of similar references to declining values among the *uchelwyr* these lines emphasize the drastic effects of materialism and economic resurgence on a boyant and forward-looking Welsh gentry class.

The derision suffered by the poets, it is maintained, had extended into areas and communities which shunned Welsh cultural tradition. One essential element in social development in the sixteenth century was the attraction of urban centres in England, especially London, for the younger sons of the gentry. Since they were deprived of a full property inheritance many of them either married local heiresses and set up cadet families or drifted over the border to England and sought their fortunes elsewhere as professional soldiers or in trade, commerce, the church or the law. The degree of absenteeism, even among heirs to established estates, also increased in the course of the sixteenth and early seventeenth centuries, thus gradually depriving the Welsh countryside of cultural leadership. The references made by Humphrey Llwyd to the new-type *uchelwr* indicated how social transition was affecting the more conservative elements. 'Whereby it cometh to pass', he maintained, 'that, laying aside their old manners they, who before were wont to live most sparingly are now enriched and do imitate the Englishmen in diet . . . applying themselves rather to the service of noblemen.' 'Howbeit also, of late', he commented further, 'they have very commendably begun to inhabit towns . . . and . . . there is no man so poor but for some space he setteth forth his children to school, and such as profit in study sendeth them unto the universities where, for the most part, they enforce them to study the Civil Law.'[35] This section suggests a comparison with certain aspects illustrated in poetic material: the adoption of English manners and fashions, the growth of material prosperity, service in noble households (especially by younger sons), the establishment of town residences, the growth of education locally in grammar schools and at institutions of higher learning and the Inns of Court. All these factors signify the adoption of a much more dynamic and assertive lifestyle which, among other factors, drew the gentry more frequently away from their natural environment. This trend had become a problem in England as well where aspiring scions of local gentry houses made their way to the metropolis and the royal court. Complaints were voiced that whole regions were being deprived of effective leadership.[36] In Wales, another dimension was added, namely the threat which such an exodus posed to *iaith* and *treftadaeth*, the concept of the Welsh community based on a common language and heritage. Wiliam Llŷn, for example, expressed his heartfelt grief that his patron, Sir Ieuan Llwyd of Bodidris in Denbighshire, had resided at Chester and had denied his native Iâl of a moral leadership which had been lasting and beneficial to the native community over many generations.

Câr dithau llyn, carw doeth llwyd
I'th fyw, o gylch lle'th fagwyd . . .
Tyred i'th wlad naturiawl,
Treia hiraeth, mab maeth mawl.[37]

The poet urgently appeals to him to cultivate affection for the region where he was reared and sustained. 'Return to your natural country', he remarked, 'have longing for it, you fostered son of eulogy.' He was still considered to be a remarkable person who evidently had much to contribute, in all ways, to the common welfare of his community. His appeal to him to return to his land and locality is evocative and conveys a sense of urgency. The emphasis is again on the innate virtues of gentility manifested chiefly in the local *plasty*, the norm of civilized existence, the fount of power and prestige and the nerve-centre of the communal entity. By the early seventeenth century the concepts of gentility, so closely guarded in previous generations, had lost much of their meaning and thrust in poetic eulogy. The emergence of new social factors and the detachment of individual gentry from their traditional rôle seriously damaged the quality of the literary work.[38] The *plasty*, judging by the vast number of eulogies which extolled its praises, continued to fulfil its normal functions down to the Civil Wars in the 1640s and, among more modest families, after the restoration of the Stuart monarchy.[39] Nevertheless, Welsh cultural spheres by then had become less well-endowed and were characterized chiefly by a duality which obscured the prime purpose of eulogy. *Uchelwriaeth*, however, contained certain inherent properties which did not easily lend themselves to change: they were uniquely applied to the resident lord who functioned among his people. The ideals expounded by the old bardic grammar and, in an English context, the writings of Sir Thomas Elyot and others of his *milieu* were upheld by poets of the calibre of Gruffudd Hiraethog, Wiliam Llŷn, Siôn Tudur and Simwnt Fychan who represented the last generation of the truly great Welsh professional poets. The declining hospitality hit those sections of society which were wholly dependant on material support and maintenance. Waste, wantonness and self-indulgence, it was believed, had poisoned the traditional liberality and bounty associated with the Welsh countryside.

> Mae'r wlad heb geidwad a'i gwaeth,
> A phoen yn galw ei phennaeth;
> Gweddw yw'r swyddau yn gweiddi
> Am berchen, medden' i mi.[40]

'A region without its leader', Robert Ifans maintained in his ode for Robert Salusbury II of Rug during his sojourn in London, 'is desolate and deprived of order.' 'Merioneth', the poet maintains, 'calls out for a chieftain now that the illustrious patron is deceased.' 'Offices are abandoned', he continues, 'and there is a general outcry that they be filled.' The moral vacuum, in other words, had stifled true gentility in the shire. It is this critical yearning for moral protection against the forces of change, the need for an efficient resident leadership, the exercise of supervisory control by the governor and a fulfilment of public obligation which constituted, in the view of early seventeenth-century poets, the essence of *uchelwriaeth*.

It is the lack of initiative on the part of a new generation of landed proprietors, the social climbers who had become increasingly preoccupied with weightier matters in other spheres of activity, which led to the gloomy picture drawn by the poets in the years following the Stuart succession. The long and formal odes added no more, in terms of poetic skill and content, than had been offered by the panegyrics composed in honour of more dedicated patrons in earlier generations. In fact, the professional poets who endeavoured to maintain the traditional canons of eulogy in the first half of the seventeenth century did not possess the same skills as those demonstrated so expertly by their more auspicious predecessors. It was they who had enthusiastically set about their tasks of elevating the prestige of men who had benefited in material terms from the Acts of Union in the first and second generations. Poets such as Siôn Phylip and Rhisiart Cynwal, for example, were fully aware of adverse circumstances which impeded them from portraying their patrons in the glowing terms applied to those addressed by Siôn Brwynog and Wiliam Llŷn among others of their *milieu* in the mid-sixteenth century.

The growth and consolidation of the Tudor social and administrative settlement had forced upon the gentry new pressures and strains in addition to granting them and their successors the benefits of equal citizenship. The tensions of financial inflation and continual demands in local and regional government, together with the pressing need to keep up appearances and create favourable impressions in places of power and influence had a serious impact upon those professional declaimers who sought to benefit by enjoying more lavish and sustained patronage. The negative consequences of Tudor social advancement in Wales for the bardic order, in addition to the need for drastic reform in the entire system, proved ultimately to be disastrous. The void in patronage, so often alluded to in poetic output in the latter decades of this period, symbolized a marked degree of recession which seriously undermined the manner in which the bardic order expounded the nature and concept of *uchelwriaeth*. The Welsh gentry in the early seventeenth century interpreted cultural affinities and obligations in a different manner. Their reaction to communal responsibilities and loyalties and the changing emphasis on the nature and extent of leadership rendered bardic eulogy almost obsolete. Pure formality and convention were no longer relevant in an age of transformation; indeed, more advanced concepts of *uchelwriaeth* had superseded those values which had been accepted in the past as the central features of bardism. The failure of the Welsh exponents of literary tradition to keep pace with social developments which stemmed initially from Tudor policies signified the demise of the old order in the cultural life of Wales.

NOTES

[1]George Owen, III, *The Description of Penbrokshire*, ed. Henry Owen, (London, 1906), p.56. For a detailed study of the bardic order and its relations with the Welsh *uchelwyr* in the seventeenth century see Gwyn Thomas, 'A Study of the Changes in the Tradition of Welsh Poetry in North Wales in the Seventeenth Century' (unpublished D.Phil. dissertation, Oxford, 1964-5); idem, 'Golwg ar Gyfundrefn y Beirdd yn yr Ail Ganrif ar Bymtheg', *Bardos: Penodau ar y Traddodiad Barddol Cymreig a Cheltaidd*, ed. R. Geraint Gruffydd (Cardiff, 1982), pp.76-94. See also D. J. Bowen, *Gruffudd Hiraethog a'i Oes* (Cardiff, 1958); idem, 'Agweddau ar Ganu'r Unfed Ganrif ar Bymtheg', *Trans. Cymmr.*, 1969 (Pt.ii), 284-335; J. Gwynfor Jones, 'Concepts of Order and Gentility' in *Class, Community and Culture in Tudor Wales*, ed. J. Gwynfor Jones (Cardiff, 1989), IV, pp.121-57.

[2]Glanmor Williams, *Recovery, Reorientation and Reformation; Wales c.1415-1642*, (Oxford/Cardiff, 1987), pp.78-89, 95-106; T. Jones Pierce, *Medieval Welsh Society*, ed. J. Beverley Smith (Cardiff, 1972), pp.229-50; idem, 'Landlords in Wales' in J. Thirsk (ed.), *The Agrarian History of England and Wales, IV, 1500-1640* (Cambridge, 1967), pp.357-81; D. Jenkins, *Cyfraith Hywel* (Llandysul, 1976), pp.19-21.

[3]A. D. Carr, 'Welshmen and the Hundred Years War', WHR, IV, 1968, 21-46; idem, 'The Historical Background, 1282-1550' in A. O. H. Jarman and G. R. Hughes (ed.), *A Guide to Welsh Literature* (Swansea, 1979), II, pp.11-33; R. R. Davies, *Conquest, Coexistence and Change; Wales 1063-1415* (Oxford/Cardiff, 1987), pp.391-459; idem, 'Owain Glyndŵr and the Welsh Squirearchy', *Trans. Cymmr.*, 1968 (Pt.ii), 150-69.

[4]W. Garmon Jones, 'Welsh Nationalism and Henry Tudor', *Trans. Cymmr.*, 1917-18, 1-59; R. Wallis Evans, 'Prophetic Poetry', in *Guide to Welsh Literature,* pp.278-97; E. I. Rowlands, 'Dilid y Broffwydoliaeth', *Trivium*, II, 37-46; Glanmor Williams, 'Prophecy, Poetry and Politics in Medieval and Tudor Wales' in *Religion, Language and Nationality in Wales* (Cardiff, 1979), pp.71-86.

[5]Glyn Roberts, 'Wales and England; Antipathy and Sympathy, 1284-1485', in *Aspects of Welsh History* ed. J. Gwynn Williams (Cardiff, 1969), pp.295-318; W. Ogwen Wiliams, 'The

Social Order in Tudor Wales', *Trans. Cymmr.*, 1967 (Pt.ii), 167-78; idem, *Tudor Gwynedd* (London, 1958),pp. 5-20.

[6] R. A. Griffiths, 'Wales and the Marches', in S. B. Chrimes, C. D. Ross and R. A. Griffiths (ed.), *Fifteenth Century England, 1399-1509; Studies in Politics and Society* (Manchester, 1972), pp.145-72; *Recovery, Reorientation and Change,* pp.175-89.

[7] Glanmor Williams, *The Welsh Church from Conquest to Reformation* (Cardiff, 1962), pp.247-68; *Tudor Gwynedd*, pp.18-27; 'Antipathy and Sympathy', 304-15.

[8] Ifor Williams and J. Ll. Williams (ed.), *Gwaith Guto'r Glyn* (Cardiff, 1939), XX, pp.55-6. For the background see J. E. Caerwyn Williams, 'Guto'r Glyn', in *Guide to Welsh Literature,* pp. 218-42.

[9] T. Gwynn Jones (ed.), *Gwaith Tudur Aled* (Cardiff, 1926), I, LIII, p.218; Saunders Lewis, *Meistri'r Canrifoedd,* ed. R. Geraint Gruffydd (Cardiff, 1973), pp.98-115.

[10] D. Myrddin Lloyd, 'Dafydd Nanmor', in *Guide to Welsh Literature*, pp.189-201; Saunders Lewis, 'Dafydd Nanmor', *Y Llenor*, IV, 1925, 135-48.

[11] T. Roberts (ed.), *The Poetical Works of Dafydd Nanmor* (Cardiff, 1923), X, p.26.

[12] F. Caspari, *Humanism and the Social Order in Tudor England* (Chicago, 1954), pp.112-6; J. Gwynfor Jones, 'Hanfodion Undod Gwladwriaethol, Cyfraith a Threfn yng Nghymru Cyfnod y Tuduriaid: Tystiolaeth Beirdd yr Uchelwyr', LlC, XV, 1984-86, 36-46; K. Charlton, *Education in Renaissance England* (London, 1965), pp.82-5; J. Buxton, *Elizabethan Taste* (London, 1963), pp.3-38.

[13] CLl., p.96.

[14] Ceri W, Lewis, 'The Court Poets: their Functions, Status and Craft', in A. O. H. Jarman and G. R. Hughes (ed.), *A Guide to Welsh Literature,* I, (Swansea, 1976), pp.123-56; J. Lloyd Jones, 'The Court Poets of the Welsh Princes', Sir John Rhys Memorial Lecture, *Proceedings of the British Academy*, XXXIV, 1948.

[15] Ceri W. Lewis, 'Einion Offeiriad and the Bardic Grammar', in *Guide to Welsh Literature,* II, pp.58-87; idem, 'Poetry and the Crisis in the Bardic Tradition', ibid, pp.88-111; Gwyn Thomas, *Y Traddodiad Barddol* (Cardiff, 1976), pp.177-83. See also J. E. Caerwyn Williams, 'Thomas Wiliems, Y Geiriadurwr', *Studia Celtica*, XVI-XVII, 1981, 280-316.

[16] *Y Traddodiad Barddol*, pp.149-53; E. I. Rowlands, 'Arddull y Cywydd', in J. E. Caerwyn Williams (ed.), *Ysgrifau Beirniadol*, II (Denbigh, 1966), pp.36-57. Thomas Parry, 'Datblygiad y Cywydd', *Trans. Cymmr.*, 1939, 209-31; D. J. Bowen, 'Dafydd ap Gwilym a Datblygiad y Cywydd', LlC, VIII, 1964-65, 1-32.

[17] Gwyn Thomas, *Eisteddfodau Caerwys* (Cardiff, 1968), pp.47-100.

[18] *Gwaith Tudur Aled*, I, lxxxvii-ci; *Meistri'r Canrifoedd*, pp.98-115.

[19] D. J. Bowen, *Gruffudd Hiraethog a'i Oes*, pp.4-19; idem, 'Gruffudd Hiraethog ac Argyfwng Cerdd Dafod', LlC, II, 1952-53, 147-60; idem, 'Cywyddau Gruffudd Hiraethog i Dri o Awduron y Dadeni', *Trans. Cymmr.*, 1974-5, 103-31; Francis Jones, 'An Approach to Welsh Genealogy', *Trans. Cymmr.*, 1948, 365-78.

[20] G. H. Hughes (ed.), *Rhagymadroddion, 1547-1659* (Cardiff, 1951), p. 92; Ceri Davies, *Latin Writers of the Renaissance* (Cardiff, 1981); Thomas Parry, *Hanes Llenyddiaeth Gymraeg,* trans. H. I. Bell (Oxford, 1959), pp.201-17; G. Aled Williams (ed.), *Ymryson Edmwnd Prys a Wiliam Cynwal* (Cardiff, 1987), xci-cxci.

[21] NLW MS. 12731.107; NBM, p.82.

[22] Gwyn Thomas, 'Y Portread o Uchelwyr ym Marddoniaeth Gaeth yr Ail Ganrif ar Bymtheg', in *Ysgrifau Beirniadol,* VIII (Denbigh, 1974); J. Gwynfor Jones, 'Rhai Agweddau ar y Consept o Uchelwriaeth yn Nheuluoedd Bonheddig Cymru yn yr Unfed a'r Ail Ganrif ar Bymtheg', in *Ysgrifau Beirniadol*, XII (Denbigh, 1982), pp.210-49; D. J. Bowen, 'Y Cywyddwyr a'r Dirywiad', BBCS, XXIX, 1981, 453-73.

[23] *Eisteddfodau Caerwys*, pp.11-15; D. J. Bowen, 'Ail Eisteddfod Caerwys a Chais 1594', LlC, III, 1954-55, 139-61.

[24] Glanmor Williams, 'The Gentry of Wales' in *Religion, Nationality and Language in Wales*, pp.62-3; J. Gwynfor Jones, 'Beirdd yr Uchelwyr a'u Cymdeithas', in Geraint H. Jenkins (ed.), *Cof Cenedl: Ysgrifau ar Hanes Cymru* (Llandysul, 1987), II, pp.29-59.

[25] HGF, p.37.

[26] Thomas Parry (ed.), *The Oxford Book of Welsh Verse* (Oxford, 1962), CXX, p.245.

[27] *Recovery, Reorientation and Reformation*, pp.260-78.

[28] *Tudor Gwynedd*, pp.5-37.

[29] Rhys Meurig, *Morganiae Archaiographia* ed. Brian Ll. James (Barry, 1983), p.67.

[30] *Tudor Gwynedd*, pp.22-4, 41-3.

[31] W. Ogwen Williams, 'The Survival of the Welsh Language after the Union of England and Wales: the First Phase 1536-1642', WHR, II, 1964, 67-93.

[32] Glanmor Williams. 'Dadeni, Diwygiad a Diwylliant Cymru', in *Grym Tafodau Tân: Ysgrifau Hanesyddol ar Grefydd a Diwylliant* (Llandysul, 1984), pp.74-86.

[33] *Latin Writers,* pp.14-19. See also Ieuan M. Williams, 'Ysgolheictod Hanesyddol yr Unfed Ganrif ar Bymtheg', LlC, II, 1952-53, 111-24, 209-23; A. O. H. Jarman, 'Y Ddadl ynghylch Sieffre o Fynwy', ibid., 1-18; J. Gwynfor Jones 'Beirdd yr Uchelwyr a Deddfwriaeth y Tuduriaid, 1536-43', *Taliesin*, LVII, 1986, 69-85, LVIII, 1987, 35-52.

[34] Cardiff MS. 4.101,112a.

[35] Humphrey Llwyd, *The Breuiarie of Britayne,* ed. T. Twyne (London, 1573), p.36.

[36] L. G. Salingar, 'The Social Setting' in Boris Ford (ed.), *The Age of Shakespeare* (London, 1955), pp.28-32.

[37] BWLl, LXXXIV, p.230.

[38] D. J. Bowen, 'Y Cywyddwyr a'r Dirywiad', 468-73.

[39] A. H. Dodd, *Studies in Stuart Wales* (Cardiff, 1952), pp.2-11. For more background to this theme see E. Roberts, 'Everyday Life in the Homes of the Gentry' in *Class, Community and Culture in Tudor Wales*, II, pp.39-78.

[40] NBSF, II, CCLXX, p.593.

Chapter I

Myth and Reality

Meurig Dafydd, a well-known Glamorgan poet who flourished in the latter half of the sixteenth century, experienced some embarrassment during one of his periodic visits to Beaupré in the vale of Glamorgan, the home of William Bassett whose family stemmed from Norman stock. 'He would be called a bard and a poet,' it was said of him, who resorted 'abroad to gentlemen's houses in the loitering time between Christmas and Candlemas to sing songs and receive rewards'. His efforts, however, were not appreciated because the old squire of Beaupré, having read the ode and given the poet his fee, 'therewith put it sure enough into the fire'.[1] That incident took place sometime in the 1580s and reveals interesting features of the bardic order in Glamorgan at that time. In the first instance it shows a sad lack of interest on the patron's behalf in the composition and it appears that Meurig Dafydd and his bardic colleagues were maintaining a dying tradition. Also, the poor quality of the ode—hyperbolic and flattering—as well as the derision with which the poet was treated signified the lack of respect among an increasing number of *uchelwyr*, particularly in the more anglicized areas of Wales, for eulogy in this grand manner. The poets were well aware of the crisis that had threatened their profession by the late Tudor period and were accustomed to debating the nature and purpose of their craft, vying for patronage and, at the same time, deploring the lack of support among the ruling families. At that time the practice of welcoming and granting hospitality to professional poets in their *plastai* continued strongly, particularly in north and west Wales, but, in an age of changing social and economic circumstances, the odes attributing to the *uchelwyr* and their families the highest of human virtues had seemingly little meaning or relevance. As a manifestation of an ideal it can be argued that eulogy had never had any relevance in any material sense but, in the late sixteenth century, it appeared to be far removed from the aggressive self-seeking activities of the Welsh landowning class. To what extent, therefore, does bardic composition contribute positively to the historian's knowledge and understanding of gentility in late

Tudor and early Stuart times and, more significantly, how far can it be accepted as a valid source? Furthermore, to what extent did the poets and their patrons appreciate that the exercise was pure convention and not designed to reflect the patron's true character? In view of the exaggerated tone of their verse do the poets need to be taken seriously or, in other words, were Meurig Dafydd and other declaimers of his status bluffing themselves into receiving hospitality and reward simply because they had no other means of support?

Since poetic eulogy, in a Welsh context, is devoted to fulfilling the requirements of rigid medieval conventions and is designed principally to glorify the virtues of privileged individuals in native society it has hardly been subjected to close critical analysis by literary historians. The compositions have largely been taken on their own merits, particularly by virtue of their peculiar imagery and manifestations of moral qualities.

The bardic grammar had taught the poets to praise, not flatter; their aim was to foster the concept of perfect gentility as created by divine will and personified in the *uchelwr*. The essence of classical Welsh poetry had been the subject of much controversy among poets in the Middle Ages. It surfaced in the early decades of the fifteenth century in the exchange between Rhys Goch Eryri and Llywelyn ab y Moel. The main theme of that dispute confirmed the central principles of poetic composition—that its prime function was to express approbation in the Taliesin tradition in honour of approved individuals. It involved excessive eulogy, a feature which Siôn Cent, who was sceptical of bardic standards, opposed fiercely in his debate with Rhys Goch Eryri. He attacked the *raison d'etre* of bardic approbation and, according to Saunders Lewis, he was probably influenced by the *scientia experimentalis* taught at Oxford, which declared that abstractions had no objective reality. The issue as to whether the muse should contain hyperbolic panegyric was a point of discussion in learned circles in medieval Europe. Was it a lie ('celwydd') to compose in such a vein? Did it distort God's design in creation? Siôn Cent, in his ode to the muse, overtly declared that poetry should portray man as he really was and not as an ideal, a belief that was echoed in the debates between Guto'r Glyn and Hywel Dafi and, in the 1580s, between Edmwnd Prys and Wiliam Cynwal. In this latter contention Prys accused Cynwal of betraying the true poetic craft by 'lying' ('canu celwydd') since his interpretation of the *uchelwr* was false and misleading. He sang chiefly for his own profit, it was said, by forging genealogies and offering undue praise ('Croyw foliant er cryf elwa') which Prys deplored.

Bardic eulogy, however, can in many respects be regarded as having made a significant contribution to the historian's interpretations of social values in sixteenth and early seventeenth-century Wales. It needs to be examined within the broader sphere of economic development in Welsh community life in that period. When it is considered that the poets, for the most part, emerged from the same social *milieu* as those whom they eulogized and that they were intimately connected with their families and natural surroundings it is essential to pose fundamental questions about the rôle of the bardic order in a changing society which viewed its relevance with an increasing degree of scepticism.

One of the key factors in any study of the professional poets in Wales is the geographical distribution of patronage as well as the social status of individuals who continued to support the poets, even in less secure times. How strong in fact was the tradition in the century subsequent to the Tudor settlement in the more anglicized areas of Wales, chiefly the border areas, the south-east and coastlands of south Wales? Furthermore, how did the quality of the poetry composed for patrons in those areas compare with the sturdy panegyrics offered to *uchelwyr* in the Welsh heartland? Despite social and economic change it is clear, as researchers have amply demonstrated, that bardic visits continued to appeal to a broad spectrum of families claiming gentility but its appeal was stronger in the more conservative regions where native cultural traditions died hard.

Within the patterns of a changing society the poets identified themselves with specified historic regions or provinces (gwledydd), and some were actively engaged in practising their craft in other parts of Wales. Similar bardic tributes were composed for gentry in all parts of Wales. While it is true to say that the tradition was sturdier in the shires of Gwynedd, north-east and west Wales, the degree of poetic output in other areas should not be undervalued. The Morgans, Herberts, Lewises, Bassetts, Stradlings and Mansels, for example, formed a group of gentry in south Wales who were actively engaged in supporting the bardic tradition. Dafydd Benwyn sang profusely to many individual members of these families although the quality of his verse was inferior to that of Lewys Morgannwg and Iorwerth Fynglwyd, two leading Glamorgan poets. His odes for Rhisiart Tomas ap Gruffudd Goch of Ynysarwed in Glyn-nedd, Leison ap Rhys of Llansawel and Tomas Lewys of Baglan, however, are superior to many of his other compositions. His importance lies in the fact that he provides valuable genealogical data about Welsh and naturalized Welsh families in south-east Wales. Lewys Morgannwg, a native of Tir Iarll—a cultural centre of considerable importance in west Glamorgan—sang to patrons in north and south Wales. He was the household bard of the Herbert family of Cardiff, and his elegy for Rhys ap Siôn of Glyn-nedd revealed the extent to which the traditional craft had declined in that region. Lewys Dwnn, the renowned genealogist of Betws yng Nghydewain, also addressed patrons in all parts of Wales as did Siôn Mawddwy who urged George Owen of Henllys in Pembrokeshire to seek a commission so that another *eisteddfod* could be held, and who disputed rights of patronage with Meurig Dafydd in Glamorgan. Wiliam Llŷn sang to the families at Picton, Y Gelli-aur, Abermarlais and Ystradmerthyr; his brother Huw Llŷn, addressed Walter Devereux, Earl of Essex, Tomas Fychan of Penbre, Gruffudd Dwnn of Ystradmerthyr, Siôn Llwyd of Y Cilgwyn and William and George Owen of Henllys. Huw Machno, better known as the household poet of the Wynns of Gwydir, found solace at Gogerddan in Cardiganshire, and as far south as Y Fan, St Donats and parts of Gwent. Conversely, Hywel ap Mathew, a native of Llanfair Waterdine in Radnorshire, sang to a number of south-east Wales patrons such as William Herbert, Earl of Pembroke, and Siencyn ap Dafydd of Llanarthne. Others, for the most part, clung tenaciously to defined regions, such as the Chief Poet Gruffudd Hiraethog, Huw Pennant, Siôn Phylip and Simwnt Fychan in the north, and Meurig Dafydd and Edward Dafydd in Glamorgan and Gwent. The fact that some poets travelled further than other testifies, in part, to their popularity and, in part, to the lasting contacts which the most notable among them established with reputable families, even in the period of decline.

Whatever the extent of their itinerary the professional poets created a nexus of family contacts which enabled those among them who depended entirely on the bardic round for their sustenance to foster their relationships with a clientele in familiar and congenial surroundings. Despite the decline these poets continued to maintain intimate relationships with families whose roots lay deep in Welsh culture. These cultural bonds elicited from them literary products which underlined two contrasting aspects employed to portray native *uchelwriaeth*, the archetypal nobility, and the underlying reality which motivated spirited *uchelwyr* in their quest for recognition in a highly competitive world.

The individual most commonly eulogized, of course, was the *uchelwr* himself. The image projected was normally idealized and abstract stemming principally from antiquated conventions which governed the hierarchical and patriarchal concepts of human life. What sort of people were those who were so effusively portrayed as high-ranking and divinely appointed to lead virtuous lives and to rule through their lineage and innate skills? How true to life, in fact, were those images of grandeur and moral excellence? Was the conventional description of the beneficent patron mere empty adulation based on outmoded medieval ideas and of no practical value? Furthermore, how close was this portrayal to the living *uchelwr* exercising his authority in his house, on his estate and in the courts of law? In other words, did this poetry have any specific relevance other than to depict an ideal or project a social image far removed from the realities of life and activity in Tudor and early Stuart Wales?

In order to attempt answers to these questions it is necessary to examine the meaning and application of virtue and urbanity among the Welsh gentle families, and to measure their social standing and function in comparison with the content of grandiose odes of varying length and quality composed in their honour for a fixed fee. To describe a patron as a 'generous and rare lord' or 'sovereign', a 'valiant peacock', the 'pinnacle of his land' ('Pôr brau'n d'oes . . . Paun glew . . . pinagl tir'), seems to be contrived and totally artificial. He may well have been a powerful man, highly respected in his community, but whether he deserved such accolades is a matter of conjecture. Bardic convention still clung rigidly to medieval notions of social class structure and to the customary usages of men at all levels of society. The model of the native nobleman who possessed abstract virtues and a degree of material ostentation appears consistently in eulogies and elegies. It was an immovably fixed feature in bardic tradition. Whatever the deficiencies in the patron's performance of his public duties it was not expected of the poets to exploit or emphasize them, thereby giving further publicity to his indiscretions. It is true that several poets attempted to counsel individual heads of families in their rôle as guardians of their people, to establish or maintain their good reputation, to banish the arrogant and oppressive, to secure peace, order and obedience among their dependants and to defend the integrity of their community.[2] How effective such counselling was in reality it is difficult to tell; what is clear, however, is that the poets felt themselves, by virtue of their office, able to establish a closely intimate relationship with the *uchelwr* in matters concerning his essential contribution to local community life.

It would, therefore, be a grave misconception to consider the eulogistic tradition in Welsh poetry as having been totally divorced from any reality. It cannot be accepted that the public declaimers ignored life around them; to the contrary, the nature of their verse often points to many formative features of Tudor society in Wales. *Cywyddau* and *awdlau* did contain shrewd observations on the social, economic and political climate of their day. The private and public image was reflected principally in their responses to pressures and opportunities as they emerged during their career. In fact, poetic acclamation does form a valuable source which displays the attitudes, ambitions and frustrations of estate-builders who constantly endeavoured to overcome all economic threats to their ascendancy. Poetic verse drew attention to the dangers and temptations which might lead men of repute to forsake their moral responsibilities and succumb to the ruthless demands of a materialistic age. That, in turn, would imply subversion of the law and the transgression of the rights of others.[3]

Renaissance ideals concerning the nature and function of gentility were commonly held in Wales and England. In this context, however, the poets differed essentially in the manner in which *uchelwriaeth* was expressed and interpreted. They were concerned with nourishing that peculiar concept of the Welsh Renaissance gentleman geared chiefly to maintaining qualities which befitted a life of courtesy on both sides of Offa's Dyke. When Rhisiart Phylip of Ardudwy, for example, extolled the virtues of the house of Rhiwedog in the opening couplets of an ode he, like several other poets of his *milieu*, expressed his adulation for the hospitality, entertainment and conviviality of the company which he had enjoyed. His lines portrayed a house full of grace and festivity.

> Y mae unllys ym Mhenllyn
> Mwya gyd oll am ged ynn;
> Maenol grym iawn olau gras
> Man da i feirdd mwyn dwf urddas.[4]

The description is appealing and elegant enough to command the reader's attention. 'There is one court in Penllyn', it is said, 'a strong manor-house which is the dignified centre where the poets convene.' The correlation between the image of the 'court' and Rhiwedog as a genial centre of cultural activity adds further significance to this impressive greeting. The poet considered himself to be a welcome guest at Rhiwedog, a place of gracious and dignified standing, primarily because he represented an age-old tradition which linked its owners with their ancient inheritance. He was aware that other gentle houses had either ceased to grant hospitality to his order or had not displayed their bounty as liberally as they might. To visit Rhiwedog, the poet maintained, was an inspiration and an invigorating experience in days of depression.

Many other bardic practitioners, of course, had adopted the same convention in style and imagery when expressing their desire to visit a house or when commenting on its merits. That was the very least expected of them; but some went on much further to add other exciting perspectives of gentry life and demeanour such as the architectural details of a rebuilt or reconstructed mansion, and even to describe the physical features of the master and his gentle wife.[5] Glimpses are caught of military features, particularly in the early decades of the sixteenth century, when service was considered a prime duty in the public image of the gentleman. He who was steeled from head to foot ('Drwy dy gorff, dur wyd i gyd'), who was dexterous in his handling of weapons ('Gwych âi â gwayw a chledd') and who bore the port of a gentleman ('Gŵr sad mewn gras') was considered to be a man of some magnitude.[6] Other qualities were often vividly recalled: the description of the jolly *raconteur* among his friends or the ageing patron who had retained his sense of humour in spite of his advancing years; also the diligent arbitrator or law officer acting in defence of the oppressed, and the assiduous man of affairs determined to maintain his prestige in the company of notable peers. The gentle lady, likewise, is often portrayed as a provider of a household reputed for its warm hospitality; she is a person of good countenance and well respected.

The martial appearance of *uchelwyr* attracted much less attention in Elizabethan and early Stuart Wales since, with the emergence of newer concepts of public service and gentility, more emphasis was placed on courtesy, humanity and gracious living within the *plasty* or the royal court among other institutions. Some poets expatiated at length on the niceties of gentle life, noting details of apparel, foodstuffs and luxuries which enriched the social circle, and approved a number of other domestic influences in matters regarding etiquette and conduct.[7] Increasing attention is given to the growing sophistication among the *élite*. Courtly life and attitudes were rapidly becoming the order of the day by the mid-sixteenth century. The cultural aspects of gentility exposed exciting trends and elements which the gentry considered essential for good living. Basically, however, the Welsh poets were concerned with declaring the fundamental features of a code of honour which embraced the urbanity and civility characteristic of the typical Renaissance man ('Gwŷr moesawg grymusawl'). The *uchelwr* was identified as the incorporation of *grazia* essentially in the Welsh context. Wiliam Llŷn described this feature exuberantly in his ode to Rhys Fychan ab Wiliam Fychan of Corsygedol.

> Weled pendefig, brig braint,
> A gweled merched a mawl,
> A gwŷr moesawg grymusawl.[8]

The sophisticated atmosphere of the *uchelwr*'s court is perceived in the lavish description of nobility mingling together in its hall. To see the privileged noblemen, ladies and powerful courtiers was an exhilarating experience for this poet who always praised convivial gatherings of gentlefolk. This view of the privileged *élite* among local gentry within the household resembled, on a much more modest scale, the centres of Renaissance culture elsewhere. When Rhisiart Phylip entered Rhiwedog he was aware of the sumptuous surroundings, the abundant provision and the select company of favoured individuals, all of which inspired him to record his joy in verse.[9] The *paterfamilias* was portrayed essentially in his ancestral rôle and his issue, usually referred to by name, were considered to have inherited grace and favour. The organic entity of the household formed a conspicuous feature of all bardic tributes, and each residence possessed its own distinct ethos. Rhisiart Cynwal's eulogy to Rhiwedog and Ceiswyn reveals the rare atmosphere of civilized living in a Welsh rural setting.

Mannau glwys am win a gwledd,
Muriau gwynion mawr Gwynedd . . .
A byw 'mysg pob miwsig pêr
I'w plasau a phob pleser,
A chroywder, mwynder a maeth
A chwn hela a chynhaliaeth.[10]

The poet was obviously favourably disposed to visiting these centres, and he extols their virtues in lavish terms. Nannau, he says, with its white walls, is the perfect place for wine; within it sweet music can be heard and all pleasures tasted. It is a place where gentility, good breeding, nourishment, hunting dogs and all kinds of sustenance are found. Similar in purport are the rich descriptions by several other poets who aim at drawing attention to the material delights of the *plasty* and the indulgent life that was enjoyed there.

It is of paramount importance to observe, however, that the Welsh *uchelwr* retained strong bonds of affinity with the older concepts of native noble status as well as with the newer notions of Renaissance thought as manifested in England.[11] The extravagant references to the courageous man who commanded respect in his own region ('Y dyn dewr od âi'n daraw, A dyn y wlad dan ei law')[12] and who appeared as a lion and a dauntless figure ('llew a dyn glew') and, at the same time, acted in a wise and valiant manner ('gloywddewr ddoeth'), might well have been conceived by the poet as an abstract image.[13] It would be unacceptable to consider each patron individually as a paragon of virtue. In fact it is not correct to assume that the poets and their patrons considered perfection to be attainable. Poetic eulogy, in terms of its symbolism, was essentially an artistic exercise designed to fulfil a purely social function however antiquated. It was mere convention and generally understood that its laudatory features were gross exaggerations. The value of poetic output in this period, therefore, needs to be critically assessed and interpreted within the context of its historical purpose. Doubtless genuine references do appear in this type of poetry, particularly the genealogical details and the sections which praised the holding of office and the performance of public responsibilities. The poets, by the very nature of their function, accurately recorded their impressions and described the appearance of landed houses and the landscape of estates with remarkable precision, not only to add flavour to the eulogy which had already exceeded the bounds of credibility, but specifically to create and sustain the image of total regional supremacy. Beyond that it is difficult to quantify eulogy and eulogistic standards, and it is in that context that myth and reality need to be identified, defined and evaluated.

The qualities of the ideal life are definable, in material terms particularly when applied to hospitality and effective homekeeping ('perchentyaeth'). It was also manifested in the ways and means adopted by enlightened estate owners to manage the *plasty* and protect the interests of their dependants and kindred. The very nature of 'governance' and 'governorship' ('gwladweinyddiaeth', 'gwladwriaeth') and its execution gave justice ('cyfiawnder') a specific meaning when associated with the routine dispensing of law in the local courts. There were, however, other dimensions which examined the character and qualities of the governor in office, at home on his estate or elsewhere in the public eye. Honesty, sincerity and grace were considered to be essential in attempting to apply the law in an equitable manner. Respect for the concept of justice and the institutions which upheld it was measured often against the flagrant disregard for law and legal procedure that existed among supposedly honourable men in positions of authority. Such transgressions were thrown into greater relief in periods when economic and political adversities created hardship and resentment and nurtured oppressive behaviour. Holders of the prime offices of sheriff and justice of the peace were invariably considered to be incorruptible and stood out in sharp contrast to other nefarious colleagues. Owain ap Rheinallt of Glynllugwy was described by Wiliam Cynwal as an unassailable bulwark, a classic representative of his region free from all hypocrisy and wrongdoing.

> Gwladwr megis gwal ydyw
> Gŵr a thôn ddiragrith yw.[14]

The leader is here described as a wall or rampart; he is incorrigible, scorns hypocrisy and leads a life of complete integrity. His example to others makes him an elevated and incorruptible person to be admired from afar.

Such was the prototype; thoroughly commendable and sincere in thought and deed. Odes, however, do not go far enough to prove the patron's qualities. Doubtless the moral virtues expounded by the poets were often at variance with the practices of aggressive forward-looking landowners and officials, but rarely did this become a contentious issue. It is mainly in stressful circumstances that declaimers became more inclined to express their personal feelings and form new attitudes towards self-seeking gentry in their day. It is at this point that historical evidence assumes greater significance. Court and estate records, for example, usually point in another direction and portray the *uchelwr* in a less favourable light or, at least, regard him as being less worthy than poetic eulogy made him out to be. Poets only hint occasionally at signs of devious behaviour or the tendency to act impetuously when confronted, say, by irate kinsmen or rival neighbours. While the myth of the true Renaissance gentleman still retained its credibility in bardic lore hard evidence proved it to be a fallacy. In those poems which concentrate largely on the rôle of the *uchelwr* in local or regional government much space is devoted to applauding his strength of character and protective capacities. They focus exclusively on images of power and precedence. The 'sovereign head' was normally identified with claims to prerogative and authority.[15] This claim to a realization of power, linked to 'regal' attributes, gave eulogy its most dynamic mode of expression in Tudor times. Since the political settlement in the 1530s and 40s had defined legal and legislative matters it was expected that local administrators could command order and discipline according to the demands and requirements of specific official guidelines. The mid-Tudor poet Morus Dwyfech crystallized such thoughts in a few lines as follows.

> A dôr i gloi ar dair gwlad,
> Ac ustus heddwch gwastad . . .
> Gwladwr perffaith goludawg.[16]

In these lines John Wyn ap Maredudd of Gwydir was portrayed as an asset to public order in a secluded region of Wales since his sole purpose in that region, it was considered, was to uphold and sustain the tenor and spirit of the Tudor settlement of 1536-43. 'He is a door which locks within its grasp three regions', the poet explains, 'an equitable justice of the peace and a substantial and perfect governor.' The emphasis here again is placed on the protective qualities and on the extension of the patron's custodianship over whole areas. Whether the myth of such an upright *uchelwr* can be substantiated is often questionable since, in the last resort, the authentic picture of the gentleman emerges from the historical evidence that is available to reveal his true character and the responses to his behaviour. Poets, it is believed, were often trying to hide or disregard the dubious and less complimentary activities of their hosts. It would be extremely naïve to suppose that they were totally ignorant of their misdeeds at a time when litigation and public manifestations of autocratic power were the order of the day. The constant references to the arrogant ('beilchion') and oppressive ('trawsion', 'cedyrn') presuppose that the poets knew who such transgressors were and where they resided.[17] Certainly not all patrons were paragons of excellence; they often broke the law but were also exonerated by the poets. This feature is often reflected in the poems which offered counsel to patrons, particularly those who were young and new inheritors of estates. Attempts were made to curb their audacity and obstreperous behaviour towards others, particularly jealous kinsfolk who eyed their good fortune with a degree of envy. Poets were consistently aware of the animosities that could arise from contentions of this sort, hence their emphasis on the need for peace and social harmony. They stressed the qualitative aspects which were deemed appropriate to resist temptation and evil doings. In an age of intense concern over property and allied matters inter-kindred rivalry of necessity created internecine strife and discord. The call for amity and concord all too often suggested that it was impossible to establish who, in fact, were the oppressors. Bardic evidence hinted strongly at ruthless administrators, land speculators and moneylenders as being the perpetrators of iniquitous deeds and, as economic depression caused hardship in the latter years of the sixteenth century, these comments became more incisive.

Poetic tributes accorded to their patrons immense power through their succession to ancestral inheritance and through their practical application of what were considered to be their innate skills. Simwnt Fychan, for example, sang triumphantly to Eliza ab Wiliam Llwyd of Rhiwedog, extolling his virtues, and proceeding to describe his heavy-handed actions against his most powerful enemies.

> Trais mur wyt iawn bur tanbaid ar gedyrn
> Tëyrn rhyfel chwyrn i rhyw feilchiaid
> Ôl cledd yn d'orsedd dursaid daufiniog
> A roist ŵr enwog ar estroniaid.[18]

Such powerful lines delineate the cruel attitude taken by a belligerent warrior-type *uchelwr* to his rivals and enemies. In this context, his actions could be interpreted as being those of an unworthy public figure, misusing his authority by taking vengeance on others less able than himself to defend their rights. The words are daunting and august and serve their purpose by portraying Eliza ab Wiliam Llwyd as a survivor of a past age when militarism had assumed greater proportions in bardic eulogy. 'You oppress evildoers in a fierce manner', the poet records, 'and you are a warrior king who sturdily opposes the proud'. 'On your throne', he adds, 'you have a steel two-edged sword which you, famed man, laid heavily on aliens.' Such potent remarks recall the valorous warrior image demonstrative of military might, but applied specifically to the patron in a late sixteenth century context. The emphasis is placed essentially on power, strength, fearlessness, and tenacity implying the ability to press one's individual interests, if need be, at the expense of others. The leader ('blaenor') whose authority should never be resisted, obtained his status by divine will; nevertheless, he could, depending on circumstances, appear to be a formidable tyrant and self-seeker who flagrantly misapplied his faculties to serve baser motives.[19] The gentleman, renowned for his concern to maintain law and order was, in reality, largely functioning in his own interests. In this instance (as in most others), however, this seemed not to be the case. The squire of Rhiwedog was classed as a defender of his people: by virtue of his courage and strength he kept order and discipline, a feature which universally appealed to the poets

When Siôn Mawddwy applauded a patron for behaving arrogantly only towards those who were equally supercilious ('Nid wyd . . . falch ond i'r beilchion'), and praised another for concentrating his efforts on counteracting the deeds of aggressive malefactors, he, and others of his *milieu* who sang in similar terms, merely referred to the redoubtable *uchelwr*, sound in judgement and sturdy in his stand for justice. In other words, this benefactor would deliver, in as powerful a manner, what he had received from others less worthy than himself.[20] When poets referred jubilantly to the head of the household as the 'supreme ruler' and 'firm controller' it is obvious that the ideal is stronger than the reality since such images are mere conventions.

Although patrons were normally assessed as individuals and portrayed as patterns of excellence it is well nigh impossible to draw distinctions between them except with regard to their personal details and family connections. Patrons were hardly compared in terms of their gentility since their inherent properties were assumed to be equal and universal. However, the very nature of eulogy demanded that each provider of sustenance in his *plasty* be assessed in an *awdl* and *cywydd* on an individual basis, hence the focus on moral probity and kindred virtues as reflected in the testimony provided by a single *uchelwr*. What that individual shared with his fellows with regard to rights, privileges and ancestral dignity was implied rather than stated. In the poetry, however, the patron, in the last resort, stood alone as a paragon of superior quality.

Individuality emerged from a variety of panegyrical verse dedicated to men possessing different talents, personalities and ambitions but all bound together in common gentility. The image of grace and legitimate power did not always seem appropriate, especially when the grandees in each shire community, avidly grasping at every vestige of authority, seemed to undermine the law and transgress all codes of honour. Sir John Wynn of Gwydir and his kinsman Sir

William Maurice of Clenennau were both prominent officials in their shire and were considered to be 'pinnacles of grace and favour'. Sir John Wynn was described by Siôn Mawddwy as the 'chieftain and protector of men' ('Pen gwŷr . . . a'u hurddas . . . a'u [h]amddiffyn')[21], and Siôn Phylip hailed Maurice as the 'head of his country' ('Yr wyt . . . i'th wlad wen . . . yn ben ar hon').[22] Both virtually ruled Caernarfonshire between c. 1580 and 1620 and were, on occasions, bitter rivals.[23] They were also often accused of grasping lands illegally and adding substantially to their estates at the expense of others. Nevertheless, by virtue of their status, they were recognized as patterns of perfection, true governors and public figures of the highest esteem.

Every patron was assessed, not only by means of his material qualities, but also by his moral calibre. Whereas Siôn Tudur, for example, poured his wrath vehemently on the oppressors in Welsh society he also drew attention to the value of trust and confidence in the governor and the danger that his righteousness might be destroyed by evildoers (Y gau . . . a gâi le'r gwir').[24] In addition to unscrupulous churchmen ('Gwŷr yr eglwys . . . a lysir am chwant'), he included greedy moneylenders, the practice of usury, rapacious lawyers, corrupt justices and other officers of law and administration in shire and hundred.[25] He severely criticized office-holders who abused their positions, and lamented the situation which compelled the poets to compose false odes to unworthy patrons who lacked the fundamental features of gentility. The crooked lawyer, it was said, exploited the weak and, by legal chicanery, grasped their lands. On a number of occasions Siôn Tudur, arguably the most perceptive social commentator among poets of his generation, censured the avarice and cupidity of those who concentrated their interests wholly on the accumulation of land and riches.

Y rhai annoeth, cyfoethawg
Â'u bryd ar ei hud yrhawg,
Prynu tir yn wir a wnân',
Pentyrru canpunt arian.

'The unwise rich', the poet states, 'have set their minds on purchasing land and accumulating a hundred pounds in silver.' The rapacity of emergent gentry is deplored at a time when the more deserving among landed families were deprived of adequate means of sustenance. Siôn Tudur was indeed a remarkable poet and social commentator, not only because he was among the most prolific but also because he was one of the last chief declaimers who addressed regional patrons. He had also experienced life as an officer in the royal court and was himself a landowner of some means at Wicwair, St. Asaph.[26] His views of society are richly reflected in his wide and numerous selection of compositions; his satirical tone exposed the most fundamental flaws at the royal court in London and in native society blighted by corruption, ambition and oppressiveness at the close of the sixteenth century. Siôn Tudur's knowledge of Welsh gentry—their weaknesses as well as their sources of strength—enabled him to view the situation from two distinctly different angles—as a poet and landowner. Thus he contained in his verse the broadest possible social perspectives. The cupidity of landowners and officials in days of economic stringency, as he and others had described them, doubtless had frustrated several poets who considered that their own livelihood was being seriously threatened by the actions of unscrupulous adventurers whose motives undermined and even destroyed the concept of organic unity in native community life as reflected in the poetry.

Since the legal bonds of kinship had been loosened by the middle of the sixteenth century and men were placing greater emphasis on material wealth than on conventional views of moral probity, bitter rivalries ensued between families and individuals purely over property matters ('Câr ni 'dwaenir, Nid câr da ond acr o dir'). The opportunity allowed free exploitation and ruthless manipulation of legal practices.[27] The world was full of 'perjurers and bribers', it was said, which made a mockery of law and justice, and they thrived on falsehood and deceit. Poets like Siôn Tudur and Edmwnd Prys drew attention frequently to sinister practices and commended worthy patrons for succeeding in overcoming temptation and avoiding evil courses.[28] A suspect or tainted reputation, it was observed, could ruin a family or an individual and bring disgrace and ill favour. It could also sadly destroy the integrity of a region or community, hence the need to maintain honour in adversity and justice in disorder.

Since the poets were expert in genealogy they singled out those individuals whom they regarded as being worthy of eulogy even among the *uchelwyr* who were, by reputation, avid land and office grabbers. Their cupidity was matched by the powerful hold which they had on their communities. Honour, it was affirmed, could only be maintained by respecting the inheritance bequeathed to the heir. They were constantly aware of the need to nourish virtue and cultivate goodness. This was the point made by Siôn Tudur when advising Siôn Conwy of Botryddan on entering upon his inheritance.[29] A similar approach was adopted by Rhisiart Cynwal in his address to John Owen of Clenennau. In order that goodness might continue in him he was encouraged to honour God, maintain his loyalty to the Crown (in a period of intensive political strife), support and protect his tenants and defend his dignified reputation in his neighbourhood.[30] Ancestral connections alone, it was declared, could not sustain good works since moral excellence was also regarded as a vital ingredient in the character of the gentleman.

Nâd un tro gneifio dy gnu,
Gad ti yma i gotymu,
Ni thy' pennaeth, hap hynod,
Mewn un awr, eglurfawr glod.
Ni thyf glân berllan o'r byd,
Ac ni thyf gwenith hefyd
Heb gael amser, breisgdir bro,
A hoff rithiad i ffrwytho.[31]

'Never allow your fleece to be shorn', Rhisiart Cynwal maintained in these lines, 'for a chieftain will not acquire in one hour a manifestly eminent reputation.' 'No fair orchard will grow in the world', he added, 'and wheat will not grow either without having time, fecundity of land and fond germination to fructify.' In such circumstances poets put their trust in those well-experienced *uchelwyr* proficient in the liberal arts and governed by grace and just living. Those who were less familiar with the task of managing public and private affairs, either because of age, lack of training and ineptitude, had to be carefully instructed in the ways of gentility. Age or maturity, however, did not constantly ensure that the gentry had attained the rigid moral standards expected of them. It is also doubtful whether, in fact, they were at all times well-endowed with 'wisdom and accomplishment and generosity and gentleness and amiability towards his men and his friends'.[32] John Wyn ap Huw of Bodfel in Llŷn, for example, a gentleman highly acclaimed by Morus Dwyfech, was known to have harboured pirates and to have involved himself in other illicit practices.[33] He was described as 'a man of good countenance, great power, ability and friendship' in his region.[34] His neighbour and near contemporary, Sir William Maurice—*custos rotulorum* and deputy lieutenant of his shire—was summoned to Star Chamber for rioting and committing assaults and for persisting in his threats against Owen Ellis of Ystumllyn concerning a number of property disputes in Eifionydd.[35] His continuous vendettas with kinsmen and tenants revealed the continued practice of retaining in the remoter parts of Wales down to the early seventeenth century.[36] Rhisiart Cynwal sang to him confidently as a public figure who accepted no bribes and who cared for his people ('Di freib a diofer fu').[37] Tomas Prys, likewise, addressed him in an ode requesting the gift of a boat to go to Spain, and praised his status as a man of influence and magnanimity.

> Eich doethder noder glân yw
> A'ch swyddau ymharch sy heddiw . . .
> Ynillaist rywliaist yrhawg
> Gredyd ysgwiair gwridawg.[38]

The motive for the eulogy is clear, hence the exaggerated tone of the verse. The emphasis is on sagacity in the public image. 'You are noted for your wisdom and reverence in office', it is said, 'and you have earned credit through your just rule.' The opulent character emerges in the manner in which the poet creates an aura of magnanimous bearing and demeanour. An imposing person indeed, judging by that type of testimony. In official legal documents, however, he was described as 'a turbulent and contentious man . . . carrying a greedy mind unlawfully to enrich himself by other men's goods'.[39] The picture given of him by Rhisiart Cynwal is of the generous *uchelwr* disposed to distribute charity in his house. In spite of the atrocities which he had allegedly committed he was still considered a man of credit and esteem, a further indication of the nature and purpose of bardic eulogy which clung fervently to obsolete practices and conceptions.

One other example amplifies the manner in which the poets dwelt on the ideal rather than the reality in contemporary society. Cadwaladr Price of Rhiwlas in Merioneth was regarded as a ruthless manipulator of his own private affairs at the expense of others less able than he. He held office as sheriff of his shire (1593), member of parliament (1584) and deputy lieutenant (1589). He was accused, however, of stealing arms valued at £1, 000, practising extortion and illegally imprisoning others for insufficient reasons.[40] In his maturer years Wiliam Cynwal composed an *awdl* in his honour, praising his strikingly imposing appearance, grace, liberality and integrity among other qualities. In the same poem the poet hinted at his wrath and indignation towards all those of inferior status who opposed or thwarted his designs, a reference doubtless to his true nature.[41] All songs composed in his honour highlighted the more attractive attributes of power, authority and influence; his autocratic behaviour had earned for him a fearsome but respected reputation. His kinsman, Dr Ellis Price of Plas Iolyn, again a prominent governor in north Wales and the Earl of Leicester's henchman, was portrayed as a turbulent and oppressive man when dealing with public affairs. In one suit in Star Chamber he and other defendants were considered to be subtle and treacherous, Price himself being described, in this instance, as a man 'of great substance and so greatly friended in the country there that this . . . offence should be clothed and hid'.[42] In the odes addressed to him, however, he was applauded for his moral probity and devotion to duty, a 'second Moses' ('Ail i Foesen'), a leader of men ('Llu ar d'ôl llawer dyn') and a notable governor appointed by God to rule his people (Nid dyn . . . A'th gododd; Duw dad a'th gododd').[43] Wiliam Llŷn stressed his triumphs over his enemies, particularly the oppressive and arrogant.

> Balch wrth ryfalch y'th rifwyd,
> A difalch wrth anfalch wyd.
> Dewr wyd a chorff drud a chwyrn,
> Da i fwrw cad, dofwr cedyrn.[44]

Once again vestiges of military grandeur emerge as an added reinforcement to the portrayal of a man considered essential to the task of restoring order in his locality. 'You are haughty towards the arrogant and oppressive', it is said, 'but sincere and merciful towards the humble and ill-endowed.' 'You are also valiant', the poet continues, 'a man of strong physique in battle and a tamer of the mighty.' These words were far more generous than the squire of Plas Iolyn deserved in his rôle as public servant. His power was felt mostly in the north-eastern region of Wales, the province which earlier had formed part of the Marcher lordships, and it was as the autonomous custodian of the border areas that Siôn Tudur portrayed him.

> Mor sad yn y Mars ydwyd,
> Acw yng ngradd y Cyngor wyd . . .
> Nedwch ymg'leddwch ein gwlad,
> Anllywodraeth na lladrad.[45]

The image of insuperable power in a wider context is created effectively to fortify and enhance the patron's overall jurisdiction in his neighbourhood. 'You are powerful in the Marches and well positioned in the Council there', it is testified, 'and you protect our country from the effects of ill-government, theft and robbery.' Lines of this kind reveal the contribution of an effective ruler in a turbulent region to the cause of Tudor government. He also rebuilt his residence at Plas Iolyn and gave his colleagues in government a lead which enabled them to function efficiently in courts of law. Similarly, Sir William Herbert of the Friary at Cardiff, a magistrate, deputy lieutenant and member of the Council in the Marches, was involved in bitter factious rivalries in Cardiff in 1595. Both he and his servants were accused of conspiring to rescue prisoners and committing assaults on two town bailiffs.[46] Regardless of his high-handed deeds and attitudes Llywelyn Siôn elegized him as the ostentatious chieftain, a symbol of beneficence among his people.[47] Sir Richard Prys of Gogerddan in Cardiganshire, like Herbert, was brought before the courts for committing many misdemeanours in office as deputy lieutenant and for exacting *cymhorthau* for the benefit of his kinsmen.[48] As a public administrator doubtless he was cautiously respected but Lewys Dwnn composed a majestic *awdl* for him on his elevation to a knighthood to enhance further his well-earned reputation.[49] Siôn Cain also recognized that his influence extended widely over Cardiganshire and elsewhere, and readily admitted that his governorship was exemplary.[50] Yet again, the portrait of the revered public figure emerges, honoured with all the trappings of local office and a protector of his community representing the Tudor state. Several other examples could be cited of bardic eulogy to men on the upgrade, forward-looking and aggressive in their ways. The emphasis is on the marked contrast between the doctrine of gentility as expounded by the poets and the seemingly disreputable practices of the gentry.

Another prime aspect was the use and abuse of litigation which had replaced much of the retaining and feuding practised in the past. Not that this feature had disappeared altogether but more frequent resort to courts of law did help to alleviate the problems of instability in the Welsh countryside. In matters concerning riotous behaviour and extortion, however, the situation continued to be serious because those involved were often the ones appointed by law to maintain order and discipline. The government's policy, to a degree, was self-defeating to the extent that unjust practices could and did, in favourable circumstances, add substantially to a family's wealth and prestige.[51] It seems not to be the case, however, that such malpractices caused widespread disorder. The *uchelwyr* had sufficient authority and ingenuity to gain substantially from their offices while at the same time maintaining the respect of a community by virtue of ancestry. The poets, who were constantly aware of the changing fortunes of gentry life, doubtless concealed the more sinister aspects of their activities and emphasized the most honourable.[52]

A detailed examination of eulogistic composition indicates that the Welsh gentry were men of the world who were fully conscious of their qualities. They were, in effect, the hard-headed political realists, assertive and resilient. The bardic ethos, however, demanded that *uchelwriaeth* embraced higher qualities which were derived essentially from Taliesin. No professional poet of any repute could ever disregard his own rôle, nor that of his patron, in society 'because', according to the bardic grammar, 'the office of the bard is to praise' ('Kanys sswydd prydydd yw moli').[53] It was primarily a social function. Although offering advice on an individual basis did emphasize the need to curb illicit dealings the fundamentally eulogistic element was much stronger and more meaningful. Even the most flagrant lawbreakers among the gentry were described as possessing the quality of leadership, obscured though it may have been. Siôn Tudur's ode counselling John Salusbury of Rug to act honourably towards others, to destroy malicious enemies and undermine knaves and slanderers, implies all too clearly that he was constantly involved in discreditable dealings. The dominant theme of the poem, however, is that divine sanction and ancestral dignity would protect and fortify him in his task to act according to the standards appertaining to good conduct as required by convention.[54]

A matter of consideration at this juncture is the position of poets such as Morus Dwyfech, Wiliam Llŷn, Simwnt Fychan and Rhisiart Cynwal whose accolades broadly represented the chronological range of poetic output during the century after the Acts of Union. Had they betrayed their craft by addressing unworthy patrons? In view of the very nature of bardic convention and the social and economic constraints placed upon them the poets continued to perform their duties in the same manner as had their predecessors. If they had forsaken their principles so had such eminent declaimers in previous generations as Guto'r Glyn, Lewys Glyn Cothi and Tudur Aled who also offered many of their encomiums to equally dubious characters. The situation, therefore, is not clear-cut, chiefly because the poets never drew a distinction between the principles of *uchelwriaeth* and the qualities attributed to those individuals who were entitled to enjoy gentry status by virtue of their inalienable birthright.

It is also relevant in this context to consider the material needs of the poets themselves and to evaluate how crucial, in their careers, were the features of worthy housekeeping ('perchentyaeth'). References to the illiberal acts and attitudes of an increasing number of potential patrons appear on a very large scale from the late sixteenth century onwards. It could well be argued that the poets flattered their patrons principally because they depended entirely on their support and charity, and that a decline in bardic practice corresponded to an increased dissatisfaction with current social attitudes. The case, as such, cannot be denied: it is made abundantly clear in many compositions that the reduced amount of patronage was detrimental to the well-being of the bardic order. Having said that it is not easy to measure to what extent the cupidity of the gentry was entirely responsible for a decline in patronage and the severe strictures levelled at them. The impression given is that it was becoming a problem of considerable magnitude with which the poets found it eventually impossible to contend. However unworthy their most benevolent patrons may have been they clung desperately to the norm as expounded in *Gramadegau'r Penceirddiaid* and exemplified in the works of their predecessors. In spite of economic adversities it was held that the truly benevolent man would counteract all the forces of disunity and divergence.

Er ei dig, ei cenfigen
Y byd a'th cymer yn ben.[55]

Amidst all the animosities and strife fostered by social and economic forces the true *uchelwr* clings firmly to his obligations. 'In spite of indignation and jealousy', the poet remarked of Dafydd Salusbury of Llanrhaeadr, 'you are accepted in the world as a worthy chieftain.' His composure and self-possession enabled him to stand firm in his commitments to his local community in a ruffled and often insecure world.

The professional bardic code demanded that a considered evaluation of *uchelwriaeth* should be achieved by each poet in relation to the character and virtues of individual patrons judged worthy of approbation; otherwise, patronage would cease. Wiliam Llŷn, in one of his finest elegies, described the devastation which occurred on the death of Rhisiart ap Rhydderch of Myfyrian in Anglesey.[56] He and others of his *milieu* had left a void which the poets considered to be catastrophic for the well-being of the local community. Patrons were increasingly becoming non-resident and involving themselves more frequently in public and private affairs outside their estates. Poets often attempted to reconcile themselves with the situation and endeavoured to come to terms with patrons who resided outside Wales with a view to influencing them to return. On occasions poets would plead with patrons to maintain their rôle in society to avoid having to suffer destitution and disgrace. 'You are the poets' chief source of sustenance', Wiliam Llŷn maintained in such a poem to appease a patron, 'their storehouse, their sustainer and their source of wealth.'[57] In such circumstances no practitioner of the craft would withhold his eulogy; the conventions of *prydyddiaeth* (poetic craft) demanded that he apply himself completely to nourishing the chief source of his livelihood. The formal eulogy concentrated on certain well-defined and specific duties of the patron in relation to the poets and others granted hospitality under his roof. The prime reason for attending the *plasty* would be either to fulfil the natural rôle of patronage or to celebrate a marriage. The practical aspects of the *uchelwr*'s office were often deliberately obscured so as to concentrate on abstract qualities. The *uchelwr*, it was remarked, was the poet's tenant ('Tenant i'r beirdd wyt') in the sense that, since an occupier of land normally gave dues to his lord, so the *uchelwr* yielded his bounty to those who glorified his status.[58] Material acquisition, it was said, was God's gift; man's achievement emerged, however, not from his earthly possessions but essentially through divine favour. To that extent land and other sources of worldly prosperity were secondary. Wiliam Llŷn made that point clearly in an eulogy to Rhys Fychan of Corsygedol.

> Nid gallu'r byd cyngyd caeth
> A yrr gŵr i ragoriaeth;
> Nid da heddiw, nid tyddyn,
> Gallu Duw sy'n gwellhau dyn.[59]

This poet is continually concerned about the moral qualities of his patrons and emphasizes the total dependence of the individual on God's grace. 'It is not worldly power, prosperity and property', he asserts in these lines, 'but God's power alone which improves and advances a man's status'. However powerful the *uchelwr* might be in material terms his position in society is measured and governed by divine favour.

Like office-holding possession of land was interpreted basically as a means to an end and not as an end in itself. In his *cywydd* to Ifan ab Ednyfed of Trefeglwys in Montgomeryshire Owain Gwynedd devoted a complete section to describing the manner in which his patron used the resources on his land to replenish the needs of his tenants and other dependants. Income from his rents had enabled him to ensure that his yield in corn was sufficient to sustain the countryside.[60] While it is true that bounty and munificence did emerge from favourable standards of living genuine prosperity appeared as a manifestation of innate virtue ('Gwell nac aur, gwell nac arian, Ei air a'i glod . . .).[61] That virtue accounted for all excellence in word and deed. Genuine goodness, Wiliam Cynwal asserted, lay in strength of character and good works ('A'r weithred dda . . . a bery'n hir').[62] Legal involvement was praised where it was rigorously applied to maintain discipline and obedience and the unity and power of the realm. No *uchelwr* could ever attain an exalted position unless he had mastered the talent of using and applying his wealth to fulfil a higher purpose than the pursuance of self-aggrandizement. The paternal figure was both righteous and merciful; his powers were based on the practice of law within his own household and area of jurisdiction.

> Rhy gadarn, rhywiog ydoedd,
> Rhywiog a thrugarog oedd.[63]

The well-bred and merciful governor, namely Morus Wynn of Gwydir, according to Siôn Tudur, was 'the father of all law' in the sense that he bestowed on his heirs and successors all benefits and privileges which just living offered.

More conspicuous was the tribute paid to notable *antecessores*; the trustworthy *paterfamilias* perpetuated the faculties of his forefathers in the manner in which he managed his affairs ('Doeth ynod, Gyneddfau dy deidiau di'; 'Dithau, mal dy deidiau, A gaiff yn hir ei goffa').[64] Consequently, there emerged the convention that the heir to the inheritance was cast in his father's image ('Ei aer . . . yn ŵr doeth un air â'i dad').[65] Unnecessary litigation and legal chicanery was deplored: to initiate legitimate legal proceedings to preserve the paternal patrimony was considered essential.

> Un fath yr ŷd ni fetha
> I'r tir lle'r heuer had da.[66]

'The corn will not wither', it was said by Wiliam Cynwal in an elegy for Hywel Fychan ap Dafydd Llwyd of Llanuwchllyn, 'where the good seed is sown', a comment again on the basis of gentility as reflected in descent and moral aptitude.

In the odes of Siôn Tudur and Edmwnd Prys, for example, where harsh words were used against the practice of unscrupulous manipulators, offenders were regarded either as upstarts who had prospered more than worthy gentlemen or as *uchelwyr* who had forsaken their privileges for baser gain. The object of every encomium, in part, was to reveal how far worthy management of the patrimony had been modelled on the example of noble progenitors. Genealogical details were not recorded in poems merely to trace ancestry and establish a link with the remote past but, more significantly, the exercise fulfilled a practical function revealing the patron as the sustainer of a cult of gentility which had its roots well laid in the glorious British past. Efficient management of the patrimony usually established concord and social harmony which reinforced kindred unity. Poets projected the myth of gentility; in their minds, the *bonheddig* used their protective powers to seal the bonds of a common cultural tradition. 'He was the supporter of our heritage and our candle' ('Canllaw iaith a'u cannwyll oedd'), Wiliam Cynwal maintained, thereby describing the benefactor as the essence of the good life.[67] In this context the *uchelwr*'s achievement was interpreted specifically as being protective, and eulogies dwelt on an active sense of guardianship. Elegies mourned its passing: the 'orphaned and deprived countryside ('Y mae'r wlad . . . Yn amddifad'), the 'exposed and deserted region' ('Aeth y wlad . . . yn noeth') and the 'empty shire' ('Gwag ydyw'r sir').[68] The poets interpreted strength ('cadernid') in the *uchelwr* within four distinct categories: the resolute and unflinching administrator ('Cadarn i'r cedyrn eurwalch'); the proud owner of a lineage ('O ryw cedyrn'); the steadfast protector and supporter of his dependants ('Dwys gadarn, nid ysgydwir') and the sturdy governor constantly opposed to criminal malefactors ('Cadarn i'r cedyrn eurwalch').[69] The 'head and defender' ('pen ac amddiffynnydd') and 'guardian of all regions' ('Ceidwad gwŷr . . . Ceidwad gwledydd') to the poets signified nothing less than attaining security in an unstable and often inhospitable world.[70] This idea had its roots deeply implanted in the tradition derived from Taliesin. 'He who defends', Einion ap Gwalchmai maintained in the thirteenth century, 'is no sluggish man but strong to support and defend, a pillar of iron to his clan'.[71] Siôn Phylip's powerful lines to Gruffudd Fychan II of Corsygedol, over three centuries later, also recalled graphically the *uchelwr*'s skill in defence and custodianship.

> Dy ran yw cadw'r union . . .
> A chadw rhwng gwan a chadarn
> Drwy bwyll, gyfiawnder a barn;
> Cadw'r wlad rhag cad rhai cedyrn,
> Ceidw Duw ywch oed ceidwad chwyrn.[72]

'Your rôle', the poet asserted, 'is to maintain what is considered right and proper in your relations with both weak and strong.' He was urged to administer justice and exercise good judgement since he was expected to protect his countryside from the threats of menacing enemies. In that task, the poet continued, God would preserve him as a staunch and fearful guardian.

In this respect as well sixteenth and early seventeenth-century poets interpreted *uchelwriaeth* essentially as a symbol of innate goodness destined to protect and preserve the most virtuous features in society. Individual patrons were regarded as good merely in abstract terms: goodness is unattainable except as a philosophical concept. The 'chief good' ('ben ddaioni byd'), the 'prime goodness' ('iarllin benllad') and the cultivation of goodness for the benefit of all were fundamentally concepts of the mind.[73] It is in this respect that the counselling services of poets need to be diagnosed. Counsel often implied criticism but, more significantly, offered its protective powers. Eulogy never succumbed to the demands of the oppressive; good order depended totally on rescuing the supposedly honourable person from all charges of impropriety. When an *uchelwr* was advised to associate with good men, to practice virtue and to heed the wisdom of elders it appeared that the poets feared for his good reputation. At that juncture he would be admonished to follow the example of wise and proven ancestors ('Gwêl rinwedd . . . A dysg wrth hynafgwyr doeth').[74] Hence the significant emphasis on the integrity of kindred relations in preserving the organic unity of the community. Wiliam Llŷn soundly advised Siôn Lewis Owain of Llwyn, Merioneth, a powerful ruler of his shire, to seek the company of loyal men and avoid those who might become traitors.[75]

In one of his most vitriolic moods Edmwnd Prys, using free and strict metres alike, sternly rebuked officers of the law for their excessive greed and self-aggrandizement. Their infamous deeds offended him so much that he composed an ode deploring the serious transgressions of those powerful enough to manipulate all public offices skilfully to their own private use.[76] He took as an image the snow-clad hilltop, the sun melting the snow so that the water flowed in torrents to the sea. In the poet's mind the hill represented gentle status ('gwedd bonedd byd') which, by means of the fast-moving river (the rapacious officers), brought pressure to bear on the sea (the commmon people) which was not able to withstand it. It was implied that public governors, drawn from among the *uchelwyr*, imposed themselves relentlessly on the unprivileged poor through heavy taxation and other oppressions. The snow, which is converted into gushing water, symbolized heavy exactions ('A'r eira . . . Yw aml dreth')[77] Such men, the poet remarked, showed favour to the undeserving and disfavour to the oppressed. As a churchman concerned for the moral welfare of his people he emphasized the injustices of the recalcitrant and impotency of the poor. Criticism is also levelled at the negligent heir who, regardless of his father's efforts to create a consolidated demesne, gave very little attention to it but squandered his assets on the dice tables in London. It was in this manner that he forsook his inheritance and undermined his obligations to the under-privileged.

Rhaid i'r gwan ddal y gannwyll
I'r dewr i wneuthur oer dwyll.[78]

'The weak must bear the candle, 'he asserts, 'so that the ruthless may perform their callous and fraudulent acts.' The emphasis is placed again on the sharp contrast between the unjust and the worthy, the tyrannous and the submissive, and the uncompassionate and the victimized. This powerful epigram draws attention to a prevalent evil in Welsh society which deeply affected the fortunes of the bardic order.

Another poem by Edmwnd Prys, in the form of a dialogue composed in free metre between a sinner and his conscience, set out to advise men to avoid those places where good conscience would be shunned, namely the magistrate's court, the mansion of the substantial knight, the squire's *plasty*, as well as the company of men of law.[79] Morus Berwyn, when praising a patron for not harassing his tenants by doubling the rents, caustically remarked at the extortionate practices of his equals elsewhere.[80] Poets did not hide the fact that individual patrons could be angered if wronged by crooked legal or financial dealers. Wiliam Llŷn admonished William Gruffudd of Penrhyn, a violent gentleman angered by his landed rivals, to control his indignation since it would gain him nothing.

> Llid sydd flin, medd doethineb,
> Llid ni all wellhâd i neb.[81]

Again, in epigrammatic style, the poet draws conclusions from unwise acts of selfish greed and covetousness. 'Anger is vindictive', says wisdom, 'and it is of no benefit to anyone.' Rancour and malice are to be deplored for the good of the family and communal welfare. The true *uchelwr* is justly enraged only when threatened by unworthy foes. Thomas Fychan of Pant Glas, Ysbyty Ifan, was regarded as the 'scourge' of countless enemies ('nerth cadarn oedd, A ryfelai ar filoedd').[82] In the eyes of the under-privileged the good man treated the bold and arrogant fearlessly, and granted the weak and defenceless all the sustenance that they required. Virtue, it was considered, could mitigate temerity: the just governor was driven to take extreme measures when provoked by the forces of evil. Where reconciliation was possible the even-tempered *uchelwr* would at all times exercise his discretion. The reality of the situation, in bardic terms, was fossilized in the myth. The resident patron possessed the potential to right the wrong, perfect the imperfect and fortify those qualities in community life regarded as fragile. The image emerges clearly, for example, in the rôle assumed by Sir John Wynn of Gwydir in his neighbourhood: a formidable person and ruthless builder of a large estate, a remarkable manipulator of public affairs, the benign *paterfamilias* and the powerful custodian of native community life.[83] In bardic eulogy, however, he personified the ideal gentleman—sturdy and unchanging and a pattern of excellence.[84] The image counted for all: virtue was the dominant feature and riches were valued, not for their material worth only but also, and more significantly, for their qualitative properties. Wynn was described as the most illustrious of patrons, the pinnacle of honour and credit. Siôn Phylip, like Huw Machno, maintained that his status in his newly erected residence above Gwydir was symbolic of perpetual grandeur. He, the poet maintained, like his *plasty* is a steadfast tower founded on a rock.[85] The poet also drew attention to his adversaries, particularly those who wished to ensure his downfall: vengeance, it was said, had no virtue, and the squire of Gwydir was advised not to pursue his enemies in the courts of law.[86]

The conceptual features which emerged from this ode by Siôn Phylip are closely linked with the social thinking of most poets in an age of political and economic transition. Emphasis is placed on good stock as a solid buttress to all kinds of threats. Vengeance, it was thought, only perpetuated and intensified rivalries, hostility and feuding. By its very nature it could destroy reputation and it served only to degrade what had been ordained by divine will. Those who oppose virtue, whether it be in the form of a noble gentleman functioning as a tower of strength in his community or defending what he claims to be his own for the good of all, shall be punished principally by their own evil doings. The end result was that the concept of honour triumphed, the myth of innate goodness persisted in the image of the majestic *uchelwr*, the 'fountain of all excellent manners', as Sir Thomas Elyot put it, 'the whole proportion and figure of noble estate . . . apt to his dignity and accomodate to time, place and company'.[87] Such a description approximated to Castiglione's definition of *grazia* and allied qualities such as *sprezzatura, urbanitas* and *galanterie*. Wiliam Cynwal interpreted these conceptual forms as intrepidity and magnanimity in his ode composed on behalf of Morus Gruffudd of Treiorwerth in Anglesey requesting the gift of eight mares from a group of modest gentlemen.[88]

Galawnder ar bob glendid,
Gwr â'i barch uwch gwŷr y byd.[89]

'He typifies gallantry in all its purity', the poet exclaimed, 'and is a man who was respected above all men in the world.' The identification of reverence with gallantry or moral valour becomes a more prominent feature in late sixteenth century strict metre verse when

Renaissance images emerged more succinctly to offer poetic artistry of a more accomplished nature.

All such qualities signified a core of humanistic thought applied to the Welsh *paterfamilias*. In one of his powerful odes to Sir John Salusbury of Lleweni Siôn Tudor underlined the indomitable nature of *uchelwriaeth*. 'You shall not be conquered', he maintained, 'nor shall you lose your lands and properties.' 'If you are humiliated', the poet continued, 'it will cause a serious rift and obstruct the river's flow.'[90] Tribulation and misfortune, it was further observed, could destroy the negligent landed proprietor; it was the proper application of his faculties which, in the last resort, could preserve the *uchelwr* and save him from catastrophe. Hence, the controlling element in the myth combined honourable demeanour with a career of distinction in public affairs: the 'pillar' in the local election ('Piler y'th alwer at etholiad'), the 'gilded knight' exalted by the prince ('Ein prins . . . a oreurodd, Yn farchog enwog inni') and the 'autocrat' among his people ('Gweled unben . . . Yw gweled nerth ein gwlad ni').[91] These hierarchic and pre-ordained features of Welsh social life, therefore, still held sway in the eulogistic tradition down to the middle years of the seventeenth century.

The career of Lewis ab Owain of Llwyn in Merioneth, which ended in tragedy on his assassination in 1555 at the hands of the Red Brigands of Mawddwy, attracted a number of emotional odes from a group of poets who had benefited by his hospitality. According to his formal record he was a ruthless and unfeeling landowner and administrator who had prospered at the expense of others in his shire. Be that as it may, on his death he was depicted as a forceful public servant and a person constantly feared as deputy Chamberlain of Gwynedd and a Baron of the Exchequer at Caernarfon.[92] His position had created much resentment and jealousy among turbulent distant relatives and rival gentry, and he provoked the brigands into hostile action against him. Syr Owain ap Gwilym composed an *awdl* in his honour in the office of sheriff of Merioneth, and hinted sharply at the enmity and opposition he had encountered. Nevertheless, the reality of the matter lay in the fact that his conscious efforts to destroy disorder had also made him a highly respected person because he placed good government before all else. He projected a different image in his house where he appeared as a genial and humane patron ('gwaraidd hynaws') who abhorred infidelity and oppression ('trawsineb'). Lewis ab Owain was assassinated on his return journey from Welshpool assizes.[93] The deed, at the time, signified the triumph of evil over good, and several poets sang his elegies, portraying his callous fate at the hands of villains. There are hardly any words in those poems which suggest the warmth of hospitality at Llwyn and the patron's cordial disposition, but the deceased is cast in the rôle of defender of his region in a warlike and turbulent society. Gruffudd Hiraethog set the tone in the opening phrases of his elegy.

> Llawen gan herwyr . . .
> Llid wrth ddwyn llywodraeth dda.[94]

The 'llywodraeth', namely equitable and sustained government, is a paramount feature: 'Outlaws are happy in their anger', the poet maintains, 'to dispossess a country of good government.' The loss of one ward or protector, in other words, deprives the shire of that essential moral sustenance considered to be the corner-stone of communal integrity.

Huw Arwystl, while deploring the evil deed at Mawddwy which brought grief to the region ('Oer yw dolur y dalaith'), saw hope for the future in the heir to the inheritance whom he encouraged to seek revenge on despicable assassins.[95] Owain Gwynedd went further and demanded that all who valued law and order should preserve the family's good name by suppressing the brigands. The governor, regardless of his harsh actions, represented the rule of law. Stress is placed on fortitude in adversity and the need to maintain the integrity of the corporate entity of the region in an age of political and religious tension. Simwnt Fychan, likewise, had been saddened by the audacity of evildoers who perpetrated a crime to defeat the rule of law.

> Cadarn oedd yn cadw er neb
> Acw ordor y cywirdeb.
> Llid fawr gan y gwylliaid fu,
> Llaw hwn oedd i'w llonyddu.[96]

The 'rule of law' ('ordor y cywirdeb') was essentially a manifestation of Tudor policy and had been entrusted, in this instance, to the sheriff of Merioneth. The malefactors of Mawddwy, the poet reported, with vengeance and hatred had destroyed the force established to control them.

Adulation was best demonstrated against a background of strife and conflict because such conditions disclosed in the honourable *uchelwr* the powers of unrelenting opposition to iniquity. Regardless of his personal weaknesses Lewis ab Owain had retained his honour. The eulogy in fact offered a new dynamic perspective on his life and career. As a divine appointee destined to maintain impeccably high moral standards he stood in a category of his own at that time. Since his demise had destroyed the image of the governor ('gwladwr') as it had emerged in his own career, and had sapped the energies of bardic declaimers who drew sustenance from its preservation, the poets were constantly aware of the need to protect those forces which would guarantee its survival.[97]

Curious though it may appear bardic eulogy exposed both the myth and the reality in a harsh and unsympathetic world where individuals were notorious for their self-seeking and avaricious activities. One prime example was Morus ab Eliza ap Morus of Clenennau in Eifionydd. He and his father had been instrumental in raising the house to a position of eminence through the purchase of lands and properties. This estate grew in an atmosphere of tension and animosity. Feuding persisted and in June 1550 Morus, eldest son of Eliza, together with others, murdered a rival contender for property rights. He was eventually brought to trial at Caernarfon where the charge was reduced to manslaughter, and by devious means he secured his own discharge.[98] It may well have been that Morus's father, himself a prominent justice of the peace in the shire, had taken part in the sordid affair. Nevertheless, both these perpetrators of the crime continued to maintain their local prestige and were heartily greeted by poets such as Wiliam Cynwal, Morus Dwyfech and Wiliam Llŷn.[99] The eulogy painted a markedly different picture and, judging by internal evidence, was composed sometime after the deed had been committed. They were hailed as 'pinnacles' of Wales ('pinagl holl Gymru') and the heads of privileged ancestral seats.[100] The death of Eliza, it was said, had deprived the region of a gracious squire descended from Owain Gwynedd. In addition to his physical strength and resoluteness his skills in subjugating the proud and the provision of a worthy heir were features paramount in the career of any estimable *uchelwr*. He was the archetypal leader, the wise and hospitable chieftain whose death was welcomed only by thieves and fugitives who were given respite from the law. Morus, likewise, in his maturer years was considered a suppressor of injustice and a loyal housekeeper.[101] Yet, both these characters had, for many years after the Tudor settlement, created discord and strife in one of the most conservative area of north Wales, principally for their own benefit. The odes addressed to them projected the surviving image of primordial grandeur which focused on the power of myth over the realities which governed the routine life of the landed gentry in Wales.[102]

Wiliam Llŷn, in his *awdl* to commemorate Eliza ap Morus, perceived what, to him, was visibly commendable: the integrity of his stock, he remarked, was manifested in laudable deeds. The words are forceful if rather staid and idealized.

> Pen eu gwlad a'u pinagl oedd
> A'r wlad ar ei law ydoedd;
> Er hyn ni wnâi . . . Ond f'ai iawn.[103]

The basis of good living, in the poet's view, lay in the transcendent glory of the *uchelwr*. 'The head of their country and their pinnacle is he', Wiliam Llŷn maintains, 'and in his region all lay securely in his authority, and nothing was performed by him that was unjust and outrageous'. His innate glory is exemplified in his predisposition to do good.

The convention is admirably preserved in an age when hardy freeholders were intent on creating as much power as possible for themselves in a strife-torn and conservative community. The situation, however, became increasingly more difficult for the exponents of eulogy because satire had begun to creep more discernibly into their work by the closing stages of the sixteenth century.

Satire had always been a feature of eulogistic verse but it appeared even more subtly in late sixteenth and early seventeenth-century verse. The gentry were mocked simply because their inadequacies as 'paragons of justice' and 'benevolent leaders' had been exposed. This feature, tinged with irony, was an important literary convention of the day in England and it emerged in Welsh verse in such a manner that it virtually destroyed the ethos of *uchelwriaeth*. Tomas Prys of Plas Iolyn was among the most vituperative who sang in this vein. He, like Siôn Tudur, had seen much more of the world than had the vast majority of other contemporary poets. Although he did not rank among the most accomplished of strict-metre practitioners he grasped the opportunity to dwell on the less worthy features in some of his fellow gentry. His ode to Sir John Wynn of Gwydir, for example, signifies the attempts of a poet—and in this instance a landowner—to ridicule the pretensions of another. It serves as one example among several which sought to expose the hypocrisy of gentility and the futility of elaborate panegyrics.[104] And it did not stop there because the poets had taken it upon themselves to satirize each other as the bardic contests of the age served to show.

The most important bardic debate of all—as has already been mentioned—was the protracted contest between Edmwnd Prys, archdeacon of Merioneth, a perceptive social commentator in his age, and Wiliam Cynwal.[105] Prys attempted to convince the conservative poet from Ysbyty Ifan of the need to change the poetic ethos and introduce learning and godliness into the strict-metre tradition. He revealed himself as the representative of the new Renaissance man, an exponent of Protestant humanism who portrayed a very dark view of cultural standards in his day. Cynwal resolutely defended the eulogistic convention—'y canu mawl traddodiadol'—chiefly on the basis that it had served the *uchelwyr* of Wales admirably over many generations. His arguments, however, were trite and flat and offered nothing spectacular. Consequently, Prys had very little to contend with since his rival's responses revealed the sad state of the bardic order in the latter half of the sixteenth century.

But what of the poets and patrons—would they have entertained the adoption of new modes of bardic artistry as advocated by Edmwnd Prys? In spite of the increase in education and the broadening of cultural interests among the Welsh *uchelwyr* it is doubtful whether in fact they—excepting perhaps those who could maintain themselves—would have welcomed a radical change in the way in which they were addressed by the poets. Although the appeal of strict-metre eulogy was weakening it is a fact that the remaining patrons enjoyed the occasional morale booster which served to remind them, in a tense and callous world, of their true worth in their native community. To that extent the impact of Welsh poetic tradition should not be discounted since it still had, in many quarters, a rôle to play in sustaining the virtuous status of the *uchelwr*.

The declaimers themselves would certainly not wish to depart from accepted conventions. It is true that Welsh humanist scholars had severely criticized them for their deceitful practices, their lack of learning and ineloquence as well as their stubborn reluctance to reform and publicize the conventions of their order, and had gone even further to publish works themselves on the bardic metrical craft; for the poets themselves, however, it was a matter of survival to uphold the old system. The forces set against them were sapping their very lifeblood, an aspect which is clarified in Siôn Tudur's remarkable ode criticizing the poets for prostituting their craft. In his view keeping up appearances was a matter of grave concern, but it was the growing tendency among his fellow practitioners to attract the wrong type of patron and not excessive hyperbole which caused him most anxiety.[106]

By that time leading *uchelwyr* had mastered the technique of combining hereditary leadership with their newer and more dynamic rôle associated with the new Tudor administration. Whereas previously loyalty was regarded largely as a clan or kindred matter, under the Tudors it gradually became a concern of the state. The articulate and hard-headed Welsh gentry were aware of their progressive trends and responsibilities and had helped, in some measure, to dim the potency of myth. The emphasis on a medieval code of honour had been seriously undermined, principally by the actions of a go-getting and ruthless group of landed proprietors and professional lawyers. The poets had also become aware that the Elizabethan power structure was having damaging effects on their craft. The conventions of Taliesin had very little to offer families and individuals whose social and economic horizons had widened considerably.[107] The Tudor myth, based on the common belief in British citizenship, assumed broader dimensions which served the needs of the growing sovereign state. Bardic concepts, however, while they endeavoured to adapt to the changing situation, were necessarily narrower and aimed at maintaining a cultural unity based on a fully-integrated privileged *élite*. Doubtless the poets, like many of their patrons, had experienced the agonizing dilemma of coming to terms with a society in transition.[108] The *uchelwyr* sought their own solution based on a more dynamic social strategy, while the poets clung fervently to the symbolism of a primeval order. 'You are Arthur personified' ('Arthur byw wyd'), Wiliam Cynwal remarked effusively in a poem to John Salusbury of Lleweni. Other similar references to early British heroes exposed the heroic grandeur of the past: the 'descendant of Urien's stock' ('o irwydd Urien'), he who shared Urien's virtues ('rinweddau Urien wiwddoeth') or he who was, by learning and nature, a Taliesin to his people ('Trwy ddysg a phob natur dda Taliesin wyt').[109] Old concepts died hard.

The defence of honour was interpreted in an essentially different context by the latter half of the sixteenth century. *Uchelwriaeth* had, by its very nature, been viewed almost exclusively in terms of regal power applied to the office of the regional or national governor. The essence of this *uchelwriaeth* to the poets was unchanging, and was a stabilizing factor in unstable social conditions. The aim was to preserve the organic cohesiveness of the social entity: the bonds of obligation governed the individual gentleman's movements and attitudes and designed his actions. The Taliesin tradition, however, could no longer protect the ancient privileges or command obedience to the medieval order of things. The bardic enterprise in past centuries had, by the middle years of the seventeenth century, gradually lost its *raison d'être*. This phenomenon was frequently reflected in the nebulous and trite manner in which eulogies lamented the decline of the craft. Poets bemoaned the covetousness of the gentry and emphasized the adverse economic climate which had obscured the ideal. Siôn Mawddwy, for example, considered the chief features of that ideal to be good lineage, innate goodness and virtuous living ('Bonheddig o waed, Ac o dda . . . Ac o arfer . . . dyna'r tri bonedd').[110] Wiliam Cynwal, likewise, appealed to a patron to maintain Urien's reputation as a staunch leader of conservative values in an age of ruthless ambition.[111] The ethos of gentility had fundamentally changed. The opening couplets of Siôn Tudur's famous ode condemning the poets for abusing their craft, exposed the dire effects of their declining rôle. The bardic vocation, he maintained, no longer has any dignity ('Swydd y beirdd sydd heb urddas').[112] He then proceeded to list the traditional hierarchy of worthies from the Godhead—*ens perfectissimum* —down to the landed proprietors, warriors and churchmen of noble stock. He upheld the concept that the universe was essentially theocentric and that reputable men shared an active part in it. Dignity in status was identified with the cosmic order and the rôle of humanity within it. Siôn Phylip, one of the most erudite and perceptive late Tudor poets, expressed deep sentiments in this respect when he endeavoured to recapture the essence of the myth in the character and function of Gruffudd Fychan II of Corsygedol, one of his most bountiful patrons.

Beth yw dyn byth da inni
Na bywyd dyn hebot ti . . .
Gwaraidd Frytanaidd wyt ti,
A thyner i'th ddaioni . . . .
Uniondeb sy'n d'wyneb di,
A fo union a fynni,[113]

'What is man or life to us without you', the poet asked, 'since you are the civilized Briton, gentle in your goodness: your countenance reflects that integrity which you exercise appositely. ' The words seem to have a hollow ring about them. The poet, like others of his *milieu*, had become aware of divided loyalties and, as time went on, the purely antiquarian value of the bardic craft assumed a more prominent function. The poets, in fact, failed to appeal to the urbane *civilita* which an increasing number of their patrons found exceedingly attractive.[114] Huw Machno deeply felt the consequences of changing attitudes when he gave expression to the tragic void in the patronage system in the opening lines of his ode to William Gruffydd of Caernarfon.

Byd da a fu i Gymru gynt,
Byd hael bywyd da welynt . . .
Hoffi'r iaith a'i phur weithwyr
A wnâi'r teidiau gorau gwŷr
Oes neb i'n croesawu ni
O'r rhain fel eu rhieni.[115]

The contrast between the glories of the past and the dire circumstances of the present is painfully revealed in these lines. In the past, the poet records, our forefathers protected and sustained the ancient culture and heritage of Wales, but now there is no one among the gentry to welcome the poets as in previous generations. The hiatus that had gradually been emerging in Welsh society had reached alarming proportions and had become an issue of considerable magnitude in bardic circles.

The Welsh *uchelwyr*, by the early seventeenth century, had maintained a good measure of independence, chiefly in the spheres of politics and administration and within the broader influences of marriage and the family. Such factors had become more positively identified in the works of Siôn Cain, Siôn Phylip, Simwnt Fychan, Rhisiart Phylip, Edwart ap Raff and Huw Machno among others. The world of true poetic craft, it was said, had become a thing of the past ('Mae'r byd a'r gelfyddyd faith . . . yn mynd ymaith') and with it disappeared all that was considered meaningful to the poets.[116] Excessive hyperbole had become the most common feature in eulogy by the seventeenth century, which indicated the futility of the efforts to keep pace with the idea of the *pays legal* which had superseded the older concept of the *pays réel* in private and public affairs.[117] Personal loyalties and attachments were being replaced by wider territorial affinities in gentry life. The sense of community had been adapted to meet the challenges of a new exciting world wherein the concept of British citizenship was interpreted anew against a background of political and economic advancement. The surviving cultural heritage, from now on had to compete with other extraneous factors which, at once, confined its impact and broadened concepts of nationhood and cultural bonds of affinity. Owain Gwynedd, singing to Edward Herbert of Cemais, one of his most prominent Montgomeryshire patrons, at a time when economic pressures bore heavily upon him, acclaimed him as one who had identified himself consistently with the essential myth. The poet expressed the perplexity which characterized others of his generation, and his despondency clearly emerges in parts of the poem.

> Deall y bûm dull y byd
> Dull hwn âi'n dywyll ennyd . . .

Dyn yw Edwart, da'i nwydau
A dyf y rhod i'w fawrhau;
Rhannai Dduw, serch rhinwedd Siôn,
Ar hwn ddawn yr hen ddynion.[118]

'I understood the ways of the world', the poet explained, 'but its ways are now dark to me.' 'Edward is a person with admirable faculties highly esteemed in the world', he continued, 'and God has bestowed upon him the skills of his father, John, and ancient men.' In a world of changing trends and attitudes such sentiments gave the poet an opportunity to perpetuate the myth, but unfortunately the reality had, by that time, rendered it almost meaningless.

It is in this context that the contribution of the Poets of the *Uchelwyr* needs to be examined. When the fundamental question is posed whether or not poetic declaimers were setting the standard for their patrons rather than praising them for having achieved it there is no denying that, from the purely conceptual viewpoint, eulogy was identified with personal achievement. Each composition positively revealed firm qualities which survived and had been preserved by notable descendants of medieval forbears. Taken at face value manifestations of exemplary behaviour cannot be accepted as being historically genuine since they distorted the true image of the practical *uchelwyr* functioning at home or on his estate or in the courthouse. In this context the shortcomings of the poets need to be reconsidered. Since convention demanded that they addressed those whose qualities had been cultivated by virtue of their descent the less exemplary were expected to improve themselves by fostering those qualities which lay within their grasp. To the poets the concept of eulogy was unique. Although they were well aware of human weakness among the high born it was with the passage of time that they felt compelled to emphasize how the principles of *uchelwriaeth* had been undermined. As economic problems became more acute and patronage less popular so also were unworthy attributes made more pronounced in the *cywydd* metre. Patrons were warned to resist temptations and cease to act discreditably. The criticism is often obliquely implied. It is not the individual himself but rather the potential which lay within him which inspired the poets. To that extent the norm in eulogy is the unworthy, and it was with these considerations in mind that the concepts of gentility in Tudor and early Stuart Wales are best appreciated.

NOTES

[1]J. Stradling, 'The story of the lower borowes of Merthyr Mawr', ed. H. J. Randall and W. Rees, *South Wales and Monmouthshire Record Society Publications,* I, 1932, 71-1; Ceri W. Lewis, 'The Literary History of Glamorgan from 1550 to 1770', GCH, IV, pp. 539-40.

[2]NBSF I, XLIII, p. 99; H. I. Bell, *History of Welsh Literature,* pp. 149-54. See also Thomas Parry, *Hanes Llenyddiaeth Gymraeg hyd 1900,* pp. 116-27; G. E. Ruddock, 'Siôn Cent', in *Guide to Welsh Literature*, II, pp. 183-7.

[3]See NBSF, II, CCCIV, pp. 687-8 for an example of an attempt made by Owain Gwynedd to conciliate between two kinsmen involved in land disputes.

[4]NBSF, II, CCCXLIV, p. 756.

[5]NBM, pp. 42, 83. See also E. Roberts, 'Everyday Life in the Homes of the Gentry', in *Class, Community and Culture in Tudor Wales*, II, pp. 39-46.

[6]SLl, XXVIII, p. 206; CLl, p. 115.

[7]E. Roberts, *Bwyd y Beirdd 1400-1600* (Bangor, 1976); D. J. Bowen, 'Agweddau ar Ganu'r Unfed Ganrif ar Bymtheg', *Trans. Cymmr.,* 300 et seq.

[8]CLl, p. 53; GEUGH, XV, p. 76.

[9]NBSF, II, CCCXXXI, p. 725.

[10]Ibid. , II, CCCXXVIII, pp. 718-9. See also A. Ll. Hughes, 'Rhai o Noddwyr y Beirdd yn Sir Feirionnydd', LIC, X, 1969, 184-5.

[11]E. D. Jones, 'Brogyntyn Welsh Manuscripts', NLWJ, VI, 1949, 3-4, 27.

[12]GSM, LXXXIX, p. 285.

[13]Ibid.

[14]GWC (1), I, VIII, p. 28.

[15]'Hanfodion Undod Gwladwriaethol', 34 et seq.

[16]GMD, VIII, p. 54.

[17]*Oxford Book of Welsh Verse*, CXX, pp. 244-8; GST, I, CL, pp. 602-5.

[18]NBSF, II, CCXCIII, p. 644.

[19]GEUGH, XXII, p. 108.

[20]GSM, XXVIII, p. 98.

[21]Ibid., XX, p. 66.

[22]'Brogyntyn Welsh MSS', NLWJ, V, 1948, 243, 260.

[23]E. N. Williams, 'Sir William Maurice of Clenennau', *Trans Caerns. Hist. Soc.*, XXIV, 1963, 88-91.

[24]GST, I, CXLVI, p. 583.

[25]Ibid. , I, CL, pp. 602-4.

[26]Ibid., I, CXLIX, p. 596; E. Roberts, 'Siôn Tudur', LlC, II, 1952, 82-96; idem, 'Siôn Tudur yn Llundain', *Trans. Denbs. Hist. Soc.,* XVIII, 1969, 50-82.

[27]GST, I, CLII, p. 615.

[28]Ibid., I, CCII, pp. 803-8.

[29]Ibid., I, V, p. 18.

[30]'Brogyntyn Welsh MSS', VI, 1949, 7-8, 35.

[31]Ibid.

[32]G. J. Williams and E. J. Jones (ed.), *Gramadegau'r Penceirddiaid* (Cardiff, 1934), p. 16.

[33]NLW Brogyntyn MS. 3. 143.

[34]I. ab O. Edwards (ed.), *Star Chamber Proceedings concerning Wales* (Cardiff, 1929), p. 32.

[35]Ibid., p. 154.

[36]D. Mathew, 'Some Elizabethan Documents', BBCS, VI, 1933, 74-7.

[37]'Brogyntyn Welsh Manuscripts', VI, 1949, 3, 33.

[38]CCM, pp. 152-3.

[39]C. H. Gresham, *Eifionydd: A Study in Landownership from the Medieval Period to the Present Day* (Cardiff, 1973), pp. 115; Edwards, op. cit, p. 155.

[40]Edwards, op. cit., p. 90; P. Williams, *The Council in the Marches of Wales under Elizabeth I* (Cardiff, 1958), pp. 121, 125-6.

[41]NBSF, II, CCCC, p. 867; GWC (1), II, Atodiad II, pp. 866-7.

[42]E. Roberts, 'Teulu Plas Iolyn', *Trans Denbs. Hist. Soc.*, XIII, 1964, 70-83; A. Ll. Hughes, 'Rhai o Noddwyr y Beirdd', 192-3; P. Williams, *Council in the Marches*, p. 268; Edwards, *Star Chamber Proceedings*, p. 4.

[43]BWLl, XX, pp. 48, 50.

[44]Ibid., V, p. 13.

[45]GST, I, XLVI, p. 189.

[46]Edwards, op. cit., p. 81; GCH, IV, pp. 188-9. See also H. G. Owen, 'Family Politics in Elizabethan Merionethshire', BBCS, XVIII, 1959, 185-91; P. Williams, 'Controversy in Elizabethan Glamorgan: the Rebuilding of Cardiff Bridge', *Morgannwg*, II, 1958, 38-46; G. E. Jones, 'Local Administration and Justice in Sixteenth-Century Glamorgan', ibid., IX, 1965, 11-37.

[47]MDLlS II, II, p. 323-4.

[48]Edwards, op. cit. , p. 40.

[49]D. H. E. Roberts, 'Noddwyr y Beirdd yn Sir Aberteifi', LlC, X, 1968-9, 93.

[50]Ibid., 94.

[51]G. D. Owen, *Elizabethan Wales; the Social Scene* (Cardiff, 1962), pp. 30-5, 170; P. Williams, 'The Welsh Borderland under Queen Elizabeth', WHR, I, 1960, 19-36.

[52]G. E. Jones, *The Gentry and the Elizabethan State* (Swansea, 1977), pp. 20-7 et seq.

[53]*Gramadegau'r Penceirddiaid*, pp. 35, 133; Ceri W. Lewis, 'Poetry and the Crisis of the Bardic Tradition', in Guide to Welsh Literature, II, p. 101.

[54]GST I, XIX, pp. 74-5.

[55]CCM, p. 62.

[56]CLl, p. 108.

[57]Ibid. , p. 75.

[58]SLl, LXXXVIII, p. 401.

[59]CLl, p. 71.

[60]NBM, p. 14.

[61]'Brogyntyn Welsh Manuscripts', VI, 1949, 33.

[62]GWC (1), I, X, p. 36.

[63]GST, I, XXX, p. 126.

[64]NLW Llansteffan MS. 122, 28. Cf. 'Cynnyddfawr yw'r cyneddfau', CLl, p. 10.

[65]Cf. Wiliam Llŷn: 'Da'r imp a gad ar ei ôl'. NBSF, II, CCCCXXI, p. 909.

[66]GWC (Mostyn III), I, LII, p. 164.

[67]GWC (I), I, VI, p. 21.

[68]GWC (Mostyn III), I, VIII, p. 24; II, CV, p. 325; GSM, XCVIII, p. 314.

[69]GWC (Mostyn III), I, XLVI, p. 144.

[70]GSM, XLIX, p. 153.

[71]R. Gurney, *Bardic Heritage: a Selection of Welsh Poetry in Free English Translation* (London, 1969), p. 64.

[72]NBSF, I, XXXVII, p. 81.

[73]Cf. 'pennaeth', 'blaenaf' 'D'wyneb ym mhob daioni'. GEUGH, XLVIII, p. 214.

[74]NBSF, II, CCLXXXI, p. 618.

[75]Ibid., I, CLVI, p. 351.

[76]*Oxford Book of Welsh Verse*, CXX, pp. 244-8.

[77]Ibid., p. 244.

[78]Ibid., p. 246.

[79]T. R. Roberts (ed.), *Edmwnd Prys, Archddiacon Meirionydd* (Caernarfon, 1899), pp. 231-3.

[80]CCM, p. 379.

[81]CLl, p. 78.

[82]Ibid., p. 125.

[83]E. G. Jones, 'Sir John Wynn of Gwydir', *The Welsh Review*, V, 1946, 187-91; J. Gwynfor Jones, 'Syr John Wynn o Wedir: ei Gefndir a'i Gymeriad', *Trans Caerns Hist. Soc.*, XXXVI, 1975, 13-52.

[84]See Owain Gwynedd's *cywydd* in his honour and Siôn Mawddwy's *awdl*. GOG, I, XLVII, pp. 155-8; GSM, XX, pp. 66-9.

[85]Cardiff MS. 4, 101, 64b-66b, 73a-74b; BGHM, XXXIV, pp. 75-6.

[86]NLW MS. 9052E. 278; G. Roberts, 'Biographical Notes', BBCS, XVII, 1956, 46-9.

[87]Caspari, op. cit. , p. 108.

[88]J. A. Mazzeo, *Renaissance and Revolution: the Remaking of European Thought* (London, 1967), pp. 144-6.

[89]GWC (Mostyn III), I, XXXII, p. 98.

[90]GST, I, XIV, pp. 54-5. See also W. J. Smith, 'The Salusburies as Maintainers of Murderers', NLWJ, VII, 1951-2, 235-8, GCH, IV, pp. 175-91; G. E. Jones, 'Local Administration and Justice in Sixteenth-Century Glamorgan', loc. cit.; P. Williams, 'Controversy in Elizabethan Glamorgan; the Rebuilding of Cardiff Bridge', loc. cit.

[91]SLl, CXXI, p. 484; CXXIII, p. 488.

[92]J. Y. W. Lloyd, *History of ... Powys Fadog*, IV, p. 285; J. Gwynfor Jones, 'Law and Order in Merioneth after the Acts of Union 1536-43', *Journal of the Merioneth Historical and Record Society,* X (i), 1986, 128-30.

[93]NBSF, I, lVI, CXXXVIII, p. 314.

[94]Ibid., I, CXLI, p. 320.

[95]Ibid., I, CXLII, p. 322.

[96]Ibid. , I, CXLV, p. 328.

[97]'Law and Order in Merioneth', 130-2.

[98]*Eifionydd*, pp. 182, 315-6; W. O. Williams (ed.), *Calendar of Caerns Quarter Sessions Records,* I, 1541-1558 (Caernarfon, 1956), lxxx-lxxxii.

[99]CLl, pp. 100-2.

[100]GWC (1), II, XIX, p. 597; II, XXVI, p. 629.

[101]T. Jones Pierce, *Welsh Medieval Society*, pp. 239-49.

[102]G. D. Owen, *Elizabethan Wales,* pp. 30-3.

[103]CLl, p. 101.

[104]NLW Mostyn MS. 112, 234; T. Gwynn Jones, 'Cultural Bases; a study of the Tudor Period in Wales', *Y Cymmrodor,* XXXI, 1921, 174-5.

[105]*Ymryson Edmwnd Prys a Wiliam Cynwal*, loc. cit.

[106]D. J. Bowen, 'Gruffudd Hiraethog ac Argyfwng Cerdd Dafod', 147-60; idem, *Gruffudd Hiraethog a'i Oes,* pp. 61-8.

[107]D. J. Bowen, 'Y Cywyddwyr a'r Dirywiad', loc. cit.

[108]Ibid.; J. Gwynfor Jones, 'Welsh Poets and their Patrons c.1550-1640', WHR, IX, 1978-9, 262-77.

[109]NBSF, II, CCCVI, p. 672.

[110]GSM, LVI, p. 182.

[111]GWC (Mostyn III), II, XCIV, p. 292.

[112]GST, I, CLI, p. 606.

[113]NBSF, I, XXXV, p. 76.

[114]D. J. Bowen, 'Y Cywyddwyr a'r Dirywiad', loc. cit; 'Welsh Poets and their Patrons', loc. cit.

[115]NLW Llansteffan MS. 122, 523.

[116]D. J. Bowen, 'Y Cywyddwyr a'r Dirywiad', loc. cit.

[117]Gwyn A. Williams, 'Twf Hanesyddol y Syniad o Genedl yng Nghymru', *Efrydiau Athronyddol*, XXIV, 1961, 24-5.

[118]GOG, I, IX, p. 30.

Chapter II

Concepts of Gentility

Wiliam Cynwal, that master of the strict-metres in the mid-sixteenth century, during one of his customary visits to the house of his patron, Siôn Lewis of Pengwern, Ffestiniog, composed a grandiloquent ode (*awdl*) in his honour. The verse was conventional and similar in style and purport to many other eulogies offered as tributes to deserving patrons. Siôn Lewis was descended from minor gentry stock and played but a modest part in public life as did many others of his *milieu* in Merioneth who claimed gentility or *uchelwriaeth*. In this *awdl*, however, the poet praised him for his cultural status and for attaining the peak of achievement as a reputable landed gentleman. By virtue of his ancestry, courage, generosity, good-breeding and geniality Siôn Lewis, in the poet's view, had been elevated to the highest position to which gentlefolk could aspire ('Brig bonedd . . . brig dewrder . . . Brig gwrolder . . . Brig haelder . . . Brig rhywiogrwydd').[1] This patron, judging by the evidence, had performed no remarkable feats but did function as a justice of the peace in his native shire. To Wiliam Cynwal, however, like others of his rank, Siôn was considered worthy of praise by virtue of his learning, his righteousness, his elevated lifestyle, and his ability to establish peace and security among his people. His innate goodness, it was believed, emerged indisputably in his social bearing and demeanour as well as his cordial relations with others of all ranks in his community. The poem is characterized by frequent references to this person's integrity and upright manner, his concern for the welfare of his dependants and his determination to maintain what he considered to be essential to the well-being of his family and kindred. The eulogy is expressed in terms which revealed the features of the typical Tudor gentleman, keen to safeguard his own reputation. Wiliam Cynwal attempted to present, in a formal and highly conventional verse-style, the concept of the perfect gentleman—in a purely Welsh context—as it had evolved in contemporary life and thought in Renaissance Europe.

The Welsh poets of the sixteenth and early seventeenth centuries were constantly occupied with the task of exalting the station or institution of the gentleman whose social features, as they emerged in Renaissance England, were partly Christian and partly pagan.[2] Emphasis was regularly placed on statecraft and public decorum in peacetime and honourable conduct of affairs in periods of war when the defences of the realm became a consideration of prime concern. Such ideas had developed during the Middle Ages and had achieved their fulfilment by the latter half of the sixteenth century. The revival in Platonic studies had re-introduced into intellectual circles a study of Greek concepts of justice (*ius*)and the ideal state as well as modes of education to achieve knowledge and understanding of the perfect rulers or guardians. The Platonic ideal of the good and just state ruled by an *élite* of governors had caught the imagination of English humanists since the notions of polity had some elements in common with the political features of the emergent national sovereign state, with its emphasis on aristocracy and privilege, and the selection and training of future rulers. In the sections of the medieval bardic grammar which deal with the attributes of the Godhead the influence of supposed Platonic ideas is revealed chiefly in the philosophical basis of the traditional eulogy.

In a purely Welsh context, following the Tudor settlement, the *uchelwr* class broadened its intellectual horizons. It was gradually trained by legal and administrative experience by establishing firmer bonds of loyalty and by formal education to respect and serve the national state. It is conceivable that ideas regarding new concepts of gentility circulated in the regional institutions of government, the *plastai* ('llysoedd') of the gentry and educational centres. It was among the privileged order in local mansion houses where the gentry resided doubtless that the professional poets would become familiar with concepts of the true Renaissance gentleman.

The ideal public servant represented a combination of Aristotelian concepts concerned with developing moral qualities in community life as well as the Christian virtues of charity and humility. The doctrine of the model courtier, as portrayed by Baldassare Castiglione in his major work *Il Cortegiano* (1528), assumed English dimensions in 1561 with Sir Thomas Hoby's translation, but the publication of *The Boke named the Governour* by Sir Thomas Elyot in 1531, had given the notion of the accomplished English gentleman a more precise and positively active definition in public life as the guardian and defender of virtue and moral probity. Although the connection between the poets and Aristotelian principles cannot be established it is doubtless the case that the concepts of honour and justice incorporated in the panegyrics did contain similar basic features. No link either can be established between the encomiastic imagery in bardic composition and the neoplatonism of the Renaissance. The poets were inextricably bound to their conventions and were inadequately equipped, by the very nature of their craft and their outlook, to absorb or even accept themes which dominated intellectual life in Europe of their day. Nevertheless, the increase in educational training among the Welsh gentry at local privately-endowed grammar schools, the inns of court and English universities together with the growing importance in their spheres of interest of the royal court and, more particularly, the Council in the Marches at Ludlow, where many of the gentry obtained political education and became acquainted with social niceties of the day, had facilitated the gradual spread of intellectual ideas into the Welsh country *plastai*. Poets, during their customary visits, were effective news gatherers and disseminators, and would normally be in constant contact with heads of families and other dignitaries who enjoyed hospitality at these cultural centres. Fresh ideas would also spread into the modest towns of Wales and the border areas as well as episcopal palaces and other clerical residences in various parts of the country. In such ideal surroundings contemporary poets doubtless would at least be made aware of newer interpretations of gentility and deference and would apply them in such a manner that they enriched their own concepts as laid down in *Gramadegau'r Penceirddiaid*. It is evident that the increasing degree of intermarriage with English families and the growth in the numbers of officials who moved in Welsh social circles brought the poets into direct contact with the sophisticated lifestyles of the privileged. Regardless of the rigid doctrines adhered to in the bardic schools it appears that the spread of educational and commercial activities into Wales as well as the strengthening of the Tudor governmental structure created a new and exciting intellectual environment within an *élite* circle of poets.[3]

In contemporary thought it was considered that the gentleman was privileged fundamentally because he possessed honourable status in the hierarchy which formed, according to accepted principles, a key component in God's universe. All parts of God's creation, it was assumed. performed a specifically pre-ordained function. The emphasis was constantly on 'degree, priority and place'. 'Take but degree away', Shakespeare maintained, ' . . . And hark what discord follows'.[4] A demonstration of pride in ancestry was interpreted as a method of upholding the formal social hierarchy and maintaining communal integration. It was, as Lawrence Stone described it, 'the welding of a homogeneous group of seemingly respectable lineage from a crazy patchwork of the most diverse and sometimes dubious origins'.[5] The emphasis on degree was a constant feature of bardic tributes. Eulogy, in its varied forms, presupposed attachment to degree and order ('Euraidd iachoedd gradd uchel')[6], and a fixed plan in an eternal chain of existence. 'He who is benign and gentle', declared Wiliam Cynwal in one couplet to John Salusbury of Lleweni, 'shall be exalted in the links of a golden chain.'

Ac a fo caredig fwyn
A godir mewn aur gadwyn.[7]

The concept of order in God's creation was the basis of medieval thought on degree, order and status, and it emerged distinctly in the Welsh bardic grammar, particularly in those sections which declare how the worthy are to be praised in poetry.[8] It is a universal order which, with its numerous gradations, possesses distinctive features, a design which provides the poets with a rich source of artistic imagery. It is hardly surprising that the Welsh *brëyr* or *bonheddig* is often compared to a deer (carw), lion (llew), eagle (eryr), large spreading oak-tree(caterwen), rose (rhosyn), vineyard (gwinllan), ploughing ox (rhychor) and similar manifestations of strength, firm leadership and virtue. The poets considered such images to be the most natural methods of expressing concepts of power and grace in their compositions. The social philosophy was implied and the unity of the community factor was based on the principle of an 'integrated Christendom' which had evolved as an essential component in the divine order.[9] Although that organic unity no longer existed following the tumultuous changes of the Reformation, the idea of God's purpose in creation—the universal plan—was strictly maintained because, to the Welsh poets, it formed an essential part of bardic convention and because, in an age of rapid and subtle social and economic growth, they could find no safer anchor than an integrated well-ordered society guaranteed to safeguard the highest qualities of life.[10] Wiliam Llŷn, in his *cywydd moliant* to Thomas Madryn of Llŷn, dwelt on the theme of the chain of being and the sanctity of God's ordination.

> Rhai'n wŷr o stad fawr rad rin,
> Hoff radau rhai'n gyffredin.[11]

Some, the poet says, are born to high and virtuous estate but others come from less imposing stock. Those ordained by God are sufficiently well-endowed with good ancestry, the basis of gentility. Such was the purport of Wiliam Llŷn's address to Rhys Fychan of Corsygedol.

> Dawn a gefaist yn gyfa,
> Ag arwydd dawn yw gwraidd da.[12]

The ethos is succinctly revealed in a crisp couplet of this kind. 'You were granted all the skills', it is stated, 'and the mark of the chiefest among them is good ancestry'. Rhys Cain similarly exposed the rigidity of the hierarchical system and God's endowment to man, according to his standing and reputation.

> Bid aml yn y byd yma
> Arwyddion Duw ar ddyn da;
> Duw nefol, dedwyddol dad
> A rôi'r rod ar ei rediad;
> Graddau teg ar ddeutu hon
> A ordeiniwyd i'r dynion
> Rhai'i ostwng ryw ystod
> Fo lyn rai ar flaen y rod.[13]

The order as declared by divine favour, in these lines, elevate the *uchelwr* to a position of prestige compared to his inferiors who had no option but to be content with their lot on the lower rungs of the social ladder. 'The marks of God are often seen on good men', the poet remarked, 'and it is God in heaven who placed the world on its axis and ordained grades of status for the benefit of mankind, some of lower rank and others more elevated.'

Siôn Phylip, who was an equally perceptive commentator on the social implications of gentility in the crucial period which spanned the late Tudor and early Stuart age, manifestly declared how significant a rôle the chain of being assumed in the life of the exalted gentleman. His reference to the organic unity of mankind is unmistakably succinct.

> O deli drwy bob dolen
> Raddau dy ffordd hyd ei phen.[14]

'You hold degrees through each link in the chain to the head', the poet maintained to a prominent patron at Gwydir fully aware of his status and obligations, thus encapsulating crisply the social theories in vogue at the time.

The Welsh gentleman or *uchelwr* was granted a privileged position: his virtues were considered to be innate and his standards exemplary in the execution of public duty. He cultivated the prime qualities of grace, honour and integrity, the chief manifestations of good manners and composure. The belief in degree and order as the basis of man's existence was clearly exposed in the Welsh bardic grammar which regulated the ways and means by which various grades in the social structure should be accorded praise.[15] Those of gentle breeding, it was stipulated, were given the following distinguishing features:

> A lord is praised for power, and ability, and military prowess, and courage, and strength, and pride, and meakness, and wisdom, and accomplishment, and generosity, and gentleness, and amiability towards his men and his friends, and also beauty of countenance, and a dignified bearing, and magnanimity of mind, and nobleness, and other honourable and kindly qualities.
>
> The nobleman is praised for bravery, valour, power, strength and fidelity to his lord together with wisdom, discretion, liberality,

> comeliness, a dignified bearing and gentility of stock as well as other creditable things.[16]

The most honourable features were shared, on equal terms, by the lord and the nobleman, and in Wales both social degrees were, to all intents and purposes, considered synonymous:power and ability, strength, wisdom, liberality and a dignified bearing were common aristocratic characteristics which were constantly displayed in the life and public demeanour of the Tudor *uchelwr* as portrayed by the professional poets. The superiority achieved by the nobility sprang initially from lineage and ancestral affinities although some theorists considered innate skills and achievements, together with a degree of tenacity, to be the more praiseworthy features of gentility. The Welsh poets, steeped in learning, genealogy and heraldry, who continually referred to 'gilded gentility' ('aur fonedd'), the 'gentility of blood' ('fonedd gwaed') and the 'glorious pinnacle of bounteous stock' ('loyw binagl hael bonedd'), regarded birth and agnatic connections to be paramount features of true nobility in the Welsh context.[17]

The Tudor age in England saw the demise of the traditional nobility as the dominant element in politics and public affairs. Gradually, their rôle in military leadership and service diminished. In their place emerged the civil servants of the Tudor polity who used their skills to buttress and defend the new state vested in its sovereign head and its regional institutions of government. The military features in Welsh poetry, however, died hard, and numerous poems referred consistently to the military attributes of well-seasoned patrons. Highly esteemed was the 'steel-armoured powerful Welshman' ('Y durgrys Gymro dewrgraff'),[18] the dexterous *uchelwr* with a notable reputation for wielding the steel spear and shining sword passionately in the province of Gwynedd.

> A dur wayw glân a dewr gledd
> A bâr gwynias bro Gwynedd.[19]

The description is awesome and fearful and depicts the warlike leader with his 'clean steel spear and valiant sword' making 'white-hot the region of Gwynedd'. His dominance on the field of battle had created, in the poet's mind, an image of aristocratic grandeur which demonstrated military power and glory to be the most striking features of *uchelwriaeth*. The hardy warriors, the 'valiant lion in the army' ('rhyfelwr'; 'llew o fewn lluoedd'), and the precious and intrepid leaders of men on the field of battle ('brau a dewr iawn mewn brwydr') were still considered to be persons of immense authority; their temerity and powers of leadership were traits of character which continued to attract the attention of professional poets. The nature of military obligation, however, had changed and more emphasis was being placed on service rendered in specific campaigns in royal armies rather than on prolonged military operations. The dauntless and chivalrous knight had yielded to the less spectacular but equally virtuous governor or administrator of the state either at the centre or in local government, and the royal court had, in conceptual terms, become a pivot of gracious living and influence.[20] New and exciting social trends emerged when the Tudors 'tamed' the aristocracy and encouraged the emergence of new and attractive qualities of civility and urbanity. The change of emphasis appears more distinctly in the movement from military to civil areas of activity and leadership. The mainstays of the new order of gentility, armed with social and economic resources, were peace, security and prosperity which were established through allegiance and loyal service to the reigning sovereign. Those families and individuals who made the grade because of their increased participation in government and law, growth in landed wealth and social connections were not all necessarily descendants of reputable ancestors. Divisions into ranks became progressively more blurred since artisans, yeomen and merchants took an upward trend in the social scale, a process which had profound effects on the nature and character of the eligible *uchelwr* in his public rôle as governor.

The order of gentility dependent on good fortune and tenacity was broadened to include a wide range of individuals and their families—not all of whom were prosperous in material terms—which laid claim to a favoured position in the hierarchy. Through increased educational activity and a broader understanding of human responses and behaviour the qualities of courtesy, humanity and civility became the order of the day among those best able to appreciate them. Above all else *noblesse oblige* identified the worthy gentleman in his social environment.[21] The Welsh poets combined the values of public office with ancient lineage, a feature which became a prevailing theme in numerous odes of praise and lament. It was considered easier for them, however, to describe rather than define gentility. Those public officials who lacked the essential qualities did their utmost to acquire them, and those who, by virtue of their birthright, had inherited them staunchly resisted their attribution to others. The 'excellent gentleman' ('gŵr da rhagorawl') who was regarded as 'an example to his age' ('Siampler i'w amser'), was he who had normally descended from good stock since the poets were rigidly conservative in such matters.[22] Although they acknowledged that the gentle strata in Welsh society were broad and all-embracing they considered the *nobilitas minor*—the rank below the conventional aristocracy in the English social hierarchy—to be equally privileged and well-rooted in history and antiquity. Nobility, in a purely Welsh context, was an explicit manifestation of this very phenomenon. Gentility was continually thought of as being inherent and fixed: in reality, privileges of rank were not exclusively dependent on birthright, but the professional poets designed their compositions in such a way that they stressed what they considered to be the fundamental links between rank and favoured inheritance. The value of pedigree assumed prominence in an age when the 'battle for status' became a crucial issue.[23] Society in England and Wales was patrilinear, patriarchal and primogenitural, which were invariably the chief bastions of the social structure. Siôn Mawddwy, a much-travelled poet of his day, established these features succinctly in an *awdl* designed to eulogize Rhydderch ap Rhys Fychan of Llandudoch, a worthy patron in Pembrokeshire.

> Myn eiriau dy deidiau di . . .
> Dyn wyd a dull daioni dy daid . . .
> A daed ydoedd dy deidiau
> Yn nhop y rhod yn parhau.[24]

'Seek the words of your ancestors', the poet maintains, 'for you are a man who possesses the good manners of your forbears who were men of excellence, determined to sustain a prestigious bearing.' Such lines disclose the honour with which a visiting poet viewed his patron. The focus is minutely on worthy ancestry tied to the essential quality of goodness. The words reflect the yearning of a poet steeped in bardic lore for those virtues which the traditional *uchelwyr* of Wales cherished, but at the same time they express joy because worthy patrons possessed sufficient strength of purpose in their native community to preserve them. *Uchelwriaeth*, while it languished as a medieval concept, continued to flourish in some gentry houses because of a conscious feeling of loyalty among their owners to the cultural affinities of their respective communities.

Various attempts had been made to reinforce the decaying social framework as it had affected the principal patrons of *uchelwriaeth*. This was done by giving prominence to stratification by title, power, wealth and other equivalent attributes, the sum total contributing to the growth of social harmony. Constant references appear in the poetry to the *uchelwr* enjoying his sumptuous life in auspicious surroundings ('Da gwreiddiai o dŷ graddol'), the heir to dignified *antecessores* ('Aer graddol, orau gwreiddyn') and the leader of a reputable house whose chief features were untarnished status, probity in action and skill in the performance of his public functions. He could command the support and allegiance of others since his word and innate skills inspired confidence and trust. It was in this context that Rhisiart Cynwal addressed Siôn Llwyd I of Rhiwedog.

> Gwrdd wladwr graddol ydyw,
> Gorau un esgwier yw.[25]

'He was a man of good ancestry and upright character', the poet maintained, 'a squire of character who possessed powers to perform his duties by virtue of his status.' This concept relating to impeccable lineage was distinctly underlined by Wiliam Llŷn in one of his epigrammatic couplets.

> Byw ar gam trwy bower gau
> A dynn dynion dan donnau;
> Byw i'ch tir fal y bu'ch tad
> A wna'ch cadw yn eich codiad.[26]

The lines remind the four sons of John Wyn ap Maredudd of Gwydir of the basis of their power in an oppressive world. Subversive activity, the poet maintains, destroys good living. Conversely, if the patron emulated his father by guarding his estate and people his status would be upheld. The correlation between the tangible source of wealth in land and moral affluence assumes prominence often in Wiliam Llŷn's poetry.

The emphasis in these lines is clearly on just living and upholding family honour based essentially on an inherited territorial patrimony. The heir was obviously endowed with natural virtues, the most explicit symbol of which was good lineage. In bardic vocabulary the nobleman—rendered variously as 'pendefig', 'pennaeth', 'penadur', 'arglwydd', 'gwrda', 'blaenor' and 'llywiawdwr'—was normally equated with the attributes of gentility such as 'bonheddig', 'bonedd', 'ysgwieriaeth' and 'barwniaeth'.[27] Both concepts were frequently linked with regal status derived from ancient progeny.

Men of reputable stock were granted an elevated position compared to that enjoyed by the early Brythonic rulers of Britain. Their standing in local community life required that they be vested with the inheritable qualities of illustrious forbears. In a sixteenth-century context they were described as the descendants of a primitive line of rulers, and their deeds were considered to be so worthy that their descendants took immense pride in their inherited sovereign status. The antiquity and primitive grandeur of the Brythonic world is re-created in powerful poetic images which denote the majesty of *uchelwriaeth*. The 'old and sturdy royal oak' ('henbraff brenhinbren'), the 'lineage of majesty' ('brenhingyff'), the 'baron of ancient royal stock' ('barwn henwraidd brenhinrhyw') and the 'descendant of old kingly roots' ('hengyff brenhingainc') were all images which enriched the portrait of a governor whose virtues were as much derived from ancestry as they were from the natural skills of government.[28].

It was universally accepted among the bardic fraternity that the qualities normally associated with the gentry sprang principally from their royal connections as leaders and supporters of their people. The emphasis was continually on moral probity and justice in all aspects of public life.

Bron raslawn cyfiawn ei caed,
Breiniau hwn o'r brenhinwaed.[29]

The focus on regal status indicates how the poet, in these lines, is able to identify it with the elegant bearing of the country gentleman. 'He was gracious and just', he says, 'and derived his privileges from old majestic stock.' In that one couplet the poet expressed the essential qualities of justice in a person whose prerogatives were long standing.

Nobility, in the bardic context, was associated with the image of the Christian gentleman of the highest order who was endowed with the virtues of self-discipline, grace and exemplary leadership. These qualities were ordained by divine sanction which meant that the community leader in his *plasty* obtained his powers directly from God ('Duw'n rhoi nawdd dyn rhinweddol'). The godly patron was essentially good and highly favoured ('Gŵr duwiol iawn, gair da'r wlad ... gŵr da ydoedd').[30] Wiliam Llŷn, who is recognized universally as one of the most eminent sixteenth-century Welsh poets, consistently referred to God's central rôle in gentry life and the fundamental powers exercised by divine law in the fulfilment of public responsibilities. It was not man but God, the poet stated in his address to the powerful Dr Ellis Price of Plas Iolyn, who elevated the strong and wise *uchelwr* to power and, in matters of law and justice, to become a 'second Moses' ('ail Moesen'). It was by God's grace alone that he was able to maintain himself in a position of privilege.

Nid dyn byw, nid da na barn
A'th godo ŵr doeth gadarn.
Duw dad a'th godo di dwng,
Dyna dysg na all dyn d'ostwng.
Duw a'th roes yn ail Moesen,
Duw'n barch a'th adawo'n ben.[31]

The words emerge in the form of a moral precept:'It is not man nor goodness nor just action which exalt you', the poet maintains, 'but God the father.' 'No man can demote you', he continued further, 'since God has raised you to become a second Moses, and by His grace your chieftaincy will be preserved.' Such mildly Augustinian views probably governed the poet's thinking on these matters and led the patron to reflect on his rôle in society in a more contemplative manner than would normally have been the case.

The natural instinct to excel and display moral virtues (doniau) was interpreted as a gift bestowed by God. He who had been well endowed with virtue usually prospered in the material world, and he to whom God had granted eminent stock flourished in old age. His family and successors in land and office would be morally fortified and would maintain peace and good order through divine intervention.

A wreiddio Duw o wraidd da,
Ar gynnydd y brigwynna.

'He whom God had well-rooted', it is observed, 'will prosper by the very nature and substance of his stock.' That substance was given tangible form in the material assets which the family grouping possessed.[32] Nobility of status implied that the privileged *uchelwr* should rationally apply his skills for the good of all. The virtuous gentleman ('bonedd o rinwedd') was equitable and impartial in his responses to and treatment of others above and below him in status. He was renowned for his civilized actions ('Iraidd a gwaraidd'), a benign gentleman who commanded total allegiance.[33]

Gorau dim o gred yma
Yw dyn a rhinweddau da.[34]

'He who cherishes good virtue in life', it was said, 'is of the highest order', enterprising and humane. His power and energy to serve transcended all other considerations and attracted the forces of goodness to aid him in his duties.

The principles involved were conveniently expressed in two couplets by Rhisiart Cynwal to Sir William Maurice of Clenennau, one of his most respected and public spirited Caernarfonshire patrons.

Nid cadw'i dda a wna'r union ŵr
Ond cadw'i glod, cu deg wladwr;
Gwell nac aur, gwell nac arian
Ei air a'i glod i ŵr glân.[35]

'The true gentleman', the poet maintained, 'cannot keep his material possessions but can retain his honour.' 'He is the fine, kind gentleman', he explained further, 'whose fame and renown is more valued than gold or silver.' The emphasis was continually on the application of moral standards to the resourceful man whose chief qualification for service was his innate gentility ('bonheddig cynhwynawl') which often defied strict definition. He who demonstrated an unblemished character ('mawrwych lân gymeriad') also displayed a measure of equanimity and self-control.[36] It was through his example that the true nature of virtuous existence became a reality. Welsh nobility was created out of good lineage, virtuous living and the cultivation of skills in the exercise of public responsibility. The accent in the mid-Tudor period, following the major bureaucratic reforms of the 1530s, was essentially on loyal service to the Crown. In Welsh bardic tradition the 'statesman'or 'governor' (gwladwr; ceidwad; llywiawdwr; colofn gwlad), in a national or regional context, was he who maintained goodness ('Dyn a bair daioni') for the common welfare of his people ('Daioni cyffredinol').[37] Only the good man could attain a state of perfection as manifested by social theorists of the day ('Ni wnaeth Duw . . . ddyn berffeithiach'). 'There is talk of your goodness' ('Mae sôn am eich daioni'), Siôn Tudur maintained, when addressing a patron in his public capacity as regional administrator and benefactor.[38] Furthermore, Wiliam Llŷn, in one of his eulogies, interpreted the *uchelwr*'s prosperity as having been inherited from noble forbears: his faculties or qualitative attributes (cyneddfau), benevolence, grace and moral stature emerged as the most praiseworthy features of his righteousness ('Cyneddfau y teidiau a'r tad'). His behaviour or demeanour was characterized by a sense of integrity, discretion and loyalty ('Digynnwrf, da ac union, Dedwydd a sad').[39]

The nobleman's accomplishments also signified a well-defined unity of purpose which stemmed from divine favour. In such a manner Siôn Tudur sang the praises of John Salusbury of Rug.

> Urddwyd eich tad yn wladwr;
> Ar Dduw gwyn mae urddo gŵr.[40]

The concept of the sublime *paterfamilias* is made apparent in this couplet: 'Your father was ordained a statesman', it is said, 'and a man's investiture as leader stems from God.' The 'statesman' ('gwladwr') is placed in context as a ruler or leader. That unity of purpose which he had created and maintained, chiefly through exercising government and control within his own household and his region, had enabled the heir to cultivate qualities which the past, as represented by his father, had bequeathed to him. All this entailed a display of honour and magnanimity in the gracious life ('Bid gras ag urddas . . . bonedd a rinwedd . . . anrhydedd, mawredd a chymeriad').[41] The poet who confidently hailed his patron as the benign paragon of gentility ('llariaidd o benllad bonedd') or as the most prosperous 'vineyard' among gentlefolk ('ben gwinllan bonedd'), accepted such qualities as being of the highest order.[42]

Nobility had acquired two well-defined features which emerged frequently in poetic tributes in the sixteenth century, namely 'nobility native', based on power and authority fostered through ancient lineage, and 'nobility dative', which highlighted distinct merit in the art of government. Those who claimed 'nobility native' were generally in the ascendant; they were the *uchelwyr* born to their status by divine will. They maintained their privileged position chiefly because of their inherent claim to superiority: indeed, they magnified their claim to ancient birthright by being consciously aware of the prerogatives enjoyed by ancient forbears.

> Y gwenith nid egina
> Wedi tes heb hadyd da.[43]

It was in this epigrammatic manner that Wiliam Cynwal explained the roots of good ancestry and the benefits derived from it in an ode to Simon Thelwall of Plas-y-ward. 'No wheat will grow', he maintained, 'unless it comes from good seed.' His view of gentility was as fixed and immoveable as it had been in the compositions of his predecessors. Those considered unworthy of status owing to inferior pedigree would never achieve the renown enjoyed by others who were blessed with good descent. Sir John Wynn of Gwydir, for example, perplexed by the fact that one branch of his family had been 'mangled' by disruption while his line, which he claimed to be the senior group, had remained 'in credit and show in their country' offered no valid explanation other than to suggest that it was 'God's mercy and goodness towards the one more than the other' which chiefly accounted for this fortunate phenomenon.[44] He even quoted the scriptures to support his argument:

> as God said in the Book of Moses 'I will have mercy on whom I will have mercy, for they lived in the same commonwealth and under the same storm of oppression, so as if God had not left us a seed we had been like Sodoma or compared to Gomorra. Nevertheless, by the goodness of God we are and continue in the reputation of gentlemen from time to time sithence unto this day.[45]

Wynn, like the poets whom he so generously patronized, was concerned to establish the source of innate gentility, and discovered that birthright was as close as anything to a strict definition of privilege. Wiliam Cynwal, in a more sophisticated fashion, dwelt on the same theme: it was the sun, he said, shining amidst the dew on mountain pastures, which brings forth fruit, and it is inclement weather or fire which destroys it. Similarly, he continued, natural growth in nature is sorely affected. It is by God's grace (the warm climate) that the heir to an estate is nurtured. It is the poet's instinctive confidence in the virtues of 'nobility native' which enabled him to compose his verse in such an exuberant fashion, to eligible gentry, principally in view of their probity and sense of justice.[46]

Not all gentlemen were so richly endowed or naturally inclined to reveal such benevolence. Not all either engaged themselves diligently in the service of the state on a national or regional basis. They may well have been able to acquire or inherit fame and fortune by diverse ways but human nature, given adverse circumstances, could and did create and perpetuate enmity and upheaval. The esteem accorded to their forbears did not necessarily imply that virtuous living would necessarily be maintained: 'The fame and wealth of their ancestors', Sir Thomas Smith maintained, 'serves to cover them so long as it can, as a thing once gilded . . . till the gilt be worn away.'[47] Who else did the Tudor and early Stuart poets in Wales have in mind when they referred to the 'cedyrn', 'beilchion', 'ffeilsion', 'cneifwyr', 'traws trwm' and the like—all indicative of illegal power and oppression in society—if not those among the gentry who forsook their dignified status in order that they might gain at the expense of others.[48]

Economic strains and stresses did often expose violent and undesirable features among all ranks of Welsh *uchelwyr*, as the records of legal proceedings amply prove.[49] The poets, however, endeavoured to eschew the issue by declaring that the *uchelwr*, by the very nature of his office, was inclined more towards virtue although the hard facts of his career seemed to suggest otherwise. Regardless of the temptations to act in a repressive or oppressive manner the governor in his locality, it was considered, possessed an innate skill to serve for the common good of all. In his ode to God and the world Siôn Tudur censured the unwise rich, principally members of alien families who had settled in the native areas, who had purchased properties and accumulated wealth for purely selfish reasons.

> Y rhai annoeth, cyfoethawg
> A'u bryd ar ei hud yrhawg.
> Prynu tir yn wir a wnân',
> Pentyrru canpunt arian.[50]

His words are pure satire. 'The unwise rich', he maintains, 'bent on accumulating wealth, proceed to purchase land and accumulate hundreds of pounds in silver'. Siôn Tudur's point is that undeserving gentlemen, presumably in administrative or legal service, had taken advantage of their base status to advance their fortunes in order that they might achieve prominence among the more respected ranks in community life. Such lines, taken out of context, seem perplexing. To whom did the poet actually refer? Would it not be fair to assume that members of his own class were also subject to his disapproval? That seems to be the case when it is realized that the Welsh gentry were continually involved in manipulating land transactions and concerning themselves with expensive litigation. In the poet's mind those who are unwise woefully misapplied their energies to unworthy ends. The perfect *uchelwr* transcended all that was regarded by him as disreputable: in fact, it became a matter of conscience in cases where hospitable and benign gentlemen, renowned for their virtue and respectable demeanour, were on occasions distraught by feelings of their own unworthiness.

Trysor da'i gael, ni ffaelia,
I ddyn yw cydwybod dda;
Os anesmwyth llwyth ych llog
Dau gwaeth gydwybod euog. [51]

'A good conscience', Huw Llwyd of Cynfal remarked, 'constituted a precious possession which will not fail the righteous man.' If the hired ox's burden is uneasy and strenuous, then a guilty conscience is twice more. The base and ignoble were continually attracted by vice and impropriety and increasingly usurped the privileges of 'nobility native' by robbing it of its exclusive rights of pedigree. Siôn Tudur cited the most serious misdealings of some of his colleagues in the bardic profession who had bowed to pressures and had accorded false pedigrees to unworthy individuals who sought to improve their status. Dishonourable behaviour of this kind led to a flagrant abuse of privilege. The desire for material gain, the poet retorted, had blunted his profession's sworn duty to uphold the genuine features of gentility. In such dire circumstances no poet could ever proclaim the qualities of the refined gentleman ('gŵr brau') and uphold the honour of his profession at the same time. [52]

The essential link between birth and virtue became almost a controlling theme in the bardic repertoire. It constantly dominated the eulogistic theme since it clung tenaciously to the concept of privileged descent. Uppermost in their minds were the chief manifestations of the qualitative life ('o ran dawn a rhinwedd') and the standards expected of the well-born ('ei had o'i wraidd hir . . . Rhinweddau'r rhain a wyddom'). [53]

Rhoi'r bonedd it a wedda
Rhoi'n nydd rhinweddau da. [54]

Gentility and virtue achieved the perfect blend, Tomas Gwynedd remarked in an ode to Eliza ab Wiliam Llwyd of Rhiwedog: without the combination no public servant employed by the state could perform his duties with any degree of exactitude or authority. Richard Moryson, the mid-sixteenth-century commentator, elevated virtuous living and considered it to be more significant than birthright in the lives of the nobility. 'True nobility', he commented, 'is never but where virtue is.' Material wealth was not regarded as the essence of a prime *uchelwr* although it shaped much of his background in real terms. The qualities of moral behaviour were fostered by instruction in good deeds and actions ('Trwy ddysg a phob natur dda'). 'Nobleness', Moryson continued, 'resteth neither in riches nor in blood but in a free and noble courage . . . exercised in cunning and virtue.' 'He who had been endowed with courage', he maintained further, 'deserveth best to be called noble, worshipful and excellent.'[55]

The poets referred often to the vital link between origin and achievement since it was believed that ancestry was the true foundation of gracious living and a buttress to the chief values of a civilized community. Eulogies and elegies alike emphasized constantly the superiority and grandiloquence of the individual patron ('Blaenor pawb . . . Bu'n fawr . . . Bu'n bennaf yn ben bonedd . . . Pencenedl . . . pennaeth gwyn'). He would untiringly defend his honour and the peace and security of his neighbourhood, thus revealing distinct signs of regional authority as well as the qualities of self-discipline.[56]

The practice of honour stood foremost in the social demeanour of the native *uchelwr*. All reputable features were considered to be inheritable. The well-governed state relied heavily on 'nobility native' because dynastic aspirations were considered paramount. The dependence of the family estate on the integrity of the eldest son or legitimate heir led poets to hail the esteemed successor to the property as being a symbol of the virtues of hierarchy, patriarchy and legitimacy, all of which, it was believed, stemmed from the most revered concept of nobility. Power was always wielded for the common good; the true inheritor to a well-ordered estate reflected the qualities of his predecessors.

> Dy dad oedd da dedwyddol;
> Duw a'th wnaeth dithau'n ei ôl.[57]

Wiliam Llŷn was consciously aware of the innate qualities of an inherited wisdom: 'Your father', he declared to Siôn Prys of Eglwyseg, 'was a good and genial person, and God has created you in his image.'

Heirs devoted to the welfare of their estates and local communities normally increased the status of their properties in conceptual terms, and their achievements reflected the glory of worthy *antecessores*. It was this feature which inspired Wiliam Cynwal to predict a splendid future for the Gwydir estate in the possession of reputable heirs.

> A'r rhain gwedi'r hen godiad,
> 'Wyllys Duw a wellhâi'u stad.[58]

Again, the focus is on the past: 'And these [heirs]', it is said, 'through God's will and illustrious forbears, will maintain and improve their estate.' The gracious *paterfamilias* will provide a 'gilded imp' to succeed him. Wiliam Llŷn maintained in his ode to Robert Llwyd of Y Waun, Is-y-coed:

> Y gŵr da a gair duwiol,
> A eura imp ar ei ôl.[59]

Siôn Phylip, in his elegy to Morus Wynn of Gwydir, joyfully proclaimed that the paternal image of the *uchelwr* would not decay on his death so long as a virtuous heir succeeded him.

> Y ddiareb oedd eirwir,
> Nid marw yw'r tad mawr o'r tir;
> O bae etifedd rhinweddol
> A roe Duw'n aer da yn ei ôl.[60]

This dynastic factor is fundamental to any understanding of bardic attitudes to the survival of the noble estate ('Gwedd a rhinwedd yr hynaif') and the renown of progenitors.[61] In view of the abstract values associated with gentility the nature of the succession became irreversibly linked with the honour normally accorded to estate founders. Indeed, the ethos of the gentry was inextricably bound to honourable inheritance and the survival of essential qualitative features. 'Children are our hope' ('Plant yw'n gobaith'), Siôn Phylip exclaimed at a time when the principle of primogeniture had become almost exclusively the mode of arranging succession to land and property. The Tudor battle for status entailed far more than maintaining and even improving one's rank in society for the good of posterity; it also involved securing the future in the hands of reputable heirs, regardless of legal wrangling, the pressures exerted by the state and the envy of kinsfolk. Hence the attention given to the good heir ('aer da'), the leading inheritor ('Yr aer . . . a dynn ei wlad'), and the chivalrous successor whose courage resembled that of his father (' . . . mawr ei godiad; Aer dewr yn un â'i dad').[62]

Times, however, were changing even though a social doctrine defending the existing hierarchy was still being expounded. Egalitarian features were becoming more frequently noticeable in Tudor literature. The principles of Plato and Aristotle were adapted by a number of Tudor commentators in an attempt to justify hierarchism in the social order. The Welsh poets continued to uphold what they considered to have been the mainstays of an ordered social structure and appeared to dismiss, for the most part, the emergence of new dynamic concepts, with special reference to urban communities, designed to increase mobility by exploiting economic and administrative resources and acquiring education.[63] Consequently, new trends gradually undermined the existing framework and frustrated the attempts of the traditionalists among poets and patrons alike to maintain the *status quo*. The gradual rise in the status of yeomen freeholders and artisans, the methods adopted by the commercial and legal classes to acquire and enjoy gentle status and the increased prosperity which accompanied landed wealth were all leading factors in the breakdown of the old order. Land mobility introduced significant changes in the social and economic structure regardless of the fact that the basic stratification survived. A more vigorous approach to the system of landownership enabled the old and new type of proprietor to benefit by the fluidity in the property market which was to have widespread repercussions on gentry attitudes and status. The centrality of land to the basic concept of gentility was maintained chiefly because of its association with power and influence, and it was in this context that the Welsh poets interpreted the essential features of proprietorial rights in relation to the concepts of virtuous living.

> Dyrchafiaeth dir a chyfoeth,
> A henw'i daid i hwn doeth.[64]

Thus said Siôn Tudur in honour of Ithel Wyn of Ystrad Alun. The accent on ascendancy and growth had become almost an obsession in bardic eulogy, and even the elegies increasingly laid greater emphasis on this theme when viewing the future of the estate in the hands of a competent heir. 'This patron', this poet observed, 'achieved promotion through land and wealth derived from an eminent grandfather.' 'Gwreiddyn gras', ('the source of gracious living'), it was maintained, lay essentially in the ancestral phenomenon and in the manner in which it manifested itself in the demeanour of 'nobility native' or innate *uchelwriaeth*.

Gentility also entailed the sharing of obligations, both moral and functional. Although social theorists endeavoured to cling firmly to principles which were gradually becoming outmoded they were forced to acknowledge the presence of new trends. The strict-metre poets in Wales, however, maintained a rigid concept of man's rôle in community life whereby they measured his standing and innate skills primarily by applying a strict code of conduct. To them and the traditionalists the terrestrial hierarchy created by divine will corresponded to the celestial order. Such a belief betrayed medieval even classical origins as portrayed in the power of the *optimates*, the new nobility, and the *equites*, the knights who performed their respective tasks independently, thus retaining their separate identity. [65] In a bardic context Shakespeare and Spenser were considered to be the prime exponents of a divinely-ordained hierarchy in sixteenth-century English literature, and in Welsh tradition the professional poets performed the same task. In a changing social and economic climate they acted as social and political thinkers armed with the essential genealogical and heraldic expertise. Regardless of the pressures which undermined the relevance of conservative notions the poets, in the period c.1540-1640, stubbornly clung to usages and postures which had characterized their predecessors.

While it was considered necessary to maintain the 'good name and fame' of reputable gentry houses, to bring others needlessly into disrepute was deplored. Indignation and jealous rivalry between kindreds were equally discouraged since maintaining harmonious relations between families and other agnatic groups was regarded as essential to preserve the code of law and order, obedience and discipline in the body politic of the realm. Negligence or public disgrace because of unworthy behaviour, was deemed to have had more detrimental effects on 'good blood' than on upstarts. 'I will have this our Courtier', Castiglione asserted, 'to be a gentleman born and of a good house.' 'For it is a great deal less dispraise for him that is not born a gentleman', he continued, 'to fail in the acts of virtue than for a gentleman. If he swerve from the steps of his ancestors he staineth the name of his family.' Hence, in bardic vocabulary, the emphasis on deference, the cultivation of virtue and the fostering of good family relationships was a feature to be encouraged and widely praised. Petty wrangling and hostility could only do harm, a point driven home forcefully by Siôn Tudur in his advice to the petulant John Salusbury of Lleweni in Denbigh in a poem offering counsel to him after he had injured his kinsman, Captain Owen Salusbury of Holt, in a duel.

> Drwg gyngor a dyr cangau.
> Nad grino dy garennydd,
> Na thor gainc unwaith o'r gwŷdd.
> A dyr coed dewr caeëdig
> Ni thy'n y fron weithion frig.[66]

This poet is expert in giving advice on the need for harmony in social relationships. 'Bad counsel', he declares, 'destroys the boughs' and he continues by describing how the kindred bond can wither. 'He who cuts down sturdy trees', he maintains further, 'will not himself grow to become strong.'

More crucial than the discord and antipathy aroused by kindred rivalries was the permanent effect which such animosities had on family reputation. The concept of gentility was concerned with maintaining the *mores*, the honourable customs and habits exercised in a sophisticated environment. Although the poets favoured good 'stems and roots' they were obliged also to regard the fruit on the boughs as symbols of a gentleman's worth in his community ('O bren a gwraidd . . . Daw brig da, bêr ei egin').[67] Countless references of this nature appear in bardic compositions highlighting such images as the 'dignified stock' ('cyff urddasol'), 'sturdy ancestry' ('coed pybyr'), the 'gilded leaf' ('aur ddeiliog') and 'gentle stock of the neighbourhood' ('dwys goed bro').[68] Unless the boughs flourished the roots, however strong and firm, would be of no value. The nurturing of well-endowed boughs signified seasoned and healthy roots: by themselves they were of no consequence.

> Y pren a fo pur yna
> Arwydd y dwg wreiddiau da.[69]

'The pure tree signifies that it has good roots', the poet declared to Sir Thomas Bruwton, a cleric, and he continued to acclaim the patron's excellence over several lines on that count. These were the carefully-structured lines composed by Wiliam Llŷn, one of the most circumspect among poets of his generation. He seemed constantly occupied with establishing the rightful place for all families which claimed gentility and, in pursuing that end, he measured his words carefully in symbolic terms. The purer the tree, he maintained in his address to Robert Llwyd of Y Waun, the more delectable the fruit.

> Y pren fydd pur yn ei fôn
> A bair afalau'n burion.[70]

'The tree which is pure at its base', he informs, 'will yield fine apples', an image, based on a conservative interpretation of burgeoning trees, which was immensely popular in bardic lore. Wiliam Cynwal also interpreted good gentility as having stemmed from sturdy origins in this couplet to Robert Wyn ap Siôn of Y Wernfawr, Llanbedrog.

> Uchel yw'i brig uwchlaw bron
> Oddi ar winwydd ddâr union.[71]

'Its bough', he says, 'is above all else and stems from a straight and sturdy tree.' Normally, references of this kind relate to oak-trees in view of their stout durability. It was a commonly held concept that gentle roots bred lusty and robust heads of gentle families: prosperous living sprang essentially from auspicious lineage. He who is firmly enrooted, it was maintained, would grow and mature ('Ef a dyf mae'n gryf y gwraidd'). To enhance the family reputation the *paterfamilias* had to nourish the foundations previously laid by worthy forbears.

Eginodd mawr rediad,
A'r rhain gwedi'r hen godiad,
'Wyllys Duw, a wellhâi'u stad.[72]

The family had germinated in a resplendent fashion, Wiliam Cynwal maintained in his elegy to Siân, the wife of Morus Wynn of Gwydir, and the heirs will doubtless improve their status as their forbears had done by God's will and favour. In the same context Sir Thomas Elyot expressed a desire that gentle offspring might cultivate virtues regardless of good ancestry. He 'had ever esteemed the stock by the fruit and not the fruit by the stock', and went on to explain further that 'no man commendeth the boughs or branches because the stem of the tree is long or straight': 'if the stock be never so fair', he stated further, 'if the boughs be rotten or seer the owner will shred them and throw them into the fire.'[73]

Another significant body of thought had emerged by the latter half of the sixteenth century specifically to combat the exclusivity of gentle virtues in the determination of rank and order. Virtue, it was contended, was granted essentially by divine will, and its cultivation revealed excellence. 'Nobility dative' presumed that personal merit and the acquisition of honours were absolutely necessary in determining rank and prestige. Important though they may have been they were not considered essential since no one *uchelwr* could assume nobility merely on the basis of his own basic skills or authority. The College of Arms conferred honour chiefly on the gentleman who bore arms. So notorious had the granting of arms become by the close of the sixteenth century, particularly to unworthy individuals, that the heraldic device had become meaningless.[74] The *nouveaux riches* had achieved a social ascendancy resented by their more conservative peers, and it is hardly surprising that Sir Thomas Smith declared that gentlemen could 'be made good cheape in England'.[75] 'A greater grief it is', Sir John Wynn of Gwydir retorted, 'for upstarts and gent of the first head to look back into their descents being base in such sort.'[76] He added that *parvenu* gentry, who had done well out of the political and administrative system, hated the 'nobility native' 'in their hearts for no other cause but that they were gent'—yet another scathing comment on their dishonourable and unjust claims to gentility. The major features which identified true gentle stock were the ties of blood ('cadarn o waed'), regal status ('Brenhinwaed o'r brenhinoedd') and genuine noble upbringing ('gwiw fonedd'), and Sir John Wynn and other traditional *uchelwyr* defied the forces of social mobility by adhering to concepts which had gradually faded by their day and age.[77] So critical had the situation become that often the distinction between what might be considered gentle and ungentle had become artificial and fabricated. The poet Rhisiart Cynwal was evidently bemused by the fashion to elevate those who had very little in concrete terms to recommend them in the race for status. He found it consoling, nevertheless, to sing to reputable houses; a song to 'puny gentry', he explained in his ode to Sir William Maurice of Clenennau, was unseemly because it obscured true greatness. 'The song is better', he continued, 'where appropriately addressed.' The unworthy ('mân fonedd'), in this context, did not refer to the smaller less eligible freeholders but rather to those who had very little to support their claims to honourable status.

> Ond rhwydd rhoi moliant yrhawg
> A chanu iachau enwawg;
> Nid hawdd cân i fân fonedd,
> Mae'n well y gân man lle'i gwedd.[78]

The poet explicitly draws attention to the distinction which existed between the ranks of gentility and which emerged in the manner employed by the local community to distinguish between those who were the most deserving of the highest position. 'It is easy to give praise and sing to famous stocks', the poet relates, 'but it is not easy to sing to inferior gentlemen.' 'The song is better where appropriate', he added, expressing his smug satisfaction with the way in which he himself had graded families according to their worth.[79]

Siôn Tudur, who was himself a gentleman born and well-acquainted with the features of gentility, severely reprimanded his fellow poets for betraying their craft by granting false pedigrees to those of base origin. The bardic profession, he maintained, had lost its prestige ('Swydd y beirdd sydd heb urddas'). It was the recognized traditional leader only, he declared further, who could justly claim superiority.[80] On the death of a gracious patron, another poet elegantly lamented the demise of an inbuilt concept of royalty. In this instance, the passing of Rowland Fychan, Porth-aml, Talgarth a scion of the famous Vaughan family, signified losing an heir to regal status, a person renowned for his liberality, purity and courage.

> Bwrw nai henbrins brenhinbren . . .
> Aeth haelder, glander, glendyd,
> Aeth dewredd i'r bedd o'r byd.[81]

The pensive manner in which words of this nature are expressed to create a sense of despondency draws attention to the grief felt at the demise of enlightened leadership. 'The nephew of an ancestor of regal stock has passed on', the poet laments, 'bounty, purity and valour have all gone to the grave.' These words have a curious foreboding about them and the elegy, in its entirety, dwells morbidly on the demise of munificent patronage and magnanimous *uchelwriaeth*. A constant reference to honourable reputation in bardic tributes presupposed the need to remind *uchelwyr* of the necessity to maintain and reinforce the character of their gentility. Siôn Tudur often revealed a deep concern for eligibility when addressing his most loyal patrons. The *nouveaux riches*, regardless of their material assets, in his view lacked reputable descent and virtue. Prime qualities were regarded as essential for the public servant, and no man, however powerful, could ever serve in an administrative capacity unless he had inherited well-defined characteristics and had cultivated innate skills. Not all the poets, however, were prepared to cling rigidly to traditional notions of gentility which barred them from according praise to the new forward-looking *uchelwyr* of their day. In fact, they combined in their verse to a broad spectrum of patrons features of the historic *uchelwriaeth* and the characteristics of the new rich.

The acquisition of wealth, usually in the form of landed property, enabled the patron to extend his bounty. Where ancient stock was lacking the poets would attribute social distinction normally to God's grace and favour. In the case of Richard Clough, the prosperous Denbigh merchant, for example, divine goodness, Wiliam Cynwal remarked, had been instrumental in raising his status and adorning him with the salutary features of gentility.

A godo Duw, geidwad Iôn,
Eirchiad dawn, perchid dynion . . .
Dyn a godo Duw'n geidwad
A gaffo gras, goffa i Gred.[82]

'He whom God raises as a person of skill and aptitude', it is said, 'should command the respect of men, and he who is elevated as a defender of his people is equally graced in his office'. This explanation of moral probity, as vested in revered gentlemen, is positively associated with the quality of perception and discretion. It was principally the exercise of virtue in a public capacity which enabled the perfect gentleman to justify himself and provide munificently for others: 'for gentility', Lord Burghley remarked, 'is nothing but ancient riches, so that if the foundation do sink the building must needs consequently fall.'[83] In a purely Welsh context 'riches', as such, were hard to come by so that greater emphasis was placed on the *uchelwr* distinguished by blood and good breeding. Landed wealth, where applicable, was also often considered essential to enhance reputation, but the broad-based Welsh social structure generally maintained that brand of gentility distinguished by descent and virtue. 'It is a happy occasion', one poet remarked, 'to eulogize the main progressive gentry' when referring to those endowed in this way. Another poet considered it a joyous occasion to sing the praises of the 'chief elevated gentry' ('prif fonedd prifiannawl') of his neighbourhood.[84] He proceeded to qualify his statement by referring to the rôle of divine will and favour ('dawn Duw'n ei dâl') in the creation and sustaining of gentility.[85] The nobleman's natural talents (daioni, gallu, rhywiogrwydd) were all combined to create the 'bounteous soul' ('enaid gwych'); the versatile leader granted natural sustenance ('Porth . . . yn porthi haid'); he possessed the 'virtuous soul' ('enaid da'i rinwedd'), and was the head of the household and substantial *paterfamilias* whose solidity and prudence transcended all in the native community.[86]

The fundamental assumption was that some were born to govern and the remainder to be governed: 'some must govern, some must obey', Henry Herbert, second Earl of Pembroke, maintained in his response to the gross mismanagement of public administration by two recalcitrant local administrators in north Wales in 1591, thereby upholding the principle of law and good government which highlighted the features of leadership sanctioned by divine will.[87] It was this phenomenon which enabled the poets to dwell on the qualities of the superior being in the hinterland regions of Wales: the 'gilded pinnacle of the region' ('A phinacl aur a phen gwlad') and the 'radiant personality' ('gŵr odiaeth uwch gwŷr') always ranked supreme in poetic artistry. Wiliam Cynwal, delighting in the antiquity of his patron's lineage, made him constantly aware of his standing among others of his *milieu*.

> Ni wn yr un yn yr iach
> A ddygwn foneddigach,[88]

The poet attempts to focus attention on one person, in this case Tomas Wyn ab Wiliam of Treborth, as the sole representative of the ideal which he is aiming to portray. 'I know of no other in the pedigree', he reassuringly states, 'who is endowed more with the qualities of gentility.' Such a couplet corresponds to the short but apt descriptions of grandeur and exalted status supplied by all the poets: the 'apex of all privileged status' ('pinacl a . . . châr arglwyddiaeth pob bonedd') was the chief manifestation of honourable citizenship in the Welsh context.[89]

The poets, however, found the egalitarian forces too strong to withstand. In the materialistic age of the late sixteenth and early seventeenth centuries, it appeared that defending the old order had become a thing of the past. Increased economic stresses had obscured the relevance of the formal and static interpretations of 'nobility native' in the community structure. The fountain-head of elegant living, however, was still considered to be divine grace from which source the gentleman obtained his natural skills to act in his people's interests ('Duw'n rhoi nawdd dyn rhinweddol')[90] Indeed, any examination of true nobility exposed the prime features of hereditary kingship and the theory of 'triumphant virtue', regarded also as a hereditary trait, and aristocracy by consent. Such a concept led to the emergence of the kingly figure, secure in his position, and it is hardly surprising that the poets associated their patrons with illustrious forbears in the British tradition. The 'emperor', ruler or governor ('llywiawdr'), and head of the kindred (pencenedl), were official designations employed to portray kingship sanctioned by prerogative powers.[91] It was kingship in action which attracted Morus Dwyfech when he referred to the achievements of John Wyn ap Maredudd of Gwydir, descended from royal stock.

> Ysgwier ffres gorau ffrwyth
> O bren henllin brenhinllwyth;
> A fu ddyn fwy'i ddaioni?[92]

This mid-sixteenth-century poet continually viewed his patrons in resplendent military terms and considered their worthy ancestry to be a paramount feature of their expert handling of affairs. 'You are an exuberant squire of the best fruit', he declared, 'descended from an old line of kings', and he wondered whether a better man could ever be found.

Others considered to be 'barons' ('Barwn henfaeth brenhinfawl') and military leaders were inclined, in their own defence, to demonstrate their honour and glory when confronted by adverse elements which posed a threat to order and security. They were elevated for their resilience and courage and were equally regarded as men of regal status who were resolute and divinely ordained to fulfil their tasks.[93]

Renaissance scholars adapted for their own purpose earlier medieval concepts which presupposed the survival of the theory governing the ruling class. Thus was maintained the hypothesis that all privileged individuals, from the highest to the lowest among freeholders, possessed well-defined common features irrespective of social and economic divisions. The Earl of Pembroke, for example, would be accorded similar virtues to those attributed to the mere gentry. In this context, social rank and ostentation was irrelevant since the poets interpreted the chief features of gentle life to be common to all. The keyword was 'virtue' (rhinwedd). 'You are a gilded hawk among other smaller birds', one poet maintained to his patron whom he regarded as a noble hero and figure of excellence.[94]. Ill-government and disunity, it was stated further, will corrupt a man's lineage and defile his posterity.[95] Maintaining order entailed preserving God's peace ('Cynnal heddwch Duw'). The gracious leader commanded loyalty among residents in his community since they were normally linked to him by bonds of kindred or tenancy.

> Un gŵr sydd a gras iddaw
> Yn dwyn ei wlad yn ei law.[96]

The gracious nobleman exercised full command in his area of jurisdiction, Siôn Cain declared in his eulogy for Gruffudd Nannau, and demonstrated his capacity to govern using all his available resources. The defender of order genuinely upheld the common welfare of the state. Stability in society was totally dependant on hierarchy and the exertions of those vested with power to preserve and administer law and justice. In his community, Wiliam Cynwal remarked of Wiliam ap Gruffudd ap Tomas, a modest gentleman from Bangor, he was uniquely endowed with all good virtue.

> Yn ei ardal bu'n wrda;
> Hwn a ddug bob rhinwedd dda.[97]

Good virtue, he observed, made the *uchelwr* a loyal subject and obliged him to impose that loyalty on others. He was a custodian of his people, a head and protector (' . . . yn geidwad, A phen ac amddiffyniad')[98] and a symbol of stability whose grandeur surpassed all. Such magnificence is demonstrated most impressively in *awdlau* where such properties are revealed in the most profuse manner. Power portrayed in material terms usually symbolized authority and leadership. Symbolically, the leading ox in the furrow was normally taken to be the highest and most senior officer of the law among eligible gentry. 'The magnificent emperor of Gwynedd', said Wiliam Cynwal of a patron, 'was a leader and governor of the whole region.'[99] His ambitions, he continued, were aimed at producing a favoured heir to maintain the line of succession. Dynastic stability was accorded a prominence in bardic thought on the concepts of *uchelwriaeth*, and eulogies constantly referred to the revered succession and the preservation of the estate for posterity ('Gorau sylfaen . . . sail i barhau').[100] The seed, it was maintained, would germinate and grow and divine patronage would preserve men of status ('Cadw'r ydych .

. . Y gras Duw mal gŵyr o stad').[101] God graces the house which provides an heir to preserve the common heritage to the future.

> Nid marw'r tad, er ymado,
> A ad fab yn ei dŷ fo.[102]

'The father who leaves a son in his house will not die although he has departed', Siôn Tudur maintained when mourning the death of Wiliam Mostyn. The concept of maintaining the inheritance in perpetuity pervades all eulogistic verse and enables the poets to focus on the functions of unceasing patrimonial government. The privileges of birth, inheritance, land and education among others would be bestowed upon the 'gracious heir, prestigious and sagacious, who lives peaceably and charitably'.[103] His actions will reveal him as a man of high esteem whose noble attributes will serve as an example to all in his community. He possessed qualities superior to those displayed by his inferiors and even some among his less reputable peers.

> E wyddai'r hyn a oedd rhaid,
> Nis gŵyr mân ysgwieriaid.[104]

This *uchelwr*, judging by what Siôn Tudur said about Sergeant Pyrs Gruffudd of Caerwys, knew better than any man of lesser status what needed to be done to maintain the common welfare of his people and dependants.

Such couplets demonstrate clearly that manner adopted by sixteenth-century poets to distinguish between the true and false claimants of gentility. The gentleman did not acquire his rank merely by accident of birth but rather by the cultivation of qualities which his inheritance obliged him to practise in action and thought. 'So ought a gentleman', the writer of *The Institucion of a Gentleman* observed, 'by his conditions, qualities and good behaviour to excel all other sorts of men.'[105] Personal attainment in any specific field was one thing; applying it to the good of all was another. Such references in bardic compositions are very difficult to quantify but they are consistently manipulated in such a way that the patron appears as the essence of justice, the 'soul' of his region ('Yn y tir enaid da'), the 'head and body' ('Y pen oedd ef'), reigning supreme over his dependants who were considered to be the various parts of the corporate entity ('A'r wlad oedd yr aelodau').[106] He was constantly portrayed as the 'prime jewel' in his land endowed with civilized traits ('Gŵraidd yw . . . glana dyn a glain nod iaith'). Such pretentious declarations were not considered to be meaningless since such persons deemed worthy of possessing them were usually devoted to pursuing a career of public service in the state. Emphasis was increasingly placed on performing loyal duties to the Crown and leadership. With the decline in military service and the feudal concepts of homage and fealty there emerged in Renaissance Europe a gradual but significant increase in laymen who acquired learning and aspired to the highest positions of administrative and legal service on a national or regional scale. The *noblesse oblige* became more prominently noticeable in the manner in which the poets referred to office-holding and a sense of obligation to the body politic of the realm.

Dawnus ym mhob daioni
Drwy'r deyrnas yw'ch urddas chwi.[107]

Focus was placed on talent in the exercise of public duty. 'You are talented in all goodness', Gruffudd Phylip reminded his patron John Jones, attorney of the common pleas, of Dol-y-moch, Ffestiniog, 'and your prestige is well-known and respected throughout the whole realm'.

The references to public service retained close links with the classical interpretation of true citizenship. Responsibility, like power and privilege, developed essentially from attaining a privileged position. It had to be fostered and, if neglected, it could lie dormant and become ineffective. In one of his *cywyddau* counselling a young heir, Siôn Conwy of Botryddan, on the ways he should approach his task as the prospective head of a privileged family, Siôn Tudur emphasized the need for the young squire to offer genuine service to the community in which he resided. His talents, the poet maintained, had been bestowed upon him by God; instead of aiming to suppress them the young heir apparent should rather apply them to foster goodwill and moral prosperity among his people.

Bydd gywir ar dy dir di . . .
Câr dy wlad, cordia ledwg,
Cais beri draw cosbi'r drwg . . .
Rhan dda iawn, rhan Dduw yna
Yw rhoi y dawn i'r rhai da.[108]

The lines emphasize a combination of moral probity and firm patriotism. 'Be true to your land, love your country and endeavour to destroy wrongdoing', it is said, 'because your rôle has been granted to you by God who offers talents to those who, by nature, are good.' He who replenished the needs of Wales ('porthi holl Gymru'), who stood magnanimously as a leader in the land ('Dwyn mawredd holl Gymru') and who functioned as the very heart of his country ('calon y wlad') displayed the most vital aspects of his region's moral well-being and gave it added vitality.[109]

In the course of the social and economic changes which gradually occurred in the Tudor century it was considered necessary to accept the forces of new gentility and attempt to accord to it the features of the traditional Welsh prototype. The qualities which Morus Dwyfech and others of his generation acknowledged to be innate and immoveable in members of such families as Bodwrda, Cefnamwlch or Penrhyn had to be applied with equal meaning to members of the *advenae* class, the Stradlings, Mansels and Salusburies in Welsh community life. The acquisition of wealth and influential family connections inside and outside Wales was rapidly displacing the respect conceded to native pedigree as the norm of reputable gentility, and the poets found it incumbent upon them to grant to the *nouveaux riches* equal status with others who claimed 'nobility native'. Indeed, such was the pressure upon them that an increasing number of strict-metre poems were composed in honour of individuals who had stemmed from English stock but who had married into leading Welsh families and had in that way acquired a new reputation.

The Tudor monarchy was primarily intent on fostering and preserving loyalty and allegiance and promoting efficiency in government. The group of new men who became involved in such activities grew in number and prestige, particularly after the Acts of Union. Consequently, the essential differences between social degrees became more blurred and meaningless. Conversely, emphasis on business skills and acumen became more marked and the honour accorded to the old concepts of *uchelwriaeth* lost much of its appeal. The demand was increasingly for expertise in administration and law as well as good governorship. 'The aristocracy of the pen', as Fritz Caspari put it, 'began to invade and even displace that of the sword.'[110] Within that context, and under changing conditions, it became abundantly clear that the old order had to acquire learning if it was to survive in such a competitive society.[111] The recipients of eulogy in the latter half of the sixteenth century displayed some military expertise, but more frequently they demonstrated their administrative and peace-keeping talents. Ancestral connections were more often supplemented by the acquisition of office and territorial influence. In other words, public service demanded skilful and dedicated laymen from diverse backgrounds who were vitally interested in fortifying their own material position and, at the same time, maintaining the integrity of the Tudor state.

New attitudes and obligations, however, did entail adhering strictly to a moral code of behaviour which poets stressed with persistent clarity in their eulogies. They conveniently accommodated the *nouveaux riches* by applying to them the customary formal modes of address and attributing to them the qualities which the old *uchelwriaeth* had possessed. Newer concepts were gradually emerging following the influence of the European Renaissance and the publication of manuals on the manners and status of gentlefolk in the making. Those who are born with grace, Castiglione observed, are resplendent: 'they seem not to have been born', he maintained, 'but rather fashioned with the very hand of God, and abound in all goodness, both of body and mind'. 'The Courtier', he further remarked, 'beside nobleness of birth . . . and by nature to have not only a wit . . . [has] also a certain grace and a hue.'[112] In a similar context one Welsh poet commented on the gracious reputation of his patron as the norm of gentility ('Ysgwiair dwys a gair da').

Goodness was accepted universally as the essence of gentility; it was traditionally regarded as the innate quality which stemmed from noble ancestry. Owing to social circumstances which strengthened contacts with English families the qualities of 'goodness', as interpreted by the poets, were extended to include individual persons—men and women—who sprang, either wholly or in part, from privileged non-Welsh origins. It had to be cultivated if the highest virtues were to be preserved. Basically, goodness comprised all those attributes overtly displayed in the gentleman's mode of life. It was God's paramount gift and it entailed the skill to govern well and also, through example, the power to make all men good. The poets frequently felt obliged to consider the nature of that goodness which characterized their patrons, chiefly as a manifestation of moral probity. It was a feature which, in the last resort, justified the eulogy. Good virtue ('rhin dda') constituted the gentleman's prime faculty ('cyneddfau gorau gŵr'), and it is not altogether surprising that the prime eulogistic themes hinged on this concept of moral probity which stemmed from the supreme good. The countryside would thereby be fortified by the actions of the reputable governor, and his attributes would be adorned with a befitting demeanour, the highest grace and the paramount good (*summum bonum*: 'iarllin benllad'). In this illustrious manner the poets would applaud their patrons and would draw attention to their grace and integrity ('Â gras ewch i'r gris uchel'). The Welsh *uchelwr* was considered to be superlative in the art of gentility ('bonedd y sy bennaf') and thus earned the highest accolades which professional declaimers could bestow upon him.[113]

Constant efforts were made to place the good man within his social environment, a task which was undertaken by Sir Thomas Elyot, Sir Thomas Smith, Roger Ascham and others in England. In Wales, the major interpretations of gentility are found in poetic compositions. The *uchelwr* was accorded his rightful position in his public and private capacities as an upright governor of his region or as a benign manager of his landed and household affairs in his *llys* or mansion house.

Ystad beirdd yn studio byd,
A dymuno da mynnych
I bob Emprwr a gŵr gwych.[114]

The poet's task, Wiliam Llŷn observed in his ode to Sir Edward Herbert, is to study the world and wish well to all rulers and men of excellence. In this context he interpreted his rôle as being that of a percipient observer of human nature at its most elevated. 'You are good and noble by nature', Edwart ap Raff explained to his patron,

Morgan ap Robert of Branas, Merioneth, 'also learned, amusing, wise and gentle.'

> Da notabl yw dy natur;
> Dysgedig, diddig a doeth.[115]

In practically every poem composed purely as a panegyric references abound to innate features which normally included benevolence, charity, munificence and moral rectitude. Owain Gwynedd associated Tomas ap Huw of Pumwern, Pennal with that goodness essentially linked with liberality and sagacity in word and deed.

> Da iawn yn rhoi da i'n rhaid,
> Daioni Duw i'w enaid.[116]

The words are resounding and equally reassuring for the heir of an *uchelwr* who was regarded as exemplary in the manner in which he granted to the bardic fraternity their needs; 'God's goodness', he added, 'lay securely in his soul'. That goodness had emerged as a leading feature in his character by virtue of his inalienable birthright and the noble qualities which that had created. Elyot drew attention to traits of this kind when describing the powers of the statesman or ruler in the sovereign realm: he is the person of influence and authority whose contribution to public life was regarded as being essential to the common good of the state. Similarly, the poets depicted their patrons, whether they held office or not, as symbols of moral excellence, exercising power in the institutions of law or managing their affairs privately in their own country mansions.

> Bu ŵr grasol bur groeso,
> Bu hyfryd ei fywyd fo;
> Da oedd fo dyddiau'i fywyd,
> Trwy iawn barch yn trin y byd.[117]

It was thus that Gruffudd Phylip assessed the contribution of Lewis ap Simwnt, grandson of Baron Lewis ab Owain, of Hafod-dywyll, Brithdir. It is a difficult task to judge how many prime talents the poets expected to discover in the manner in which the *uchelwr* attended to his duties and responsibilities. In the Middle Ages the concept of knighthood included well-defined Christian features, and such qualities as devotion, courage, charity and courtesy were given prominence. This religious dimension, although not entirely abandoned in the sixteenth century, was largely superseded by practical material factors aimed at improving the efficiency of secular government or promoting business acumen. In poetic terms, however, goodness constantly implied Christian charity, and virtues were regarded as being granted by divine sanction. In other words, God's will perfected gentility in action.

> Dyn a euro Duw'n unig
> A gyrraedd braint, gwraidd a brig;
> A ddonio Duw o'i ddynion
> A ddaw'n hyd y ddaear hon.[118]

'It is the man whom God honours only who achieves ancestral privileges', the poet comments with a view to exposing the rare combination of talents. 'They whom God endows with talents', he continues, 'will succeed in this world', an assurance to the patron that all was well in his case. Such lines clearly manifested God's central rôle in the creation with regard to the structure and development of gentility.

The concepts of gentility, as defined in the Tudor and early Stuart periods, were basically Aristotelian and associated with the values expounded by Augustine and Thomas Aquinas and later Renaissance scholars. To them the principal virtues were justice, prudence, fortitude and temperance. Allied with these was the sense of public duty in both military and civil spheres of activity. Even Christian ideals were identified with older Aristotelian concepts in so far as they upheld and enriched the image of the moral being. To that extent they were conveniently blended with those of pagan origin and were considered to be among the most noteworthy traits of native *uchelwriaeth*. Not that the poets had been influenced directly by such ideas as has been noted earlier, but the concepts of gentility adhered to in the bardic schools revealed some of their fundamental principles. The patron who was regarded as the 'crown of goodness' ('coron daioni') was, in fact, in possession of both pagan and Christian virtues but they were interpreted essentially as being endowed by God—the fount of virtue—for the benefit of humanity.

Aristotelian teaching differed essentially from basic Christian principles because it expounded inequality of status as the basis of the social structure. Christianity accepted that inequalities are unavoidable in secular life but clearly emphasized that, in the sight of God, all human beings are equal. The numerous poems composed in honour of the Godhead and the Trinity make concrete references to central beliefs of this kind and examine God's eternal goodness towards mankind. In secular life, however, it was considered that perfection in this world could only be attained by the privileged few at the expense of their dependants. Thus was combined an awareness of secular virtue: he who has wisdom and grace, one poet maintained, symbolizes human integrity in an imperfect world.

> Synnwyr a gras sy ynod . . .
> Dy air sy lawn dros y wlad.[119]

Siôn Salusbury of Rug's good judgement, grace and trustworthy demeanour, Siôn Tudur declared, were fully respected over the region where he reigned. The territorial concept of magnitude assumes significant proportions at all times in bardic panegyrics of this kind. The couplet implies that the *uchelwr* had adeptly applied his essential goodness to the needs of the secular world.

The professional poets divided human virtues principally into two main categories, public and private. In his relations with others the *uchelwr* was considered to be renowned for his sense of justice, courtesy and liberality. He himself would practice temperance and prudence, the qualities of self-discipline regarded as essential for attaining public acclamation. Who else, in bardic estimation, could become the' author of virtue'('awdur rhinwedd'), the 'epitome of grace' ('uchelder gras'), the 'vineyard of gentility' ('Gardd win y rhywiogrwydd'), the 'summit of aristocracy' ('brig pendefigaeth') and the 'gilded pinnacle of his region'('A phinacl aur a phen gwlad') if not the person who contained within himself the perfect blend of public and private virtues. In this sense the good man was equated with the sublime ruler. The faculties which enabled the *uchelwr* to rule with distinction constituted an extra dimension to private morality as expounded by Elyot in *The Governour* where justice, fortitude, magnanimity, temperance and wise judgement were collectively regarded as uppermost. Furthermore, a sense of majesty added significantly to the creation of the perfect gentleman, displaying strong traces of humanity, grace and liberality.

Of all the virtues justice was considered to be of the highest order, followed by prudence, courtesy, liberality and integrity in word and deed. These prime features were overtly displayed in the sixteenth-century concept of the Christian gentleman as he emerged in public life.[120] In Welsh poetic compositions the just patron was placed at the top end of the social scale. He possessed inbuilt moral resources and was strong, resolute and unyielding in his opposition to the forces of evil. Justice embraced those rich qualities which befitted the ideal Tudor governor, all of which were reflected conspicuously in the *awdlau* and *cywyddau* of the age. Thus Siôn Phylip addressed Gruffudd Fychan II of Corsygedol in this context:

> Drwy bwyll gyfiawnder a barn;
> Cadw'r wlad rhag cad rhai cedyrn . . .
> Duw a'th roes ar wlad i'th ran,
> Do yn bennaeth dyn byw anian.[120]

Through the constant application of reason, justice and law the *uchelwr* was able to defend the country from all its oppressors. God had placed him, with his active concern for law and order, as the cherished leader of his country. In these lines justice prevails as the most dominant feature and it also served admirably as a secure guide to determine the rights of others, to consolidate natural bonds of affinity and also to bind men together in a common cause to defeat the forces of evil.

In his rôle as landed proprietor, a man of law and social benefactor, the just person was unyielding and firm in his defence of righteousness. His service revealed undeviating loyalty to the acknowledged sovereign power in the state. No man could function in any capacity unless he had displayed his willingness to safeguard all the public institutions that were considered honourable in the realm. Justice was regarded as an all-embracing feature in the moral character of the gentry, and was hailed as the foundation of all virtues. No community could prosper without just leaders to govern and protect the common welfare of its inhabitants from external threat and internal dissension.

Prudence was another virtue portrayed as being uppermost in the character of the model *uchelwr* who exercised wisdom in managing his affairs. Prudent behaviour called for circumspection in thought and action and signified how dexterously the public figure responded to his responsibilites at community level. The prudent gentleman was normally taken to be rational, discreet and tenacious. Emphasis was placed on the exercise of controlled action. Irresponsible or irrational reactions to public and private duty would have detrimental effects on community welfare. He who rose to pre-eminence acquired honour principally through restrained and unselfish action.

> O chodaist yn barchedig,
> I ben y braint, bôn a brig;
> Cynnal dy ffortiwn cennyd
> Drwy bwyll wrth air Duw a'r byd.[121]

The poet remarks that this munificent patron had been elevated respectfully to the highest point of privileged gentility, and had maintained his fortune in a rational and equitable manner. The preservation of 'privilege' ('braint') entailed maintaining close ties with kinship ('gwaedoliaeth'). These lines disclose the true *uchelwr* as he who displayed tenacity and astuteness in matters which required delicate and decisive action. The perfect gentleman is constantly portrayed as a man of deliberate action and honesty who has a fine mind and humble disposition.

> A synnwyr hen sy ynod
> Ar bob enw ar bawb yna
> A'th ddysg a naturiaeth dda.[122]

The *uchelwr* and his stock possessed ancient reasoning powers, the poet remarked, and thereby nurtured learning and a good nature which strengthened his hand when dealing with subversive powers in his territory.

In every *awdl* and *cywydd* which draw attention to the *uchelwr* and his surroundings the emphasis is constantly on his ability to rule and extend his authority in his region on behalf of the sovereign realm. George Owen of Henllys, who possessed all the normal traits of a typical Tudor gentleman in Wales, was admiringly described by Siôn Mawddwy as the local governor who held sway in his native Dyfed with abundant wisdom and prudence: similarly scores of other patrons throughout Wales were endowed with the magnificence and prestige of the provident leader.[123]

In addition, the virtues of courtesy and liberality added significantly to the picture of the gentleman who commanded respect and obedience within his household and area of jurisdiction. His courtesy displayed an urbane demeanour and a state of grace, and such a quality appealed immensely to the social commentators of the age. Courtesy, to Sir Thomas Elyot, constituted a gracious bearing—the sense of decency and dignity—which betrayed elements of majesty in action. 'In a governor as man having in the public weal some great authority', he stated, 'the fountain of all excellent manners is majesty.' Grace, or *grazia*, elevated the *uchelwr* to a position of moral supremacy, creating him almost as a work of art, the emphasis being chiefly on the affable, honourable and comely rather than on the arrogant and uncivil. 'When a noble man passeth by, showing to men a gentle and familiar visage', he continued, 'it is a world to beholde how people lack the comfort, how the blood in their visage quickeneth, how their flesh stirreth and hearts leapeth for gladness.' Castiglione, on the other hand, concentrated solely on courtesy, stressing *sprezzatura* or effortlessness in accomplishment, *urbanitas*, the cultivation of polished demeanour, and *gravita reposata*, the majesty of bearing. *Sprezzatura* became the chief visible manifestation of grace which, in itself, was a gift of nature, In England and Wales, the man who possessed such faculties ('aeddfed cyneddfau') owed his existence to God, but the fashionable Italian concept also appears to have had an impact on the Welsh poets, particularly with regard to ideas about good judgement and ease of accomplishment. These are not easily definable terms when applied to practical affairs but, when translated into active conditions, they reveal the practical wisdom which Renaissance scholars linked with the *vita activa*. Such a rich combination blended high moral principles with the public sense of duty in the efficient governor. Sir Thomas Hoby's epistle in his translation of Castiglione's masterpiece, set out to 'garnish' the minds of young gentlemen 'with moral virtues and their bodies with comely exercises . . . and . . . the most necessary implements for the conversation, use, and training up of man's life with courtly demeanours.' Virtues, as exemplified in the *uchelwr*, were interpreted essentially as 'a harmony of parts' which was normally manifested in good conduct and propriety.

Tyfodd ei foliant hefyd
At ras a'i barch tros y byd.[124]

In these lines Eliza ab Wiliam Llwyd I of Rhiwedog was described by Huw Pennant as a man who deserved eulogy which accentuated his grace and reverence, qualities which he permanently enjoyed.

Poets interpreted the virtuous *uchelwr* against a broader civilized background invariably associated with the royal or aristocratic court: 'it is a sober and discreet behaviour', Castiglione explained when referring to the essential features of courtesy, 'that in court winneth both credit and commodity.'[125] Such grandiose concepts find their place in bardic tributes as well since the 'dignified bearing' and magnanimity of mind and 'nobleness of actions', according to the medieval bardic grammar, were prominent features in the strict-metre panegyrics. The dignity of gait, stately bearing and appearance, the grace which emerged from good breeding as well as God's beneficence to the privileged, were all features which assumed prominence. Courtesy and its attendant features, however, were not considered merely as abstract qualities since they were amply demonstrated in the pursuance of the practical aims of the sovereign state. The *uchelwr* noted for his just character would maintain the honour of his estate and degree and would prosper as the superior leader in his *tiriogaeth* or region of jurisdiction. It was in this fashion that Wiliam Cynwal described Huw ap Siôn of Rhosllanerchrugog.

Cyfiawnder a chymeriad . . .
. . . os deil a geidw ei stad;
Gwych y tyf . . . gŵr ffynadwy
Cadarn . . . mewn goruchafiaeth[125]

A man of justice and good character, it is said, if he survives, will sustain his estate and grow splendidly; he will also be prosperous and firm in his ascendancy. It is this persistent recall to supremacy or superiority in the native environment which adds splendour to lineage in all bardic accolades.

The emphasis on character and justice associates the perfect gentleman with his public rôle in society: his ascendancy reflected his innate virtues. Over-indulgence, however, could breed contemptible features such as arrogance, pride and jealousy, traits which were strongly deplored in such sophisticated verse. Siôn Phylip cautiously counselled the young heir of Corsygedol in Merioneth to shun pride ('balchder'), flattery ('gweniaith'), falsehood and fabrication ('celwyddawg . . . ffug'), jealousy and envy ('Cenfigenwas . . . ffals') with a view to maintaining his self-respect and the good reputation of his stock.[126] To Sir Francis Bacon gracious behaviour was 'the garment of the mind that was not to be over-indulgent and over-expensive'. It ought to be shaped in such a way that it reveals 'any virtue of the mind'. On the other hand it should not hinder a man from acting honourably in his own interests and for the benefit of his family. The chieftain in his region ('pendefig gwlad'), the superior among his people and the head of all public affairs in his neighbourhood ('pennaeth gwladwriaeth gwlad wych') was the munificent patron who extended his influence over the countryside protecting the welfare of all in his care as the 'very soul' of his locality. His grace, pride and peaceful demeanour revealed a posture characteristic of the governor in the course of his duties. The 'civilized and gracious' person ('gwaraidd a llariaidd') was highly reputed for his effortlessness in accomplishment. Grace and courtesy did not entail over-exertion or over-indulgence but rather allowed the normal features of human virtue to manifest themselves in their natural environment.

In the bardic tradition the concept of grace signified the perfection of form as symbolized in the courtier as well as the spirit which controlled individual activity and attitudes towards others. Grace, it was believed, was a divine gift extended to the privileged order, and the origin of gracious living ('gwreiddyn y gras') stemmed from God's bounty to those who had been granted sublime pedigrees. When the poets referred to the 'crown of grace' ('coron y gras'), the 'godly grace' ('duwiol gras'), 'gracious living' ('grasoliaeth') and the 'gentleman of abundant grace' ('gŵr aml ei ras'), they emphasized the principal features of decorum and moral integrity blended in such a manner as to create a self-possessed and self-controlled individual. The gracious person practised wisdom and handled efficiently the affairs of his region. He is the *exempla* of magnanimity, equanimity, composure, serenity and refinement. Owain Gwynedd expressed all these qualities in one powerful couplet in an ode to Tomas ap Huw of Pumwern.

> Gŵr didwyll, gŵr da ydoedd,
> Gwir be byw, gŵr i bawb oedd.[127]

He was regarded as a sincere and good man, truthful in all that he accomplished and a man who served all with exemplary exactitude.

The *uchelwr* who demonstrates grace, it was said, commanded the allegiance of his people. In place of the flamboyant features of the Italian courtier the English commentators and Welsh poets portrayed the sturdy upright governor who still shared a good number of the common virtues which constituted the gracious being. The *vita activa* emerged succinctly as the external manifestation of perfection. Goodness was normally equated with excellence of purpose and achievement, and led others to a condition of gracious living through example.[128] In this context the Welsh poets strenuously endeavoured to portray their patrons as constituting the ideal in their *tiriogaeth* and, for the most part, set about to associate virtue with the specific duties of statesmanship. It assumed a functional rôle and was manifested in the character of the public servant, the hospitality offered in the *plasty* and the charity which the landowner distributed among his tenants. Such features are distinguished by references to the 'gracious Solomon' ('Selyf gras'), the 'gracious host' ('gŵr grasol') and the 'godly and sagacious being' ('mor rasol, mor dduwiol ddoeth'). Guided by expediency he would acquire from others of all ranks what he considered to be his due, and grant to them what they deserved. Each *uchelwr*, parading his virtues, was endowed with the noble qualities equivalent to the traditional aristocracy of England. The nobleman ('pendefig'), in poetic terms, represented the most illustrious among a group of eligible gentry.

Bu ysgwier mawr uwch llaw'r lleill,
Yn ragori rag eraill.[129]

He was doubtless accorded the virtues of the esquire who excelled all others and manifested his superiority in word and deed.

Emphasis was also placed on the qualities of liberality or munificence. Eulogistic poetry had constantly referred to the benefits of hospitality to the under-privileged, and during the sixteenth century its demise as a source of sustenance was deplored. Liberality was the essence of good living in the country mansion, a sustaining feature of the bounteous gentleman displaying his abilities to serve the needs of his community. This bounty was normally identified with the Christian virtue of charity and had emerged from the ancient Germanic concept of generosity to companies-in-arms as a demonstration of magnanimity by a self-respecting leader of men in battle. Among gentle qualities generosity ('haelder'), sustenance ('cynhaliaeth'), care and succour ('ymgeledd'), welfare ('gwellhad a lles') and household patronage ('perchentyaeth') ranked among the most conspicuous. Such bounty was well-controlled: rewards were not distributed unless fully deserved. Granting hospitality to the ill-favoured cast doubts on the veracity and trust of the gentleman and might undermine his privileged status. Generosity was also considered to be the most explicit form of virtuous living bestowed by divine will. The *uchelwr* symbolized moral fortitude acting as a buttress against the forces of mis-government and poverty. In these terms Wiliam Cynwal, representing others of his *milieu* who sang lavishly the praises of modest gentry, interpreted the *uchelwriaeth* of his day as a manifestation of innate goodness.

A dibarha yw da dyn;
Da a gair i'r rhai da'u gwedd,
A'r da dderfydd o'r diwedd,
A'r weithred dda . . . a bery'n hir.[130]

The poet exemplifies the power of goodness as highlighted in Morus Wynn of Gwydir, principally through the survival of his good deeds into the future, even after his death. In addition to perpetuating the good name and fame of the house and strengthening the public image of reputable gentry such munificence also concentrated on the *uchelwr* as the paragon of excellence whose good offices would survive his mortal life. Siôn Phylip, in a poem to Rhisiart ap Dafydd ap Tomas, a minor gentleman from Hendrefechan in Llanaber, Merioneth, stressed his acumen and discretion as well as other honourable features. His accumulation of land and property, he maintained, did not prevent him from attending to other essential duties which elevated his moral stature among his dependants. The focus in the following lines is on the nobleman's self-discipline and skill in avoiding worldly temptations to prosper by devious means.

Dy olud di a welir
A ddylai'n hawdd ddal yn hir,
Ni wnaethost mewn anoethwedd
I gynnull hwn, gannwyll hedd,
Drawster na thaerder na thwyll,
Dyn iawnbarch, ond unionbwyll,
Na thrwy drais, eithr Duw a'i rhodd,
Duw weithian a'i bendithiodd.[131]

His prosperity, it is manifested, should survive long because the patron's material wealth had not been accumulated unwisely or fraudulently through oppression or deception. 'You are highly respected', the poet added, 'since God has granted you your bounty and has blessed it.' The lines record the prestigious position assumed by the *uchelwr* who practised virtue in property affairs.

Material rewards were considered secondary to moral sustenance and refined living enjoyed by the *uchelwr* in his mansion. The lord's court was often regarded as the soul of the countryside ('i'th lys enaid i'th wlad'), and his good lady, by the very nature of her gentle upbringing and benignity, was equally praised for her charity and hospitality. It is in this context that Siôn Dafydd sang to Siân, the wife of Siôn Llwyd, Ceiswyn, Talyllyn, who was himself a prominent patron of poets.

Cadwodd ei thŷ mewn codiad,
Oll ar les i wellhau'r wlad.[132]

This gentlewoman kept house, as did so many others of her *milieu*, in a dignified manner for the good and well-being of the countryside. Liberality knew no bounds and was considered to be a paramount feature of gentle life. Excessive generosity was deplored since it could lead to corruption and dissoluteness. The beneficent patron gave according to his means, and the sixteenth-century poets drew attention increasingly to the lack of initiative on the part of the Welsh gentry in matters relating to these basic functions. Furthermore, the loss of patrons, through death or misfortune, signified the demise of hospitality and the creation of a void never again to be filled. Such a theme had become more pronounced by the latter half of the century: whereas in previous generations it was considered that a man's character lived after him in his heirs, in the period of cultural decline elements of dispair and despondency were underlined more frequently.

In purely materialistic terms liberality was based essentially on wealth ('golud'), but the poets did not attach too much significance to visible manifestations of prosperity. In fact, poetic tributes endeavoured to maintain an equilibrium between the practical and abstract qualities of *uchelwriaeth*. The possession and accumulation of landed property did not necessarily diminish the gentleman's reputation unless any sharp practice on his part cast doubts as to his motives. Without material gain the *uchelwr* could not afford to extend generous hospitality. One Merioneth patron was compared with fertile land which yielded a good crop through God's grace.[133] Virtue, it was said, might well be innate but it also had to be nourished. Castiglione drew upon another not dissimilar comparison: 'as the bee in green meadows flyeth always about the grass, choosing out flowers', he explained, 'so shall our Courtier steal his grace from them that to his seeming have it.' Without liberality the *uchelwr* was denied true gentility. 'This man, therefore, that can thus govern', it was said, 'and moderate the motions of the mind, hath won the love of temperance, and shall be honoured of all men as one inclined with a rare and singular virtue.'[134] Temperance acted as a firm control on excessive passion and over-indulgence; its exercise fortified the gentleman when beleaguered by evil forces. When Edward Dafydd of Margam hailed his patron, Siôn Powel of Maesteg, as the fount of knowledge ('gwybyddiaeth'), learning ('athrawiaeth'), military sagacity ('gwrolaeth'), humanity ('dynoliaeth'), godliness ('duwoliaeth') and renowned ancestry he referred specifically to the skills associated with the revered Welsh *uchelwr*, well-disciplined in his actions, versatile in his accomplishments and influential in public affairs.[135]

Constant references to the patron's courage ('gwrolder') and valour ('glewder') pointed yet again to another noble trait which portrayed the *uchelwr* at his most chivalrous. His unqualified successes in all actions and responses made him a figure of admiration and essentially a protector of his people. In the Middle Ages the virtue of courage was interpreted largely in a military context, but, by the sixteenth century, it had been applied to describe the individual whose superiority lay in his ability to overcome and master adversity. Indeed, fortitude and endurance were yet again features which dominated the good life of the *uchelwr*, particularly in the task of maintaining law and order and preserving the organic unity of his community. Courage and tenacity were required to master the traditional feats of accomplishment which the gentry were expected to perform with agility. Such qualities aided him in his task of suppressing all vestiges of opposition or threat to his position or to the security of his people. In the poetic tributes courage was identified with strength of purpose, tenacity, fortitude (or valour) and resilience ('cryfder', 'grym', 'sadrwydd', 'goruchafiaeth', 'nerth'). It symbolized direct action and created heroes of young heirs. Such features also consolidated the protector's hold over his property and helped to increase it.

> Aer o bower a bywyd
> Ai'r un barch aer yn y byd.[136]

The heir to power and a privileged life, Siôn Phylip sang in an ode to Gruffudd Fychan II of Corsygedol, earned for himself universal respect. He possessed courage and valour which no man inferior to him could ever hope to attain. Courage, in this context, is regarded as being more dynamic than Christian fortitude: its aim was to defend the body politic of the realm and protect the good as well as ruling and controlling a region and supervising an estate. 'The duty of every gentleman', it was said, 'is to keep his courage with wisdom' or, as the poet explained, the *uchelwr* amply demonstrates his courage, generosity and wisdom principally in his public appearances.

> Am ddewrder a haelder hwn,
> Am synnwyr mwy a soniwn.[137]

In such abundance did the munificent patron support his own virtues that more again can be related, the poet exclaimed, about his courage, liberality and reasoning powers.

The magnanimous host ('iraidd wych', 'gwrolwych') was placed in a higher position because the qualities of clemency and forbearance contained those virtues constantly found in the individual functioning in a public and private capacity. Those qualities also gave expression to the high-mindedness which directed his actions, hence the continuous references to the 'fine resplendent pinnacle'('pinagl gwych') and to the person who had 'prestigious ostentation' ('rhwysg urddas'). Such forbearance gave the *uchelwr* a sense of honour which constituted the prime reward for virtuous living. 'The deeds of virtue', it was said, 'be worthy of honour, the which are put in execution by exercising magnanimity.'[138] Personal worthiness was increased and the individual became more aware of his duties to the state.

In England the governor was described as a statesman in the sense that all he accomplished in public and private life was directed towards the good of the body politic. The benefits of the state constituted his major concern; thus he attained the status of lord or leader in a purely political sense. Such a patron who devoted his time and energy to furthering good works displayed equanimity, composure and self-discipline. He judged individuals primarily by their virtues and was consequently hailed by all as the most distinguished figure in his locality.

> Dangosaist . . .
> O'th fawr barch i'th fro bur;
> Haelder, galawnder, glendyd,
> A rhan gŵr yw rhain i gyd.[139]

He amply demonstrated generosity, gallantry and purity because of his inherently acquired dignity, the very norm of gentle conduct. It was in such abstract terms that this poet, like his colleagues, set about his task of delineating the principal features of *uchelwriaeth*.

All these balanced virtues were intended to portray the ideal gentleman, principally as a man of action. Equanimity in conduct presupposed fair-minded action in estate management, legal affairs or in the service of the state. The Welsh poets, like Elyot, attempted to picture the patron as a person who maintained a moral composure in an unchanging community structure. That, of course, was not practicable since Tudor society experienced economic change which threatened its very foundations. Honour, in reality, had to be displayed against a background of distress and social mobility, and the poets strove to preserve reverence, dignity and moral probity in an age which placed greater emphasis on material gain. One inspired poet described the features of integrity in his address to one of his worthiest patrons.

> Gofalu a wna gŵr da doeth,
> Gofal, ac nid am gyfoeth;
> Gofal am fyw yn gyfiawn
> Bob dydd yw'r llawenydd llawn.[140]

When considered in isolation honour signified the execution of duties justly and with due valour. In bardic terms an illustrious person had a 'godly visage' ('duwioldeb i'w wyneb'): he was amiable and incomparable ('gŵr hawddgar, digymar gwych) and emerged as the 'apex of the gentle order' ('pinagl a chanllaw pob bonedd'). The aim, it seems, was to picture the righteous man as infallible in his judgement of human affairs; never unwise, and acting at all times in a circumspect and discreet manner. The virtue of honour was the prime test of integrity in adversity, and was consistently associated with a man's goodness when defending his reputation. By God's will and the law of nature the privileged were compelled to do good and to hand it on as an inheritance. 'I have had the breeding of a gentleman', Sir John Wynn of Gwydir remarked in his own defence, 'and am free from drunkenness and frenzy.'[141] 'My former life shall witness amongst those that know me', he continued, 'that I used not to be lavish in words (especially in their absence) towards my very enemies.' Morus Dwyfech described such qualities in a reference to

Wynn's uncle, Dr. John Gwynn, Fellow of St. John's College, Cambridge, whom he regarded as wise and dignified ('Pybyrddoeth mewn pob urddas'), qualities which blended integrity ('uniondeb') with majesty ('rhyw brenhinol').[142] This code of honour included a demonstration of personal aggrandizement as well as undertaking responsibilities in public affairs. 'A noble gentleman' was known either for 'the gravity of his wisdom or the authority of his person, or his service to the commonwealth', and he could be identified by 'his singular excellency or the favour of all men toward him being loved of every man and hated of no man'.[143] In practice, of course, such an ideal was unattainable: enemies, lawbreakers and rivals constantly tested the resilience and fortitude of the good man. There would always be contenders for power and authority, and patrons were constantly counselled never to enter into unnecessary litigation lest they might, by so doing, jeopardize their reputations.

The concept of the Christian gentleman emerges distinctly in the Welsh bardic tributes where the Godhead is regarded as the essence of creation. The chain of being, as exemplified in the sixteenth-century Welsh tract entitled *Graduelys*, accorded to God the highest status as the supreme creator, and benefactor of mankind. The same doctrine was often expressed in the verses of Wiliam Llŷn who emphasized the qualities of degree and order in the divine plan.

> Duw a'th wreiddiodd, doeth raddiwr,
> Duw wyn a wna dyn yn ŵr.[144]

'God gave you secure roots', the poet declared to Siôn Lewis Owen of Llwyn, Dolgellau, 'and it is God who makes a man a person of status.' The correlation between the godly attributes and moral rectitude emerges strongly.

The concept is also expressed in the works of other contemporary poets who endeavoured to place man in the divine creation. His inbuilt attributes are often associated with the mundane objects visible in that creation. He is regarded as the 'trunk' ('hengyff brenhingoed'), 'orchard' ('purllwyth perllan') and 'pillar' ('piler', 'canllaw', 'trawst', 'post'), and many military features were attached to him to remind him of his protective powers ('gwayw', 'paladr', 'tarian', 'aesawr'). Such symbols denote rank and ennoblement and reveal the divinely-appointed position enjoyed by the *uchelwr* in Welsh society.[145]

Piety was also considered a key factor in any assessment of the proper gentleman. Christ was assumed to be the true pattern of all nobility and pious works were increasingly associated with God's favour towards the privileged. Pious attributes were accorded to gentlewomen as well as men: Elin, widow of Gruffudd Nannau II, it was maintained, spent the remainder of her life after her husband's death in 1609 in the service of God and did not remarry.[146] Siôn Cain, in a couplet and on another occasion, portrayed the Christian gentleman at his most pious.

> Duwiol freiniol frau uniawn,
> Dwys, doeth wyt a distaw iawn.[147]

He was described as godly, privileged and upright in all his actions; he was also regarded as sincere, wise and discreet in his relationships with others in his community. Such qualities had to be acquired and cultivated. That could be accomplished in various ways, such as good breeding, exemplary living and education. Renaissance scholars believed that God had given man the impulse to perfect himself: his very nature directed his path towards self-advancement but, more specifically, towards moral accomplishment.

> Gŵr da rhwydd a geirda rhawg
> A wna'i wlad yn oludawg.[148]

Prosperity, in a relative sense, in these lines by Wiliam Llŷn to John Salusbury of Rug, is interpreted principally as the yield of the just and versatile gentleman. The upright and resolute protector, the poet maintained, enriched his community since he was disposed to perform good works. The medieval bardic grammar firmly stipulated how praise was to be accorded to gentility characterized by blood, liberality and innate goodness. Central to such a doctrine was ancestry derived from worthy forbears. Wiliam Cynwal expatiated at some length on the qualities of lineage in his ode to Sir John Salusbury of Lleweni.

O ran ffynnu 'ryn ffunud
Yw beunydd barch bonedd byd . . .
Bonheddig, goronig wŷr
Yw gwaed pawb o goed pybyr . . .
Pan beidio'r gwaed, na wnaed neb
Ddiwael daith ar dduwioldeb,
Yno y derfydd, nod oerfawr,
Beunydd maeth y bonedd mawr.[149]

These lines again are associated with the image of the prosperous individual who outshines others in his community. 'To prosper', the poet observes, 'sound gentility of blood is absolutely essential.' 'When the blood affinity ends then the thriving gentility will wither and perish'.

When gentle families cease, owing to lack of heirs or kindred disasters, the prime nourishment of ancient nobility by ancestry is destroyed at its very source. Within families of repute, however, there existed the innate ability to survive, a feature which characterizes eulogistic themes on a grand scale in this period of intense economic and cultural pressures. No man, Tomas Berwyn maintained in another poem to Sir John Salusbury, could obscure the image of the *uchelwr* who, through divine grace and wisdom, had been firmly rooted in noble stock.

Y gŵr sydd â gras iddaw
A dynn y wlad dan ei law . . .
A raddio Duw ei wreiddyn
O ŵr doeth, ni wyra dyn.[150]

The emphasis is yet again on the virtues of grace, authority and an acknowledged status. 'The gracious gentleman possesses full sovereignty within his region', the poet explains: 'he to whom God has granted status through eligible stock no man can distort or destroy.' It is a powerfully expressed viewpoint which embraced all that other poets of his *milieu* were prepared to appraise in the perfect gentleman. It was universally accepted but, in this context, was given further meaning and relevance and was more forcibly expressed by another poet who, in his lament to a favoured patron, exclaimed helplessly that, on his death, the majesty of noble life had descended to the grave: 'Aeth i'r bedd fy mawredd maith'.[151] What he had not realized, however, was that the potent and compelling new features in the social structure of his community were causing a significant breach and cleavage in social and cultural loyalties in matters relating specifically to the doctrine of gentility in Tudor and early Stuart Wales.

NOTES

[1]NBM, pp. 172-3; GWC (1), II, XXVII, pp. 633-7.

[2]R. Kelso, *The Doctrine of the English Gentleman in the Sixteenth Century* (Massachusetts, 1964), pp. 12-15.

[3]Charlton, op. cit., pp. 81-92; Thomas Elyot, *The boke named the governour* (London, 1531): ed. H. H. S. Croft (London, 1883); Baldassare Castiglione, *Il libro del cortegiano* (1528), trans., Thomas Hoby, *The courteyr of Count Baldessar Castilio* (London, 1561); F. Caspari, *Humanism and the Social Order,* chaps. I, IV, pp. 1-15, 76-109. See also Glanmor Williams, 'The Renaissance', in Glanmor Williams and R. O. Jones (ed.), *The Celts and the Renaissance: Tradition and Innovation* (Cardiff, 1990), pp. 1-15; R. Geraint Gruffydd, The Renaissance and Welsh Literature', ibid., pp. 17-39 (esp. pp. 25-9); G. H. Hughes, (Ffasiynau'r Dadeni), in *Ysgrifau Beirniadol*, V, (Denbigh, 1970), pp. 62-70; I. M. Williams, 'Ysgolheictod Hanesyddol yr Unfed Ganrif ar Bymtheg', 111-24, 209-23.

[4]*Triolus and Cressida*, act 1, scene 3; Caspari, pp. 99-101.

[5]L. Stone, *The Crisis of the Aristocracy* (Oxford, 1965), pp. 21-3; A. O. Lovejoy, *The Great Chain of Being* (Massachusetts, 1936), chap. II, pp. 24-66; J. E. Mason, *Gentlefolk in the Making* (Philadelphia, 1935), pp. 23-54.

[6]Francis Jones, 'An Approach to Welsh Genealogy', *Trans Cymmr.*, 1948, 368-78. See also E. M. W. Tillyard, *The Elizabethan World Picture* (London, 1960), pp. 7-15, 23-76; J. Huizinga, 'The Hierarchic Conception of Society' in *The Waning of the Middle Ages* (London, 1955), pp. 56-6; W. G. Zeeveld, 'Social Equalitarianism in a Tudor Crisis', in *Foundations of Tudor Policy* (Massachusetts, 1948), pp. 190-225.

[7]SL1. , XLII, p. 271.

[8]Ceri W. Lewis, 'Einion Offeiriad and the Bardic Grammar', in *Guide to Welsh Literature,* II, pp. 58-84; Gwyn Thomas, *Y Traddodiad Barddol*, pp. 204-12.

[9]Saunders Lewis, *Braslun o Hanes Llenyddiaeth Gymraeg hyd at 1535*, I (Cardiff, 1932), chap. IV, 'Beirdd yr Uchelwyr', pp. 51-69; idem, *Gramadegau'r Penceirddiaid* Cardiff, 1967); G. J. Williams and E. J. Jones (ed.), *Gramadegau'r Penceirddiaid*, xxxix et seq.

[10]Lewis, *Braslun o Hanes Llenyddiaeth*, chap. VII, 'Y Ganrif Fawr 1435-1535', pp. 115-33; E. I. Rowlands, 'The Continuing Tradition', in *Guide to Welsh Literature*, II, pp. 298-321.

[11]CLl., p. 68.

[12]Ibid., p. 70.

[13]NLW Peniarth MS. 69, 107. See J. Gwynfor Jones, 'The Merioneth Gentry in the Social Order: Bardic Evidence c. 1540-1640' (Pt. i), *Journal of the Merioneth Historical and Record Society*, IX, 1983, 278-86.

[14]Cardiff MS. 4. 101, 59b.

[15]Kelso, op. cit., pp. 70-110.

[16]Ceri W. Lewis, 'Poetry and the Crisis in the Bardic Tradition', in *Guide to Welsh Literature*, II, pp. 59-93; G. J. Williams and E. J. Jones, *Gramadegau'r Penceirddiaid*, pp. 55-6.

[17]D. J. Bowen, 'Agweddau ar Ganu'r Unfed Ganrif ar Bymtheg', 286 et seq.; J. Gwynfor Jones, 'Awdurdod Cyfreithiol a Gweinyddol Lleol yng Ngogledd Cymru yn y Cyfnod 1540-1640 yn ôl Tystiolaeth y Beirdd', LlC, XII, 1972-73; 190-3; Caspari, op. cit., pp. 10-15.

[18]Caspari, op. cit. , pp. 10-15.

[19]NBSF, II, CCCI, p. 662.

[20]Caspari, op. cit. , pp. 1-15; J. E. Mason, *Gentlefolk in the Making*, pp. 23-54.

[21]Kelso, op. cit., pp. 16-17, 111 et seq.; Stone, op. cit., pp. 672-83.

[22]NBM, p. 107.

[23]Stone, op. cit., pp. 21-35.

[24]GSM, LXXXIX, p. 286.

[25]NBSF, II, CCCXXIX. p. 721.

[26]CLl., p. 64.

[27]J. Gwynfor Jones, 'The Welsh Poets and their Patrons c. 1550-1640', 250-4.

[28]Ibid., 245-50; Gwyn Thomas, 'A Study of the Changes in the Tradition of Welsh Poetry in North Wales in the Seventeenth Century', chap. III, pp. 427 et seq.; idem, 'Y Portread o Uchelwr', pp. 110-29; S. T. Bindoff, 'The Stuarts and their Style', *English Historical Review*, LX, 1945, 204-5.

[29]J. Gwynfor Jones, 'Merioneth Gentry', loc. cit.; idem, 'Welsh Poets and their Patrons', 245-8.

[30]Bobi Jones, 'Beirdd yr Uchelwyr a'r Byd: II Wiliam Llŷn ac Awdurdod Dinesig', in *Ysgrifau Beirniadol*, VIII, (Denbigh, 1974), pp. 36-42. See also R. M. Jones, *Llên Cymru a Chrefydd: Diben y Llenor* (Swansea, 1977), pp. 274-80.

[31]Ibid., p. 39; CLl., p. 52.

[32]BWLl, VIII. p. 20; J. Gwynfor Jones, 'Hanfodion Undod Gwladwriaethol', 61 et seq.; idem, 'Merioneth Gentry', 280-4.

[33]'Merioneth Gentry', loc. cit.

[34]GEUGII, XIX, p. 93.

[35]'The Brogyntyn Welsh Manuscripts', NLWJ, VI, 1949, 4, 33.

[36]Kelso, op. cit., pp. 70-82.

[37]Ibid., 'Merioneth Gentry', loc. cit.

[38]GST, I, XLII, p. 174.

[39]'Merioneth Gentry', loc. cit.

[40]GST, I, XIX, p. 75.

[41]GMD, p. 117.

[42]GWC(1), II, V, p. 541.

[43]Ibid., I, XLIX, p. 171.

[44]HGF, pp. 14, 16.

[45]Ibid., pp. 14-15.

[46]GWC(1), I, XLIX, p. 171.

[47]J. Gwynfor Jones, 'Awdurdod Cyfreithiol', 190-1; Thomas Smith, *De Republica Anglorum* (1583), (Menston, 1970 ed.), p. 26.

[48]E.g. GST, I, CXLVI, pp. 584-5.

[49]Kelso, op. cit., pp. 21-4; G. D. Owen, *Elizabethan Wales: the Social Scene*, pp. 29-33; GCH, IV, pp. 175-92. For a further examination of the problems of law and order see Nia M. W. Powell, 'Crime and the Community in Denbighshire during the 1590s: the Evidence of the Records of the Court of Great Sessions', in *Class, Community and Culture in Tudor Wales*, VIII, pp. 261-94.

[50]GST, I, CXLIV, p. 596.
[51]'Brogyntyn Welsh Manuscripts', V, 1948, 253, 263.
[52]GST, I, CVI, pp. 606-9.
[53]Cf. relevant references to the heir as a true representative of worthy stock in GWC (Mostyn III), I, XIX, p. 56: 'Aer yw o ryw, ir ei wraidd'.
[54]NBSF, II, CCCVIII, p. 675.
[55]Charlton, op. cit., p. 74; W. G. Zeeveld, 'Richard Moryson, Official Apologist for Henry VIII', *Publications of the Modern Languages Association,* LV(i), 1940, 406-25; idem, *Foundations of Tudor Policy*, pp. 209-95.
[56]Kelso, op. cit., pp. 50-1.
[57]BWLl, XXXVIII, p. 95.
[58]GWC(1), II, LI, p. 749.
[59]BWLl, XXXVII, p. 93.
[60]J. Gwynfor Jones, 'Priodoleddau Bonheddig yn Nheulu'r Wynniaid o Wedir: Tystiolaeth y Beirdd', *Trans. Cymmr.*, 1978, 127; Cardiff MS. 4. 101, 114. See also J. Gwilym Jones, 'Cyfnod Olaf y Beirdd yng Ngwedir (1627-74)', *Ysgrifau Beirniadol*, XV, (1988), pp. 121-41.
[61]Stone, op. cit., pp. 589-92.
[62]GWC(1), I, XVII, p. 60.
[63]D. J. Bowen, 'Canrif Olaf y Cywyddwyr', LlC, XIV, 1982-84, 10-32; J. Gwynfor Jones, 'Y Bardd a'r Uchelwr 1540-1640: Rhai Argraffiadau', *Taliesin,* XXXIX, 1979, 13-22.
[64]GST, I, XCI, p. 357.
[65]Kelso, op. cit., pp. 11-30.
[66]GST, I, XIV, p. 53.
[67]Charlton, op. cit., pp. 83-7.
[68]SLl, intro.; Saunders Lewis, 'The Essence of Welsh Literature', *Wales*, VII (27), 1947, 337-42.
[69]BWLl, LXI, p. 164.
[70]Ibid., XXXVII, p. 92.
[71]GWC (Mostyn III), I, II, p. 5.
[72]Cf. CLl. pp. 54, 106, 108.
[73]Charlton, op. cit., pp. 78-9.
[74]A. R. Wagner, *English Genealogy* (Oxford, 1960), pp. 102-21; Francis Jones, 'An Approach to Welsh Genealogy', 350-73.
[75]Smith, *De Republica Anglorum*, p. 27.
[76]HGF, pp. 36-7.
[77]J. Gwynfor Jones, 'Priodoleddau Bonheddig', 127 et seq.
[78]'Brogyntyn Welsh Manuscripts', VI, 1949, 3, 33.
[79]Ibid.
[80]GST, I, CLI, pp. 606-8.
[81]Ibid., LXXVI, p. 303.
[82]GWC (Mostyn III), I, XXVI, p. 79. For more information on Clough see R. Gwyndaf, 'Sir Richard Clough of Denbigh c. 1530-1570', *Trans. Denbighshire Hist. Soc.*, XIX, 1970, 24-65; XX, 1971, 75-101.
[83]A. L. Rowse, *The Elizabethan Renaissance: the Life of the Society* (London, 1971), pp. 75, 118-11.
[84]NBM, p. 117.
[85]NLW Cwrtmawr MS. 204, 26b; NBM, p. 117.
[86]J. Gwynn Williams, 'Rhai Agweddau ar y Gymdeithas Gymreig yn yr Ail Ganrif ar Bymtheg', *Efrydiau Athronyddol*, XXXI, 1968, 43-7; 'Hanfodion Undod Gwladwriaethol', 92-8.
[87]T. Jones Pierce (ed.), *Calendar of Clenennau Letters and Papers* (NLW, Aberystwyth), Suppl. 1V (Pt. i), 1947, XLVIII, p. 15.
[88]GWC(1), I, XIX, p. 67.
[89]'Merioneth Gentry', loc. cit.

[90]Bobi Jones, loc. cit.
[91]'Welsh Poets and their Patrons', 256-60.
[92]GMD, XXV, p. 54.
[93]Francis Jones, 'Welsh Pedigrees', in L. G. Pine (ed.), *Burke's Genealogical and Heraldic History of the Landed Gentry* (London, 1952), lxxi-lxxvi.
[94]BWLl, XLVI, p. 119; XLVIII, p. 122; LXXXVII, p. 209.
[95]J. Gwynfor Jones, 'Awdurdod Cyfreithiol', 188-93.
[96]NBSF, II, CCXXI, p. 486.
[97]GWC(1), I,I, p. 2.
[98]GSM, XLIX, p. 151.
[99]GWC(1). II, VI, p. 544.
[100]GEUGH, XV, p. 77.
[101]CLl, p. 65
[102]GST, I, XXIII, p. 94.
[103]Ibid., XLV, p. 187.
[104]Ibid.
[105]Kelso, op. cit., pp. 38-9.
[106]GST, I, XXII, p. 87; 'Brogyntyn Welsh Manuscripts', VI, 1949, 40.
[107]'Brogyntyn Welsh Manuscripts', 19, 38; NBM, pp. 64-6.
[108]GST, I, V, p. 19.
[109]GWC(1), II, LI, p. 749, LIII, p. 758.
[110]Caspari, op. cit., pp. 12-18.
[111]D. J. Bowen, 'Canrif Olaf y Cywyddwyr', 26-30.
[112]J. H. Whitfield (ed.), *The Book of the Courtier* (London, 1975), p. 33.
[113]GWC (Mostyn III), II, CVI, p. 330; MDLIS, II, X, pp. 483, 485.
[114]CLl, p. 60. Kelso, op. cit., pp. 70-5.
[115]NBM, p. 11.
[116]Ibid., p. 193.
[117]Ibid., p. 108.
[118]GEUGH, IX, p. 46.
[119]GST, I, XIX, p. 73.
[120]NBSF, I, XXXVII, pp. 81-2; Charlton, op. cit., pp. 78-90.
[121]NLW Peniarth MS. 69, 189. Kelso, loc. cit., Caspari, op.cit., pp. 106-9.
[122]J. Gwynfor Jones, 'Hanfodion Undod Gwladwriaethol', 46 et seq.
[123]J. A. Mazzeo, *Renaissance and Revolution: the Remaking of European Thought*, pp. 142-3, 145-8; Charlton, op. cit., pp. 82-4.
[124]NBSF, II, CCCI, p. 662.
[125]GWC (Mostyn III), II, CVII, p. 332. 'Cyfiawnder a chymeriad'; 'Cyfion mewn goruchafiaeth'.
[126]NBSF, I, xli.
[127]GOG, I, LXIV, p. 214.
[128]Mazzeo, loc. cit.
[129]NLW Peniarth MS. 72, 17. Cf. 'Ysgwiair gwrdd', 'Ysgwiair dwys', 'Ysgwiair gwych', GWC (Mostyn III), II, XC, p. 278; ibid., I, LVIII, p. 179; GWC(I), I, IV, p. 20.
[130]GWC(1), I, X, p. 36.
[131]NBM, p. 112.
[132]Ibid., p. 39.
[133]NBSF, I, XXXV, p. 75.
[134]Kelso, loc. cit.; Whitfield, *Book of the Courtier,* pp. 89-104.
[135]EDDN, I, p. 106. For more information on the background see J. Gwynfor Jones, 'Reflections on Concepts of Nobility in Glamorgan c.1540-1640', *Morgannwg*, XXV, 1981. 11-35.
[136]NBSF, I, XXXV, p. 75.
[137]NBSD, p. 92.

[138]Kelso, loc. cit.

[139]Cf. NBSF, II, p. 738 ('Da rhoe Dduw . . . Dy lawnder wrth dy lendid')

[140]Cf. CLl, p. 111, where Wiliam Llŷn draws attention to the true qualities of Robert ap Morus of Parc, Merioneth, who showed little concern for material prosperity ('Ni bu chwannog . . . Na thaer am dda na thir').

[141]NLW Add. MS. 465E. 247; J. Ballinger (ed.), *Calendar of the Wynn (of Gwydir) Papers c. 1515-1690* (Cardiff, 1926), no. 247.

[142]GMD, XXI, p. 122; DWB, pp. 329-30.

[143]Kelso, loc. cit.

[144]NBSF, I, CLVI, p. 350.

[145]SLl, pp. 23-35.

[146]NBSF, I, xcvii. For a detailed investigation of the feminine aspects of gentility see R. Kelso, *Doctrine for the Lady of the Renaissance* (Illinois, 1956), especially pp. 1-37.

[147]Gwyn Thomas 'Y Portread o Uchelwr', p. 118.

[148]NBSF, II, CCLXIII, p. 578.

[149]SLl, LXXX, p. 383.

[150]Ibid. , XCVI, p. 421.

[151]'Brogyntyn Welsh Manuscripts', VI, 1949, 34.

Chapter III

Rank and Status

The *uchelwyr* who were commemorated in bardic tributes because of their elevated position in Welsh society were often regarded as the descendants of kings and princes; hence the grandiloquent references, for example, to the 'roots of kingly descent' ('wraidd raddau brenhinaidd'), the 'bosom of royal pedigree' ('bron henwaed brenhinoedd'), and the 'nobleman who assumes a privileged princely rôle' ('yn bendefig a brig braint').[1] Some poets compared their patrons to the 'emperor' of world-wide reputation ('emprwr gwlad'), which adds yet another significant dimension to concepts of regality.[2] The *Graduelys* listed the emperor as the highest in status in that category followed closely by the 'crowned king' ('brenin coronawc'), the 'regional prince' ('tywysoc taleithiol') and the 'privileged ruler' ('tywysoc breiniawl').[3] In sixteenth and early seventeenth-century strict-metre verse there appeared to be very little distinction between such designations, principally because they referred to the *uchelwyr* of native stock who incorporated the qualities of their illustrious forbears. The emperor, king or prince would normally assume sovereign power and, in the eulogistic context, would be compared to the native *brëyr* or nobleman who exercised complete authority in his community like a ruler or benign chieftain of regal status.

The dynastic element in Welsh poetry, closely identified with concepts of sovereignty, constituted one of the most prominent features of nobility. The status of lord or territorial baron ('arglwydd', 'barwn') was consistently acccredited to the enterprising and well-endowed gentleman of good lineage ('bonheddig'). Common ancestry was regarded as the essential feature of all corporate functions performed in the interests of the commonweal, and was established as the basis of fame and renown ('gŵraidd rywiogaidd').[4] The aim was to establish a noble pedigree, associating the *uchelwr* and his line with the privileges of regality and supreme power. According to Wiliam Llŷn, the patron who was descended from the ancient line of any one of five royal dynasties was considered worthy of pre-eminence. In a bardic context, he had been elevated primarily because of his ancestral connections.[5]

Since the native land structure in medieval Wales prohibited the outright alienation of property and since aspiring *uchelwyr*, in the two centuries before the Acts of Union, had been hindered from expanding their material interests as freely as they desired it is hardly surprising that *uchelwriaeth* was based essentially on a firm pedigree rather than ostentatious proprietorship. While it is true that strict-metre poetry linked power, in the Welsh context, with land and its occupation, doubtless it is descent and the *uchelwr*'s ties with the soil which primarily drew the poets' attention. Status was derived essentially from a man's standing within the kindred grouping. Regardless of his independent nature his status was fixed: in bardic tradition his privileges as a freeholder stemmed from his kindred links with the neighbourhood.

All bardic tributes contained detailed genealogical and heraldic references which identified the *uchelwr* with an eminent past. Royal status carried with it unique privileges, exposing the honour of kindred ('cenedl'), the close-knit network of blood affinities which tied the patron to well-established agnatic groups: hence the references to 'kingship' ('brenhiniaeth'), 'the fruits of regal stock' ('ffrwyth y brenhinllwyth'), 'ancient royal kindred' ('hen genhedlog') and the 'tree of royal lineage' ('hengyff brenhingainc').[6] The concept of kingship associated the Welsh Tudor gentry with political privileges and prerogative rights which enabled them to participate in matters of state by virtue of distinct ancestry. This authority exposed a number of strands which emphasized the peculiar rights enjoyed by all those who claimed *uchelwriaeth* in Wales. The aim was to expose what potential lay within the individual patron, namely magnanimity in bearing and majesty in the execution of public office. Poetic commentators were fully aware of his political authority to rule over a *patria* or recognized territorial unit ('gwlad', 'rhanbarth', 'tiriogaeth'), and his sense of justice when governing for the good of all.

Braich a llaw hylaw haeledd—a dorrwyd;
Dibenwyd twf bonedd;
Bron gwin brenhinbren Gwynedd
Brau oer byd bwriwyd i'r bedd.[7]

'The generous arm and hand have been severed', Siôn Phylip maintained in an ode to Eliza ab Wiliam Llwyd I of Rhiwedog, 'and flourishing gentility has been destroyed.' In his view also the 'heart of Gwynedd's royal line' had been coldly lowered into the grave. In that disconsolate fashion this poet described the passing of a typical Tudor landed gentleman who, in his native region, had paraded as a powerful kindred chieftain. In such majestic and lofty lines Siôn Phylip displayed how the demise of a notable patron could destroy the concept of regional unity and have far-reaching repercussions for the government of Gwynedd. He underlines the imposing powers which Eliza ab Wiliam Llwyd of Rhiwedog possessed, and explains that his death had disrupted the organic unity and concord which his presence had created and sustained in his community.

Such concepts had their roots well laid in the Middle Ages because Welsh territorial units were largely based on the commote ('cwmwd'), hundred ('cantref') and kingdom ('gwlad'). Lordship in these areas of jurisdiction was essentially royal, the native king exercising full sovereign rights over his subjects. Thus was evolved the concept of political power, during the centuries which followed the conquest of Wales in 1282, among the emergent gentry who prided themselves on having acquired a unique inheritance stemming essentially from the prerogatives of tribal kingship. The portrayal of *uchelwyr* in such a fashion concentrated chiefly on regional or provincial jurisdiction. In the fifteenth century Welsh poets emphasized the authority of individuals in broader regional terms, one of the most conspicuous being Sir William Gruffudd III of Penrhyn, Chamberlain of Gwynedd, who died in 1531. He was born the scion of an illustrious north Wales family related to the Tudors of Penmynydd, Anglesey, and stemming from the line of Ednyfed Fychan. His inheritance was indisputable and Tudur Aled considered him to be highest in rank in his region ('Pen bonedd Gwynedd'), a person of magnitude and immense political skill and authority ('Ar dy wlad, dal dy law').[8] Sir William Herbert of Raglan in Gwent, likewise, was described by Guto'r Glyn as the greatest power in south Wales, a figure who demonstrated military prowess and political tenacity.[9] On a more modest scale numerous other *uchelwyr* were granted honours normally attributed to kings and their successors. Maredudd ab Ieuan ap Robert, the ancestor of the Wynn family of

Gwydir, was hailed by Tudur Aled as the protector of Snowdonia because of his successful defensive tactics against brigands and malcontents.

> Dy wayw'n friwdan, Faredudd,
> Dy lafn, rhaid i lifo'n rhudd,
> Dur nis deil, dyrnaist aliwn,
> Dor nid gwiw rhag dyrnod gwn.

These lines were composed at the turn of the sixteenth century when the commote of Nanconwy was in a turbulent condition subject to the attacks of marauders from the nearby Hiraethog borderlands. Maredudd's success at Dolwyddelan in curbing their activities inspired the poet to describe his martial prowess and praise his exploits fervently. 'There is less oppression on the righteous and weak', Lewys Môn maintained, 'less threats from a nest of thieves, less anxiety in your time for the whole of Snowdonia.' The relief expressed by this poet revealed the trust and confidence which poorly-endowed peasant communities had placed in a military adventurer who had made the upper reaches of Nanconwy his adopted home and had created order out of a state of anarchy.[10]

Later in the sixteenth century Siôn Mawddwy described John Salusbury of Lleweni as the 'keeper of the two provinces of Gwynedd', thus following the revered tradition established by previous generations of poets who considered their patrons to be among the most illustrious political leaders.[11] Such concepts reveal magnanimity in action or a sense of obligation to the native communty similar to the authority wielded by kings in their respective realms. The concept of territorial power as a means of indicating prestige and virtuous rule over others survived in the bardic tradition in later generations at a time when the quality of poetic content had shown distinct signs of decay. References abound to 'gwlad', 'tiriogaeth', 'talaith', and 'bro', but they had no particular relevance except to indicate the nature of the power exerted by the *uchelwr* over his tenants, kindred and, in a political or legal context, his shire community. Thus the head or ruler of a lordship ('pennaeth arglwyddiaeth gwlad') or the defender of the realm ('clo teyrnas') or the supreme chieftain, born of noble stock, who justly rules ('pen gwlad

. . . gwladwriaeth cyfion . . . eigion pendefigaeth') was regarded as a person who, by virtue of his innate talents, enjoyed the fruits of good 'statesmanship' ('gwladwriaeth') within a closely-defined area of jurisdiction.[12]

The marcher areas, where Anglo-Norman lords had exerted power and authority over many centuries as independent sovereign rulers exercising full prerogative powers, were also conceived as territories to be safeguarded as ancient native patrimonies, and their lords or deputies as inheritors of exclusive regal rights by virtue of their *uchelwriaeth*. Their distinct areas of political influence were closely reviewed in poetic eulogy and were valued on the same basis as the qualities of rank and status which were manifested in their public image. The families which contended for the 'sovereignty of the country' were principally applauded in view of their rights of gentility, and in that context political power was interpreted essentially as regional sovereignty.[13] Thus emerged references to territorial lordship ('gwlad'), custodianship ('ceidwadaeth') and governorship ('llywiawdwriaeth . . . lawn o'r Mars'). Political leaders were likewise regarded, for example, as the 'lion of the March' ('llew'r Mars') and the 'soul of Gwynedd's two provinces' ('enaid dwy Wynedd').[14] However obscure and anachronistic such terminology may appear, in a sixteenth-century context the poets were aware of the need to magnify the prestige of men who had the potential to rule and maintain the social order.

> Marcus foliannus flaenawr
> A llew i'r mab llaw hir mawr;
> Maen o radd, mynor ydwyd,
> Maen i'w ddallt am Wynedd wyd . . .
> Blaenor wyd be blinai'r wedd
> Pia blaenu pobl Wynedd.

Morus Wynn of Gwydir, in these couplets, is portrayed as a well endowed custodian and is favourably compared to Marcus Aurelius, the Roman Emperor who cherished the virtues of nobility and emphasized the rôle of moral probity in man's material advancement. He was a tower of strength to his son and heir. 'You are a marble stone of rank recognized in Gwynedd', the poet added, 'a leader who heads the people of that region.'[15] Powerful words indeed, expressed by a poet who was aware that, in reality, his patron's sovereign power was concentrated within the confines of his landed estate or shire community. Such prominence, however, was given to those who wielded territorial power in governmental posts, particularly after 1536. A select group of *uchelwyr* governed Wales and the borderland from Ludlow, the headquarters of the Council in the Marches. Such broad-based authority, focused on this small Shropshire town, highlighted the concepts of regional authority. It was there that such potentates as the Herberts, earls of Pembroke, and lesser ranking gentry buttressed their political domination, and the bardic approbations, particularly the *awdlau*, profusely refer to the delights of an honourable birthright which they enjoyed. The emphasis in such odes was principally placed on grace, humanity and the administration of justice. The image of the sovereign maintaining his court in full sway also survived, and the magnificent descriptions suitably matched the impressive metres employed in the *awdl*.

> Aur dëyrn dewr chwyrn doe eirchiaid i'th blas
> Yno y bu urddas i naw byrddaid;
> Gwirodydd yn rhydd i'n rhaid a lenwir
> Gwin hoff a elwir gan ffiolaid.[16]

The portrayal of Eliza ab Wiliam Llwyd I of Rhiwedog is imposing and stately. 'The gilded sovereign, powerful and fearful, who grants hospitality to those who eat around nine tables' is given prominence, and his wine is distributed freely to 'replenish the needs of the poets'. In such bold terms Simwnt Fychan expressed his joy in the presence of a munificent patron who had assumed regal features. The 'good noble lord' ('pendefig nodedig da'), the 'chieftain among men' ('penaig gwŷr'), the 'lord who owns the patria' ('Pendefig . . . perchen y wlad') were all in fact symbols of the ostentatious rites associated with kingship and applied, in the most pretentious manner possible, to the *uchelwyr* in the Welsh countryside.[17] In short, their status and position was compared to the rôle of monarchy, and poets reminded their patrons of the need to maintain the link between noble and regal ancestry which stemmed from the same roots.

Links between regality and ancestral nobility, however, were often tenuous and, in the sixteenth-century, would be applied only to the *nobilitas maior*. They constituted families which had been elevated to the peerage owing to their specific services to the Crown. In Wales their number was small, the most powerful being the Herberts of Chirbury, and the earls of Pembroke, Worcester and Essex, to whom a succession of poets sang in the same vein as they did to lesser mortals among the landed gentry.[18] The terms 'baron' ('barwn'), 'lord' ('arglwydd') and 'leader' ('llywiawdwr') were associated with the features of the traditional English aristocracy:however, the traits of nobility were attributable to all who claimed honourable gentility. Judging by the style employed by Gruffudd Hiraethog, when describing Huw Gwyn, one notable Merioneth patron from Hendwr, who maintained ancestral baronial connections with the northern March, he ranked highly among his peers. He was considered to be the towering and stately baron descended from prime regal stock.

> Farwn henbraff frenhinbren;
> Brenhinbren mawr gerllaw'r llaill,
> Brwyn dŵr barwniaid eraill.
> Nid un enw, nid un anian,
> Yw barwn mawr a brwyn mân.[19]

Once again, the ostentatious turn of phrase adds a touch of arrogance. A baron of ancient royal stock is compared favourably to others of inferior status. The poet jubilantly extols his virtues, principally as a regal figure, imposing in his grandeur, and awesome in his exercise of authority over his region. As a baron of the March he undertook his duties to quell disorder and exert his influence over all within his jurisdiction.

Uchelwyr throughout Wales were proclaimed as prime representatives of nobility. Whatever distinction Gruffudd Hiraethog wished to imply in his verse he, like his fellow declaimers, attributed gentility to all those of noble stock. They all enjoyed primacy among their kindreds, and individuals were described as the 'head of all gentility' ('pennaeth pob bonedd'), the 'gilded baron' ('barwn euraid'), the 'respected lord' ('parchus Iôr'), the 'magnanimous kindred leader' ('Pencenedl mawrchwedl') and the 'baron who stemmed from ancient Welsh regal stock' ('Barwn hendir brenhindai').[20] The terms 'baron' and 'barony' were normally associated with the feudal structure, and although alien to the Welsh social framework in the Middle Ages they were gradually accepted as recognizably Welsh designations of nobility. This came about principally through intermarriage and land inheritance as well as the interaction between both Welsh and English sectors of the border community over the centuries. Consequently, such terms became meaningful and acceptable in Welsh cultural circles and were used synonymously with lord ('pennaeth'), prince ('pendefig') and gentleman ('bonheddig').[21] The ancient barons of Edeirnion, for example, had, over a period of three centuries, sadly experienced a marked decline in status and had, by the sixteenth century, become mere gentry. Neverthless, poets continued to hail them as being among the most illustrous and forthright who still maintained their patrimony in north-east Wales. They formed part of the new gentry order and were attributed with the honourable status of *nobilitas maior*.[22] Whatever their material disabilities may have been they continued to uphold the rank granted to them by divine will. Their honour lay in their antiquity although their lifestyle in Tudor times was equivalent to that of the lowliest of gentlefolk. Poets, eager to extol their virtues, ignored their economic problems and concentrated positively on their modest possessions as concrete evidence of superiority. The title 'head' ('pennaeth') or 'ruler' ('penadur') applied to the gentleman in his *plasty* as it did to the descendants of lords on their private estates. This common identity of interests combined all ranks of gentry in bonds of unity:the poet who sang to an *uchelwr* as a prince among his people ('Da i'th wlad . . . pendefig wyd'), who personified gentle stock ('corff bonedd') and who paraded his material assets ('goludog') incorporated in his verse the prime features of the typical squire who prided himself on status.[23] Such glory was adequately expressed in the lines of Owain Gwynedd in one of his most perceptive *cywyddau* to Siôn Lewis Owen of Llwyn.

> Dyn, â grym, da iawn ei gred,
> Dug o Wynedd, da y'i ganed . . .
> Pennaeth arglwyddïaeth gwlad
> Parch mawr pôr â chymeriad . . .

Ni ad hwn eniwed, hael,
Ar y dref, er ei drafael,
Nac ar y sir, nac er swydd,
Oresgyn na gorysgwydd.[24]

In four couplets this poet sets about to depict the 'man of power and a duke of Gwynedd' who was the acknowledged head of his lordship; a person of dignity and sublimity who resists all forces which intend to usurp his power in the town or shire. His supremacy is the all-embracing feature in this section of the *cywydd*, and relates how character exposes the true value of the individual in his native environment. Furthermore, these couplets reveal the prime features of honour and dignity accorded to the lord or baron within his community, and signify how majestically he undertook his responsibilities and protected those dependent on him.

The essential difference between the terms 'lord' and 'king' is not easily defined but the emphasis in bardic composition is constantly placed on the unity of purpose and resilience displayed by the *uchelwr* when performing his obligations. Siôn Mawddwy wove three different concepts into his eulogy to Sir Walter Rhys of Dinefwr and created a sense of unity between them, drawing them together, not as distinctly independent units but rather as the 'harmony of parts' and as the core or kernel of privileged power. He blended together the 'truly privileged sovereign' ('Pendefig eurfing wirfraint'), the most elevated among the 'aristocracy' ('pendefigion') and the 'native kindred chieftain' ('pencenedl'), all three factors bearing the marks of an essentially Welsh brand of nobility.[25] All three images also represented the levels of gentility acquired and cherished in the Middle Ages and highly acclaimed down to the mid-seventeenth century. The concept of kingly power was paramount: the peer or baron ('brëyr') was synonymous with the kindred chieftain ('penteulu'; 'penaig', 'pencenedl'). At grass-root level he assumed the rôle of the master binding together his community in perfect harmony as exemplified in Wiliam Llŷn's verse to Siôn Prys of Newtown.

Da i'th wlad, nid aeth elw well
Ddisgyn dan dy ddwy asgell;
Dy dad oedd â gair di dwn

A phen y wlad a'i phiniwn;
Pont a phen pan'd da i ffynni
I'r wlad wedi'r tad wyt ti.[26]

Jubilantly the poet records that this young *uchelwr* was an inspired moral leader in his country: 'there is no better', he says, 'and he follows his father, a man of reputation, the bridge, opinion and head of his region, with equal mastery.' The testimony in these lines reveals as much the capacities of the father as it does the gracious activities of the son and heir. Wiliam Llŷn gave priority to the magnanimity which characterized the country squire resident in his native community and enjoying the rich resources inherited from a renowned father. Similarly, Wiliam Cynwal addressed Captain William Thomas of Coed Alun, Caernarfon, as a potent leader and a warrior of repute as well as a protector and sustainer of the weak and stern defender of his people.[27] The 'kingly arrogance' and 'unrivalled majesty' were symbols of moral responsibility as well as privilege. The 'protector' ('ceidwad') and 'prop' ('llorf') was as essential as the lavish displayer of material prosperity. In addition to fulfilling his duties as leader of the clan group and avenging the wrongs done to the kin the *uchelwr*, on a more elevated plane, came to terms with his obligations to society at large, hence the references to regional lordship ('arglwyddïaeth gwlad'), order and control ('rheolaeth') and territorial protectorship ('cefn gwlad'; 'gwarcheidwad gwlad').[28] Not that this concept of lordship assumed any significant rôle in society, but the stress on blood kinship ('gwaedoliaeth') implied lordship attained by ancestral privilege ('cenhedlog waedogaeth') and the powers of protection ('cynheiliawdr') rather than royal prescription or ancient Anglo-Norman bonds of affinity.[29] In the Welsh context he is equated with the 'brëyr' *(optimates)*, the nobleman who, in customary law, succeeded to his patrimony as a free clansman and became identified in eulogy with the highest degree of gentility. In one *cywydd* he is described as the hindermost, or leading ox, in the furrow ('ych bôn, ucha bonedd'), the creature which pulls the greatest weight as the team nears the headland ('talar').[30] Such a rich comparison found favour with many poets who wished to enhance the image of power and responsibility in the higher ranks of Welsh gentle society.

Ych bôn a'i gŵys uwchben gwŷr,
Ac uwch pawb, ŵr gwych pybyr.[31]

'He is the leading ox in the furrow', Wiliam Llŷn explained in his couplets to Rhys Fychan of Corsygedol, 'highest of all, a resplendent figure among others.' This experienced poet prided himself on his skill in portraying imposing individuals in such artistic terms.

The bountiful leader transcends all and is granted priority which Siôn Mawddwy magnifies when referring to 'the exalted ox of regal status' ('brenhinbren uwchben ych bannog') and the 'well-cultivated ox' ('Ych bôn tal uwchben tylwyth').[32] Wiliam Llŷn again addressed the ploughing ox which plodded along the furrow ('rhychor bôn'), comparing it to the unswerving and upright *brëyr* fulfilling his essential tasks and, in view of his superiority, assuming the greater amount of responsibility. In such circumstances rank implied the performance of specific duties in periods of war and peace.[33] This comparison is alluded to in couplets by Siôn Tudur to a Marcher patron.

Chwi, nos da iwch, yw'n ystôr,
Chwi yw'r ych na châi rychor.
Tro di gŵys, taro dy gyrn
Tan goed nis tynnai gedyrn.

Again, in similar mood to Wiliam Llŷn, this declaimer proceeds to compare the single-minded patron to the leading ox. 'You are our store and our ox', he maintains, 'who turns the furrow.' 'Your horns lift up under trees', he continues, 'in a manner that no oppressors could.'[34] The contrast between two distinct sources of strength, good and evil, adds significantly to the repute and pre-eminence of the ideal gentleman. Nothing could hinder the ox from cutting the furrow and completing its task. Similarly, the worthy gentleman humiliated all those who were not approved by him and who tyrannized his subjects. It was not in a state of pride and arrogance, the poet maintained, that the patron achieved his goal but principally through the weight and authority of his reputation based on privileged ancestry.

Among the few noble families in sixteenth-century Wales the Herberts ranked highly in bardic estimation. William Herbert, first

Earl of Pembroke of the second creation and Baron Herbert of Cardiff, was a firm supporter of Welsh cultural activities. Gruffydd Robert, the exiled Welsh Catholic grammarian, presented his Welsh grammar to him in 1567, and considered him to be the 'most honourable lord' ('anrhydeddusaf benadur'), the 'unceasing patron of the language' ('a'i diball nodded') and a 'chieftain in rank' ('pennaeth mewn gradd') who intermingled freely among the highest in the realm.[35] He was also commended by Sir Thomas Wiliems of Trefriw as the most munificent and highly adorned earl in his position as Lord President of the Council in the Marches, the 'eye of all Wales' ('llygad holl Gymru') and a conspicuous patron of poets.[36] In spite of his close connections with the royal court, having served under four monarchs in succession, he was widely acclaimed by Wiliam Llŷn, Siôn Brwynog, Lewys Morgannwg, Dafydd Benwyn, Huw Arwystl and others as the classic among patrons.[37] Sir William Herbert was succeeded by an equally renowned son, Henry Herbert, second Earl of Pembroke, who also found bardic favour. Lewys Dwnn sang to him at Cardiff castle and commemorated his death in 1601.[38] Others of the family were well disposed towards the poets, and a substantial *corpus* of eulogistic matter relating to that family has survived.[39] Wiliam Cynwal addressed Edward Herbert of Welshpool and, in line with all other bardic tributes, the verse followed the customary conventions which reflected the pronounced regal features displayed in all eulogy.[40]

Eulogy, composed in elegant Renaissance style, was usually incorporated in the contemporary prose dedications composed by humanist scholars to individual patrons of aristocratic stock. Sir Henry Herbert, for example, was called the 'bright and resplendent star of the British nation' ('seren ddisglair a llachar y genedl Frytanaidd');[41] Sir Edward Stradling as second to none among his contemporaries in virtue ('nid ydych . . . yn ail i'r un ohonynt o ran rhinwedd, yr ydych yn hyglod ar gyfrif bonedd eich hynafiaid'),[42] and Morus Wynn of Gwydir and Edward Thelwall of Plas-y-ward, among others, were regarded by Sir Thomas Wiliems as gentlemen ('boneddigion') of honourable nobility ('gwyrda clodforus').[43] His contemporary, Siôn Dafydd Rhys, drew attention to the three ranks of nobility, gentility and commonalty ('pendefigion a boneddigion a chyffredin'), and considered the two upper sectors to have firm distinguishing features.[44] One factor is clear: the poets attributed to the aristocratic and gentle sections of society one common tradition from which Welsh *uchelwriaeth* sprang. Deference and lineage were complementary; gentility, consanguinity and descent were prime characteristics of that *uchelwriaeth*. In the same way as Sir William Herbert was described by Wiliam Llŷn as a sturdy servant of the state, foremost among earls, and a baron of ancient British lineage,[45] so also Meurig Dafydd paid a warm tribute to Sir Edward Stradling as a baron of worthy pedigree.[46] Morus Wynn of Gwydir was constantly reminded by a number of poets of his illustrious descent from Gruffudd ap Cynan.[47] Such attributes were equally accorded to gentry of lesser status who, though they often lacked claims to regality, did aspire to bardic favour by means of their acquired deference.

Contemporary thought on matters regarding gentle status identified gradations of title normally with defined levels of wealth in the belief that hierarchical gradations were meaningless unless they were identified with notions of material advancement. Social stratification, however, was never constant, and economic power did not always relate to rank. In an age of social mobility it was an insuperable task to quantify the order of gentility in Wales and associate it with any specific level of prosperity. In a Welsh context, however, considerations of this kind were regarded as irrelevant since greater emphasis was placed on the quality of life linked to pedigree and virtue. 'Your robust status and degree', one poet observed of a patron, 'were incorporated in your noble lineage' ('A'ch gradd iach yw'ch gwraidd uchel'). In Wiliam Cynwal's words, the basis of gentility lay in kindred affinity ('gwraidd dyn . . . ydyw cenedl').[48] He compared good pedigree with a sturdy oak-tree: good roots were its essence; without them the growth would wither, and the same was true of family pride. 'Temporal possessions', it was maintained, 'are the life of man, and by riches is worship and honour preserved in families': 'virtue followeth oftest noble blood', it was further observed elsewhere, and the emphasis was placed primarily on lineal descent.[49] To the Welsh poets 'gentility of blood' ('bonedd gwaed') was paramount. Whereas English social commentators would concentrate on material resources as an indication of gentility bardic schools stressed qualitative features which were normally applied to descent, territorial power and official status.

When generic features are considered, especially in relation to the *advenae*, successive generations of poets became aware of the need for a single organic concept of gentility which would embrace all shades of rank and status in Welsh and border community life. Racial harmony had become a potent factor in the lives and careers of the majority of the old and new gentry in Wales. Indeed, *uchelwriaeth* as a concept was in the process of acquiring less exclusively Welsh features.[50] Such high-ranking families as the Herberts, Salusburies, Thelwalls, Perrotts, Mansels, Stradlings, Kemeyses, Hanmers and Conwys of Botryddan,[51] among others, were praised with as much lavish ostentation as any other native family in Carmarthenshire, Cardiganshire, Llŷn or Anglesey, since blood relations, agnatic affinities and a constant fusion of inter-family interests blended all these groups together into one cultural mould termed *uchelwriaeth*. Siôn Tudur amply demonstrated the agility and intellectual prowess of members of the Conwy family in a series of odes depicting their public spirit and obligations in their native environment in north-east Wales.[52] The hospitality granted by the *advenae* was second to none in the Principality, and their prestige was often way above that enjoyed by their modest peers elsewhere. In spite of his Anglo-Norman ancestry Sir Edward Mansel of Margam was regarded by Meurig Dafydd of Llanisien as having rightfully descended from several royal lines and as a paragon of excellence in his own community in Glamorgan.[53] Likewise, Sir Richard Bassett of Beaupré in the vale of Glamorgan was hailed by Edward Dafydd, another local poet of some repute, as having legitimately stemmed from ancient British stock.[54] Regardless of origin the squire who could combine in his person the features of princely dignity, who was confident of his rank and status and who commanded universal respect and allegiance was hailed as the noble inheritor who bequeathed his virtues to posterity.[55] The 'pinnacle of gentility' ('loyw binagl bonedd'), it was maintained, signified qualities far superior to any that the material world could offer.[56] Such was the nature of the tribute given by Siôn Phylip to Gruffudd Fychan II of Corsygedol, a prominent Merioneth squire.

I'th gorff perffaith gywirffydd
A'th galon ffrwythlon hoffrydd;
O natur bur ond rhiw bod
Dewrder gydag awdurdod.
Awdur dwywlad aur dalaith
Wyd tëyrn at euro'n iaith . . .
Duw a'th roes ar wlad i'th ran
Do yn bennaeth dyn byw anian.[57]

The description is fully devoted to outlining the prime features of this patron's gentility. 'Your body is itself perfection', he says, 'and your heart is fruitful.' 'You have a refined nature', he continues, ' and are courageous, powerful and honourable. You are the embodiment of two provinces and a royal being who enriches our culture. God has granted you your position as the active head of your region'. This patron's vivacious personality had obviously attracted Siôn Phylip, principally because of his resoluteness in performing his services.

The struggle to establish and retain status in a rapidly changing society constantly occupied any person with a claim to gentility in the sixteenth century, and constituted a powerful force in the routine daily life of a social order which was often hard hit by the economic realities of the day. The Tudor poets were aware of such tensions but were more immediately concerned with defining status as a source of moral excellence. Welsh gentility, in their view, had withstood the pressures of economic forces; in moral terms, it was believed that *uchelwriaeth* equalled all that high-ranking and ostentatious families had to offer elsewhere and endured the hardships by virtue of its primitive grandeur and divine support. Moral affluence was uppermost and was maintained through inheritance. Siôn Phylip, one of the most percipient of commentators in his age, again pronounced succinctly on this matter in what might be regarded as his most notable eulogy. The survival of the inalienable birthright in the succession of a worthy heir ('etifedd rhinweddol') stands out as a formative indication of dynastic integrity. In the case of Sir John Wynn of Gwydir it was said that the concept of the overbearing *paterfamilias* in his court would never fade so long as the patrimony is preserved for a legitimate successor.

Oes unlle'r penllad llu
Aer well ei air a'i allu?[58]

The focus on the succession of the worthy heir inspired this poet to see confidently into the future. 'The proverb was true', he maintains, 'that the father does not die if God's will provides a worthy heir to succeed him'. Then, in his reference to this individual heir at Gwydir, he posed the question whether there ever had been a better heir of credit and skill than he who had succeeded as the leader of men?

Noble succession was another factor considered to be high among the priorities of claimants to gentle status. It is hardly surprising that most eulogies contained lavish references to birthright and inheritance as well as the proliferation of agnatic relations. The poets were concerned with the identity of pedigree, wherever possible with Welsh origins. Although William Herbert of St. Julians in Gwent was praised by Dafydd Benwyn, arguably the most professional among poets of his day in Morgannwg, chiefly because of his descent from English forbears, he was proclaimed as a worthy Welshman because some Welsh blood flowed in his veins.[59] This kind of noble descent served to buttress bonds of kinship, to enrich family tradition, to maintain a distinct cultural ethos and to preserve the organic unity of the community. It was in the late sixteenth century that poets became increasingly aware of changing times and attitudes among the most ambitious gentry and detected the *malaise* which consequently was to have detrimental effects on Welsh bardic tradition.

Aristocratic attributes featured conspicuously in verse which displayed particularly the virtues of public office and standing. References abound to the claims of patrons to knighthood by virtue of their accomplishments in royal service. Such esoteric claims were often linked, in bardic convention, with the need to buttress reputation and identify levels of attainment among the most aspiring squires of the day. Wiliam Llŷn's lines to Siôn Prys, a Montgomeryshire squire whom he considered, by virtue of his public achievements, worthy of a knighthood, serve to illustrate the point.

Ysgwier braisg ger ei bron
Y'th elwir bennaeth haelion;

Nid wyd farchog cefnog wych
Ni obeithir na bythych.
D'euro'n llew derwen lluoedd,
Felly Siôn fy wyllys oedd.[60]

The reputation of such a renowned patron, in the poet's mind, fully justified further promotion by the Queen. 'You are regarded as a sprightly squire and generous chieftain', he observes, 'and although you are not [by designation] a substantial knight it is not my wish that you do not attain that position.' The poet continues by expressing his heart-felt desire that a knighthood be formally conferred upon him.

In 1611 James I created the rank of baronet chiefly to obtain further sources of income.[61] The sale of honours was to prove more damaging to the Crown's reputation than at first realized. The lavish creation of knighthoods on the king's accession in 1603 soon became a disreputable feature of the new sovereign's reign because it degraded the honour. Furthermore, the order of baronets, devised in 1611, was but another method adopted to solve the Crown's pressing financial crisis. This new status was originally intended for only 200 prime gentry considered to be sufficiently worthy of attaining minor noble rank, but the honour was granted to any substantial squire who could afford to pay £1,095 for the privilege. The position was expected to serve as an intermediate step between the order of knighthood and the lower ranks of the peerage. Candidates for the title had to prove that their families had enjoyed armigerous status for at least three years and that they owned property to the annual value of £1,000. Although the creation caused considerable opposition among the younger sons of barons who claimed precedence over the 'audacious and unmannerlie' upstarts in the social hierarchy, the first year saw keen competition among eligible gentry for the title.[62] It was a matter of prestige for families of the highest order in county society to contest with each other for the honour, thus perpetuating old kindred feuds. The title of baronet, however, did place the recipient at the top end of the gentry scale and complemented the prestige which he and his kin had already enjoyed. While the elevation of gentry into the aristocracy created opposition in English circles on the grounds that order, degree and precedence were ignored, in a purely Welsh context the new honours served admirably to buttress ancestral eminence as well as the ascendancy achieved by some prominent families. The poet Robert ap Rhys Wyn, for example, observed that Sir John Wynn of Gwydir, who was among the first in Wales to receive the title, had justly deserved his position primarily on grounds of descent and deference. He closely linked the privileged baronet ('baronet teg a braint da') with the baron or lord claiming royal pedigree ('barwn henwaed brenhinol'), and by so doing identified Wynn's promotion with the rôle of kings.[63] The baronet of elevated stock, it was further maintained, deserved his dignified position by virtue of his line of descent from Welsh kings. The couplet by Rhisiart Cynwal succinctly explains this view of an acquired status.

> Baronet hael burion tylwyth,
> Bron hen llin y brenhinllwyth.[64]

'He was the opulent and generous baron of pure stock', the poet maintained, 'a descendant from an illustrious line of kings.' The identification of kingly attributes with the privilege acquired by Wynn in 1611 served to highlight the superiority of official status in Welsh public life in those days.

The auspicious baronet ('baroned breiniawl') was constantly identified with the ambitious *paterfamilias* and chieftain in the old tribal context. The benevolent leader, described concisely by Huw Machno as the heart and soul of his hall at Gwydir, fulfilled his rôle admirably by lavishly entertaining poets and official dignitaries.

> Gweled y baroned oedd ben—
> Llywydd, a phawb yn llawen,
> A'i Arglwyddes rhoe'i gwleddoedd,
> A'i phlant ar ffyniant hoff oedd.[65]

The situation was idealized as the poet portrayed the *paterfamilias* in his court surrounded by his household and guests. 'To see the baronet presiding over all the proceedings and everyone contented', he said, was a remarkable and satisfying experience. His lady would organize the feasts and his children would enjoy the sumptuous atmosphere of their home. His central rôle in presiding over his household was doubtless a memorable occasion for the poet. His contribution as *paterfamilias* was largely reflected in his lasting service to his immediate family and local community. To that extent, as regional leader, he was equal to the true nobleman with whom he shared majestic features. Siôn Phylip considered one *uchelwr* to have emerged as the very essence of nobility ('eigion pendefigaeth'),[66] and Siams Dwnn, the Montgomeryshire poet, dedicated an entire *cywydd* in honour of Sir Richard Prys of Gogerddan on his promotion to a baronetcy.[67] In it he emphasized the comparison between the virtuous and well-endowed squire skilled in all public relations and the inheritor of ancestral grace and tenacity. The office was a means by which men of quality could apply their authority to maintain and defend the commomweal.

The few in Wales who did successfully attain the rank of baronet were doubtless representatives of the most eligible families who ruled at the time. Among the earliest to be honoured were Sir John Stradling of St. Donat's, Sir Thomas Mansel of Margam, Sir John Wynn of Gwydir and, in 1619, Sir Henry Salusbury, all of whom were considered, in bardic tributes, to be benign heads of their communities. Not only were they seeking to consolidate their positions within county society and creating for themselves opportunities for self-advancement but were also concerned with cultivating family connections and identifying their interests with the baronage of England while, at the same time, exercising those privileges within a specifically Welsh context.[68] Before Henry Salusbury of Lleweni was elevated in this way Siôn Cain jubilantly forecast the event observing that he would ultimately be honoured or 'gilded' ('euro') by James I as a sign of virtuous living. Within his portals, the poet maintained, his ostentatious bearing equalled that of ten earls,[69] and that was the type of testimony given also to his son Thomas Salusbury, second baronet, who was commended for much the same reason.[70] He wore a gilded collar, the poet explained, and was more renowned than the traditional nobility for his integrity and bearing. His baronetcy, the poet continued, would soon be changed for a peerage since his increasing grandeur augured well for the future. His gentility, it was maintained further, qualified him for the highest honours which any sovereign could bestow on a man of his status, the title of earl or marquis being well within his reach.

Baronetcies were considered, therefore, to constitute the first major step forward towards attaining full English aristocratic status. The true *uchelwr* had again achieved, in a practical sense, the goal which his forbears had claimed to be their inalienable birthright within the context of the ancient traditions of the Isle of Britain.[71] The position of baronet enabled its holder to perform duties relating to the total well-being of the realm. What their ancestors had accomplished in regional terms in the past was now extended and enhanced to embrace the body politic at large. Indeed, by the early seventeenth century the Welsh gentry had become well aware of the intrinsic features and needs of British citizenship: the accession of the Stuarts had bound the nation in a common bond of unity, and the affairs of state became increasingly more relevant to them personally and enabled them to acquire and appreciate a more global view of public life and activity as well as contribute successfully to it.[72] They continued to regard themselves as the true inheritors of the 'island empire' which had existed before the Saxon invasions, and in a more positive sense they now considered themselves, by virtue of public office and authority, to form an essential part of the newly-united Britain which emerged with the union of the two crowns in 1603. By maintaining their links with the Crown, thereby establishing stability in the realm, the prime gentry safeguarded their own interests and manifested, in the most overt manner, their dignity as the latter day *nobilitas* of Wales. The concept was succinctly expressed in one crisp couplet by Huw Machno to his chief patron at Gwydir.

> Braint da doeth barnet i'w dai,
> Y brenin Siams a'i breiniai.[73]

The *uchelwr* is shown to be the 'privileged, good and wise baronet in his house', contentedly positioned because King James had honoured him. The identification of the newly-established Stuart dynasty with 'honour, prestige and privilege' among Welsh gentry added yet another significant feature to the social demeanour of the traditional Welsh gentleman.

In the years subsequent to 1611, immediately below the rank of baronetcy, stood the order of knighthood to which several privileged Welsh gentry aspired during the course of the sixteenth century. Its history in the development of the gentry extended back to the fourteenth century when prominent individuals, well-proven in their loyalty to the Crown of England, were honoured, especially for their feats on the battlefields of Europe. In his *History of Wales* (1697), William Wynne of Garthewin in Denbighshire, recorded a tradition concerning Tudur ap Goronwy, one of the fourteenth-century descendants of Ednyfed Fychan and an ancestor of the Penmynydd family in Anglesey. It is said that he had received the honour of knighthood without royal sanction, and had consequently been summoned before Edward III to explain his seemingly audacious pretence. Tudur explained that he had acquired the title 'by the laws and constitution of King Arthur', and then proceeded to enumerate his three principal qualifications. First and foremost, he maintained that 'he was a gentleman; secondly, he had a sufficient estate, and thirdly, he was valiant and adventurous, adding this withal; if my valour and hardiness be doubted of, lo, here I throw down my glove and for due proof of my courage I am ready to fight with any man whatever he be.' It is alleged that the king, admiring his pluck and self-assertion, agreed to confirm the status of knighthood which the redoubtable warrior had already assumed.[74] Whether Tudur ap Goronwy really qualified for knighthood, strictly in material terms, is debatable, but, in view of his imposing Welsh ancestry, his pretence is noteworthy and is to be applauded.

The honour of knighhood was not normally conferred on *brehyrion* or *gwyrda* (Welsh nobility or *optimates*), excepting those elevated because of their distinguishing features in military service. It is certain, however, that the status was coveted by leading gentry, although it was essentially an alien feature in the annals of Welsh *uchelwriaeth*. In England, with the decline of military service, knighthood gradually became a compulsory obligation on all freeholders who owned property valued at £20 a year. In Wales, on the other hand, emphasis had customarily been placed on noble lineage rather than on feudal gradations as the chief criterion for gentility.[75] This feature was increasingly connected to the acquisition of property and kindred privileges. Below the *brenin* (king), *tywysogion* (princes) and *brehyrion* (nobility), stood the *bonedd* and *bonheddig*, which emerged as a popular term for privileged status in poetic composition in the late Middle Ages. Welsh gentility differed essentially from the English concept where the emphasis was placed on family distinction and economic competence and superiority. English gentility gave prominence to dynastic elements, the practice of primogeniture and largely to the perpetuation of the senior branch. Welsh genealogy, however, gave equal consideration to all family groupings, and gentility was often measured by identifying blood affinities with a common ancestor. Poets normally eulogized family groups which stemmed from that ancestry so that, in due course, with the rise of cadet families by the fifteenth century, the pedigrees of younger sons were also given publicity in bardic eulogy.

The three *bonheddig* arts, according to the Welsh lawbooks, were the bearing of arms, horsemanship and hunting.[76] Doubtless, the most eligible among the Welsh *uchelwyr* were privileged by virtue of their links with free warrior clansmen noted for their military prowess, a trait which persisted among their fifteenth-century descendants who assumed distinctive features of 'privileged nobility' (*uchelwriaeth freiniol*). Kinship loyalties and obligations were jealously guarded, and Welsh law emphasized the leadership offered by the king in warfare. Owing principally to economic pressures the warrior classes gradually settled permanently on land, and clan-founders in the twelfth and thirteenth centuries based their property rights on free *gwely* tenure.[77] Such rights entailed the division and sub-division of clan holdings which unavoidably led to fragmentation of property rights within the clan structure. Thus emerged new clan holdings from the disintegrated condition of the old, and the *uchelwyr* continued to enjoy those privileges inherited from the original *gwely* founder. It is hardly surprising, therefore, that sixteenth-century poets continued to remind descendants of such family groupings of their military glory. Indeed, in the Tudor period, there emerged a large and amorphous group of freeholders who, owing to the unstable economic climate, rose to prominence, claimed gentility and assumed the ascendancy, not so much on account of their landed means but rather because of their pedigrees. It has been interpreted as a purely Welsh concept of *bonheddig* which displayed a broad and very modest social dimension, varying degrees of material wealth and competence as well as qualities commensurate with the aristocracy of England. Principally, poets were expected to praise their sponsors for their strength, valour and military accomplishments,[78] but were also expected to promote the 'courtly' attributes of their worthy lords.

The order of knighthood was normally reserved for a select band among the prospering *uchelwyr* who had made the grade. The material inadequacies of the majority of claimants to gentility strikingly reflected the economic poverty of Wales. The broad-based framework led to the existence of a sizeable majority of yeomen-freeholders who constituted the lower ranks of landed proprietors. In Gwynedd, for example, in the mid-Tudor period subsidy assessments indicate that *uchelwyr* who owned goods to the value of £10 a year and lands worth £5 were considered to be worthy of gentle status.[79] Rowland Lee's stricture that very few Welshmen above Brecknock could 'dispend £10 land' was not, in fact, far off the mark.[80] In the 1543 assessment for Gwynedd, for example, the gentry with goods valued at £10 or more numbered only 7%, the remainder forming a large group of small freeholders possessing a disproportionately much smaller amount of wealth. Thus emerged a social entity in which the largest *corpus* of families claimed gentility purely on an ancestral basis, a feature which is revealed most conspicuously in the strict-metre compositions to gentry of all ranks in the Welsh social context. Rhys Fychan of Corsygedol in Merioneth, a modest squire who assumed considerable power in his community, was accorded praise by Wiliam Llŷn in the following lines.

> Dawn a gefaist yn gyfa,
> Ag arwydd dawn yw gwraidd da;
> A'ch anrhydedd chwi'n rhediad
> A'ch gras Duw uwch gwŷr o stad;
> Ych bôn a'i gŵys uwchben gwŷr
> Ac uwch pawb ŵr gwych pybyr.[81]

This well-known section portrays the potentiality which lay within the privileged *uchelwr*. 'You have obtained all the talents', says the poet, 'which are indicated clearly in your illustrious ancestry.' 'You possess honour and God's grace', he maintained further, 'which has elevated you above all others. You are the chief ox in the furrow, significantly higher than all others in rank.' Such lines indicate the power and dignity which such a leader enjoyed in a remote part of the Principality regardless of the economic constraints imposed upon him. The emphasis is placed principally on good ancestry and the benefits which were bestowed on him and his family.

The most eligible among Welsh *uchelwyr* in the sixteenth century were designated knights (marchogion), squires (ysgwieriaid) and gentlemen (boneddigion). Numerous unsuccessful attempts have been made to distinguish between these ranks since wealth varied at different levels in that period and social designations often varied according to the economic climate. In the 1530s the squire was broadly regarded as a man valued between £20 and £40 in land a year, and the gentleman between £3 and £20.[82] Status, however, depended largely on impression and the way in which the community viewed an individual and his family: his prestige was derived essentially from common consent to the degree of gentility he could legitimately claim. The poets sang profusely to patrons who were endowed with nobility based on this very factor, ancestral eligibility. It was considered to be a firm buttress to all pretensions and a manner of justifying their lavish hospitality in the *plastai*. Indeed, the status of squire (ysgwier) was officially designated as being immediately below that of knight, and those regarded as worthy had attained a balanced and acknowledged degree of gentility. 'May God preserve the progeny of good squires', Wiliam Cynwal maintained, 'because they shall never go astray.'[83] The ideal squire was a mirror in whose image men should judge themselves. According to the *Graduelys* three types of squire existed, two royal appointees and a third marked by lineage. From his rank would spring the most auspicious leader who would aim at promotion and provide a worthy succession.[84]

> Ysgwier drwy wychder draw
> Wyd i aros dy euraw.

This opulent squire, Hywel Fychan of Glanllyn, Llanycil, was considered to be so refined that he eagerly expected the royal court to promote him. The pattern had been well laid by then in gentry circles. These words by Wiliam Llŷn reflect the image of the ambitious landowner aspiring for further promotion in view of his public services. Simwnt Fychan also drew attention to the glory of dynastic succession in landed affairs.

Ysgwîair gair rhagorol
Y daw sgwieiriaid i'w ôl.[85]

'He is a squire who enjoys an excellent reputation', it is said of John Salusbury, 'and he will produce other squires to succeed him.' The dynastic trait is again very much in evidence and is registered in the poet's mind. Elevation, in this context, implied a rise to the grade of knight which some substantial gentry in Wales had successfully achieved in the last quarter of the sixteenth century.

The traditional concept of knighthood in England, based on feudal ties and military service, was no longer a marked feature of the social structure, and the honour became largely a means by which men of rank and substance who loyally served the state achieved priority in public life. In a Welsh context as well the professional poets had become acutely aware of the need to stress proficiency in domestic duties relating to local or regional government. Not that military service ceased to have any importance because the gentry were called upon constantly to supply men and leadership in times of military pressure at home and abroad. Sir Richard Trefor of Trefalun in Denbighshire, for example, was a soldier, politician and administrator who was knighted in Ireland in 1597 for his services as head of the shire levies in the Irish campaigns. He owned a large estate in north-east Wales and, in spite of his military commitments, played an impressive rôle in local politics and administration.[86] Sir John Perrott of Haroldston in Pembrokeshire served as Lord Deputy of Ireland between 1584 and 1588, but found enough time to attend to his landed affairs in his native shire.[87] Knights of this order, who were rewarded for military service, became prime objects of lofty and pompous eulogy.

Knighthood in Wales was conferred on a very narrow group of gentry. In his *Description of Wales* (1602) George Owen of Henllys could name only fourteen knights out of a total of 124 *generosi* in the shires of Pembroke, Radnor, Monmouth, Brecknock and Glamorgan. In the remaining shires the numbers were even smaller.[88] Judging by the knighthoods conferred on Welsh members of the Council in the Marches in Elizabeth I's reign it appears that the honour was very rare. Between 1560 and 1603, out of a total of a 100 members only 21 came from Wales and of those only 9 had been knighted.[89] Elizabeth was not lavish in her disposal of knighthoods but an increase did appear in the last two decades of her reign, principally for distinguished military service. This was confirmed by Sir Thomas Smith in *De Republica Anglorum* when he stated that knights were 'made either before the battle to encourage them the more to adventure their lives, or after the conflict as advancement for their hardiness and manhood.' He also drew attention to the honour being conferred 'for some great service done or some good hope for the virtues which do appear in them.'[90] It was the age when the Renaissance spirit was gradually converting the old concept of the chivalrous knight into a gentleman identified more for his courtly etiquette and services to the state. Ideals of nobility were being more closely associated with the qualities of civil life, the urbane and gracious. Sir John Salusbury of Lleweni, in the late sixteenth century, was acclaimed by Tomas Berwyn as a man of grace and favour sprung from a wise and discreet stock. His benignity, the poet maintained, permitted him to govern the countryside efficiently, and much of his prosperity stemmed from his knightly rank and sagacity.

> Y gŵr sydd â gras iddaw
> A dynn y wlad dan ei law . . .
> Dawn o ras da iawn a rodd
> Yn ei wyneb a 'nynnodd.
> A raddio Duw ei wreiddyn
> O ŵr doeth, ni wyra dyn . . .[91]

The picture again is familiar: 'The gracious man has the ability to control his region', the poet declares, 'and he obtains good grace in order to do so.' 'No person,' he states further, 'can destroy rank sanctioned by God', a timely reminder of the insuperability of *uchelwriaeth*.

The Tudors needed able, willing and experienced administrators to maintain the peace and good government considered essential to promote the interests of the new sovereign state. Military campaigns were given less attention in poetic exercises, and the order of knighthood became ostensibly identified with those individuals who had distinguished themselves in civil government.[92] Prosperity was the preserve of the *uchelwr* who revealed business acumen, who skilfully applied it to enhance the reputation of his family and the state, who demonstrated enough ambition to prosper materially and who successfully climbed the social ladder with the greatest of ease. His chief qualifications were educational and a good working knowledge of and instinct for public service. The lay administrator became more relevant in the late sixteenth-century context. The new capitalist features enabled those who were able to out-manoeuvre their peers to seek higher preferment. The concept of knighthood, in Welsh eulogy, became readily identified with the virtuous *uchelwr* who applied his learning and allied virtues for the benefit of others, residing in his *plasty* and attending to the needs of his estate and tenants. His reputation was often considered to be superior, as Siôn Cain exclaimed, in his address to Sir John Bodfel of Llŷn following his promotion.

> Y marchog aur hebog hir
> Y mae d'arswyd am deirsir;
> Marchog wyd, osglog disglair,
> Mwy na'r iarll am enw a gair.[93]

The image of the 'gilded knight' again emerges, 'awesome in his power over three shires.' 'You are a knight higher than any earl in reputation and credit', he continued, suggesting that, in a Welsh context, his range of qualities equalled, even excelled, the best that England had to offer. His public authority was augmented, the poet maintained, because of his rise in status, implying that the highest privilege demanded total commitment to public duty. The Tudor settlement had intensified the struggle for recognition among the Welsh gentry in judicial and administrative capacities. It not only made individuals ambitious but also inspired those who were culturally associated with them to declare their elegibility and vaunt their dynastic ambitions.

The Welsh knight in the Tudor and Stuart periods, in poetic terms, was hardly distinguishable from native squires on a grand scale: the titles 'lord' (arglwydd), 'earl' (iarll) and 'knight' (marchog) were interchangeable and universally recognised in verse as common denominators. In an attempt to mediate discreetly between Sir John Salusbury and Sir Thomas Myddelton of Chirk Castle, in a case of legal wrangling, Robert Ifans referred to them as two notable esquires sadly distraught by mutual jealousy and hatred ('Dau sgweier . . . dau o gynnyrch digofaint'). Huw Machno, however, wished to go further and, in his poem, added substantially to Salusbury's reputation after he had been elevated to a knighthood in 1601.

> Ysgwier ydych, gwaisg, ar rediad,
> O gorff Elsbeth, difeth iawn dyfiad;
> Marchog hefyd, mawr ucha' cofiad,
> Y'th raddiai, doniai iawn ordeiniad,
> A'th frenin, da'i rin, Duw a'i rad—drosto
> A ŵyr ddwys d'urddo, urddas darddiad.[94]

'You are an esquire of the body to Elizabeth', it is declared, 'and a knight of high rank.' 'Your talents are ordained', it is further manifested, 'because your sovereign has conferred the honour legitimately upon you.' Salusbury had been fully acknowledged as a governor of his communty through royal favour, the poet observed, and was renowned in Wales for his good government. Siôn Tudur, likewise, gave attention to the external manifestations of knightly glory in his congratulatory ode to Sir Thomas Mostyn on receiving his distinction in 1599.[95] He was a courageous knight, the lines ran, and accomplished his feats in exemplary fashion, his court being a worthy lodging for the whole of Wales.

Such testimonies added a touch of harsh reality which normally distinguished the practical man of affairs. Conferring knighthood did not necessarily add authority to the family although it could, to some degree, repair a tarnished reputation. Poets often speculated whether some of their most illustrious patrons might achieve knighthoods and, in some cases, foresaw the event. ('Cei d'euro'n wir').[96] Adorning the squire with a gold collar ('aurdorchog') was indeed considered a symbol of excellence since it had established military associations. '[In] or out of the wars', William Harrison explained in *The Description of England* (1577), 'for some great service done or for the singular virtues which do appear in them (and then are they named *equites aurati* as common custom intendeth).'[97] In that context, therefore, a Welsh appointee to knighthood, for example, would be addressed as the 'sternly valiant knight with gilded torque' ('Marchog aurdorchog dewrchwyrn') or, less pretentiously, as the knight of good descent, a man of power, mercy and other similar properties.

> Croeso i farchog rhywiog wraidd
> Nerthog, trugarog gŵraidd.[98]

The poet jubilantly records his patron's distinguished appearance: 'Welcome to the elegant knight of gracious stock; powerful, merciful and manly.' In the same context, Siôn Tudur proceeded to describe the act of dubbing Sir John Salusbury in 1601, knowing full well that the act symbolized the highest honour which the squire could achieve. He was called the 'dubbed knight' ('marchog urddawl') honoured by the Queen herself.[99] In Tomas Penllyn's view Salusbury might again be promoted by virtue of his dignity and ancient Welsh ancestry through Henry Tudor's line. In the case of Sir John Wynn of Gwydir, one poet took the opportunity of linking his privileges with those of an ancient chieftain of memorable stock.

> Hwn a'i gledd anrhydeddawl
> A'i hurddodd mewn harddwedd mawl . . .
> Urddiad hardd ei waed ei hun;
> Un yw Syr Siôn . . . fry'r hanoedd o frenhinwaed.

It is an impressive description, referring to the manner in which the sword was elegantly placed on the recipient's shoulder, much in the same way as Siôn Tudur splendidly described, but in greater detail, the same honour given to Sir John Salusbury of Lleweni.[100] Poets also referred to knights as 'coursers' ('cwrseriaid') and 'riders' ('reidars'), terms normally associated with a swift war-horse and mounted warrior, thus adding substantially to the image of grandeur, military prowess and benign leadership.

The knight, therefore, had emerged as a combination of the scholar, soldier and courtier noted for his versatility. He possessed courage, endurance, adaptability and knowledge of military science as well as the qualities of justice, prudence, self-discipline and liberality characteristic of the courtier.[101] Siôn Dafydd Rhys portrayed the perfect gentleman when describing Sir Edward Stradling in his preamble to his *Cambrobrytannicae Cymraecaeve Linguae*

Institutiones in 1592. He referred to him as a man of learning, resourceful and enterprising in his defence of the kingdom against disorder and external threat. He had received the training of the scholar and administrator, and his virtues were considered valuable for their utilitarian rather than aesthetic properties. As a courtier, he blended the qualities of the well-bred, self-disciplined man of affairs.[102] The redoubtable warrior ('marchog ewinog o ŵr'), as Lewys Môn portrayed a patron in the early sixteenth century, had been converted, in the words of Siôn Mawddwy to another patron, into 'the leader . . . under the Prince, the guardian and chief defender' ('A blaenawr . . . Dan y Prins yn geidwad a phen ac amddiffyniad'), traits which reveal prime virtues in war and peace.[103] Not only does the ideal gentleman need to know his ancestry but also, as Sir John Price, the humanist scholar observed, he must care for the benefit of all. Thus he would maintain the same features expounded by Sir Thomas Elyot and others who labelled the knight as a civil servant. 'A knight', Elyot explained, 'hath received that honour, not only to defend with the sword Christ's faith and his proper country . . . but also, and that most chiefly by the means of his dignity . . . should more effectively with his learning and wit assail vice and error . . . having thereunto for his sword and spear his tongue and his pen.'[104] Sir Robert Salusbury of Rug in Merioneth was hailed a notable figure knighted for his service in Ireland in 1593. He combined, it was said, the qualities of the redoubtable warrior and county administrator. His poet esteemed him both as a 'knight of war' ('marchog o ryfel') and as a royal servant in his locality 'ordaining peace'.[105] Sir Walter Rice, a descendant of Sir Rhys ap Thomas of Dinefwr, was distinguished, it was further stated, as a 'dignified knight' ('marchog urddawl') who functioned prominently in the government of Carmarthenshire. Some Welsh gentry rose through the ranks to attain knightly honours. Sir Gelly Meyrick, for example, was elevated because of his services in the household of the Earl of Essex,[106] and others of his *milieu* were honoured in the same way.

James I extravagantly created knights on his accession in 1603. During the first four months of his reign he had created 906 of them compared to the grand total of 878 by Elizabeth during her long reign.[107] The 'inflation of honours' by then had reached its peak:

knighthood had become merely a method of rewarding courtiers and officials who possessed influence and some degree of proficiency in the art of government. Sir William Herbert of St. Julians in Monmouthshire, in his reply to another squire who claimed equal status, remarked that 'if he be as good as myself, it must be either for virtue, for birth, for ability or for calling and dignity'. 'For virtue', he continued, 'I think he meant not for it is a matter that exceeds judgement.'[108] Virtue, in this context, was identified with the code of conduct practised by Renaissance gentlemen, symbolizing probity and justice. 'Without it', Elyot maintained, 'none other virtue may be commendable.'[109] In the Welsh poetic tradition any person considered to be of sufficient status was invested with innate qualities of excellence. Rhisiart Cynwal, in his ode to Sir William Maurice of Clenennau, knighted in 1603, admiringly portrayed him as the typical Welsh country squire elevated to knighthood on the threshold of a new and exciting phase in his career.[110] He rejoiced in his success at court, the poet explained, 'he was the Moses holding office under James, and he paraded on equal terms with earls and other dignitaries'. The true gentleman, he maintained further, does not emphasize wealth or material welfare as much as he does his reputation. 'Better than gold, better than silver', he stated, 'is his name and dignity to a gentleman.' Thus was conceived the image of the Welsh *uchelwr* as a proficient courtier who concurrently maintained fundamental characteristics which linked him with his distinguished lineage.

Below the higher ranks of gentry trailed the large numbers of modest freeholders who claimed gentilty by descent. Materially, the majority were dangerously close to subsistence level, concerning themselves with tilling the soil and attending to the routine business of managing their estates or tenancies. In England, according to Sir Thomas Smith, one prime feature of the gentleman was the opportunity he enjoyed to 'live idly and without manual labour'.[111] Such a luxury would not normally be available to the Welsh gentlemen who often struggled to make both ends meet. 'Gentlemen', Smith added, 'be those whom their blood and race doth make noble and known', a feature which emerged, with equal prominence, in the concept of Welsh gentility. The poets concentrated on the 'privilege of blood affinity' ('braint gwaed'), 'wholesome gentility' ('da'r bonedd'), the 'ties of blood' ('gwaedoliaeth') and so on.[112] Such qualities drew from the poets hyperbolic imagery but, at the same time, enabled them to place *uchelwriaeth* in its native setting. Good virtue, it was said, stemmed from noble progenitors. No gentleman, it was further perceived, existed *in vacuo*. To develop his personal resources implied that the *uchelwr* had to rely on his innate moral qualities, hence the constant references to 'roots' ('gwreiddiau') and 'degree' ('gradd').

> Graddwyd ef o'r gwraidd dyfiad,
> Urddas doeth o radd a stad.[113]

In these lines Siôn Tudur was eager to point out that the *uchelwr* had been graded from good stock, that he was dignified and wise in degree and estate and able to defend his reputation among his kinsmen and dependants in his neighbourhood. It was generally considered that a gentleman of reputation, by definition, could claim the rank deemed appropriate for him.[114] The poets endorsed this by attributing to such individuals their own designations such as 'esquire' ('ysgwier'), 'chieftain' ('pennaeth'), 'the magnificence of gentility' ('mawredd bonedd') and 'statesman' ('gwladwr'). To say that the patron represented the peak of his social order did not necessarily imply that he had descended from the most illustrious stock, but rather that his virtues resembled that code of behaviour which revealed good breeding. 'In you there is gentility' ('Ynod . . . mae bonedd'), Siôn Mawddwy maintained, in his poem to a gentleman of very modest proportions, meaning that his qualities compared favourably with any others displayed by the gentle order.[115] The man of good breeding would, by nature, offer hospitality and entertainment with the style and deference of a revered nobleman. The concepts of the 'soul of munifience' ('enaid haelioni') and the 'gilded pinnacle and head of his neighbourhood' ('A phinagl aur a phen gwlad') created images which, in esthetic terms, make it difficult to decide what the real worth of a gentleman was in terms of land and property and other sources of material wealth.[116] Very rarely are references made to the indigence of several patrons although the decline in hospitality in the late sixteenth century did imply that some gentry found it impossible to continue their customary services to the bardic order. Recipients of the eulogy, however, were complimented for their valour and strength of character, normally through office-holding and good housekeeping. George Owen of Henllys doubtless exaggerated when he remarked that many gentlemen in Wales were, by his time, valued at £100 a year and that 'there is no shire in Wales but is able to yield sufficient number of gentlemen' of that sort.[117] While it is true to say that social advancement had, in many respects, stabilized the various social gradations, it is equally correct to assume that the forces of inflation, poor agricultural conditions and heavy domestic expenses had taken their toll in hinterland areas. If a person of the standing of Sir John Wynn of Gwydir could bitterly complain about the adverse effects of the economic climate of his day on his living standards in the 1620s it is only reasonable to suppose that less well-endowed gentry freeholders felt the pinch much more severely. The poets sang frequently to middling and lower range gentry, and the purport of their verse revealed hardly any distinction between them regarding status and rank. In fact, poetic licence allowed them to interpret gentility as the organic entity of moral excellence. Lewys Morgannwg sang to Sir John Wynn's grandfather, emphasizing his principal features.

> Tri chyfoeth wyt, tra chyfiawn,
> Y tri yw: dysg, natur, dawn.[118]

'You possess three major sources of wealth', the poet observes in his reference to this prominent administrator and landowner in the commote of Nanconwy, 'and the three are learning, demeanour and talent.' He had perceived that the new social order, as it gradually emerged under the Tudors, demanded newer modes of behaviour sustained by a nation state which had all to offer the perspicacious public figure. Learning, in this context, embraced all other admired qualities, and the gentleman's character and nature displayed his grace and courtesy. He possessed the integrity which created him an exemplary leader and protector of his region.

While holding office and enjoying official reputation were features to be admired in the Welsh *uchelwr* they were subordinated in verse to other more fundamental characteristics. Historically, he acquired reputation principally on the basis of his innate qualities and protective powers within his community rather than any show of public service. Promotions and higher office might enhance prestige but would have virtually no bearing on the true status of the Welsh *uchelwr*. 'Even in direct poverty', Humphrey Llwyd, the Tudor antiquary, remarked, 'they never forget their gentle origins'. Social class and affiliations in Tudor and Stuart Wales have, in recent times, been interpreted as 'highly elastic and comprehensive',[119] lacking the features of a 'caste system.' Added to descent and lineage, and closely allied with them, were the patriarchal and patrician properties, the constant recall to noble attributes stemming from ancient Brythonic tradition. It is in this context that *uchelwyr* were granted regal status. He who owned extensive lands, it was said, deserved honour and glory, but he who kept a worthy reputation deserved even more. Good character and probity were more highly esteemed than material wealth and power.

> Ni ddug, mae'n dda i'w ogylch,
> Na thai'r gwan na thir i'w gylch,
> Eithr dwyn â'i weithred yna,
> Aeddfed iawn, gyneddfau da;
> Cyfiawnder a haelder hwn
> Cyfa' i'r oes y cofiwn.[120]

In Huw Machno's view the patron does not oppress the poor or take from them their homes; rather, he cultivates new and mature faculties, namely justice and beneficence which he abundantly displays. The lines reflect much that was deplored in an age of rapacity and economic tension which was exhibited in the legal activities of many Welsh gentry of all ranks in this age.

In the early seventeenth century the gradual withdrawal of gentry patronage and the increasing degree of absenteeism among landowners forced the poets to emphasize more insistently the benefits of good housekeeping. Heirs and their progeny were regarded as symbols of continuous traditions in lands, offices and housekeeping. There was a marked lack of confidence among the poets in their addresses to absentee heads of families, a feature that was offset by dwelling profusely on public image as the norm of admired gentility. Such sentiments were more often expressed in elegies (marwnadau) where the demise of a memorable patron gave a fit and able heir the opportunity to govern his patrimony with equal dexterity and trust.[121] In his eulogy for Huw Nannau I Gruffudd Hafren drew attention to the hope which his community shared in the presence of a suitable heir.

> Ni ad yr aer hynod rwysg
> Nannau i lawr union loywrwysg;
> Efo'n ben a fo yn byw
> Ar ewythredd mawr wythryw.[122]

The poet was reassured that the remarkable heir, resplendent and dashing, would not forsake his home at Nannau. The house would continue under his leadership which combined the power possessed by several kindred strands. The potency of such couplets is unmistakably succinct: the coming of the heir to his inheritance, in these lines, is fortified by lineal descent of some magnitude. The force of divine intervention was also considered essential, as Huw Machno points out in his elegy to the same patron.

> A Duw drwy ei rad a'i rodd
> Doe a'i waith a'i bendithiodd.
> Yno i weled yn wiwlu
> Plant i plant ar lwyddiant lu.[123]

God, according to the poet, through his grace and favour yesterday blessed the patron, and his posterity continued to flourish in each succeeding generation. Some poets were obliged to counsel young heirs when they came to their inheritance because of their tendencies to involve themselves in expensive lawsuits and wrangle among their kindred and others for power and position. The belligerent heir was often severely censured and given firm guidance on how to act in a just and equitable manner. A classic example of such sound advice is found in Siôn Phylip's *cywydd* to the young Rhisiart Fychan I of Corsygedol on his return to his native country after a prison sentence at Coventry for opposing the Earl of Leicester's designs in the Forest of Snowdon affair.[124] The tone of the poem is similar, in most respects, to those which greeted heirs on achieving their responsible office as heads of families. The poet dwells on the evils of society which the heir should eschew, and underlines the dignity and bearing expected of him on his succession. The lines form an ardent plea that the new patron should respect the stock from which he had sprung and practice virtue.

> Nâd hiraeth yn y tiroedd
> Am dy dad, pen dwywlad oedd . . .
> Nâd ar dy wlad o ledwg
> Dreth drom na gwladwriaeth drwg.[125]

'Let us not long for your father, the head of two regions', was the poet's plea, 'and do not oppress the countryside by exacting heavy taxes and imposing corrupt government.' The message is clear and direct: lineal descent is considered worthy only when it bequeaths to successive generations the moral bounty of august *antecessores*. To lose face owing to undignified bearing and oppression was deplored as a condition of decadence. Practically every line in Siôn Phylip's poem expresses concern for the well-being of the local community and manifests the rôle of the true leader and protector. Justice and loyalty implied attaining status and performing obligations, and, in that context, evinced the most efficacious of virtues. The heir of grace was better off for having possessed the eloquence and bearing worthy of the inheritance. The man of good lineage profited more because of his trustworthiness and credit.

> Gŵr o waed a gair ydoedd:
> A gŵr o ddawn a gradd oedd.[126]

'He was a man of good reputation, talent and degree', the poet maintained: his 'credit' went far to fortify his position in the countryside where he ruled. His 'reputation' was positively identified as the basis of his authority and influence.

It is evident that the Welsh gentry were far from being the homogeneous group they were taken to be although the poets classed them as such. The familial entity was emerging more clearly thus giving more precise definition to the status of the *paterfamilias*.[127] The strong traces of cousinage and kindred ties continued to betray firm conservative elements of ancient gentility; social patterns changed very slowly, but gradually loyalties became less personal and more territorial with the consolidation of royal power over Welsh community life. The poets gave precedence to the *paterfamilias* over the kindred unit, strongly advising him to maintain amicable relations with his kindred of all degrees. Reputable standing depended on maintaining the integrity of the kindred. It is easier, Tudur Aled declared, to destroy a house than to build it ('Bwrw tŷ sy haws . . . Na'i godi') The moral integrity of the chieftain was manifested, in its broadest context, in his regard and respect for the rights and privileges of others.[128]

Y gŵr a fawrha'i geraint
A geidw'i frig gyda'i fraint.[129]

'The man who respects his kindred', Siôn Tudur maintained, when addressing Siôn Wyn ap Cadwaladr of Rhiwlas, Merioneth, 'sustained his elevated status and prestige.' The innate ties of consanguinity transcended all in matters concerning social and familial harmony and drew together the formative features of enlightened *uchelwriaeth*. Wiliam Llŷn went as far as to suggest that the benevolent *paterfamilias* revealed more grace and wisdom in dealing with kindred than he did in managing his own business affairs because strife between blood relatives created more devastation and ill-will than any other source of contention.[130] Greed, it was maintained, rapidly destroyed the cohesive and common bonds which preserved law and order. Siôn Tudur, the most critical of late sixteenth-century poets, emphasized the need to safeguard the individual's position in kindred matters, and Wiliam Cynwal, likewise a stalwart among perceptive commentators of his day, stated that amicable kindred relations served primarily to buttress the power and prestige of good men.[131] Such attitudes underlined the moral code which established paternal authority since discipline and obedience were considered to be the main props of public order. The nuclear family had gradually undermined the medieval concept of kindred feeling and, to the poets, establishing a unity of purpose within familial ranks demanded control in thought and action. The individual was interpreted as being a microcosm; his relations with the kindred reflected his attitudes towards the broader concept of the state or political realm. Bad counsel, it was stated, could subvert the cause of justice; the *uchelwr* who valued his station also respected his agnatic affinities, a point to which Siôn Tudur drew attention.

> A garo'i dŷ fry, a'i fraint,
> A gâr yn fawr ei geraint . . .
> Na rowch glust i rai o'ch gwlad
> A dry gynnen drwy gennad.[132]

'He who respects his house and status', Siôn Tudur observed in his *cywydd* to the impetuous John Salusbury of Lleweni, 'also has the power to respect his kindred.' 'Do not heed the advice of those in your region who promote contention and strife', he added further since all discord breeds discontent and disorder. The poet, who had served in the royal court earlier in his career, had appreciated the benefits of loyalty, service and the exercise of justice. Without good order, he maintained, no worthy patron or his family and estate could ever endure: without sustaining patronage virtuous living would perish.

The words of Siôn Phylip, on another occasion, also indicated how significant a factor kindred harmony had become in a society dominated by a sovereign power intent on maintaining unity within the realm. Kindred animosity, he maintained, could inflict greater harm on individual reputations than all other divisive forces put together.[133] Concord between relatives was imperative with regard to the conduct of property and other material affairs: reputations could be stained or lost completely if violence and ill-will ensued. 'I have ever more accounted of a true friend than a kinsman', Sir John Wynn of Gwydir retorted on one occasion to his heir, 'for many kinsmen there are but few friends.' He urged his heir to 'learn to know your friends from your enemies'; 'as I shall leave you friends', he continued, 'so also enemies whose chief motive is that I prosper.'[134] The poets cautioned their patrons against all manner of disruptive behaviour and deplored extortion, oppression, greed, audacity and jealousy. In an attempt to entice Ifan Llwyd of Bodidris in Iâl back from London Wiliam Llŷn assured him that his position in his native area would be secure because his kinsfolk and dependants continued to respect him.[135] The nature of good kinsmanship, Siôn Tudur maintained, never changed or withered; a trustworthy relative, he continued, was more valuable to a reputable house than any material possessions.

> Naws carennydd nis crina,
> Cywira dim yw câr da;
> Gwell ydyw ac o llidir
> Gâr yn d'ôl nag aur neu dir . . .
> Urddwyd eich tad yn wladwr,
> Ar Dduw gwyn mae urddo gŵr.[136]

'The nature of kindred never withers', the poet observes, 'a good kinsman is righteous and is of better value than gold and landed possessions.' 'Your father was a statesman', he continued in his counsel to the young heir, 'because God confers honour on the true nobleman.' Attention is drawn again to the powers of good inheritance which enabled the ruler to display his integrity.

Although it appears, judging by the evidence of legal and other records, that family feuding was gradually in decline by the early years of the seventeenth century, the animosities which arose from property disputes increased, normally through intensive litigation in a variety of common law courts. Beleaguered tenants often took proceedings against allegedly oppressive landlords in a period when the completion of the Tudor land settlement was in its final stages. In addition, social mobility and the inflation of honours had created insecurity and apprehension among the gentry, and the battle for status still caused local jealousies and faction, all of which was reflected in the cautionary note struck by the poets. To them personal power and authority were subordinate to the dignity and privilege of ancestral virtue. In purely material affairs a belligerent kinsman might, in other respects, perform the duties of the benign and beneficent host. Leadership in war and peace displayed two complementary aspects designed to buttress the common welfare of community life.[137]

In a world of insecurity the professional poets of Wales continued to maintain their views of class and status irrespective of harsh social change which, by the mid-seventeenth century, had obscured much of what they had to say. The social structure which they upheld had been eroded by factors well beyond their control, and those declaimers who sadly lamented loss of status and prestige ('Beirdd sydd heb urddas heddiw') revealed a deep-seated dissatisfaction with the *bonheddig* who had largely abandoned their cultural heritage.[138] Gruffudd Phylip, in a powerful ode to Wiliam Fychan III of Corsygedol, a sturdy Merioneth patron, endeavoured to emulate the former high-ranking poets of a past generation when he described his qualities of leadership.

Pennaeth helaeth ei haeledd
Pen brodir wen breuder wedd;
Dal i fyw mewn duwiol fodd,
Dy waedoliaeth da daliodd . . .
Eurawg aer gan ragori
Enaid Brytaniaid wyt ti;
Corf o urddas cryf wir ddoeth
Cyneddfol, deddfol a doeth.[139]

'You are a generous and bountiful chieftain, godly and well-descended', the poet remarked, 'you are the gilded heir, the very soul of the Britons, a pillar of dignity, sagacious, just and fully in possession of your faculties.' Such a resplendent and flattering address would doubtless enhance the poet's reputation within his patron's house as well as strengthen the bonds of affinity between the bardic order and the vital source of its existence. These lines, composed in the years before the Civil Wars, recall the glories of ancient traditions and the qualities of the virtuous *paterfamilias*. He is accorded Brythonic attributes and is regarded as a worthy descendant of heroes. All the prime virtues are encapsulated in those four couplets which disclose how restricted the poets were to the prescribed code of their craft, Their abstract manifestations of grandeur, however, did enable them to preserve that untarnished image of nobility which survived all the changes in Welsh society in that period. To them virtue was changeless, station and degree indestructible, authority and leadership unfailing. The poets had identified the weaker traits in Welsh concepts of *uchelwriaeth* as it had emerged in the early Stuart century and had incorporated them into the context of their verse. Absenteeism and a marked change of attitude towards what they considered to be fundamental to the well-being of an organic community structure, was interpreted by them as the 'great betrayal'.[140] The lofty references to promotion and to the potential among very modest gentry to aspire higher than they could, rendered the eulogistic tradition less meaningful and redundant. The point is poignantly made, for example, in Siôn Cain's poem to Sir Thomas Salusbury of Lleweni who continually sought promotion and status. The lines sound empty and pretentious, the poet merely following convention to please his patron.

> Dithau unwaith, doeth wyneb,
> Onid ei'n iarll, nid â neb . . .
> Mae naid d'oed a'm nod dedwydd:
> Marc sy fwy iwch, Marcwis fydd.[141]

The true meaning of rank and status had, by the early seventeenth century, been obscured in strict-metre poetry by the use of trite and tired images. In the past, even as late as the remaining two decades of the sixteenth century, when the last generation of great Welsh poets continued to sing profusely to the *uchelwr* in his traditional rôle, the concept still appeared to carry some meaning. It was constantly associated with the resident *uchelwr* who regarded his *plasty* as the fulcrum of cultured living. Status was demonstrably linked with favour and privilege. The preservation of *yr iaith* and *treftadaeth*—the community spirit and cultural entity—implied that social rank had formed an essential component in the texture of a refined and qualitative lifestyle. It also entailed a lasting allegiance to moral duty buttressed by divine sanction which shaped and justified *uchelwriaeth*.

> Nid dyn byw, nid da na barn
> A'th gododd, ŵr doeth gadarn;
> Duw Dad a'th gododd di-dwng,
> Dyna dyst n' all dyn d'ostwng.[142]

'It is not any living man nor possessions nor just behaviour which has elevated you, strong wise nobleman', Wiliam Llŷn maintained in a powerful ode to Dr Ellis Price of Plas Iolyn, 'but rather God the Father, and this is sufficient testimony that man cannot demote you.'

The link with divine sanction is again given prominence above all other factors in the social make-up of the Welsh gentleman in his natural environment. Rank and status, according to Wiliam Llŷn, were granted by divine will to all practitioners of gentility by virtue of their descent, gracious living and residence. They were given the power to fulfil their obligations and to cultivate those properties which they considered essential to establish unity, concord and good order. The broadening of gentry interests in Wales, however, had gradually undermined that image and had isolated bardic patronage.

NOTES

[1]NBSF, II, CCXXV, p. 709; GSM, LXVIII, p. 220. For general discussions of rank and status see GCH, IV, pp. 77-92; H. A. Lloyd, *The Gentry of South-West Wales, 1540-1640* (Cardiff, 1968), V, esp. pp. 200-4; Kelso, loc. cit.; Stone, *Crisis of the Aristocracy,* pp. 66-97, 589-93; W. H. Greenleaf, *Order, Empiricism and Politics, 1500-1700: Two Traditions of English Political Thought 1500-1700* (Oxford, 1964), pp. 14-20, 58-67; F. Caspari, *Humanism in the Social Order,* pp. 132-56.

[2]NBSF, I, XXIX, p. 62; GSM, XXIII, p. 79 ('Rheolwr yw'n emprwr ni').

[3]*Gramadegau'r Penceirddiaid,* p. 201; D. Jenkins, *Cyfraith Hywel,* pp. 28-31.

[4]'Welsh Pedigrees', loc. cit.; GWC(1), II, XIV, p. 578.

[5]CLl, p. 133.

[6]CSB, p. 119; MDLlS, II, XV, p. 505.

[7]NBSF, II, CCXCVII, p. 653.

[8]*Gwaith Tudur Aled,* I, XXXIII, pp. 145, 147.

[9]*Gwaith Guto'r Glyn,* XLVII, p. 126.

[10]*Gwaith Tudur Aled,* I, LIV, pp. 220-1; E. I. Rowlands (ed.), *Gwaith Lewys Môn* (Cardiff, 1975), XLVIII, p. 173.

[11]GSM., XXXII, p. 110; XXXIII, p. 113.

[12]Cardiff MS. 4. 101, 52b.

[13]HGF, p. 41.

[14]GWC (Mostyn III), II, LXXXVI, p. 265; GSM, LXVIII, p. 222.

[15]CLl, p. 64; F. C. Cross and E. A. Livingstone (ed.), *Oxford Dictionary of the Christian Church* (Oxford, 1954), p. 871.

[16]NBSF, II, CCXCIII, p. 644.

[17]GSM, XXV, p. 86; CSB, XLV, p. 100.

[18]GCH, IV, pp. 161-4.

[19]NBM, p. 118; GGH, XXI, p. 78.

[20]GSM, LXXVI, p. 250; NBSF, II, CCLXIII, p. 578.

[21]R. R. Davies, 'Owain Glyndŵr and the Welsh Squirearchy', 150-4.

[22]Kelso, op. cit., pp. 19-23; A. D. Carr, 'An Aristocracy in Decline: the Native Welsh Lords after the Edwardian Conquest', WHR, V, 1970, 103-29.

[23]GSM, LXIX, p. 224.

[24]GOG, I, LI, pp. 169-70.
[25]GSM, XV, p. 49.
[26]CLl, p. 57.
[27]GWC(1). I, VI, pp. 19-22.
[28]BWLl, XVI, p. 35.
[29]GSM, XXIX, p. 99.
[30]GWC(1), II, VI, p. 544; F. G. Payne, 'Cwysau o Foliant Cyson', *Y Llenor*, XXVI, 1947, 4-8.
[31]BWLl, VI, p. 15.
[32]GSM, X, p. 31.
[33]Cf. 'ych bannog'. GSM, V, p. 15; XXV, p. 86; 'rhychorion', BWLl, VI, p. 15.
[34]GST, I, CVI, p. 418.
[35]H. Lewis (ed.), *Hen Gyflwyniadau* (Cardiff, 1948), I, p. 1.
[36]*Rhagymadroddion,* p. 114.
[37]BWLl, XXVIII, pp. 72-4.
[38]NLW Peniarth MS. 96, 125.
[39]G. J. Williams, *Traddodiad Llenyddol Morgannwg* (Cardiff, 1948), pp. 182-3 et seq.; E. I. Rowlands (ed.), *Gwaith Iorwerth Fynglwyd* (Cardiff, 1975), VIII, pp. 24-5.
[40]GWC (Mostyn III), II, XCIII, pp. 286-9.
[41]C. Davies (ed.), *Rhagymadroddion a Chyflwyniadau Lladin*, 1551-1632 (Cardiff, 1980), p. 94.
[42]Ibid., p. 75.
[43]*Rhagymadroddion*, pp. 114-5.
[44]Ibid, p. 78.
[45]BWLl, XXVIII, p. 73.
[46]MDLIS, II, XV, pp. 504-5; XXXIII, pp. 574-5.
[47]GWC(1), II, V, pp. 540-1.
[48]GWC (Mostyn III), I, XLVI, p. 144.
[49]Stone, op. cit., pp. 746-7.
[50]'Welsh Pedigrees', loc. cit.
[51]See DWB for further information about these families, their kindred relations and public offices.
[52]GST, I, i-ix, pp. 3-36, VI, p. 23; E. P. Roberts, 'Seven John Conways', *Trans. Flintshire Historical Society*, XVIII, 1960, 61-74.
[53]GCH, IV, pp 541-2; MDLIS, II, CVI, p. 461.
[54]EDLIS, II, XV, p. 504; *Traddodiad Llenyddol Morgannwg,* p. 99, GCH, IV, pp 555-7; EDDN, XII, pp. 189-90.
[55]D. Jenkins, *Cyfraith Hywel*, loc. cit.; F. Jones, 'An Approach to Welsh Genealogy', 350-8.
[56]Cf. GOG, I, XXX, p. 103, XXXIII, p. 112.
[57]NBSF, I, XXXVII. pp. 80, 82.
[58]Cardiff MS. 4. 101, 55b; J. Gwynfor Jones, 'Syr John Wynn o Wedir: ei Gefndir a'i Gymeriad', *Trans Caerns. Hist. Soc.,* XXXV, 1975, 48.
[59]J. Kyrle Fletcher (ed.), *The Gwentian Poems of Dafydd Benwyn* (Cardiff, 1909), XLV p. 23.
[60]BWLl, XXIX, p. 75.
[61]Stone, op. cit., pp. 82-8.
[62]*Calendar of Wynn of Gwydir Papers,* nos. 624-7.
[63]UCNW Mostyn MS. 8, 10r; 'Awdurdod Cyfreithiol', 190-1.
[64]UCNW Mostyn MS. loc. cit.
[65]BGHM, XX, p. 43.
[66]Cardiff MS. 4. 101, 52b.
[67]D. H. E. Roberts, 'Noddwyr y Beirdd yn Sir Aberteifi', 93.
[68]'Hanfodion Undod Gwladwriaethol', loc. cit.
[69]SLl, CLXIII, p. 575.
[70]Ibid., CLXXXV, p. 612.

[71]A. H. Dodd, 'Wales under the Early Stuarts', A. J. Roderick(ed.), *Wales Through the Ages* (Llandybie, 1960), pp. 55-61.
[72]Idem, 'Wales's Parliamentary Apprenticeship, 1536-1625', *Trans. Cymmr.*, 1942, pp. 9-15.
[73]UCNW Mostyn MS. 8, 5r.
[74]D. Powel, *Historie of Cambria,* ed. William Wynne (1697 ed.), p. 314; G. Roberts, *Aspects of Welsh History*, pp. 190-1.
[75]'Welsh Pedigrees', lxix-lxxvi.
[76]Idem, 'An Approach to Welsh Genealogy', 360-5.
[77]T. Jones Pierce, *Medieval Welsh Society*. pp. 333-5; W. O. Williams, 'The Social Order in Tudor Wales', 167-8.
[78]*Gramadegau'r Penceirddiaid*, p. 132.
[79]R. Stephens, *Gwynedd*, 1528-1547; *Economy and Society in Tudor Wales* (Ann Arbor, Michigan, 1975), pp. 27-31, 79-80.
[80]CSPFD, 1536, no. 453, p. 182.
[81]BWLl, VI, p. 15.
[82]W. O. Williams(ed.), *Calendar of the Caernarvonshire Quarter Sessions Records; 1 1541-1558* lxviii-lxx.
[83]GWC(I), I, IX, p. 31.
[84]*Gramadegau'r Penceirddiaid*, p. 202.
[85]CLl, p. 66; SLl, XLVII, p. 290.
[86]DWB, pp. 980-1.
[87]Ibid., pp. 747-8.
[88]*Penbrokshire*, pp. 289-360.
[89]P. Williams , *The Council in the Marches of Wales under Elizabeth I,* pp. 342-61.
[90]*De Republica Anglorum*, pp. 21-2.
[91]SLl, XCVI, p. 421.
[92]Stone, op. cit., pp. 71-82.
[93]NLW Peniarth MS. 117, 235.
[94]SLl, XCIII, p. 413; CXVIII, p. 475.
[95]GST, I, XXVII, p. 111.
[96]CLl, p. 162.
[97]CCM, p. 205; G. Edelsen (ed.), *The Description of England* (New York, 1968), p. 102.
[98]Ibid.; 'Awdurdod Cyfreithiol', 193-5.
[99]GST, I, XVI, p. 62; SLl, CXXI, p. 484.
[100]GST, I, XVI, pp. 62-4.
[101]Kelso, op. cit., pp. 42-7.
[102]*Rhagymadroddion a Chyflwyniadau Lladin*, pp. 71-5.
[103]GSM, XLIX, p. 151.
[104]Kelso, op. cit., p. 50.
[105]NBSF, II, CCLXXII, p. 596.
[106]For further details see NBSG, passim, and DWB s.n..
[107]Stone, op. cit., pp. 71-3.
[108]A. L. Rowse, op. cit., p. 109.
[109]Caspari, op. cit., pp. 92-109.
[110]'Brogyntyn Welsh Manuscripts', VI, 1949, 3-4.
[111]*De Republica Anglorum*, p. 27.
[112]Ibid., p. 26; GSM, LXXVI, p. 248; NBSF, II, CCC, p. 661.
[113]GST, I, XCVIII, p. 389.
[114]GCH, IV, pp. 77-82.
[115]GSM, LI, p. 160.
[116]NBM, p. 172.
[117]*Penbrokshire*, p. 57.
[118]NLW Cwrtmawr MS. 12, 131; Cardiff MS. 4. 101, 35a.

[119] A. H. Dodd, *Studies in Stuart Wales* (Cardiff, 1952), pp. 1-4.
[120] BGHM, X, p. 20.
[121] G. Thomas, 'Portread o Uchelwr', pp. 110-29.
[122] NBSF, I, CLXXXI, p. 402.
[123] Ibid., CLXXXII, p. 404.
[124] Williams, *Council in the Marches*, pp. 237-40; A. H. Dodd, 'North Wales and the Essex Revolt', *English Historical Review*, LIX, 1944, 348-70.
[125] NBSF, I, XIX, p. 39.
[126] NBSG, p. 337.
[127] Stone, op. cit., pp. 589-93.
[128] *Gwaith Tudur Aled*, I, LXVI, p. 266.
[129] GST. I, XLIX, p. 204.
[130] CLl, p. 78.
[131] GWC(1), I. XLIV, p. 154.
[132] SLl, CIV, p. 440; GST, I, XIV, p. 53.
[133] NBSF, I, XIX, p. 39.
[134] NLW MS. 9059E. 1188.
[135] BWLl, LXXXIV, pp. 228-30.
[136] NBSF, II, CCLXI, p. 575.
[137] Cf. NLW Llansteffan MS. 122, 509 (Watcyn Clywedog's ode to Colonel John Bodfel)
[138] D. J. Bowen, 'Y Cywyddwyr a'r Dirywiad', 468-73.
[139] NBSF, I, LIII, p. 124.
[140] Bowen, op. cit., 456-67.
[141] SLl, CLXXXV, p. 612.
[142] BWLl, XX, p. 50.

Chapter IV

Law, Order and Government

The century between the Acts of Union (1536-43) and the Civil Wars constituted one of the most significant eras in the evolution of modern institutions of local and regional government in Wales. Out of the social and economic changes following the Glyndŵr Revolt there emerged a new landholding structure which featured the rise of capitalist estate-owners who adopted new methods of tenure and agricultural practice. In Wales the *uchelwyr* constituted that group of free clansmen who had gradually crept up the social scale and had established their rights in land regardless of communal and kindred ties. They had built up landed estates based essentially on English property laws and had acquired some considerable influence in local or regional government.[1] The decline in the medieval institutions of law and administration gave the opportunity to a small but powerful group of aggressive, forward-looking and tenacious landowners to rise to power and influence in the Principality and the Marches. They had been able, in diverse ways, to avoid the harsher consequences of economic hardship which had devastated the clan structure in the Welshries and the feudal manor in the lordships. They had been able to build up for themselves a new confidence in public affairs which enabled them to exploit the existing framework of government and to perform their duties as competent administrators, with few exceptions, in all but the highest offices. Gradually, during the course of the fifteenth century, however, even the offices of Chamberlain and Justiciar were granted to trusted and resourceful gentry which indicated how well the new order in Welsh society had overcome the pressures imposed upon it after 1284 and during the century following the Lancastrian penal enactments of 1401-2. The contributions of families such as the Mostyns, Salusburies and Gruffudds of Penrhyn in north Wales, the Prices of Gogerddan in Cardiganshire, the Stradlings in Glamorgan, Morgans in Gwent and the house of Dinefwr in south-west Wales, were regarded as essential to the maintenance of order and good government in the localities in the fifteenth century and, by the Tudor period, they had become fully experienced in all aspects of administration and were prepared to share in managing the public affairs of their respective regions under the new political dispensation. Indeed, by the early sixteenth century, the Welsh *uchelwyr* had become aware of their political obligations and had familiarized themselves with legal and administrative procedures.

The desire to hold public office and share in regional government became a matter of prestige. It was considered to be yet another method of displaying grandeur and authority and imposing law, order and obedience on their dependants. So eager were they to wrangle among themselves for positions that John Salcot, Bishop of Bangor, scornfully expressed his view of the situation in 1527 in a letter to his steward. 'For the nature of a Welshman', he stated, 'is for to bear office and to be in authority'. 'He will not let to run through the fire of hell', he continued, 'and to sell, and give all that he can make of his own and of his friends for the same.'[2] The ambition to hold office characterized all ranks within the gentry order, and members of the most modest of freeholding families became actively engaged in running the affairs of the hundreds and parishes. The experience gained served to establish a new tradition whereby such people identified themselves, even more firmly than previously, with the interests of the Crown, and it was this feature which emerged as the most conspicuous in the decades leading up to the Acts of Union and subsequent to them.

The Tudor monarchy doubtless was very loyally and ably served, and Thomas Cromwell's pragmatic view of the situation buttressed the allegiance of a virile and perspicacious section of the community to a dynasty which had everything to offer it in terms of material advancement. The Acts of Union added significant dimensions to the broad structure of government which aimed at securing uniformity in law and administration.[3] Not that the condition of the Welsh countryside was in any respect conducive to the establishment of good government before the Tudor settlement. Indeed, the social scene was often fraught by dissension and strife and old revered customs were being sadly abused in the Principality and the Marches. The long-term effects of war, plague, revolt and civil dislocation created insecurity, strife and tension, and Welsh poetry, in the latter half of the fifteenth and early sixteenth centuries, often referred to the threatening activities of dissidents and criminals, the incursions of private armies, the serious retaining of liveried servants and the flagrant misuse of the law. The works of Tudur Aled and Lewys Môn, for example, portray graphically the harsh realities of the world in which up and coming gentry families, confident in their authority, asserted their domination and, in some respects, endeavoured to establish order in reputedly anarchic conditions. References appear to the elusive bands of brigands ('gwylliaid nos'), fugitives ('rhodwyr') and the dens of thieves ('nyth lladron'). Under such circumstances further emphasis was placed on the military prowess and might of the regional leader entrusted with the task of restoring peace and security. Tudur Aled's ode to the powerful Sir Rhys ap Thomas is almost unique in its descriptions of the patron's martial bearing and valour in battle. He, like others of his *milieu*, assumed territorial jurisdiction; law and order was interpreted as being a matter of wielding the sword and coercing whole communities into a state of obedience.[4] Owing to Maredudd ab Ieuan ap Robert's gallantry and strategy, Lewys Môn maintained, the wild commote of Nanconwy had been reduced to a state of order. He had surmounted the dangers posed by brigands and renegades who assailed the area from the Hiraethog frontier areas of the north-eastern Marches. The poet's words are powerful, indeed fearful, in the manner they depict the ruthless fashion in which order was restored.

> Llai tyrfâu gwylliaid tra fych,
> Llai o rodiaw lle'r ydych,
> Llai treisir gywir a gwan,
> Llai draw nyth lladron weithian;
> Llai pryder yn d'amser di,
> Llai ar wŷr holl Eryri.[5]

'Fewer bands of brigands and dens of thieves, less oppression and anxiety', the poet maintained, 'have eased the pressure on the men of Gwynedd.' In a world of social and economic readaptation this percipient observer draws attention to the expertise demonstrated by the exemplary leader of men in an attempt to quell sources of strife and discord. The focus is placed on the redoubtable leader's initiative and personality exerting his self-acquired authority over his dependants under unfavourable conditions. A picture of territorial grandeur is created out of which emerges a concept of responsible behaviour modelled on military glory and based essentially on a gentleman's natural right to establish peace and security. This feature emerges clearly as well in the poems composed in praise of Sir William Gruffudd of Penrhyn, Sir John Puleston of Caernarfon, Sir William Herbert of Raglan, Sir Thomas Salusbury of Lleweni and others who had assumed responsible office on a territorial basis.[6] The awe inspired by Ieuan ap Robert in Eifionydd, Tudur Penllyn explained, was felt over three shires ('A'i arswyd ar deirsir').[7] Likewise, Sir John Puleston and Sir William Gruffudd were portrayed by Tudur Aled as figures of considerable magnitude in the Principality of North Wales. Welsh poets in the fifteenth century were keenly aware of the need to restore order, and they interpreted their patron's tasks largely in that context. Their military power in foreign and domestic wars, it was said, could conveniently be adapted to further the cause of peace and good government. The just *uchelwr*, under these circumstances, was he who manned offices and administered all reputable institutions designed to uphold legitimate authority. It so happened that, in poetic terms, such a task lay with those individuals characterized by good lineage and a good measure of ambition and tenacity. The strict-metre poems of the early sixteenth century were more concerned with establishing the public image of individual warrior-leaders than they were in applying that image to the mutual relationship which was growing between the Welsh gentry and the Tudor Crown as a natural symbol of justice.[8]

The Tudor settlement of the 1530s and 40s remedied a situation which had caused the Crown much perplexity. To further the concept of the national sovereign state Thomas Cromwell, aided by leading *uchelwyr*, designed to increase royal power over Wales and the Marches through the careful manipulation of circumstances which already existed in the social and administrative life of the country. The dissolution of the Marcher lordships as political units was a major step forward in the creation of uniformity. Henceforth, government would be exercised from the centre through the agency of the Council in the Marches based at Ludlow and the Courts of Great Sessions. English law was imposed in all matters relating to legal and administrative affairs, and the Welsh people enjoyed equality of status.[9] Emphasis was again placed on the rôle of hierarchy and the organic entity of community life: the rule of law was to apply to all parts of the land and particularism was destroyed. To the aspiring gentry the Tudor settlement provided all that was needed to establish their prosperity. They were confirmed in their positions as local governors by a convincing show of loyalty and allegiance to the sovereign state.

During the course of the sixteenth century, regardless of pressing economic strains, Tudor social commentators, including the Welsh poets, considered the new obligations of the *uchelwyr* to be overwhelmingly beneficial to all sections of the community.[10] The balance of power depended largely on combined efforts in the localities to maintain loyalties and apply the rule of law. It was further considered that responsible service to the state constituted one of the prime features of *uchelwriaeth* in an age of benevolent government, and references appeared in poetic tributes to the 'substantial and perfect statesman' ('gwladwr perffaith goludawg'), the man of virtue who possessed abundant resources to enable him to command respect and exercise his will in the king's name.[11] His virtues to undertake this task were those granted to him and vested in him by the very nature of his gentility. As a local leader ('penadur', 'penllad') he reserved for himself the right to exert legitimate authority; within him lay the prerogative rights exercised by his *antecessores*, identical to regal power in a defined geographical community. The Welsh *uchelwr* tradition had elevated the concept of responsible leadership; the embodiment of law and justice and other symbols of integrity emerged as features inherently fixed in the perfect statesman. Where references appear in sixteenth-century verse to the 'sound ruler of the kingdom' ('synnwyr teyrnas'), the 'pillar of the community' ('piler gwlad')and the grave and 'righteous governor of the shire' ('uniondeb dros wyneb sir'), they all extolled the virtues of individuals who, because of their status and natural abilities, willingly served the state for the benefit of all.[12] Two couplets composed by Morus Berwyn to Huw ab Wiliam of Gwerclas, Llangar, a Merioneth patron, summarise conveniently this view of the upright gentleman fully occupied in governing his neighbourhood.

Gwladwr oedd, ar glod yr aeth
Gwaelod ar bob gwladwriaeth.
Cefn ardal, cyfion wrda,
Cynghorwr a dyddiwr da.[13]

'He was a highly esteemed statesman', the poet remarked, and was regarded as the foundation of all good and honest government. He functioned also as the chief support of his region, a just man, counsellor and able arbitrator in legal disputes. His example served the poet admirably since his chief purpose was to identify an ideal with the functional responsibility of government. By the mid-sixteenth century concepts of justice and public service were interpreted less in military and more in civil terms. The versatile *bonheddig*, dispensing justice in court and within his own *plasty*, usually became the acknowledged portrait in poetic eulogy. This interpretation highlighted the polished and humane individual who, by exercising his self-discipline and restraint, applied his talents in the service of the commonweal. His sagacity ('doethineb'), justice ('cyfiawnder'), and protective capacity ('gwarcheidwadaeth')—the three major virtues in the public governor—were all given equal prominence in poetic eulogy.[14] The image of regal power exerted over a territorially defined area would often be used to underline the sovereign attributes of *uchelwriaeth* in government. Some poets even composed in terms of imperial power, as did Siôn Mawddwy on one occasion in an ode to Dr William Gruffudd of Penrhyn.

Rheolwr yw'n emprwr ni,
I'r hael e'i gwedd rheoli.
E ddeil hwn heb eiddilhau
Ystad ei dad a'i deidiau.[15]

The words are expressed in the most elevated fashion: 'Our emperor is a ruler', it is stated, 'and he maintains fully the estate of his predecessors.' The magnificence of the address and the portrayal of sublime majesty gives this poem a quality which surpasses many others composed by this poet. Such a person vested with grace and wisdom, the poet explained, would by nature preserve the rights inherited from illustrious forbears. Wisdom implied that the governor could distinguish between good and evil and exercise self-discipline. It also signified the skill to forsee, devise and protect what he considered to be most beneficial for his people, and it reflected the ability to dispense justice equitably. His acumen, perspicacity and judicial cunning were constantly exposed to rigorous examination. Every Solomon ('Salmon', 'Selyf'), wise statesman ('gwladwr doeth') who was also recognized as a 'fount of justice' ('gwraidd cyfiawnder'), symbolized common responsibilities and privileges among those who assumed leadership.[16] He who was endowed with the 'reason of Moses' ('synnwyr Moesen') and who was considered to be a bastion of law ('rhywiog a thrugarog . . . a thad pob cyfraith') served the Tudor state in the most accomplished manner.[17] It is hardly surprising that poets, in a period when emphasis was placed on good order and uniformity, should refer to the excellence of patrons as custodians and protectors of the commonwealth. The successful performance of public duties presupposed a knowledge and understanding of law and administration as well as integrity and equanimity. The lines of Wmffre ap Hywel to Siôn Llwyd I of Rhiwedog make the point clearly.

> Ni bu sgwier ir bêr iach
> Nag un ustus gonestach . . .
> Yn dy swydd yr oen Duw sad
> Wyt ŵr gwrol trwy gariad . . .
> Fe ddaw i bawb drwy ffydd bêr
> Fendith a wnêl gyfiawnder.[18]

The poet revelled in his patron's acumen in administrative affairs. 'There was never a better nor more honest squire and justice', he commented; 'in office he was gallant and well affected.' 'All those who practise justice', he further remarked, 'shall constantly receive God's blessing.' In such terms emerged the features of the privileged officer defending the state ('gwladwriaeth'). By divine sanction only would he obtain and exercise his power. Justice was his main virtue; thus was he able to resist bribery and corruption and counsel others to act likewise. The equanimity and probity of the regional governor became virtues which others were expected to cultivate. His civilized demeanour in his *plasty* was demonstrable as well in the court-house, in the presence of dignitaries and among lowly tenants on his estate. Any malpractices on his part would not only destroy his reputation and impair his sense of justice but would also threaten the integrity of the state. Richard Madryn, a Llŷn *uchelwr*, who ranked highly among the worthy governors of his region, was esteemed by Owen Gruffudd for his moral rectitude in the following lines.

> Yn gwrando llawn gywreindeb
> A gwylio na wnelo neb
> Flot na math gamwriath gau
> I'r didwyll awdurdodau . . .
> O fewn sir ni fyn sôn
> Wrthwyneb cyfraith union.[19]

The alert patron, the poet maintains, heeds all that occurs around him and ensures that the quality of government in his care is not impaired. In his shire he will not tolerate lawlessness and a vicious defiance of good order. Power lies in him, he continued, by virtue of his innate energies which drive him to combat the forces of evil. The poet's awareness of his obligations and sense of duty highlighted those qualities which were admired in regional governors. To misrepresent or corrupt the course of justice would threaten the organic unity of the shire or hundred and bring disorder. When Wiliam Llŷn addressed Simon Thelwall of Plas-y-ward in Ruthin, he referred to this concept of justice and used the image of the ploughing ox to illustrate his point. As the straight furrow yields a good crop, he maintained, so also the upright and honourable governor of his land follows the paths of justice and equity.[20] The squire who attends diligently to the needs of his household and dependants will also apply himself to fulfil the needs of the community in which he is resident. Residence, in fact, was considered to be a prime requirement since *uchelwyr* in public service formed the essential link between the localities and the central government and were considered to be vital components in the maintenance of law and good government. To Owain Gwynedd that order depended principally on four social categories, the Crown, the Church, the law and the native community and they, in their various capacities, were expected to maintain peace and social harmony and establish the 'common good'.[21] This idea, allied with the sense of loyal citizenship, is manifestly present in poetic eulogy, and although little attention is given to the lower orders in such laudatory exercises the picture of social integration and harmony does emerge whereby the dependants ('gweiniaid') are constantly protected under the powerful wing of the *nobilitas*. In a purely Welsh context all this implied that the virtuous *uchelwr*, who wielded the *imperium* within his own domain, also maintained order and obedience.

The concept of the *imperium* had been expressed fully in the 1530s when Henry VIII assumed his position as Supreme Head of his realm in all matters spiritual and temporal. Any resistance to that authority constituted an act of treason. The sovereign power protected those who served under its authority and, in turn, expected them to maintain peace and suppress rebellion in the land.[22] Any show of opposition had to be destroyed, and the just and firm leadership offered by local gentry was deemed sufficient to strengthen loyalty to the Crown and its institutions. The striking comparison in eulogies between the benign attitudes adopted by the justices of the peace towards the under-privileged, and the harshness with which they would deal with the oppressive and traitorous, was designed to focus on the judicious character of the ideal gentleman. The contrast between the weak and the strong and the constant plea to destroy all vestiges of corruption and injustice is a common feature in *cywyddau* and *awdlau moliant* alike. The expert judge ('ustus dawnus') would exercise his wisdom regardless of impending threats to law and order, and the magnanimous *uchelwr*, resident in his *plasty*, would care for the welfare of his people. It was his death which left a rift or void in community life and enabled the forces of evil to intrude and devastate the harmonious equilibrium achieved unless a like-minded heir succeeded to his office. Siôn Tudur expressed his feelings of despair on the death of one such leader; the region, he observed, was devoid of effective government and direction and he posed the vital question.

> Beth yw gwlad am geidwad gŵr
> O bai gwlad heb ei glewdwr?[23]

'What source of protection has a region', it was asked, 'if it has no valiant governor to rule over it?' The words echo a feeling of utter despondency at a time when the demise of the *paterfamilias* had created a tragic void. How will a community exist, he lamented, without a proper statesman to lead it? The 'gwlad', in this context, constituted the political entity of the realm identical to the medieval Welsh kingdom. In the sixteenth century it was applied to mean the organic regional entity over which the *uchelwr* exerted his powers sanctioned by the state. Such a region constituted what might be called the microcosm of the body politic of the realm. Local judicial and administrative institutions were interpreted essentially as cogs in the machinery of the central government. As the sovereign ruled supremely in the state so also, at regional level, the gentry towered over their subjects and exercised unquestioned authority. The concept of the shire community had gradually emerged to displace the territorial grandeur of former generations, and loyalties were being manifested in a regional context.

The sense of corporate unity, as revealed in the structure of shire government became, in the course of the century, a prominent feature of poetic eulogy.[24] Local or regional identities were normally associated with specific areas of jurisdiction with which the poets were familiar. Shire organization, following the new structure imposed by the Tudors in the 1530s, had, by the mid-century, become universally recognised as the chief organ of local government. Although the poets persistently referred to the older territorial designations, such as Gwent, Gwynedd-is-Conwy, and Powys, they were well aware that the fulcrum of power lay in the shire and its institutions. Since the poets were accustomed to travelling the length and breadth of Wales to obtain patronage they would naturally identify the *uchelwyr* with the older regions. Phrases such as the 'captain of Merioneth' ('capten Meirionnydd'), the 'gilded prince of Ceredigion' ('Tywysog eurfrig Ceredigion'), the 'soul of Glamorgan' ('enaid Morgannwg'), the 'arm of Brecknock' ('braich . . . Brycheiniawg') and the 'lord of Denbighshire' ('unben sir Ddinbych') appear abundantly in verse to buttress the image of the resourceful governor.[25] Government was entrusted to a broad spectrum of gentle families in all hundreds, but corporately they would represent the shire entity, and the 'country' would normally be identified with the territorial limits of the shire. Sir John Wynn of Gwydir, for example, was considered to be a 'good governor of his country' which, in his case, signified a wide area.[26] Since his powers extended well beyond the confines of his native shire it is assumed that 'country', in this particular context, implied Denbighshire and Merioneth if not the whole of north Wales. His kinsman, Sir William Maurice, the archetypal squire, was also called a 'chief magistrate' of his shire because of his territorial credibility and wide reputation in government.[27] Odes composed in honour of both these leaders echo resplendently the type of eulogy which Tudor administrators in Wales would normally merit. One *cywydd*, dedicated to Sir Thomas Mostyn, set out to identify the basis of his power and discovered it in the medieval *llysoedd* of Pengwern, Trecastell, Mostyn and Gloddaith. Consequently, because of this illustrious background, the panegyric proceeded to survey and glorify the range of Mostyn's authority in north Wales. The words used to describe him are both imposing and laudatory.

> Y llywydd mawr galluog . . .
> Llywydd ydwyd llwyddedig
> Llew wyd o fraint ieirllwaed frig . . .
> Llew fyth wyt ti yn holl Fôn,
> Llywydd yn sir Gaerlleon.[28]

The description is impressive and draws attention to the ostentatious surroundings of the *plas* (mansion) and the reality of Mostyn's powerful jurisdiction. He is described as a 'lion in Anglesey', a 'leader in Cheshire' and a nobleman with extensive landed interests and influence in north Wales. The picture drawn is reminiscent of the English feudal aristocracy clinging firmly to their prerogatives by virtue of their ancestry. The eulogy in these lines relate directly to the qualities of leadership as they emerged in ancestral links established over the centuries. References to the 'lord of the shire' ('iôr y sir'), the 'chief of the neighbourhood' ('pen brodir'), the 'good head and ruler of the shire' ('Da i sir benadur'), and the 'soul of the shire' ('enaid y sir'), among other images, are chiefly reminiscent of the power exerted by the princely stock of Wales to defend their patrimonies.[29]

The problems which confronted local administrators in conducting routine business varied immensely according to the circumstances at the time. New and dynamic economic factors attracted more attention during the course of the sixteenth century compared to the emphasis placed on social and political insecurity in its earlier decades when the poets considered military strength to be the governor's main asset. Thus Lewys Môn interpreted the career of Thomas Salusbury at the end of the previous century.

> Cyn dy fod, trwy amod trwch
> Nid oedd hawdd gael dydd heddwch . . .
> Llaw Dduw droes, lle'dd wyd rasol,
> Llywodraeth well draw i'th ôl.[30]

'Before your time', the poet remarked, 'it was difficult to establish peace.' By means of God's grace and protection, however, this steadfast patron had been well-endowed with virtues which enabled him to impose more effective government on his region. Poets, earlier in the century, had lamented the atrocities committed by outlaws, and it is in the mid-sixteenth century that more effective long-term remedies begin to take effect. Once the new administration had been established co-ordinated efforts were made in the shires, supervised by the Council in the Marches, to create a greater degree of coherence in government. In spite of all the hazards which precluded the effective administration of the shires Tudor government did not falter in its aim to extend and fortify the Crown's authority. The increase in the number of justices of the peace doubtless entailed a marked degree of malpractice and inefficiency but it also created new opportunities to maintain the performance of essential duties to the state.[31] When Wiliam Cynwal, for example, observed that his patron never acted unwisely he implied that deceit and dishonesty plagued administrative offices. The poets consistently set their benefactors apart as paragons of excellence beleaguered by a world of avarice, intrigue and shameless ambition.[32] Office-holding is commendable, Wiliam Llŷn stated, only when expeditiously exercised by the 'moderate and balanced officer' ('cadernid cymesurwydd'), steadfast in duty and exemplary in demeanour.[33] He was appointed solely to establish and maintain stability, hence the popularity of references to the patron as an arbitrator or daysman ('dyddiwr', 'cyflafareddwr', 'cymodwr') outside the courts who would bring peace among contending factions or dissident kindred groups. Owain Gwynedd devoted several lines in a satirical ode to justices and prelates to explain the judge's specific task in a court of law. It was his duty, the poet explained, to weigh the evidence carefully according to the dictates of his conscience: it is unfortunate, he added, that dishonesty and bribery so often destroyed the course of justice.

> Ei glorian ef, eglur nod,
> Gwiw dyb, yw ei gydwybod . . .
> Eto aeddfed hyd Dyddbarn
> Yw da'r byd i wyro barn;
> Gŵr a'i gyr ag aur i'w god
> I gyd heb ei gydwybod.[34]

'His scales are his conscience', the poet maintained, and proceeded to show how worthily he behaved in a depraved world. The material values of life, he continued, distorted any sense of justice; men seek gold greedily without any conscience. Such bitter criticism highlights the subversive and less attractive features of newer economic tendencies which forced families and individuals to contest fiercely for supremacy in their respective regions.

The blunt and consistent exposition of unjust activities in courts of law signified the nature of corrupt practice among men of status. Dr David Lewis, Judge of the High Court of Admiralty, and a native of Abergavenny, expressed his deep concern with the unsatisfactory state of affairs, particularly in the south-east parts of Wales in the 1570s. In a letter to Sir Francis Walsingham he explained that Wales 'is so far out of order . . . as doth require severe remedy, and in every commonwealth severity used with indifferency of justice to all men is more commended than lenity'. He set out to suggest certain remedies, one being that 'such as profess the laws of the realm . . . should not be in fee with any gentlemen within the limits of their commission'.[35] Retaining of this nature was discouraged also by the poets who considered the ruthless manipulators of the law ('beilch', 'beilchion') to be the instigators of dissension and discord. The 'destroyer of the proud' ('plygwr beilch') and he who 'binds in chains outlaws and coarse men' ('rhwym herwyr a gwŷr geirwon') doubtless did take steps to curb disorder but that, it was considered, was not enough.[36] There was also need for a change of heart among all those involved in government and who prided themselves on displaying as well as abusing their own skills rather than serving for the common good. Pride and arrogance, it was further observed, did not befit the proper gentleman ('Dyn balch yn wrda ni bydd'): conversely, he was disposed to act in all goodness. The governor, it was considered, displayed his virtues in humility: 'And therefore,' William Lambarde enquired, in one of his strictures on equitable government in the localities, 'if we shall come hither for show only, or for fashion's sake, and shall not both seek and ensue the amendment of manners and correction of misdoers, what do we else but wittingly betray the life of the commonwealth into the hands of such as lie in await to take it?'[37] What had emerged as a single uniform secular state in the sixteenth century achieved its period of fruition in the newly-established Protestant polity in the reign of Elizabeth I. The forces of local or regional government served principally as bulwarks to the overriding authority of the Crown and fortified the secular arm of the Tudor realm. Thus, as expressed in another source and context, the emphasis is placed on worthiness and equitable rule.

> Cefn y fainc wyd, cyfiawn farn,
> Ceidwad rhwng gwan a'r cadarn.[38]

These are indeed powerful words expressed by Wiliam Llŷn to Robert Llwyd of Y Waun to illustrate the chief manifestations of control and influence exerted in positions of authority. The resilient patron is described as the moral bulwark on the bench of magistrates, a protector of the weak against the oppressive and a just person in word and deed. The exercise of mercy and good judgement in local courts of law was desired in view of the governor's intimate knowledge of his community ('A phen y wlad a phiniwn').[39] Justice had to be exercised publicly for the good of all in those institutions designated for that purpose. The governor would, by his very nature, avoid all kinds of oppressive behaviour ('trahausdeb', 'trawster') and, regardless of the multifarious duties heaped upon him and his colleagues, would be expected to maintain his 'good name and fame'. As property owners, who held close family links with the neighbourhood, the governing *uchelwyr* were further counselled to discount their own private interests. The misuse of office for selfish reasons defeated the end of law; the preservation of that law created wholesome government which, in turn, sustained and defended the sovereign state. It also fortified the concept of organic unity in the localities and enhanced the prestige of the *bonheddig* in their public capacities. It is the chain of command, linking government at the centre with the shire community, which strengthened the bond of unity in the body politic. Gruffudd Hiraethog drew attention in verse to the merits of the counselling *uchelwr* who directed others to a just and upright way of life.

> Sy i'w weled dros y wlad draw
> Sadrwydd ustus dewr ddistaw.
> Os dewiso ustusiaid,
> Y nifer hyn a fu rhaid.
> Os dyn ni ŵyr eiste'n iawn,
> Dysg ef, dydi sy gyfiawn.[40]

The advice is sound and unchanging: the patron's stalwart appearance is noticeable and dominates throughout the region. 'If you choose magistrates to serve the cause of good government', the poet observed, 'do so for the essential purpose of maintaining peace.' Since he was just he was in a position to instruct those who were either inexperienced or untrained in the office, a comment doubtless on the inadequacies of a large proportion of justices of the peace in mid-sixteenth-century Wales. It appeared that, to most professional poets, the ideal of justice in the performance of duties was of greater significance than the routine details of the patron's activities in and out of the court of law. Persons are fallible, it was maintained, but virtues are unchanging and incorruptible. Very rarely would eulogies divert from this standpoint. Although the gentry used power and authority to improve their own rank and status the poets did not necessarily regard private affairs as relevant to their task of defining and interpreting qualities. To dwell on inadequacies alone was retrogressive; the aim was to apply the faculties of talented men to the needs of the time. On an *uchelwr*'s death it was usual for the poet to assess his rôle in local government and to lament the moral impoverishment which ensued. The countryside, it was said, would lack focus, moral sustenance and leadership.[41] It was often in such a despondent manner that poets expressed sorrow when a region was deprived of its very lifeblood. Such were the thoughts uttered by Rhisiart Cynwal on the death of Huw Nannau I.

> Aeth i'r llawr bennaeth o'r llys,
> Aeth hen lywodraeth ynys.[42]

The lines are majestic in their purport: 'The head of the court had been interred', the poet dolefully recorded, 'and the ancient governorship of the isle [of Britain] has passed on.' The emphasis on an imposing and noble past adds significantly to the grandeur of this elegy. The couplet focuses on the integrity of the patron's rule in Merioneth where he had proved his worth. The ability to interpret the law was but one aspect of the gentleman's expertise; the skill to practice it justly was another. It created a new dimension to moral values because vengeance on wrongdoers was achieved often through the use of law rather than by the use of force.

Within the shire organization in Wales in the century following the Tudor settlement a number of key offices or positions were considered to be the chief agencies of law and good government. Bardic tributes constantly glorified the rôle of patrons in public office, especially as sheriffs and justices of the peace.[43] The shrievalty, which was eagerly coveted, was normally held by prime gentry and they, together with the justices of the peace, who were recruited from among a broader range of *uchelwyr*, were linked to the central government through the supervision of the Council in the Marches.

The holder of office under the government assumed his responsibilities by making a declaration of allegiance and service to the Crown or the princely head of state. In his elegy to William Herbert, Earl of Pembroke, a prominent patron in courtly circles, Wiliam Llŷn unhesitatingly stressed his longevity and dedicated service to four heads of state successively in Tudor England.[44] His couplets summarize effectively how important sustained service to the Crown was for the common good. The frequent references to the all-powerful position of the prince and the service he could normally expect gave added weight to the belief that fulfilling legal and administrative obligations was a condition of gentility and that the poets supported the spirit of the Tudor settlement.

The transference of loyalties to the Stuart dynasty in the early seventeenth century consolidated the firm alliance with the state and its institutions. It was interpreted as a natural development from the loyalty, both Welsh and British, which the gentry had so lavishly shown to the Tudor monarchs. They clung firmly to the concept of worthy descent from early forbears, and references to Britain and British became increasingly popular since James I had united the Crowns of England and Scotland and had recreated the image of the Isle of Britain as it had existed in pre-Saxon days.[45] Within that image the Welsh gentry claimed that they had the right, by descent, to rule or, at least, to participate actively in the government of the realm. James was hailed by Huw Machno as 'King of Great Britain', a designation which became current in the early seventeenth century to express equality of status in the political realm.

> Brenin Siams brau union sydd,
> Prydain fawr hap waredydd.[46]

In this couplet by Edward Urien King James is elevated as the redeemer of 'Great Britain' at a time when Tudor loyalties were being successfully transferred to the Stuarts and when individuals, like Sir William Maurice of Clenennau, applauded the union of interests between Wales and England. It was the optimism which accompanied this doctrine of unity that featured most prominently in Welsh strict-metre poetry at the turn of the seventeenth century. It appeared in the works of Huw Machno, Siôn Cain and Rhisiart Phylip among others. In Edward Urien's tribute to James and Prince Henry, one was compared to Charlemagne ('Sy eurlew mal Siarlymaen') and the other considered to be a worthy kinsman of the Welsh installed in office to protect and exalt the Welsh nation.[47] With equal enthusiasm Tomas Prys of Plas Iolyn praised Sir William Maurice of Clenennau, one of the most spirited supporters of the new doctrine, because of his prestige as regional governor under the new regime.

> Wyt ruwliwr i'n tir Wiliam
> Eich doethder noder glân yw,
> A'ch swyddau ymharch sy heddiw . . .
> Enillaist, ruwliaist yrhawg
> Gredud ysgwiair gwridawg.[48]

'You are a ruler in our land William', the poet notes, 'and a man renowned for his sagacity and respect in office.' He is also acclaimed as an experienced courtier who had earned for himself a good reputation in the official circles in England. He was a person, it was added, known for his 'credit' and distinction in government. Such a testimonial gave this munificent patron the moral backing he needed to sustain his powerful hold over Eifionydd and adjacent areas. He emphasized his rôle as a man of wisdom and integrity and then proceeded to list his offices in Eifionydd and in Caernarfonshire generally. This poem and other similar accolades accorded regal attributes to the high-born; sovereign power was vested in them and they enjoyed what amounted to delegated powers handed down from time immemorial. Thus they were committed to preserving the rights and prerogatives of legal kingship over the whole realm. Since the Stuarts constituted the rightful heirs in succession to the Tudors the transference of loyalties implied the continuation of ancient traditions as well as signifying the prestige which Welsh *uchelwyr* enjoyed in the process. The image of Brutus and the legacy of the British inheritance had caught the imagination of the poets once more in this transitional period, and they applied their interpretation of the 'island empire' in the context of undeviating and fervent service to the ruling dynasty. Hence, the offices held by the gentry under the Tudor and Stuart monarchs were applauded and their holders considered worthy of acclamation. Indeed, historical evidence shows that patrons were becoming increasingly more articulate in their comprehension of political issues and other matters of state and were fulfilling a more conspicuous rôle in the royal court and other governmental institutions.[49]

The offices, whether at local or regional level, were hailed as just rewards in the purely historical pattern. The credit earned by gentry demonstrated their aptitude for public service. 'For I protest', one resolute governor maintained, 'I desire not to live the day wherein I shall be ashamed of my doings or must be forced to bear so open a disgrace.'[50] Such an overt show of confidence in status was featured in all patrons judging by the content of a large *corpus* of *awdlau* and *cywyddau* composed in their honour. The gist of the adulation centred upon three prime elements, namely loyalty, skill and educational instruction which were underlined by Sir Thomas

Elyot and others in their discourses, and considered vital for the Tudor administrator.

The office of sheriff, introduced into the Principality of Wales in 1284, stood at the apex of shire government. It was a historically well-established office and its holder functioned as the chief royal representative in the shire. 'He is the chief officer of trust and credit in the shire', said George Owen, 'and the Prince's lieutenant.'[51] The prestige attached to the position enabled the poets to grant some of their patrons added glory. 'He is the bailiff of the whole shire', Owen continued, 'and the shire is termed in law his bailiwick'. 'His glory is extensive', Huw Machno maintained, when applauding one of his mentors, 'and the inhabitants of the whole shire fear him.'[52] The sheriff's authority was constantly admired since he did preserve the right to impose the royal will on his subjects ('Siryf wyd . . . grymus ragorion').[53] The concept of the valuable office ('y swydd gosdus') was often associated with a sense of duty and responsibility. Routine details of his administrative tasks were usually left unmentioned except for the occasional reference to his authority at the shire musters and in other military capacities. The main emphasis was given to maintaining law and order within his area of jurisdiction. Dr. Ellis Price of Plas Iolyn, one of the most forceful and successful of long-serving officers of the Crown in the shires of north Wales, was counted as an efficient governor essentially because of his good sense, integrity, gracious bearing and sagacity in executing his duties.[54] These qualities were amply described by Wiliam Llŷn who applauded his 'great attributes and character' ('mawredd a chymeriad') and wisdom which God's grace had bestowed upon him ('gras Duw . . . da i'th ddoniwyd').[55] Price and others of his *milieu* were often described in glowing semi-military terms since they functioned in areas, such as the notorious Hiraethog region, known for its disorder. References appear to the sheriff who mustered the levies ('mwstrio sir'), organized men and horses ('gwŷr a meirch') and upheld the cause of peace and good government.[56]

Individual odes were frequently composed to celebrate a squire's elevation to the office of sheriff, the content normally describing the highest public virtues which he possessed. The new officer would defend the good and banish the evil, and stand steadfast in his rôle as defender of the realm against external threat. He was, according to

Siôn Phylip, a figure of integrity appointed to represent the king, and a man of standing in his community. Since the office was held on an annual basis it was accorded more prestige than would otherwise have been the case. The sheriff had to prove his worth during his term of office and to create a favourable impression in the manner in which he conducted his business.[57] The dignity of the office was given prominence, for example, in the lines of Siôn Cain to Pyrs Lloyd of Y Ddol, Corwen in Merioneth, whose jurisdiction, it was said, extended over remote and unwieldy territory.[58] His contributions to law and order were viewed as a means also of buttressing his own position for the benefit of the community. The need to maintain the defensive strategy of his shire, the constant call for taxation and the general routine business of keeping law and order made the office often unrewarding in terms of the pressures placed upon him. Bardic eulogy, however, considered him to be constantly a man of endurance who performed his tasks efficiently because of his innate abilities and unswerving loyalty to the Crown. Monarchy provided order and security, and since the sheriff was its official representative it was considered that he possessed similar faculties which enabled him to pursue his most pressing duties with the highest degree of proficiency. It was in that context that Huw Machno portrayed the services of William Wynn of Glyn Cywarch, a prominent Merioneth patron in the sheriff's office.

A'i bur hedd a bair i hon
Ei breinio o lwybrau union;
Ac o flaen hyn, gyflawn hedd,
I sir Feirion, siŵr fawredd;
Siri fu, gallu teg oedd,
I hwn nodol iawn ydoedd.[59]

Queen Elizabeth had conferred the office upon him: in Merioneth, he was a renowned figure who demonstrated his skills proficiently. The lines disclose the aptitude of such a gracious person to fulfil the requirements of office and to co-ordinate the administrative tasks in all parts of the shire. His grace and favour in office, the poet continued, had enhanced that shire's prestige as well as his own. It was his contribution in royal service which had made him a notable character and had preserved the communal entity of the shire.

The office of justice of the peace also emerged to become a position of considerable prestige. It had been introduced into Wales in 1536, and was later extended into the newly-created shires in 1543.[60] It was well-established in England by the fourteenth century and was virtually controlled by the emergent landed gentry. Localities were kept firmly within the grasp of responsible middle-class governors who based their power in the court of quarter sessions. The office of justice had gradually formed a legal tradition of its own since it centred on the shire community and assisted in maintaining its independence. While the system worked efficiently within the chain of command in the realm the justices of the peace, as a body of laymen involved in government, were remarkably successful in adding to the sense of corporate unity within the shire. In Wales in the sixteenth century justices of the peace became the linch-pin of local administration, and sources show that a large proportion of the landed gentry, regardless of their rank, participated actively at this level and wielded extensive powers in office.[61] Such authority was frequently displayed in the eulogistic tradition which aimed once again to magnify and sustain the image of the public governor. Judicial and administrative responsibilities increased during the course of the century inside and outside the courts of quarter and petty sessions, and much of the routine business was conducted in the rural *plastai*. Those who held the office, according to George Owen, were 'the chiefest gentlemen in every shire': their qualities, according to the poets, were similar to those possessed by the sheriff, the main feature being their steadfast devotion to public duty.[62] The symbolism constantly reveals the person regarded as 'the author of equitable judgement' ('awdur cyfiawn farn'), the 'impartial magistrate' ('ustus heddwch gwastad'), the 'sagacious justice' ('ustus cofus cyfiawn') and so forth.[63] Like the sheriff the justice of the peace viewed his office as being designed to destroy all evil and oppression. Gruffudd Hiraethog summarized it conveniently in two couplets to Cadwaladr ap Morus of Y Foelas.

> Sylfaen o ustus haelfawr,
> Swydd wych i'm oes heddwch mawr.

Carud rhai cywiriaid draw,
Caswr lladron a'u ceisiaw.[64]

The words applaud the services of the 'generous magistrate' who zealously protected the peace, defended the weak and unyieldingly opposed the oppressor. His reputation was built on maintaining the balance between the exercise of mercy and the due execution of the law.

Another poet highly acclaimed his patron as the chieftain and guardian of his land ('pennaeth gwlad sy geidwad'), a duty which demanded the services of a person with protective qualities, such as the head of kindred or the *paterfamilias* ('pencenedl'), whose prime task it was to preserve clan unity.[65] Conversely, that image was interpreted by the poets to describe the magnanimous *uchelwr* resident in his mansion and displaying his will to hold public office under the Crown. The chief purpose of local government, according to William Lambarde, was to honour God and his laws, to serve the Crown and maintain the goodness of all.[66] Whether Lambarde's views were known to contemporary poets is doubtful but concepts of order and justice in Elizabethan England were common currency also in Wales in an age when considerable emphasis was placed on the need to maintain the organic unity of the state, a principle consistently expounded by the poets who had tacitly accepted the spirit of the Tudor legislation with regard to community affairs. When a justice of the peace is referred to as the 'emperor of all government' ('ymherodr pob llywodraeth') and as the 'good and godly leader, statesman and ruler' ('Da lywiawdr . . . da wladwr . . . Da reolwr . . . Da a duwiol'), his innate skills are pronounced.[67] Thus he would be considered as the 'foundation of his region' ('sylfaen gwlad'), its 'backbone' ('cefn gwlad') and its 'bridgehead' ('pont a phen gwlad').[68] As a pillar of strength the justices of the peace symbolized goodness and moral prosperity. The lines by Siôn Brwynog to describe one of his Llŷn patrons stressed the manner in which his probity was reflected throughout the land ('Drych ydwyd, dewr a chadarn . . . doeth yw'r farn').[69]

The justices of the peace were involved in organizing judicial proceedings in the courts of quarter sessions and administering the shires in conjunction with other officials besides the sheriff who controlled affairs in the hundreds, parishes and townships. He who protected his community ('ymgeleddu gwlad') and who was reputed to be a solemn, weighty and steadfast magistrate ('A dwys sad ustus') was recommended universally as the ideal governor.[70] His duties as protector and maintainer of the localities were clearly reflected in odes designed to highlight the chief features of *uchelwriaeth* as they were interpreted by poets who, like their patrons, became gradually accustomed to the new political and administrative system. The specific features of office enabled justices of the peace to act honourably since they were aware of the standards expected of them.

> Union at union wyt ti,
> A fo union a fynni.[71]

The poet is firm in his pronouncement that the *uchelwr* who has integrity also has satisfying influences on others. 'You desire that which is upright', he maintains further, thus portraying him, as did Sir Thomas Elyot in his discourse on the ideal governor, as a person of dignity and skill.

Integrity ('uniondeb') was accepted as the prime quality expected of a public servant. His obedience in fulfilling his duties reflected his desire to serve the state as the symbol of national unity and security. 'The very end of law', Lambarde maintained, 'is obedience, and the end of obedience is the life and safety of the commonwealth.'[72] Similarly, the poets drew attention to their patrons as just and dutiful rulers humbling the oppressive ('gwarhau cedyrn') sternly controlling thieves ('uthr lywodraeth ar ladron') and opposing deceit and arrogance ('Trahausdeb a thrawster').[73] The highly esteemed governor also displayed other urbane qualities which fortified him in his task. As a man of virtue he appeared to others as the cultivated gracious gentleman, a pillar of justice ('piler y cyfiawnder') to all who were aware of his presence.[74] To hold office was regarded as a duty as well as an honour; to attend to their multifarious tasks of office entailed strengthening the bonds between the countryside and the government at the centre. Siôn Phylip drew attention to the versatile qualities which the public figure demonstrated when maintaining peace and good government in his shire. His lines to Gruffudd Fychan II of Corsygedol, underlining his sterling qualities, were very impressive.

Dy ran yn cadw'r union
Ar dy fainc o'r deau i Fôn;
A chadw rhwng gwan a chadarn
Drwy bwyll gyfiawnder a barn;
Cadw'r wlad rhag cad rhai cedyrn
Ceidw Duw i'ch oed ceidwad chwyrn . . .
Duw a'th roes ar wlad i'th ran
Do, yn bennaeth, dyn byw anian.[75]

Such lines demonstrate the wide powers exerted by justices of the peace in one and more shires. This patron wielded his authority in Gwynedd south of Anglesey: 'you maintain peace, care for the ill-endowed and suppress the oppressive', the poet sings, 'and God will preserve you as a chieftain in your country.' The description depicts power at its most extensive, the 'country' or 'patrimony' ('gwlad') being the chief jurisdictional entity. As in all eulogies of this type the poet invokes God's blessing on the righteous governor. His task, the poet maintained further, is to uphold honour by administering justice equitably. The merciful and well-bred man of law combined in his actions the benefits of firm justice and mercy. The custodian ('ceidwad') of his community extended his power and influence beyond the boundaries of his estate and rooted his power in the shire.

It is evident that the office of justice of the peace had enhanced the reputation of the high-ranking gentry, and the poets were constantly prepared to add this awareness of public duty in their portrayal of the administrator in action. The independence of the local officer was manifested in the manner in which he was able to execute his duties with the minimum of unease; such was the partnership established between the Crown and its local servants that the functions of regional government in Tudor and early Stuart Wales were performed with dignity and a degree of efficiency. That harmony was clearly reflected in bardic eulogy. Regardless of the problems which beset administration at the local level the poets doubtless interpreted the honour of office-holding to be of the greatest significance.

The third official to attain prominence was the *custos rotulorum,* the keeper of the rolls of the court of quarter sessions.[76] The title was often rather clumsily woven into the intricate metre structure of the *awdl* and *cywydd* because the poets considered the position to be sufficiently important to deserve acclamation within the shire's administrative framework. The office, created in 1543, was intended to unify the processes of local government at that level in that the senior magistrate would co-ordinate judicial procedure by assuming the office of custodian. The position was often nominal since there were only a few formal functions to perform, but the concept of grandiloquence in administrative duty gave the poets an added opportunity to express their feelings. The *custos*, as presiding magistrate, assumed primacy; he appointed the clerk of the peace and preserved the court records so that legal precedent might be safeguarded. It was essentially the legal custodianship which appealed to the poets. Sir John Wynn of Gwydir was reminded that, in his position as *custos*, he should 'have in readiness all the records of the quarter sessions to attend the justices of the peace . . . to be seen by them and determined according to justice'.[77] In that context he was regarded as the guardian of legal precedent and was chiefly responsible, as principal magistrate, for good order and government. By his means, it was thought, legal administration might be executed more efficiently. Poetic adulation drew attention to the officer's primacy in the art of governorship, thus his description as the 'conscientious and authoritative ruler' ('awdurdod cydwybod') who coped well in all aspects of regional government.[78] Siôn Tudur described one patron as the gracious, executor of his offices in the shire.

> Bu'n ustus cariadus cryf,
> Bu'n y sir yn ben siryf.
> Cwstos hardd, câi osod swm,
> Ŵr tal, i rotwlorwm . . .
> Rhy gadarn, rhywiog ydoedd,
> Rhywiog a thrugarog oedd.[79]

The image of the powerful and awe-inspiring *custos rotulorum* emerges succinctly; 'He was an affectionate and strong magistrate', says the poet, 'a tall and befitting custodian of the rolls.' He was stalwart, merciful and gracious in the execution of all his duties. This patron, it was said, roused the bench of magistrates into action ('cynhyrfu'r fainc'), and gave counsel as a pillar of order and justice ('Rhoes gyngor . . . piler y cyfiawnder').[80] With the marked increase in the numbers of justices of the peace in the latter years of the sixteenth century the duties of the *custos rotulorum* became increasingly more varied and burdensome. Since they were completing a long and arduous period of administrative apprenticeship it was deemed necessary that an experienced senior magistrate should maintain order and discipline. It is hardly surprising, therefore, that some poets emphasized the prominent qualities of the *custos rotulorum* who was consistently described as the genuine statesman, a person of renowned descent and an individual sufficiently strong in his allegiances to be able to govern with a strong hand. Yet again, poetic eulogy interpreted his rôle as being beneficial to the welfare of the local community.

The emphasis on precedent or usage in legal matters symbolized respect for tradition, and the welfare of the community depended, particularly after the Tudor settlement, on the firm but equitable application of English common law. This established a legal tradition which, in the poets' minds would bring peace and security to the realm. It is in this light also that they envisaged the duties of the *custos rotulorum*. His primacy among others was earned essentially through the very nature of his work in co-ordinating law and legal procedures and establishing sound government, often in periods of unrest and instability.[81] Such powerful attributes were worthily recorded in the elegy composed by Wiliam Phylip to Huw Nannau II, the chief governor of his shire at the turn of the seventeenth century.

> Cwstws o'r Rhotiwlorwm
> I'w ôl y troes wylo trwm;
> O'i ddwyn ef mae heddiw'n ôl
> I'w Goron swyddog gwrol . . .
> Bron a nerth i'r brenin oedd
> A cheidwad heddwch ydoedd.[82]

He was obviously a man to be highly regarded as a gracious *custos rotulorum* who assumed his duties with great valour. 'He was a courageous officer', the poet maintains, 'the Crown's strength and a keeper of the peace.' His power lay principally in his skill in combining his regional responsibilities and his devotion to the Stuart king Charles I in days of adversity. The cornerstone and foundation of good order, the poet maintained further, had departed owing to the increasing disregard for the status of monarchy and the political tensions which ensued. The very nature of his office dictated that he should attempt to buttress royal power and jurisdiction, preserve legal custom, enhance his own reputation and instil confidence in his people. The maintainer of law, the poet added, gave to the Crown that reassurance that local government was being executed by loyal men in the interests of all and for the good of the commonwealth.

The next officer of note to which declaimers in the strict-metres gave attention was the deputy lieutenant, an administrator considered to be of the highest reputation in the shire.[83] It was introduced into Wales in the 1580s as a measure to counter the threat of Spanish attacks on the Welsh coasts after the outbreak of war in 1585. The danger of invasion from Ireland also caused much concern and anxiety, and Henry Herbert, Earl of Pembroke, who was, in 1586 appointed Lord President of the Council in the Marches, introduced the office to strengthen the defensive strategy of the maritime shires. The holders of this office came primarily from among the most eligible gentry. It was considered to be a position of immense prestige and entailed a degree of superiority over all other shire officials in matters of defence. It was an office coveted by several of the high-ranking *uchelwyr*, but it also proved to be, in times of war, an onerous and demanding post which often led to dissension among those who occupied it and also to disagreement in the Council in the Marches at Ludlow over matters of organization and efficiency in administration. 'For how can your minds be united in public defence', the Lord President asked the two Caernarfonshire deputies in 1591, 'when they are divided by private quarrels?' 'All men cannot be deputy lieutenants', he continued, 'some must govern, some must obey.'[84] This formal advice was aimed at destroying all animosities and uniting their interests in the service of the state. In poetic terms the 'all-powerful lieutenant' ('Lifftenant a meddiant mawr'), who kept a firm grip on his shire, enabled his community to survive under abnormal conditions.[85] It was he who ultimately assumed responsibility for securing order and stability by manipulating his natural skills. Without the unswerving leadership of Gruffudd Fychan II of Corsygedol in the defence of his shire, Rhisiart Phylip observed, the community would never have survived as an organic unity ('Hebddo'n ben ni bydden byw').[86] Siôn Phylip also considered this mighty leader to be the 'good man' ('gŵr da') who protected Gwynedd and who executed his duties with profiency. Through his efficient dealings with men, he continued, Gruffudd Fychan enhanced his own prestige and safeguarded his shire, and indeed Gwynedd, from disaster.

> Dwrn a braich cadarn a bron
> Wyd, a nerth i wlad Meirion . . .
> Gwaraidd Frytanaidd wyt ti
> A thyner i'th ddaioni.[87]

The customary images are employed in this section of the *cywydd* to illustrate the authority possessed by this protector of Merioneth. 'You are the strong fist and arm of the shire', the poet maintains, 'a civilized Briton, benign in all goodness.' The lines disclose the powerful hold which this resourceful *uchelwr* had on all aspects of public administration. The ancient concept of the British inheritance, as vested in this patron, is also regarded as an added virtue to his practical powers and skills.[88] The emphasis is principally on defence and protection against the forces of dislocation and anarchy.

In critical years the Earl of Pembroke advocated close co-operation between local deputy lieutenants to protect the 'common good'. 'Yet can I not but wish', he remarked, 'to think that it will now appear by your proceedings in these services how worthy you are of thc authority committed to you and what hearts you bear to our dread sovereign under whom, and to our dear native country in which, we live.'[89] Since the office demanded knowledge of wartime conditions and expertise in the management of levies designed to serve at home and abroad, it was expected that the holder of the deputy lieutenancy should be experienced in organizing and leading men and commanding their allegiance. In addition, his skills as an administrator were considered a vital asset, and within this context the image of the traditional military clan-leader emerged. One patron, according to Rhys Cain, could confidently lead a hundred loyal soldiers to battle: he commanded allegiance and provided his shire with a solid resistance against menacing transgressors.[90] In poetic terms the combination of the soldier and administrator appears succinctly in every reference to the office of deputy lieutenant, but the accomplished ruler of the local community is manifestly portrayed in his major rôle as defender, leader and organizer.

In 1536 Wales was granted the privilege of parliamentary representation. Political rights were extended to the *uchelwyr*, and although full parity of status was not achieved with regard to membership of the House of Commons the years which followed the legislation enabled prime gentry to strive among themselves for the honour and serve a period of political apprenticeship.[91] While being constantly aware of their obligations to the Crown and its institutions the Welsh members lacked experience during the first half-century of their term in parliamentary affairs. In fact, the Welsh poets hardly drew attention to the office in the middle years of the sixteenth century, and it is only gradually that the importance and relevance of representation became meaningful to them. Where references did appear they usually described the patron as the embodiment of his community in the King's high court of parliament. The very 'soul' of his neighbourhood had been granted the privilege of displaying his gentility, among others of equal status, in the most resolute and active manner. This concept emerged also when poets described their patrons in all public offices. It was in this respect that Siôn Mawddwy addressed Owain Fychan of Llwydiarth.

> Y dewr galawnt aur goler,
> Enaid parch, brenhinwaed pêr;
> Enaid y wlad wastad wych,
> Aer Llwydiarth i'r llu ydych.[92]

The fullness of this description draws upon the resourceful and substantial *uchelwr* who had been appropriately rewarded for his services to the state. 'You are the brave and gallant one wearing a gold collar', it is said, 'the soul of reverence and a person of regal stock.' Indeed, he is described as the very essence of his region, an incorporation of communal unity, a resplendent heir to Llwydiarth admired by all. He was a gracious man indeed, highly esteemed for his functional contributions to peace and security in the shire. Those contributions were considered to be the fundamental features of *uchelwriaeth* in the native environment.

Once again, the concept of integrity in public office emerges, sometimes regarded as the 'credit' attributed to individuals in high office. Sir William Maurice of Clenennau, for example, was a long-serving member of the House of Commons in the early seventeenth century who was lavishly praised by Tomas Prys of Plas Iolyn, principally because he combined in his person the prestige of rank and status and the qualities of the native cultured gentleman.[93] As in the odes which praised the deputy lieutenants this poet gave prominence to the features of defence and guardianship. It was Maurice's task to apply his own involvement in the affairs of state in London to the needs of the lower orders in society which had suffered extensively in consequence of their economic plight. His eminence was based largely on family renown and his own skills in adapting his chief political interests to serving within a much broader pattern of administrative activity. It is clear that, fundamentally, the Welsh members of parliament represented their own interests and those of their class. Emphasis was placed, not on politics, but essentially on precedence and prestige, so that it was expected that poetic eulogy would dwell largely on the ostentatious bearing and political acumen of Welsh parliamentary representatives. They were frequently regarded as symbols of sovereign power which they applied to meet the needs of their localities. The parliamentary constituency was also described as being an essential part of the harmonious relationship which existed between rulers and ruled.[94] Robert Llwyd of Rhiwgoch in Merioneth was pictured elegantly by Edward Urien as the 'gentle gracious man' ('gŵr grasol addfwyn') worthy of his position in parliament. He had served as sheriff, a position, according to the poet, which had given him further promotion in due course. He was fully in command of all legal matters and practised the law proficiently. The picture drawn of this country squire amply displays the leader of his shire in the House of Commons.

Siri fuoch gwyddoch gael
Siŵr ddwywaith y sir ddiwael:
Aethost gŵr â thyst geirwir
Er serch yn Farchog o'r sir.
Dysgaist faith gyfraith i gyd
A chofiaist yn wych hefyd . . .

Tra enwog lew trwy naw gwlad
Tynnaist y beilchion tanad.[95]

The patron's prestige as twice-elected sheriff of his shire is advanced by his newly-acquired office as the Merioneth representative in parliament. By means of these achievements he was endowed with means of suppressing oppressors and other dissidents. The poet enthusiastically considered that his patron's elevation from his position as sheriff to that of member of parliament had enhanced his services to the shire community. It had also broadened his outlook and had added new exciting perspectives to his rôle as governor. However, at local level, the emphasis was essentially on maintaining the corporate unity of the community. Hardly at all do the poets mention specific political issues or controversies because they considered that aspect to be totally irrelevant in view of the expectations of bardic convention. The *uchelwr*'s prime duty in parliament and elsewhere was to maintain the well-being of his people and locality as well as to assert his own dignity. It was the status attained through being associated with various institutions of government that appealed to the poets not the instability of political life and experience. Sir John Salusbury of Lleweni, one of the most powerful administrators in north-east Wales, served his shire as member of parliament for seven years (1597-1604) and was involved in the stormy election of 1601. Albeit, three poets sang to him as an imposing figure, Huw Pennant exclaiming that he had earned the affection of his people by his good bearing in office.[96] He was further regarded by Siôn Tudur as the chief of men and the mainstay of the Crown in precarious days. Similarly Thomas Mostyn was portrayed, on another occasion, as a skilful and spirited exponent of political integrity in the House of Commons. He was the 'stalwart pillar' ('piler cadarn') who had cultivated four prime virtues, namely valour ('dewrder'), mercy ('trugaredd'), justice ('cyfiawnder') and munificence ('haelder'), all of which assisted him in fulfilling his rôle in regional affairs.[97]

In the early seventeenth century Welsh membership of the Council in the Marches had increased steadily. The position granted further prestige to the prime gentry and enriched their political education. A succession of able and long-serving Lord Presidents in the latter half of the Tudor century had added significantly to its dignity, and it served as the chief administrative intermediary between power at the centre and in the regions. Its prime function was to supervise law and administration in Wales and four of the border shires.[98] The Council had been placed on a statutory basis in 1543 and, as George Owen maintained, it served as an essential cog in the government of Wales: 'let that house or council be dissolved but for a few years', he remarked, 'those that live now most quietly and think that court unnecessary shall first feel the smart and want thereof.'[99] In spite of its weaknesses this Council continued to function in an official capacity as a court of law as well and served, until its temporary abolition in 1641, to co-ordinate administration in Wales and maintain peace and security. The prerogative Council had become an institution of state but it was consistently regarded by the Welsh gentry as a centre which displayed the power of the king in government. Enterprising *uchelwyr* used what means they had at their disposal to augment their political responsibilities in Stuart society. Their power was lavishly praised by poets such as Huw Machno who described Sir John Wynn of Gwydir (who became a member in 1604), in his capacity as a member of the Council, as he who possessed the skill and discipline to enforce peace and order.[100] William Herbert, first Earl of Pembroke, was hailed as the 'eye of all Wales' ('llygad holl Gymru') and as a 'steadfast baron' in royal service ('Barwn sad i'w brins').[101] His son, Henry Herbert, a person with equal public talents, was viewed by Henry Salesbury as the 'bright star of the Brythonic nation', and its worthy President ('seren ddisglair a llachar y genedl Frytanaidd'). He was renowned, it was said, for protecting public interest through the exercise of justice and mercy. It was under his tutelage that an increasing number of aspiring gentry served their time at Ludlow and became familiar with the principles of government on a more sophisticated basis.[102] The office, in bardic lore, recalled the ancient allegiance to territorial control practised by a small exclusive band of privileged gentry who formed an *élite* in county society. It was in that context that Dr. Ellis Price of Plas Iolyn was described by Siôn Tudur as the 'protector' of his country ('ymg'leddwch ein gwlad') whose chief occupation was to suppress theft and disorder ('anllywodraeth a lladrad').[103] He was firmly entrenched in the Marches and entrusted with all aspects of governmental duties. Simon Thelwall, likewise, was addressed in similar fashion by Wiliam Cynwal as a 'beneficial gift to his region' ('rhodd fudd yrhawg') by virtue of his contacts at Ludlow, and Sir Richard Price of Gogerddan was deemed worthy of praise for the same reason.[104] Descriptions of men who had achieved such an honour were designed to concentrate principally on their moral rectitude.

Tra fu'n ymgeleddu'n gwlad
Y gŵr oedd fawr ei gariad;
Ni chaid yn ei fro na chwyn
Nag och unwaith nag achwyn . . .
Y fo'n rhychor blaenoriaid
Yn un o'r cyngor y caid.[105]

This person was portrayed against a background of intensive administrative and legal activity. He was the 'protector' ('ymgeleddwr') in his position as member of the Council in the Marches. 'In his position as guardian of his country', it was said, 'he was highly esteemed; his government maintaining peace and security.' 'He was the leading ox in the furrow', it was added, by virtue of his prominence in the public life of Wales. The glowing reputation earned by such an illustrious character, as this extract from his elegy shows, drew much of its meaning from the fact that the governor had manipulated all sources of power to establish himself as an admired representative of the Crown in Wales.

The emphasis in all spheres of government was placed on God's overriding power and beneficence towards men entrusted with the welfare of their communities. It was by divine sanction that the power and prestige of individuals considered worthy of holding public office were enhanced. Siôn Mawddwy, for example, is particularly succinct on this point in his ode to Robert Llwyd of Rhiwgoch, Merioneth.

Duw gadarn yw dy geidwad,
Duw roes dy law dros dy wlad.[106]

'Almighty God is your protector', the poet maintained, 'it is He who has granted you the extensive power which you enjoy in your country.' Key lines of this kind disclose how close a correlation existed between the poet's analysis of moral obligation and civil order and obedience.

The concept of the rule of law was a prerequisite of the creation and preservation of organic unity as perceived in poetic eulogy. No stability or cohesion could ever be achieved in the community unless obedience and loyalty had been achieved. 'Lose not, therefore, I pray you the benefits of so precious a jewel as law is' Lambarde said, 'being both brought home to your doors and committed to your hands.' 'Have . . . a zeal of godly justice', he continued, 'that may either amend or make an end of the evil and the bad.'[107] The poets were also constantly occupied with the concepts of law and order and the place of the virtuous ruler in localities which had to be protected if the highest public values were to be maintained.

I'ch sir oll heddwch sy raid
A chyd wylio eich deiliaid.[108]

This view of guardianship and protection entailed assuming responsibility for the well-being of whole communities. The weaknesses of the system posed a serious threat to the unity of those communities as well as the nation state. The 'good and wise gentleman' ('gŵr da doeth') and the renowned arbitrator ('dyddiwr da') represented the concerted opinion of the region ('cyngor y wlad') because they both brought peace in place of anarchy and strife.[109] One patron, according to Siôn Phylip, possessed three prime attributes in his capacity as local magistrate, namely good sense ('synnwyr'), learning ('dysg') and justice ('cyfiawnder').[110] A knowledge of the law, fortified by his humanity, gave him the attributes of the 'perfect' governor. The words of Huw Machno to a Merioneth patron revealed the skills which he deployed to arbitrate successfully between contending factions. As a 'daysman' ('dyddiwr'), he explained, the gentleman created equilibrium; his strength of purpose and latitude of mind imposed upon others the qualities of leadership which other less resourceful and enterprising gentry could never offer. 'The law itself', it was said, 'is most honourable among men, so those that should be practisers . . . might likewise to be of credit and estimation.'[111] Thus, in this context, the 'just magistrate', through his sound interpretation of law, symbolized gravity in the execution of his duties ('Dwys gadw gwir . . . Da i rannu wyd, yr uniawn'). Commentators constantly emphasized *ius*, the sense of justice embodied in the law and exposed in each measured deed.[112] Such interpretations valued just citizenship which transcended all other manifestations of urban codes of behaviour; to act unjustly implied denying to others the basic rights of citizenship. The *uchelwr*, in his rôle as judge and arbitrator, assumed the protective powers granted to him by divine favour.

Gentry who served in other official capacities on a lower level, as bailiffs, constables of hundreds, escheators, coroners, stewards and such like, were also highly acclaimed as descendants of noble Welsh stock. Their very modest incomes hindered their progress up the social ladder but they followed in the same tradition as their forbears in offering service in regional government in the less prominent but often more onerous offices. Their contribution, regardless of its inefficiency, was considered to be indispensable for the smooth running of affairs. Many of them had descended from a long line of key administrators whose services in the Principality and the Marches had been augmented in the wake of social dislocation and increasing absenteeism among landlords.[113] The Acts of Union consolidated their hold over government in the hundreds, parishes and townships at a time when Tudor rule depended on yeomen, freeholders and modest gentlemen to carry out the essential duties among the lower orders of society. An increasing number among them, of Welsh or English or a mixed lineage, earned bardic praise by virtue of their administrative posts and the prestige which they enjoyed. Such eulogy reflected their growing prosperity in a society which was placing increased emphasis on the acquisition and retention of office. Humphrey Stanley, for example, was regarded as the auspicious constable of Harlech castle and escheator of the shire,[114] and Edward Almor was equally praised as the steward of Holt. Wiliam Llŷn opened his *cywydd* to Robert Davies of Mold, a prominent officer in royal service, in imposing style.

> Y sersiant a'r meddiant mawr . . .
> Gwraidd edn mewn gradd ydwyd
> Mwy'n y radd na manwyr wyd.[115]

He is acclaimed as 'the sergeant who enjoys large possessions', 'a man rooted in good stock and superior to others of lower rank.' The couplet hints at the distinguishing features which even poets observed within the broad stratification of gentility.

It was jealousy and resentment between individuals and kindreds, the poets remarked, which often obscured the qualities of gentility in all aspects of administrative functions. Deceit and intrigue, it was stated, defeated the end of justice. The assassination of Lewys ab Owain of Dolgellau, perpetrated by defiant and vindictive freeholders in 1555, led Owain Gwynedd to lament the cause of justice in Merioneth.[116] Ill-will subverted good government and destroyed social cohesion. He who preserved such harmony was divinely appointed to rule and challenge the forces of evil, thus the patron was normally called the 'perfect and prosperous statesman' ('gwladwr perffaith goludawg') and the 'fort and lock who unifies his region' ('caer a chlo i uno'i wlad').[117] Huw Pennant drew the comparison well between the man of power and the consoler and maintainer of the poor in Gwynedd in an ode for Sir William Glyn of Glynllifon. His innate privileges afforded him the opportunities to dispense justice and charity as an essential part of his services.[118]

It is hardly surprising to find the poets, during the century which linked the Acts of Union with the Civil Wars, giving more of their time to distinguishing between the virtuous and conscientious ruler and the powers of evil in society, and also between the oppressors and the under-privileged and long-suffering peasantry. Couplets ceaselessly refer to the gross injustice ('anghyfiawnder'), naked oppression ('trais') and selfish arrogance ('trahausdeb') of aspiring merchants, lawyers, moneylenders and landowners.[119] The strong and tyrannous ('cedyrn eurwalch') and the bold and disdainful ('dewrion beilchion') destroyed the organic unity of the shire community.[120] Lengthy descriptions refer to the cupidity, pride and insincerity of individuals who rose to power in unstable economic circumstances. The just governor, on the other hand, was the complete antithesis: his deeds are honourable, and he is well disposed. 'Your prosperity lies in the qualities of your character', one poet remarked of his patron, 'and you practised the law calmly without deceit to achieve your aims.'[121] The image was outlined by Roger Ascham who stated that 'only good men by their government and example make happy times in every degree and state'.[122] The essence of this probity was innate goodness. The Aristotelian concept of the governor who commanded obedience and established security is highlighted, with equal glamour, in the *awdlau* and *cywyddau* of the period 1540-1640. Rhisiart Phylip's accolade to Edmund Meurig of Ucheldref in Merioneth, a prominent administrator in the early seventeenth century, contains those features which contemporary commentators readily applauded.

> Sir wych o lwys air a chlod,
> Swyddwr hon sydd ŵr hynod . . .
> Yn lân ddoeth, ni lyn i'w ddig,
> Yn ddwys gadarn ddysgedig . . .
> O gofynnwn gyfiawnwaith,
> Gŵr yw a'i myn, gwiwrym waith.[123]

Yet again the laudation is clearly directed towards exposing the 'wise, powerful and learned' man in society. He is fully accomplished in public affairs and his sense of justice and equity is reflected in the well-governed shire entrusted to his care. Such individuals deserved to be admired and emulated. 'They sit, as it were, on a pillar on the top of a mountain where all the people do behold them', Sir Thomas Elyot explained, and in bardic tributes the images of the 'pinnacle', 'pillar' and 'immoveable power of gentility' ('Tŵr bonedd safedig') are very popular.[124] The governor was the 'mirror of his land' ('drych y wlad') and a worthy reflection of goodness.[125] He and his colleagues should 'seem to all men', Elyot explained in his discourse on the ideal public governors, 'worthy to be in authority, honour and noblesse, and all that is under their governance shall prosper and come to perfection.'[126] He referred further to them as 'a precious stone in a rich brooch', an image which again was applied in some panegyrics to describe the illustrious *uchelwr* as the 'fair jewel' ('glain teg'), the 'immensely honoured jewel' ('glain dirfawr glod') and the 'wise gem' ('glain doeth').[127] It is clear that views of gentility in this period coincided with concepts of regional statesmanship and communal integrity. Siôn Mawddwy crisply summarized, in two couplets in praise of the squire of Bodfel in Llŷn, the fundamental feature of the just governor.

Dwys gadw gwir, dysgedig iawn,
Da i rannu wyd, yr uniawn.
Hyn sydd glod mewn swydd gwladwr,
Hyn sydd dda mewn swydd i ŵr.[128]

The basic features of veracity and trust emerge in the manner in which the poet construes how the *uchelwr* had participated effectively in government. Keeping the truth and exercising justice, the poet continues, is a commendable facet of the governor's office and a nobleman's station.

The medieval bardic grammar declared that the professional declaimers of verse should also address worthy prelates and other ecclesiastics, principally as governors of the church and also because they shared the same virtues and descended from the same privileged stock as the gentry.[129] In addition, their offices in the church in the period of the Reformation, were considered to be equally important with the establishment of the new Protestant state, and it is specifically in that context that they are included in this study on the concepts of order and authority. Clerical gentility contained qualities which buttressed the *imperium* established by Henry VIII and consolidated within a Protestant structure by Elizabeth I. The firm and resolute spiritual leadership, as envisaged in poetic works, was detected in the pioneers of the Elizabethan church in Wales established in 1559. It supplied a succession of able and dedicated higher clergy who were resident, learned and well-descended, and who also were to become the spearheads of the new faith in the four Welsh dioceses.[130] The long series of Roman Catholic bishops were replaced by some high-powered Protestant exponents who interpreted their task principally as a vindication of the church as a political as well as a religious institution and as a bulwark of unity and uniformity in the realm. It is this stalwart leadership which, in periods of strain and tension, assisted greatly in settling the realm and maintaining internal security. The professional poets who favoured the new faith sang ardently to the bishops of all four dioceses, particularly Thomas Davies and William Hughes (St. Asaph), William Morgan (Llandaff and St. Asaph), William Bleddyn (Llandaff), Nicholas Robinson and Henry Rowlands (Bangor) and Richard Davies (St. David's).[131] Most of these prelates came from north Wales: their courage and tenacity in pursuing their duties, regardless of their insuperable difficulties, were highly esteemed by poets such as Wiliam Cynwal, Siôn Mawddwy, Siôn Tudur, Wiliam Llŷn and Huw Machno who composed sublime *awdlau* and *cywyddau* emphasizing their status as leaders of spiritual life and governors of the new church establishment.[132]

Such notables represented a religious order whose prime task it was to defend the doctrine of the church and, at the same time, identify that church with the fundamental principles of the new Protestant state. The odes sung in praise of prime religious leaders normally contained six major elements which applied just and gracious living to the ecclesiastical context. Eulogistic patterns in these poems placed emphasis on gentlebirth, spiritual leadership, moral sustenance, theological skills, parochial duties and a defence of the Protestant settlement. Taken together, these factors signified the concepts of gentility interpreted within an ecclesiastical structure and based on the traditional virtues of honour and privilege.[133]

Among the Protestant leaders of the Reformation William Morgan doubtless ranked uppermost and attracted the largest number of poetic tributes principally because of his feat in translating the scriptures.[134] In addition the odes composed in his honour contained specific references to his sterling qualities as governor of his diocese and to his defence of the Protestant tradition which he represented as priest and prelate. Most of the odes, in commending the Bible, significantly gave attention to the foundation of the Anglican church which was persistently threatened by external and internal forces. Huw Machno, for example, noted the change of heart which had occurred in Wales following the government's policy, to foster the new faith through the effective preaching of God's Word.

Lle bu'r niwl bob llwybr i ni
Ac i wledydd galedi.
Barn hynod ein Brenhines
A barodd, do, ebrwydd des;
Rhoes inni, o'i gras uniawn
Ffydd dda i'n mysg, dysg a dawn.
Ordeiniodd wŷr da, enwawg,
Gwaith rhwydd, i bregethu rhawg.[135]

These couplets reflect the honour bestowed by Elizabeth I on the Welsh nation by allowing the Bible to be translated into the native tongue. 'Where there was obscurity and hardship', it was said, 'the Queen, of her grace and favour, gave us the good faith and ordained renowned and good men to preach the Word.' These lines associated this privilege specifically with the goodwill and benignity of the sovereign head of state—as did William Morgan himself in his dedication of the Bible to the Queen. It was considered that the government had maintained national unity and enriched Welsh identity within the secular realm, a feature which is fundamental in any understanding of Tudor policy in Wales.

Thomas Davies, the first long-serving Elizabethan bishop of St. Asaph, was principally distinguished for his administrative and legal skills. As an ecclesiastical lawyer his contribution to the Reformation lay chiefly in organization and discipline with regard to church government and administration. Lines by Wiliam Llŷn reflect his firm attachment to the new faith, his good offices symbolizing the 'quality of grace' ('ansawdd gras').[136] Richard Davies was hailed by the same poet as a scholar of repute, a formative leader of his people, a conscientious governor on behalf of the Crown and a dedicated provider for his flock. The bishop was compared to St. Paul in his dedicated service to his people, a 'key to learning' ('agoriad ffydd') and a 'complete exponent of Christ's way' ('Agoraist ffordd Crist o'i phen').[137] In all the odes to ecclesiastical leaders, chiefly from the accession of Elizabeth I onwards, the emphasis was essentially on spiritual gentility and virtues designed to preserve order in church government, discipline, control and grace in the execution of public duty. In both secular and ecclesiastical spheres gentility manifested itself most profusely in the virtuosity, vibrancy and versatility of individual members of society who honoured obligation and benign leadership as paramount.

In spite of his notorious reputation as a pluralist and poor administrator of his diocese William Hughes, Bishop of St. Asaph (1573-1600) was, like his colleagues in the church, also considered to be an accomplished scholar, a person of reputable ancestry and a warm supporter of the Welsh cultural tradition.[138] It is hardly surprising that his virtues as a churchman were extolled and his learning cited as an example to others, again in the context of spiritual governorship.

Wiliam Llŷn and Wiliam Cynwal, among others, portrayed him as a worthy descendant of noble Welsh stock, a man of trust and discretion, a leader of courage and tenacity, a skilled scholar and eager propagator of God's Word. Regardless of his weaknesses he was considered to be a pillar of the established order. His virtues projected the image of the Protestant faith among poets who considered its protection and defence to be tantamount to maintaining the security of the state. Wiliam Llŷn captured all this in sturdy couplets when referring to William Hughes's acceptance of the Queen's favour.

> Cawsoch yngwydd arglwyddi
> Groeso hardd gan ei gras hi.
> Am iawn weddi mae'n addas
> Rodio'r grym lle rho Duw'r gras.
> O codaist yn ŵr cadarn,
> Cefn y fainc mewn cyfiawn farn.
> Nid da neb nid dyn a'i air,
> Duw a'th gododd di i'th gadair.[139]

The words reflect the gracious and authoritative nature of his rule as prelate at St. Asaph and magnify his close contacts with spheres of power and influence beyond its boundaries. 'In the presence of lords', it is said, 'you were welcomed by her grace the Queen'; it was most seemly that he should walk in God's grace as a man of courage and strength, a supporter and sustainer of the episcopal bench where his word and judgement are respected. It is only a man of his word, the poet maintains further, who can be considered virtuous, and William Hughes had been elevated to the episcopal chair for that very reason. Royal favour, God's grace and the bishop's innate virtues had raised him to a position of renown. In the poet's estimation his reputation as a leader in the Protestant church was untainted. His excellence transcended all other less worthy considerations. His services to God had amply testified to his unfailing integrity of purpose. He had been appointed and maintained in office under the Tudors by grace and favour. As secular governors were exalted because of their devotion to law and order so were prelates portrayed as defenders of moral standards and effective leaders of the Reformation. The Protestant tradition was manifested in both spheres with equal enthusiasm and served appropriately to extend and defend the interests of the Tudor state.[140]

With regard to ecclesiastical leaders the poets concentrated essentially on spiritual gentility as well as those qualities fundamental to the preservation of order, justice and security in church government. Regardless of the spiritual tone of the odes sung in their honour the main thrust betrays broader features. They were primarily portrayed as leaders in their respective communities. The need to maintain political cohesiveness was manifested strongly in an ecclesiastical setting. Leadership in the church—at diocesan or parochial level—buttressed the overriding authority of the state. Prelates, parish clergy and other church dignitaries were appointed as spearheads of the new faith whose prime task it was to fortify the ecclesiastical arm of the Tudor realm. In secular and ecclesiastical spheres alike gentility manifested itself most overtly in the exercise of virtue, a show of virtuosity and a vibrant desire to govern for the common good. It is in this context that the rôle of secular and ecclesiastical governors achieves a degree of unity. Tudor and early Stuart administrators had one feature in common besides private ambition, namely their distinct awareness that their prosperity and the survival of the institutions upon which their prestige relied depended, in the last resort, on the close alliance established between them and the Crown. The innate links between that Crown, the common law, parliament and the Protestant church created that firm unity upon which the new sovereign state wholly depended. Thus would be established law, order and obedience to just rule, doubtless one of the most conspicuous features in Welsh strict-metre poetry in the decades of resettlement after the Acts of Union.

Similar odes, composed principally in the *cywydd* metre, were offered to several other clerics, at a lower level, who had become popular among the bardic fraternity. Many came from gentle stock and some, in fact, were poets themselves and often produced verse of high standard. As lower officials in secular government attended to the needs of hundreds and townships so did priests conduct their affairs in the parishes. Syr Owain ap Gwilym, curate of Tal-y-llyn in Merioneth, is a good example of a cleric who had established for himself a reputation for composing sound eulogy and offering perceptive comments on social conditions in his age.[141] Another was the redoubtable Edmwnd Prys, Archdeacon of Merioneth, who was one of a small band of scholars who aided William Morgan in his task of translating the scriptures into Welsh. His poetic output varied in nature, but his notable compositions in strict-metre, besides those composed in his lengthy debate over bardic standards and conventions with Wiliam Cynwal, were the few works aimed at exposing the major defects in community life in Wales of his day. Posing as an aggrieved clergyman, he commented bitterly on oppressive officialdom, thereby highlighting some of the most resented and deplored features in Welsh society of that age.[142] Dr John Davies of Mallwyd, the celebrated early seventeenth-century humanist scholar, was himself the object of numerous odes by Edward Urien, Gruffudd Hafren, Huw Machno, Rhisiart Cynwal, Rhisiart Phylip, Siôn Cain and Watcyn Clywedog among other lesser known bards. Most of these represented the bardic tradition in its period of decline, and this verse sadly reflected the cultural *malaise.*[143] Dr Edmund Meyricke, Archdeacon of Bangor, and William Evans, Chancellor of Llandaff (a renowned patron), for example, were among a significant minority group of Protestant clergy who sustained patronage and who drew from the poets some of the best-quality verse composed in that period.[144]

What emerge distinctly from a study of this central theme are the key concepts of privilege and obligation as applied to the Welsh *uchelwyr* and ecclesiastical leaders in their public offices. The prime objectives appeared to be to assert good order and establish national security, both of which were reflected in royal service at regional levels. The doctrine of order was regarded as a vital component in the exercise of monarchical government in the Elizabethan and Jacobean eras. Order was most strongly desired and striven for in an age of change, as was the case in Wales among the more conventional gentry in the century subsequent to the Tudor settlement. Those who held the reins of power clung tenaciously to what vestiges of authority they could because it was by means of their astuteness and unyielding loyalty to the state that they assisted in the task of achieving communal unity within their areas of jurisdiction. Stability was overtly manifested in a variety of ways but, as bardic approbation clearly symbolized, the projection of the public image, as exemplified in the awareness and exercise of power and authority, was positively regarded as being among the most effective. It was essentially the privilege of office and its obligations that were confidently sustained in the early decades of the seventeenth century and that ultimately lost much of their relevance among the traditional *uchelwyr* of Wales in the less stable and insecure days of Puritan rule.

NOTES

[1]W. O. Williams, *Cal. Caerns Quarter Sessions Records*, xl-xlix; idem, 'Social Order in Tudor Wales', loc. cit.; G. Williams, *Recovery, Reorientation and Reformation*, pp. 263-75. For a detailed examination of the practice and theory of peace-keeping see J. Samaha, *Law and Order in Historical Perspective* (London, 1974); W. H. Greenleaf, *Order, Empiricism and Politics: Two Traditions of English Political Thought, 1500-1700*, pp. 44-56; P. Slack (ed.), *Rebellion, Protest and the Social Order in Early Modern England* (London, 1984), passim; C. Read (ed.), *William Lambarde and Local Government* (New York, 1962).

[2]G. Roberts, *Aspects of Welsh History*, pp. 310-18; R. R. Davies, *Lordship and Society in the March of Wales, 1282-1400* (Oxford, 1978); E. Owen (ed.), *A Catalogue of Manuscripts relating to Wales in the British Museum,* II (London, 1903), p. 125.

[3]*Cal. Caerns Quarter Sessions Records,* xxxviii-xl; W. Rees, *The Union between England and Wales* (Cardiff, 1947), pp. 25-30; G. E. Jones, *The Gentry and the Elizabethan State* (Swansea, 1977), pp. 20-7; W. R. B. Robinson, 'The Tudor Revolution in Welsh Government, 1536-1543: its Effects on Gentry Participation', *English Historical Review*, CCCCVI, 1988, 1-20; H. A. Lloyd, *The Gentry of South-West Wales,* III, pp. 93-134, IV, pp. 135-73.

[4]*Gwaith Tudur Aled*, I, VII, pp. 38-42.

[5]GLM, XLVIII, p. 173.

[6]J. Gwynfor Jones, 'Welsh Poets and their Patrons', pp. 247-50 et seq.; idem, 'Awdurdod Cyfreithiol', pp. 154-8.

[7]T. Roberts (ed.), *Gwaith Tudur Penllyn ac Ieuan ap Tudur Penllyn* (Cardiff, 1958), XXXVIII, 70-1.

[8]*Gwaith Tudur Aled,* I, XXXIII, pp. 145-8, XLII, pp. 177-9; 'Awdurdod Cyfreithiol' , loc. cit.

[9]P. Williams, *Council in the Marches*, pp. 11-33; *Recovery, Reorientation and Reformation*, pp. 260-75.

[10]*Pembrokshire*, pp. 37, 56; Merrick, *Morganiae Archaiographia*, ed. B. Ll. James, pp. 67-8; Powell, *Historie of Cambria*. [13-14]; J. Gwynfor Jones, 'Beirdd yr Uchelwyr a Deddfwriaeth y Tuduriaid 1536-43', *Taliesin*, LVII, 1986, 69-85.

[11]GMD, VIII, p. 54.

[12]Cf. 'enaid gwŷr', 'enaid ei sir'; GSM, LVI, p. 180; 'urddas gwlad', GST, I, LXIX, p. 280; 'ymgeleddwr gwlad', NBSF, II, CCLXVII, p. 586.

[13]NBM, p. 96.

[14]Kelso, op. cit., pp. 50-3, 70-8; Caspari, op. cit., pp. 8-12, 82-6.

[15]GSM, XXIII, p. 79.

[16]Cf 'piler y cyfiawnder'. Cardiff MS. 4. 101, 101; 'cyfiawnder a chymeriad', GWC (Mostyn III), II, CVII, p. 332; 'rhuwliwr gwlad', ibid., LXXVI, p. 235.

[17]For further discussion of this point see 'Awdurdod Cyfreithiol', 184-7.

[18]NBSF, II, CCCXXXVII, p. 738.

[19]NLW Peniarth MS. 124, 76.

[20]BWLl, XXXIV, p. 84.

[21]GOG, II, LXXXIII, p. 280.

[22]G. R. Elton, *England under the Tudors,* (London, 1957), pp. 160-5, 398, 404.

[23]CCM, p. 183; GST, I, XX, p. 78.

[24]'Hanfodion Undod Gwladwriaethol', 76 et seq.

[25]GSM, LIV, p. 174; VI, p. 19; LXXXIII, p. 266; XVI, p. 52; GWC(1), I, XLIV, p. 153.

[26]*Calendar of Wynn Papers*, no. 715.

[27]*Clenennau Letters and Papers*, no. 189, p. 56. See also no. 398, p. 113.

[28]CCM, pp., 205-6.

[29]NBM, p. 197; GWC(1), II, p. 527; NBSF, I, LIII, p. 124.

[30]GLM, LV, p. 196.

[31]*Gwaith Tudur Aled,* II, XC, pp. 357-8; *Council in the Marches*, passim. See also Cardiff MS. 4. 101, 61a. Ac ustus a ddwg ystod
O'r heddwch glân rhyddwych glod.

[32]GWC(1), I, I, p. 2.

[33]'Siryf cymesurol', NBSF, II, CCCXXIX, p. 722; 'Oes ŵr gymesurach?', GWC(1), I, LVIII, p. 201; 'Siryf wyd cymesurwaith', CCM, p. 85.

[34]GOG, II, LXXXIII, p. 281.

[35]D. Ll. Thomas, 'Further Notes on the Council in the Marches', *Y Cymmrodor,* XIII, 1900, 130-1.

[36]GEUGH, XI, p. 57; GWC (1), II, XXIII, p. 617.

[37]Lambarde, op. cit., p. 95.

[38]BWLl, XXXVII, p. 93.

[39]Ibid. , XXIX, p. 77; CLl, p. 57.

[40]GGH, XCI, pp. 291-2.

[41]NBSF, II, CCLVII, p. 586.

[42]Ibid. , I, CLXXXV, p. 413.

[43]*Penbrokshire*, III, pp. 64-6; 'Awdurdod Cyfreithiol', 182-5.

[44]CLl, p. 49.

[45]A, H, Dodd, 'Pattern of Politics', 9-20. For more information on gentry interests see G. D. Owen, *Wales in the Reign of James I* (London, 1988), pp. 111-29.

[46]Cardiff MS. 19, 431; 'Welsh Poets and their Patrons', 252-5.

[47]GEUGH, V, p. 28.

[48]CCM, pp. 152-3.

[49]A. H. Dodd, *Studies in Stuart Wales*, pp. 49-65; *Recovery, Reorientation and Reformation,* pp. 471-9.

[50]NLW MS. 9055E. 716.

[51]*Penbrokshire*, III, pp. 41-2, 64, 67.

[52]BGHM, VIII, p. 16.

[53]GWC (Mostyn III), I, p. 176.

[54]See GST, I, XLVI, pp. 189-92; BWLl, V, pp. 11-14; XX, pp. 48-51.

[55]BWLl, XX, p. 49.

[56]CLl, p. 59.

[57]NBSF, I, xlii, XLI, p. 92.

[58]NBM, p. 70.

[59]Ibid., p. 82.

[60]I. Bowen (ed.), *The Statutes of Wales* (London, 1908), pp. 67-9; *Penbrokshire*, III, pp. 52-5, 59-62; *Cal. Caerns Quarter Sessions Records*, xxxiii-xxxv.

[61]*Pembrokshire*, loc. cit; T. H. Lewis, 'The Justices of the Peace in Wales', *Trans Cymmr.*, 1943-44, 120-32. For the broader background see J. R. Lander, *English Justices of the Peace, 1461-1509* (Gloucester, 1989).

[62]*Penbrokshire*, p. 53.

[63]GMD, VIII, p. 54.

[64]GGH, XXXVIII, p. 126.

[65]BGHM, XLII, p. 91.

[66]Lambarde, op. cit. , pp. 101, 110, 112-3.

[67]J. Gwynfor Jones, 'Concepts of Order and Gentility', in *Class, Community and Culture in Tudor Wales*, pp. 147-53.

[68]Cf. GSM, XX, p. 68; CLl, p. 57.

[69]CSB, XI, p. 89.

[70]BGHM, XXV, p. 56.

[71]CLl, p. 193.

[72]Lambarde, op. cit. , p. 95.

[73]GLM, LVI, pp. 181-2.

[74]GST, I, p. 126.

[75]NBSF, I, XXXVII, p. 81-2.

[76]'Hanfodion Undod Gwladwriaethol', 66-8; *Cal. Caerns Quarter Sessions Records*, pp. 25-6.

[77]*Calendar of Wynn Papers*, no. 977.

[78]'Hanfodion Undod Gwladwriaethol', 72-4.

[79]GST, I, XXX. p. 126.

[80]Loc. cit.

[81]'Hanfodion Undod Gwladwriaethol', loc. cit.

[82]NBSF, II, CCXII, p. 470; *Statutes of Wales*, pp. 76, 122.

[83]GCH, IV, p. 149 passim; J. Hurstfield, 'County Government, 1530-1660', *Victoria County History of Wiltshire, V* (London, 1957), pp. 80-110; G. Scott Thomson, 'The Origin and Growth of the Office of Deputy-Lieutenant', *Transactions of the Royal Historical Society*, IV, (V), 1922, 154 et seq.

[84]*Clenennau Letters and Papers*, no. 48, p. 15.

[85]CCM, pp. 152-3.

[86]NBSF, I, XXXII, p. 69.

[87]Ibid. , I, XXXV, pp. 75-6.

[88]'Awdurdod Cyfreithiol', 170-4 et seq.

[89]*Clenennau Letters and Papers*, no. 26, p. 8.

[90]NBSF, II, CCCCXXVII, p. 920.

[91]A. H. Dodd, 'Wales's Parliamentary Apprenticeship', 8-22; idem, 'The Dawn of Party Politics', in *Studies in Stuart Wales*, pp. 176-86; idem, 'Pattern of Politics', loc. cit.

[92]GSM, XCVII, p. 308.

[93]CCM, p. 153.

[94]GWC (Mostyn III), II, CVI, p. 329; GWC(1), I, XLVI, p. 160.

[95]NBSF, II, CCCLXIX, p. 806.

[96]E. Roberts, 'Ymryson y Salsbriaid', *Trans. Denbs Hist Soc.*, XVII, 1968, 108-46; W. J. Smith (ed.), *Calendar of Salusbury Correspondence 1553—circa 1700* (Cardiff, 1954), pp. 8-9; J. E. Neale, *The Elizabethan House of Commons*, pp. 122 et seq.; SLl, CXLI, p. 531.

[97]GST, I, XXVII, p. 113; CCM, pp. 205-6.

[98]*Council in the Marches*, chap. I. 'Wales and the Council from 1471 to 1543', pp. 3-43.

[99]*Penbrokshire*, III, p. 24.

[100]BGHM, XXXV, p. 27

[101]*Rhagymadroddion*, p. 114; BWLl, XXVIII, p. 73.

[102]*Rhagymadroddion a Chyflwyniadau Lladin*, p. 94; 'Pattern of Politics', 9-12.

[103]GST. I, XLVI, p. 189.

[104]GWC(1), I, XLVIII, p. 167; BGHM, VI, p. 11.

[105]UCNW Mostyn MS. 8, 5v.

[106]GSM, LVIII. p. 188.

[107]Lambarde, op. cit., pp. 96, 108.

[108]GSB, LIV, p. 120.

[109]Cf. 'Pennaeth y gwladwriaeth da', GST, I, XXVII, p. 113.

[110]NBM, p. 55.

[111]Kelso, op. cit., p. 51.

[112]Cf. GSM, XXV, p. 88; NBSF, II, CCIII, p. 45a.

[113]M. Gray, 'Power, Patronage and Politics: Office-holding and Administration on the Crown Estates in Wales' in R. W. Hoyle (ed.), *The Lands of the English Crown* 1558-1640 (Cambridge, forthcoming); J. Gwynfor Jones, 'Cyfraith a Threfn yn Sir Gaernarfon c. 1600-1640: yr Uchelwyr a'r Byd Gweinyddol', *Trans. Caerns. Hist. Soc.*, XLVII, 1986, 25-70.

[114]CLl, p. 96.

[115]Ibid., p. 48.

[116]GOG, I, LXXXI, p. 237.

[117]GMD, VIII, p. 54.

[118]NLW Llansteffan MS. 122, 518.

[119]Cf. Edmwnd Prys. *Oxford Book of Welsh Verse*, CXX, pp. 244-8.

[120]Usually, references to rapacious officials and their subversive activities appear in odes which specifically comment on adverse social and economic conditions. Cf. GST, I, CXVI, pp. 583-8.

[121]NBM, p. 112.

[122]Kelso, op. cit., 70.

[123]NBM, p. 214-5.

[124]Caspari, op. cit., p. 107.

[125]'Hanfodion Undod Gwladwriaethol', 57-63 et seq.

[126]Kelso, op. cit., p. 80.

[127]GSM, XIX, pp. 63-4, XLVIII, p. 146; GWC (1), I, XII, p. 42; XXXVI, p. 128.

[128]Ibid., XXV, p. 88.

[129]*Gramadegau'r Penceirddiaid*, p. 55.

[130]*Welsh Reformation Essays*, pp. 22-4.

[131]DWB, pp. 147-8, 153, 392-3, 656, 887.

[132]GWC(1), I, LI, p. 177; II, III, p. 531; XXXII, p. 658; BWLl, LXII, p. 166; LXIX. p. 187; E. Roberts, 'Canu Wiliam Cynwal i Glerigwyr', *Trans Denbs Hist. Soc.*, XIV, 1965, 120-40; C. Fychan, 'Y Canu i Wŷr Eglwysig Gorllewin Dinbych', ibid., XXVIII, 1979, 115-82. For background see W. P. Griffith 'Anglicaniaid a Phiwritaniaid: Myfyrwyr a Diwinyddion Prifysgolion Lloegr, 1560-1640', LlC, XVI, 1989, 23-39.

[133]See J. Gwynfor Jones, 'Ymateb y Beirdd i'r Cyfnewidiadau Crefyddol c. 1536-1640', LlC, XVI, 1989, 133-84.

[134]R. G. Gruffydd, *The Translation of the Bible into the Welsh Tongue by William Morgan in 1588* (London, 1988), pp. 30-83.

[135]Ibid., 135, VII p. 51.

[136]CLl, pp. 1-2.

[137]Ibid., p. 8.

[138]DWB, pp. 392-3; J. Gwynfor Jones, 'Thomas Davies and William Hughes; Two Reformation Bishops of St. Asaph', BBCS, XXIX, 1981, 320-35; J. Strype, *Annals of the Reformation* (London, 1725), 11(1i), pp. 293-4. App., pp. 62-4; 'Thomas Davies and William Hughes', loc. cit.

[139]GWC(1), I, LI, pp. 177-9, II, XXXII, pp. 658-62; CLl, p. 73.

[140]*Welsh Reformation Essays,* pp. 26-7; *Recovery, Reorientation and Reformation*, pp. 323-31.

[141]NBM, pp. 217-8; D. G. Williams, 'Syr Owain ap Gwilym', LlC, VI, 1960-61, 179-93.

[142] *Oxford Book of Welsh Verse*, CXX, pp. 244-8.

[143] For further references see Rh. F. Roberts, 'Y Dr. John Davies o Fallwyd', LlC, II, 1952 (i), 19-35, (ii), 97-110.

[144] GCH, IV, pp. 229, 546, 549; *Traddodiad Llenyddol Morgannwg*, pp. 61, 80, 84, 88-90, 280; GWC(1), II, XXX, pp. 648-52.

Chapter V

Social and Economic Dimensions

The fundamental changes which occurred in the structure of land tenure in Wales and the Marches from the mid-fourteenth-century onwards established a new social and economic framework based on the squire-tenant-labourer relationship. The capitalist landowner gradually emerged and gentry families in embryo, varying in their material wealth and power, began to assume leadership in the Welsh countryside.[1] Many of them had descended from native kindred families in the Welshries and others came from *advenae* stock in the Principality and the Marches. It is said that a 'land revolution' had occurred in the century spanning the years between the Black Death (c. 1350) and the mid-fifteenth century when the wars between Lancaster and York broke out. It was an era which saw the rise of Owain Glyndŵr and the growth of Welsh national consciousness, and in the wake of the revolt social and economic trends were intensified, transforming significantly the patterns of land tenure. The long-term consequence was the growth and consolidation of gentry houses which played a vital rôle in Welsh—and English—political life in the fifteenth century. Their progress was carefully monitored by poets such as Iolo Goch, Guto'r Glyn, Lewys Glyn Cothi, Dafydd Nanmor, Lewys Môn and Tudur Aled, and their eulogies contain well-defined features which disclosed the ways and means adopted by them to strengthen their territorial positions in land and office.[2] The houses of Tredegyr (in Gwent), Penrhyn, Mostyn, Dinefwr and Raglan, among others, were extravagantly eulogized in order to display their grandeur and imposing status in Welsh society. The holding of administrative posts and estate management in general became the prime features of individuals who had, because of propitious circumstances, been able to avoid the perplexities of a declining medieval social order. The modest estates which emerged became symbols of power, influence and rising status, as in Guto'r Glyn timely reminder to Gwilym Fychan of Penrhyn.

A'th dir a'th fraint a'th dreth fry
A'th fonedd aeth i fyny.[3]

The emphasis is again placed on the acquisition of land and property which, in this instance, had enabled the scion of Penrhyn to increase his possessions, prestige and rent-roll, all of which boosted his status in regional society.

The ties of blood and kindred continued to hinder the development of other families who failed to make the grade but who still claimed gentility on the basis of good pedigree. Small-time landholders were often involved in local feuds, and animosities grew, usually out of landed disputes, in a period when the custom of succession to property was being significantly undermined. The strife vividly described by Sir John Wynn of Gwydir in his *History of the Gwydir Family,* which traced the turbulent story of his ancestors in Eifionydd and elsewhere in north Wales in the late Middle Ages, does indicate the sort of background that did create and perpetuate instability and lawlessness.[4] Conditions of disorder were provoked further by the unsatisfactory political situation in the Welsh Marches, the lack of an effective central control in the Principality and the general effects of plague, war and revolt. Consequently, the leading *uchelwyr* were given opportunities to further their interests in law and administration and they also became the patrons of poets in their country residences. The professional bardic order considered the prime rôle of these benefactors to be maintaining hospitality and offering sound cultural leadership. In such unstable conditions, however, the emphasis was placed as well on two other features which characterized the gentry in that age, namely their relative wealth and influence based on ancestry and their obligation to protect their regions from the threats of disorder. As guardians of peace and good order they were expected to undertake their duties as custodians in the Welsh native communities. The poets drew attention constantly to these prime themes since the *uchelwr* was regarded as a protector of all that was deemed virtuous and worthy of preservation. Many also referred to their patrons' participation in local and national events such as the Forest of Snowdon affair, Tyrone's rebellion in Ireland and the Civil Wars. They pronounced as well on religious matters, and on occasions revealed significantly divergent views. A case in point is Siôn Brwynog's famous ode to the 'Two Faiths' which amounted to a satirical comment on the new Protestantism. In the majority of odes, however, the poets concentrated exclusively on formal eulogy and the rôle of the *uchelwr* and the protector of the integrated community structure. Combined with this duty to defend was the concept of the military leader whose career had a firm economic base; he projected his power and might in a world where his qualities were respected.[5] From this particular angle Lewys Môn captured the sense of awe and reverence in his description of Thomas Salusbury of Lleweni as the principal power in Dyffryn Clwyd whose material prosperity was on the increase. Economic upheaval often created a sense of instability, and the emergent gentry were viewed either as forces which established peace and conformity or which perpetuated strife and discord.

> Mae'r wlad i'th dad a thydi
> Mae d'ewinedd amdani;
> Cloi tir Dyffryn Clwyd dy hun . . .[6]

The poet wished to portray the firm control which Salusbury enjoyed over his region of jurisdiction. 'You grasp it with your nails and you lock Dyffryn Clwyd well within your possession', the poet exclaims excitedly when attempting to create an impression of complete control. This is a bold reference to the trends that were in the process of moulding a new social order in mid- and late fifteenth-century Wales, the principal features of which were the accumulation of landed power and military strength. Similarly, Tudur Aled, in his perceptive manner described Roger Salusbury's reputation as an efficient estate manager, and applauded him for improving his status by purchasing lands and tenements.

> Tyrau a bronnydd, tir a brynoch
> Tyddynnau, cwysau a bwrcasoch . . .
> Ni wys dir uchel nas edrychoch,
> Ni wys gwlad uchel nas gwledychoch.[7]

The description is confined to the landed strength of the patron which had impressed the poet beyond all measure. 'You have purchased land and farmsteads together with arable land', the lines relate; there was no part of the country, high or low, that did not fall within his grasp. The same poet addressed Morus ab Ieuan of Abertanad reminding him that the lordship of Chirk had virtually fallen into his possession since he held so much land and authority there.[8] Much of Tudur Aled's bardic output revealed the chief manifestations of social change which revolved around the standards of gracious living in refined country houses. His direct references to the move made by Maredudd ab Ieuan from Eifionydd (via Caernarfon) to the remote uplands of Nanconwy, for example, dwell significantly on trends which were becoming common among rising freeholders and other property adventurers in the latter half of the fifteenth century. The acquisition of bond townships, owing principally to economic recession among the depressed servile population, was a phenomenon which demanded attention in any attempt to describe the build-up of landed estates.

Prifiaist ym mhob rhyw ofyn,
I roi d'aur ar dir pryn . . .
Nid oes i'r wlad, asur lain
Dyn nid ydyw dan d'adain.[9]

The lines are significant in that they draw attention to the subtle economic processes that were gradually eroding customary practices in landholding, especially bond tenure. 'You prospered in every way', the poet relates, 'by purchasing land with gold, and there is no man in that country who is not under your protection.' Not only did Maredudd extend his hold over territory but also became a dominant power in his adopted region by assuming responsible leadership over restless and masterless men. Tudur Aled flattered another patron by referring vividly to the flourishing condition of his estate. He had extensive acres of arable land and all his cottages housed a tenant and his family. He owned mountains, woodlands and common land as well as meadows and sumptuous mansions. The description of such splendour represented a person of considerable magnitude in his neighbourhood.

Ba dir cŵys o bedwar cant,
Ba dy annedd heb denant?
Ba du i wlad heb d'aelwydau,
Ba le'n hon heb lawenhau?

Mynydd-dir, coetir, ti a'u cai,
Ytir, gweirglodd-dir, gwledd-dai.[10]

Such detailed references to property success increase in bardic eulogy during the course of the sixteenth century when property became more available on the market, particularly after the dissolution of the monasteries in the 1530s. Such developments were doubtless only to be expected in a period when the chief social feature was the prestige accorded to the new capitalist landowner and the pressures exerted to seek offices and positions under the new Tudor dispensation. The circulation of a money economy, together with the trade in money-lending, provided means for local gentry to augment their landed interests and strengthen their control, and the poets often commented on the availability of resources and the restrictions placed on men who abused and exploited their positions. During their seasonal visits to the *plastai* they became more aware of the benefits and stresses of gentry life, and were doubtless in a position to counsel and even reprimand where they considered it to be appropriate. One poet mentioned the ready cash which his benefactor hid in four chests in his house ('Ym mhedair cist mae d'aur coch'); another was commended for spending his money to purchase and maintain his buildings ('D'aur a fwriaist ar furiau'), their value thereby increasing.[11]

Bardic commentary of this kind focused on the establishment and settlement of landed estates in an age when property created wealth, and wealth brought power and authority in its trail. In the sixteenth century such power and control vested in land reached new and exciting proportions. In a legal sense the ties of kindred assumed a less important rôle, and the practice of primogeniture, in matters relating to the succession to land, became the only method that could be legally used after 1543.[12] It was in the mid-sixteenth century that the Welsh *uchelwyr* began to identify their new found power with a sense of regional control and responsibility under the aegis of Tudor rule. Property rights, acquired by means of propitious economic circumstances, entailed performing duties as well as enjoying privileges. The power builders were linked with the efficient and equitable handling of landed affairs whereby the legal defence of rights and the benevolent care of dependants were given precedence. The worthy landowner was further buttressed by his innate moral worth and his material prosperity sprang from his benign disposition. Wiliam Cynwal phrased it in another way when he stated, on three separate occasions, that corn will only grow from good seed in fruitful ground.

> Ar gynnydd yr egina
> Yd teg lle bytho had da.
>
> Y gwenith nid egina,
> Wedi tes, heb hadyd da.[13]
>
> Ni thy'n aml, weithian, yma
> Egin ir ond o dir da.[14]

'Good corn will grow only from fertile seed', the poet maintains, and wheat will not appear in seasonable weather without good seed.' 'This seed', he continues, 'will not grow often except on fertile land.' By applying much the same phraseology the poet underlines the significance of roots and a sense of belonging to noble stock. These comments can be interpreted in two ways: gentility will prosper only when rooted in good stock, and virtuous living stems only from conditions of stability and good living. Constant references to ambition and forthright action as well as to 'progress' ('cynnydd'), 'growth' ('twf'), 'prosperity' ('ffyniant', 'golud') and 'expansion' ('braster') imply a condition of affluence which assumed moral as well as material dimensions. These two sources enhanced the prestige of proprietors and constituted the twin features of the favoured social order in Welsh community life. The close associations established between land, virtues, official power and moral rectitude were blended naturally in the pattern of eulogy, as Wiliam Llŷn and Gruffudd Hafren reveal respectively in the following two examples.

> Da'n ei wlad annwyl ydoedd
> A da iawn yn ei dai oedd,
> O gadw tŷ gwedi y tad
> Â mawredd a chymeriad.[15]
>
> Nod a sail, enaid y sir
> Yw'ch adeildai a'ch doldir.[16]

The patron's munificence is identified in these lines with his benevolent authority in his house. 'He was beloved in his countryside and his house', Wiliam Llŷn maintains, 'and he kept house with grandeur and character after his father's death.' Gruffudd Hafren considered his patron's possessions to have been the 'apex and foundation', and he the 'very soul' of his shire, and the poet magnified the abundance found in his mansions and in the surrounding countryside.

To substantiate the hold which the *uchelwr* had over his property most poets endeavoured to allow more space to that aspect than to others. The *awdlau*, in particular, extravagantly described such lavish prosperity as if it took priority over all other factors. Wiliam Llŷn, a regular visitor to several of the *plastai*, majestically praised the possessions of Siôn Salusbury of Rug in Merioneth. His *awdl* concentrated largely on the benefactor's power in landed affairs, extolling the virtues of his husbandry and detailing the main features of the properties including parks, orchards and mountain pastures. The impression given is that the proprietor had accumulated his lands simply to display his grandeur.[17] Emphasis is placed on his good husbandry and the wide variety of sources of landed income which he enjoyed in view of his inheritance. The poet's vivid recollections on this occasion enriched the poem, primarily in terms of real property. To Wiliam Llŷn patronage revolved around the *plasty* and the territorial estate. References to the 'country' ('gwlad') or 'estate' ('stad') were occasionally applied to mean management on the broader scale, the shire or state successively being regarded as a mere extension of the family patrimony. It is increased prosperity granted by divine sanction, Siôn Tudur maintained in his elegy for Richard Clough of Denbigh, that truly enhanced a man's fortune.

> Grasol oedd gwrs ei lwyddiad,
> Gras Duw a ddwg ŵr i stad.[18]

His career, the poet observes, is a success story; he was gracious by virtue of the fact that God had endowed him with the faculties considered essential to the estate owner of high status. Since dependants worked the land *uchelwyr* were expected to support and protect them. Indeed, so impoverished were they materially that some were obliged to apply themselves to manual labour, particularly among the mere gentry.[19] The upper levels, however, were portrayed consistently as being in command of their affairs and sufficiently well-endowed to expect others to perform menial tasks on their land. Siôn Cain praised one patron effusively because his rent income from lands in two shires had augmented his wealth more than would any ten officials together.[20] One Llŷn patron, according to Rhisiart Phylip, was renowned chiefly because he gave lands to others: another of the same rank was magnified because his landed power was buttressed by his bounty, gallantry and exemplary public image.[21] Huw Pennant also drew attention to that munificence and liberality exercised in the *plasty* which surpassed all. The owner's grace and reverence ('gras a parch'), the poet maintained, stemmed, in part, from his extended patrimony.[22] The 'undefiled' succession to land and the respect earned for beneficent and protective guardianship gave meaning to the poem; indeed, the 'prime owner of land' ('Perchen perchentyaeth tir') mustered all his resources, including business acumen and an astute understanding of legal intricacies to extend his property and other dynastic ambitions. Through matrimonial ties the house of Corsygedol, for example, established a hold over parts of Llŷn and Eifionydd, thus extending its power northwards into parts of Caernarfonshire, and members of the family were praised because of that enterprising expansion of power. The poets interpreted family pride and fortune most frequently in a territorial context although Wiliam Llŷn was constantly aware of God's overriding authority in the making and unmaking of every individual.[23] The good husbandman deserved the success he achieved through careful administration of his property: the negligent owner, it was further observed, deserved to suffer the dire consequences of his mismanagement. Not only were material means important to the growth of local prestige but they were also considered absolutely necessary to maintain the welfare of the political realm. Several poets described their hosts ruling their lands with majestic power, protecting their inferiors from external threats and acknowledging the authority of the state in buttressing their public and private interests.

Un pen i gloi'n neupen gwlad
Edeirnion, nawdd Duw arnad,

Un o'i dynion daioni,
Er un a chant ni ron chwi.[24]

Yet again, in these couplets by Gruffudd Hiraethog to Huw Gwyn of Hendwr, the image of territorial grandeur emerges in lines designed to portray this individual's sway over Edeirnion. He had both ends of this region in his grasp, the poet maintains, and he is exemplary in his pursuits. The situation was familiar in the sense that the native patrimony, in whatever context, was constantly associated with *noblesse oblige*. Powerful words indeed which interpreted the *uchelwr* who possessed power ('Rhywlia dy wlad rheolwr'), who bore himself as an emperor or king in his region and who organized efficiently his family and public affairs as a prime governor and sagacious ruler of his land.[25]

After the Tudor settlement had been established the practice of primogeniture as the law of succession to land gradually created a rigidly dynastic approach to landownership. Over many generations the more forward-looking among the gentry had attempted to overcome the problems of kindred customs and had managed to base their fortunes on English practice. Sixteenth-century poets focused exclusively on the inheritance and the character of the heir apparent. Wiliam Llŷn dwelt on this point, for example, in his address to Robert ap Morus of Llanfrothen.

Pur ei chwedl mewn parch ydoedd,
Pendefig dysgedig oedd . . .
Eu parch drwy gyfarch a gaf,
A'u pen yw y mab hynaf.[26]

'He was well-known as a pure and respected ruler', the poet confirms, 'a man of learning' whom he was prepared to salute. The head of the family is the eldest son who has sustained the good name of his stock. Such a clear manifestation of primogeniture indicated that Wiliam Llŷn and his colleagues in the bardic fraternity were fully supportive of major tenurial changes that had occurred even in their own generation. This candid acknowledgement of the eldest son as the worthy successor suggests that all was well within the family. That ideal situation, however, did not materialize in other families where inheritance could and did cause strife and contention, and it is hardly surprising that the poets, while they extolled the virtues of the emerging heir to land and property, were fully aware of the pitfalls and underlined the need for conformity and unity within the kindred circle. Several poems were composed to counsel individual *uchelwyr*, particularly on their succession, in matters relating to the principles of good management and housekeeping and the ways in which amicable relations could be maintained, even in times of potential discord.[27] It was usually the case that eulogy endeavoured to expose the benefits of good kin relations and assert the value of family pride and unity. One of the chief requirements of the Tudor state was stability at regional level. The invocations of the poets were directed specifically to achieve that very harmony that was so often abandoned in family relations. Varied images were used to portray the evil consequences of rivalry in the days when the battle for status and social recognition had become intensified. Bad relations with kinsfolk, Siôn Tudur declared, could sever the vital link between the branch and the living organism in the main stem itself, and should be avoided at all costs.

> Drwg gyngor a dyr cangau . . .
> Nad grino dy garennydd
> Na thor gainc unwaith o'r gwŷdd . . .
> A garo'i dŷ fry, a'i fraint
> A gâr yn fawr ei geraint.[28]

The words, addressed to John Salusbury of Lleweni, are harsh but equally evocative; they arouse feelings of anger and dismay and also express the need for caution in dealing with clandestine family affairs. 'Bad counsel destroys the branch', the poet maintains, and he goes on to advise his patron not to deprive his kindred of sustenance nor break a bough from the main stem through rash or jealous action. 'He who loves his house and cherishes his privileges', he added, 'also supports his kindred'. He then proceeded to caution his patron because he was fully aware that persistent animosities undermined the image of the well-governed community. Such was the concern expressed with maintaining wholesome relations with kinsmen that this poet, like others of his generation, gave precedence to the just inheritance and the legitimate heir to landed property ('tiriogaeth'), the 'heir apparent' ('aer aparwnt'), as Siôn Cain called him, destined to maintain and fortify stability and prosperity on the estate.[29] They considered the rightful succession to be all-embracing in such matters; the *paterfamilias* ('pencenedl') was described as the vital link with *antecessores* of noble bearing. The ideal patriarch enjoyed the privileges of old age and good lineage and had possessed good fortune based essentially on legitimate succession. He was sometimes compared to the hefty ox in the furrow or to the chief juror ('penrhaith') proclaiming judgement in a court of law.[30] His authority was universally recognized, and he could easily pass on the inheritance to a sympathetic heir aware of his duties to preserve the traditions of his stock. The glories of a historic past were closely identified with the qualities of life in the present. Robert Ifans attempted to mediate in a dispute between John Salusbury and Thomas Myddelton of Chirk. He emphasized the need for amity between kindreds in order that peace and security might be maintained. Preserving stability in the region, it was said, assisted in establishing a prosperous commonwealth.

> Heddwch a fag hawdd wych foeth,
> A chyfion ras a chyfoeth.[31]

Memories of the father, Siôn Phylip remarked further, never faded while there was a virtuous heir, by God's grace, to succeed him ('etifedd rhinweddol').[32] 'Children are our hope' ('Plant yw'n gobaith'), the same poet maintained when referring to the security which linear succession would provide.[33] The beneficial consequences of male succession were never lost in poetic eulogy; the heir, Wiliam Cynwal observed, who had governed his lands as had his father was the dynastic ruler of his land and people.[34] The 'patriarchal sway' governed all and established effective relations between the proprietor and his tenants. References abound to the need for successful management based on peace and goodwill because no state could prosper without it. Although it is evident that the portrayal of patrons renowned for their benevolence and goodwill towards their tenants is often idealized, it does reflect the increasing emphasis on humanitarian and pietistic practices in Welsh rural society.

Dygwch drwy degwch draw
Eich deiliaid yn eich dwylaw,
A nad byth yr un diball
O'th wŷr at bennaeth arall.[35]

The element of custodianship emerges yet again in these lines with the poet's ardent plea that the patron should defend his patrimony and dependants from the covetous designs of others. 'Protect your subjects honourably', he maintained, 'and do not allow any other chieftain to usurp your power and govern them.' 'The humour of my tenants', one leading landowner remarked, 'was to take my word or my mood because they trusted me.'[36] He also recommended to his son and heir that he should honour tradition, maintain his tenants liberally and act nobly towards all with whom he came into contact. It appears again, judging by this type of evidence, that the patron did in fact heed the advice given him. These are the words of Watcyn Clywedog some years later.

Ni ddarfu i chwi o chwant
At ennill newid tenant;
Ni roech lid na newidiad
Ar weision tirion eich tad.[37]

'You did not, out of desire, change a tenant', the poet observed, 'and you did not bear grievance against your father's gentle servants.' The couplets record the poet's satisfaction that continuity and respect had surpassed all in the relationships established between a new heir and his dependants. The image of the father had been forceful enough, in this instance, to impose order and good management on the estate.

Bonds established between landowner and tenants were often in the nature of a private agreement based on a sound knowledge of family connections and history. It was considered to be the landlord's duty and in his interests to ensure that his property was fully occupied with tenants and was well-husbanded. 'What ploughed lands and what cottages are there without a tenant?', Tudur Aled asked, when referring to the prosperity of the Nannau estate at a time, early in the sixteenth century, when its owners were achieving the ascendancy in Merioneth.[38] The implication was that the survival of this substantial estate was based essentially on its economic capacity, its efficient organization and the presence of a benevolent *uchelwr* to supervise his inheritance. Respect for long-term tenancy enhanced the reputation of the landowner and exposed his successful governorship. He emerged as the well-endowed *paterfamilias*, reflecting all that was considered honourable, practical and lasting in family and regional tradition. His 'imp' ('impyn') or scion symbolized the survival of noble attributes.[39]

If the *uchelwr* was regarded as the pattern of the magnanimous protector his mansion (*plasty*) was chiefly interpreted as the centre-piece of excellence and esteem. It had emerged as the fulcrum of gracious living in its broadest perspectives, and the poets, even in the days of marked cultural decline, refer to it constantly as a haven of nobility. It has been regarded as the 'real centre of gravity' in the Welsh countryside which inspired the *uchelwr* to serve his community and offer solace and hospitality to the weak and ill-endowed. It emerged as a meeting-place for an exclusive clientele among the shire gentry as well as a shelter for the destitute and needy. Professional poets, in practically every eulogy, emphasized its rôle in Tudor and early Stuart society, many of them describing at length its appearance and architectural features and the attractions of its interior.[40] Good, efficient and bountiful housekeeping was regarded as essential ('cadw tŷ', 'perchentyaeth'), and the images employed to describe this function were wide-ranging: the 'mirror of the countryside' ('drych y wlad'), the 'notable pinnacle of bardic reputation' ('Pinacl hynod y glod'), the 'refuge for the community' ('noddfa'r wlad') and the 'second paradise' ('ail paradwys').[41] Siôn Tudur, in eloquent testimony to the merits of the court at Mostyn in the days of the redoubtable Sir Thomas Mostyn, asserted that this 'lodging' of the poets ('llety'r glêr') was renowned for its hospitality and also an open house to the whole of Wales ('Llety fu i holl Gymru i gyd'). Within its precincts were cherished the acknowledged virtues which fashioned the perfect gentleman and sustained nobility.

Dy lys, lle rhoid elusen,
Yno cyrch ifanc a hen . . .
Llety fu holl Gymru i gyd,
Lletyfwr ieirll wyt hefyd . . .

Duw iwch adawo iechyd
Am harddu holl Gymru i gyd.[42]

The lines are memorable and reflect the glorious traditions highly valued by the Mostyn family at its principal seat in Flintshire. 'In your court, where charity is distributed', the poet recalls, 'the young and old are attracted.' He considered the mansion to be a fitting lodging-house for the Welsh gentry, and a welcomed resting place for earls. 'May God grant you health', the poet continued, 'for gracing Wales in this manner'. These lines were composed after the squire of Mostyn had been knighted, when he entertained the Earl of Essex on his way to Ireland in 1599. 'In a governor', Sir Thomas Elyot explained, 'the fountain of all excellent manners is majesty; which is the whole proportion and figure of noble estate, and is properly a beauty or comliness in his countenance, language and gesture apt to his dignity and accommodate to time, place and company.'[43] Such qualities were nurtured principally in the hall ('llys'), the symbol of good reputation and excellence. In his elegy for Edward Puleston of Trefalun, Wiliam Llŷn considered these elements to be paramount.

Cynhaliai dŷ fry yn frau
I gadw'r gair gyda'r gorau.[44]

This patron had maintained his house in the most magnificent manner and thus had preserved his reputation. It had become a symbol of pre-eminence, easily recognizable and accessible.

The forms of majesty and grace emerged in the manner in which the *uchelwr* conducted himself in relation to others. His *plasty* was described as the fount of justice and a source of dignity and moral rectitude. It was also regarded as the most congenial place where poets would visit on their seasonal itineraries to enjoy succour and sustenance. The nobleman in his court, it was often maintained, would support and protect according to his status and disposition. There, the standards of civilized life would he fostered and fortified: it was often considered to be the 'hospitable anchor of the community' ('garedig angor adail'), a fort ('caer') and the 'very soul of a region' ('Dy lys enaid dy wlad').[45] As the young heir was expected to succeed honourably to the estate so also would he be encouraged to maintain a bountiful household. The poets constantly emphasized the honour and ostentation as reflected in the munificence of its interior. The bearing of Ellis Bryncir, a modest country squire from Eifionydd, is portrayed admirably in a few couplets by Huw Machno in his elegy.

Er pallu ym mhob tuedd
O wŷr gwlad yma i roi gwledd,
Llew a golud, lle gwelwn,
A llaw hael, ni phallai hwn.
Ym Mryncir pybyr hap aeth
At haelwalch i'r tai helaeth.
Fel ei dad adeiladwr
I'w fawr gôst yno fu'r gŵr.[46]

A modest squire such as Ellis Bryncir had earned the same approbation as Sir Thomas Mostyn and other prime gentry in north Wales. The couplets refer to the receding hospitality that was available in the Welsh countryside and the bountiful gifts bestowed by this patron in adverse times. 'At Bryncir', the poet observed, 'fortune went his way; like his father he had augmented his mansion and had resided there.' It was essential that the *uchelwr* remained permanently in his *plasty*. Within the sturdy tower, Wiliam Cynwal reported of Nannau, the strength and bounty of a whole region is preserved ('Tŵr bonedd safedig . . . haelder . . . rhywiogrwydd').[47] George Owen of Henllys drew a sharp contrast between the 'ruyn and decaye' of the old medieval castles of Wales and the new mansions which, by his time, had appeared in the Welsh landscape, namely the flourishing 'howses of the gentlemen' which, in part, had caused 'a ioyefull metamorphosis' in Tudor Wales.[48] To the poets, likewise, such centres were noted for their hospitality, and deserved honour as symbolic representatives of status, authority and charity. Rhisiart Phylip described Morfa Mawr in Ceredigion, the seat of Huw Gwyn, as an open court whose owner would never close its doors on any in need.[49] Furthermore, Wiliam Fychan II of Corsygedol, according to Edward Urien, had extended his hall to accommodate his guests: he had provided a paradise, the poet maintained, where he and his colleagues could retreat and enjoy solace and comfort.[50]

The *plasty* was also viewed as a base from which the *uchelwr* could extend his authority over a parish, hundred or shire. Country houses had emerged during the sixteenth century as centres of their communities, as John Leland had observed in his *Itinerary*. They represented a life of increased luxury and sophistication, established the household on a firm basis and enhanced family pride.[51] In this context the *plasty* manifested and buttressed the social order based on 'degree, priority and place'. As the royal court functioned as the focus for the entire realm so did country residences in their respective communities. Both symbolized the power and authority of a specifically defined entity possessing innate prerogative powers enabling it to impose its sovereignty on others. It was essentially from this angle that Owain Gwynedd portrayed the house of Llwydiarth as a royal place and a tower which preserved the dignity and integrity of a community.[52] The house also bound together three shires ('clo tair sir'), and was portrayed as a regal residence. Such concepts elevated the country seat to a position of unique standing as a court befitting the ideal governor. Wiliam Llŷn had this in mind in his elegy for Edward Almor.

> Da'n ei wlad annwyl ydoedd
> A da iawn yn ei dai oedd.[53]

The good and gentle *uchelwr*, it was reported, was highly esteemed in his own house where he demonstrated his power and magnanimity and exerted control over his neighbourhood. Such words by Wiliam Llŷn reveal the notion of grace and excellence in true Renaissance fashion. From it emerges the image of the resident leader in his court—the norm of justice—incorporating within himself all that was considered beneficial to community life. The absentee *bonheddig*, who denied their dependants the sustenance they required, threatened the very source of that life blood and all but destroyed the peaceful harmony which existed between landlord and tenants. Such a catastrophe was not expressed in clearer terms than in Edmwnd Prys's ode appealing to Sir John Wynn, junior, of Gwydir to return from his sojourn in Italy to reside at his home in Llanfrothen, Merioneth.

> Mae ar weiniaid Meirionnydd
> D'eisiau'n Y Wern, dewis Nudd . . .
> Eisiau bara a syberwyd.[54]

'You are urgently needed at your residence', the poet maintains, 'for the weaklings of Merioneth are in dire need of sustenance to preserve the dignity of community life.' The poets expressed similar feelings on the death of notable patrons who had left a void which could not easily be filled.

The concept of the country mansion as virtually the microcosm of the royal court was a common enough phenomenon in many bardic tributes. The patron, who was also an acknowledged governor, derived his legal ascendancy essentially from his place of residence. It was there that he carried out many of his legal functions, serving the public in all manner of affairs relating to law and government. It was only natural that the residence was considered to be a fount of justice. The notion of the *plasty* as a royal seat or fort ('caer reiol') maintained the image of honourable descent and law and just government, and was expounded enthusiastically by a succession of poets who depicted their patrons as owners of a 'privileged court' ('llys braint').[55] All the complimentary observations were meant to elevate the resident gentleman in the tradition of earlier generations of poets who emphasized a stable and unchanging social order. The redoubtable patron and governor, the embodiment of the ancient *breyriaeth*, and the *plasty* as the foundation of civilized life—were principal features that were interpreted as the mainstay of order, governance and justice.

The most expert among late Tudor and early Stuart bardic practitioners were fully aware of the ingredients which formed noble life and of the *plasty* as the focal point of that very existence. The idea of the mansion as the soul of civilized living appealed most favourably to those members of society who derived most benefit from it.[56] The portrayal of the royal court as the main attraction for all ambitious young gentry with an eye to the main chance was matched by the appeal of the country mansion where the highest moral values were protected. The obligations of both courts, at different levels, were principally to maintain or preserve a cultural heritage. The cult of kingship peculiar to the Tudor age had grown around the royal court in the same manner as the cult of gentility had emerged in the context of the *plasty*. The 'prosperous edifice of the country' ('golud adail gwlad') was an image well-worked in bardic eulogy.[57] Moral sustenance was emphasized as much as material support, if not more.

The royal court protected and enhanced the concept of unity within the realm; the patron's residence was interpreted as being the source of regional integrity. The Welsh *uchelwr* maintained his credibility by forging a valuable and lasting link between himself as the protector of his people and the national *paterfamilias*. Wiliam Glyn of Glynllifon, for example, was a renowned governor of his shire and, in his younger days, served as a squire of the body to Henry VIII. Siôn Mawddwy emphasized his prestige in that office and praised the manner in which it had fashioned his loyal services to the Crown in his native region later in life.

Cwrtio bu, cawr at y banc . . .
Tëyrn oedd, pen ein tir ni . . .
Yr haelaf o'r rheolwyr
A fu gall bendefig gwŷr.[58]

His prestige in courtly circles was immediately admired and given publicity. 'He was a giant at court, and in his native region a king', the poet ecstatically recorded and also, in his native region, 'the most benevolent and shrewdest of leaders among his people'. In his capacity as Crown servant at court and later in Caernarfonshire he was considered to be the most substantial ruler who possessed regal qualities. Wiliam Glyn was immediately identified with twin loyalties, both concentrated essentially on concepts of regality but applied in more subtle ways. Service in the royal household was not merely a means by which young gentry identified themselves closely with fashion and etiquette but it also trained them, on their return to their respective regions, to apply concepts of honour and justice. Sir John Salusbury of Lleweni, another squire of the body, was addressed by several poets as a figure who applied his experiences in that capacity to the needs of his dependants. Not surprisingly, Edwart ap Raff described him as the powerful man of reason who embodied all true virtue.

Mae synnwyr grymus ynoch
Mae glendid y byd lle boch.[59]

'You possess powers of reasoning', the poet maintained, 'and you are a figure of purity wherever you may be.' His veracity shone in a world of adversity and rapacity. Sir John Salusbury's training among men of grace and favour in London gave him added incentive to administer his locality with greater confidence.

The unblemished rôle of the perfect *uchelwr* was constantly identified with the concept of goodness. Huw Gwyn of Hendwr was thus portrayed in his *plasty* by Gruffudd Hiraethog as the 'baron of regal status' ('Farwn henbraff frenhinbren'), governing his area of jurisdiction with proficiency. He bound together his people in a common bond of loyalty, it was said, as a man of honour.[60]

So eager were the poets to convey the idea of regal grandeur and guardianship ('gwarcheidwadaeth') that their attention was often drawn to the specific details of houses, some of which were rebuilt, which dominated the rural scene. A large *corpus* of the verse described at length the distinctive external and internal features of the buildings, and descriptions were occasionally given of town houses, thus adding yet another dimension to the function and lifestyle of the gentry in an urban setting. When referring to the house rebuilt by John Wyn ap Maredudd at Gwydir Owain Gwynedd placed much emphasis on its commanding position in Nanconwy, and compared it with a glowing candle reflecting its splendour and attracting people towards it.

> Glân yw cannwyll glan Conwy,
> Goleuad teg eu gwlad hwy.
> Gorau un tŷ, gwarant teg,
> Eu grwndwal yw'r gaer wendeg.[61]

The imaginative way in which the poet describes the glowing appearance of Gwydir is, in itself, worthy of comment. 'The candle on the banks of the Conwy is fair', he observed, 'and is a fine light to their country'. Gwydir was regarded as the best of houses, a fortress and solid groundwall, and the poet signified its stalwart appearance as a centre of bounty and charity. Thus the gentleman's court is displayed as a catalyst, drawing together various elements in community life and creating an organic bond of cultural unity.

The poets were also concerned with portraying life within the mansion, dwelling principally on its hospitality and its affinities with the family. Next to the *paterfamilias* stood the lady of the house who was constantly regarded as a source of inspiration to all. She was described, occasionally at length, as the munificent, warm-hearted and benign mistress of the household displaying the same virtues as her husband, especially discretion, generosity and courtesy. By her gentle disposition she appealed to all who desired food and shelter. She brought harmony and a feminine charm into the household; added to her lineage, cordiality and charity were the qualities of prudence and sincerity which enriched the family circle and extended the house's reputation.[62] The gentlewoman assumed the rôle of the skilful partner in household management, and by her noble descent she added substantially to the prestige of her family. Although marriages were pre-arranged poetic evidence amply testified to a wholesome and productive family life and, in that context, etiquette and all that it symbolized dictated that the perfect gentleman deserved and obtained an equally virtuous wife. The need to establish familial solidarity demanded that the partnership flourished for the benefit of the household and the community at large. To the poets, the death of a noblewoman signified the loss of sustenance. As in the case of the deceased husband, the departed wife also created a tragic void which was difficult to fill. Wiliam Llŷn's lines on the death of Ellen Puleston, widow of Morus ab Eliza of Clenennau, express the woe felt on her passing.

> Cynnal plas mewn urddas mawr
> Acw'n hael cyn ei helawr,
> Rhoi aur a gwin y min môr
> Rhoi i gall ag anghall gyngor.
> Fal na bu o flaen ei bedd
> Eisiau gŵr nes ei gorwedd . . .[63]

These magnificent lines expose the true gentlewoman at her most bountiful. 'She maintained a palace in a dignified and abundant manner', the poet maintains, 'and gave gold and wine as well as good counsel to both sensible and foolish.' Before her death she assumed the tasks of her late husband with exemplary efficiency. The command and respect which such a lady enjoyed in her household among her immediate family and servants were considered by Wiliam Llŷn to be the most notable trait in her character. The poet's couplets refer to a good number of innate qualities: bounty, management, generosity, integrity, justice, discipline and good order in maintaining a household and providing sustenance in her widowhood. Harmony and concord prevailed in her house even though she was bereft of a worthy husband. Kindred solidarity and a dynastic approach to family fortune demanded that it be so. Marital harmony was considered paramount to ensure peace and good government. Lack of governance in the household threatened security in public affairs.[64] In spite of the patriarchal nature of society no head of the household could properly control his power unless he commanded full respect among his own kith and kin. It is hardly surprising that the poets referred consistently to the matrimonial bonds which buttressed gentility and drew ancestral stocks together in unity. The practicalities of patronage were essentially the gentlewoman's preserve: her sincerity, geniality and benignity were matched by her skills in playing the ideal hostess. Gruffudd Phylip described the virtues of Siôn Gruffudd III of Cefnamwlch's wife in this manner.

> Gorau da, achau dichwyn,
> Gorau'i rhodd lle gwirir hyn;
> Gorau'i dawn gyda'i gair doeth,
> Gorau'i moddau, em wiwddoeth;
> Gorau'i doniau adwaened,
> Gorau gwraig ei gair, o Gred.
> Gorau ym mhob rhagorion,
> Gorau hil a gair o hon.[65]

Extolling her virtues provided this poet with a pleasurable task. 'She is the best of all', he explains, ' and possesses a pure pedigree; she bestows the best gift, has skill and discretion in abundance, and is a wise gem.' In the poet's view she was the best lady of her word in Christendom, sharing all that was praiseworthy.

In certain spheres of activity the gentlewoman governed affairs in the mansion and was attributed with the qualities of charity and piety, the Christian virtues which ranked highly in her bearing. Odes were composed in honour of individual women considered to be worthy in their own right and, in that context, eulogy was identified with the acknowledged norms of gentility. Moral guidance and the exercise of discretion in public duty and function in the home was regarded as the counterpart of a man's contributions in the outside world. As the 'queen' ('unbennes') of the household she appropriately assumed, in a broader context, the rôle of the lady of the Renaissance.[66]

The lack of male heirs enabled women of gentle birth to share in land inheritance, and heiresses were quite common in Wales in this period. References appear to the lady who maintained a household as the prospective heiress to her father ('Hon a ddeil . . . Wres i'w thŷ, aeres ei thad').[67] After his son's decease Ifan Llwyd ap Dafydd of Hafodunnos shared his patrimony among his daughters ('A'i dda . . . A'i dir i'w ferched i'w ôl').[68] The poets always draw attention to their imposing pedigrees ('wreiddiau heirdd'), the 'lady of status' ('Gorau merch . . . gorau ystad') and the heiress of the highest social reputation ('bennes o ben bonedd').[69] The mother's property and status enabled heirs also to strengthen their landed power, and the prestige of the stately widow enabled her to preserve her dignity. The widow of Morus Wynn of Glyn Cywarch in Merioneth, for example, was described as a lady who resisted a second marriage and continued to occupy her place gracefully in her son's residence. She is portrayed as a person renowned for her good sense and dignity. She and her deceased husband, Huw Machno observed, had been content in their community sharing between them the virtues of gentility.

> Dau oeddynt yn ddedwyddawl,
> Un dôn ym Meirion eu mawl;
> Dau'n rhannu pob un rhinwedd
> I'r Glyn a rôi lawer gwledd.[70]

The partnership appeared to be perfect. They were both contented and equally prepared to ease the burdens of their region; they abundantly shared the same virtues at Glyn and distributed lavish hospitality. The situation was such that the performance of duties on equal terms at this house enabled Merioneth, as a social entity, to flourish conspicuously.

With their emphasis on benevolence, dignity and wisdom the poets were able to portray the gentlewoman as a symbol of moral probity in her own right, asserting her independence irrespective of her husband's own personal qualities. It is such a character study that emerges in numerous odes by Siôn Tudur, Simwnt Fychan, Edwart ap Raff and others for the famous Katheryn of Berain, Llanefydd and Harri Hywel's lament on the death of Marged, wife of Lewis ap Simwnt of Hafod-dywyll in Merioneth: as a person she is projected as the ideal housewife by virture of her sobriety, righteousness, grace and humility.

> Hyswi bur oedd, syber iawn . . .
> Bucheddol, rinweddol waith;
> Garedig foneddigedd,
> Gariadus groesawus wedd . . .
> Y wraig ddoeth drugarog dda.[71]

She was looked upon as a 'pure, mannerly housewife', devout and virtuous, kindly, gentle, loving and hospitable. She was a good, wise and merciful lady who owed her qualities to her personal endowments and enterprise as a meaningful housewife. The qualities of charity and devout living assumed more prominence in the early seventeenth century when it was considered that the lady's chief feature, besides maintaining her household, was to practise piety and godliness at home. References appear to her godly ways ('gwraig i Dduw'), moral integrity ('bucheddol rinweddol') and to her rôle as a good servant of God and her fellow men ('Ddaed oedd i Dduw a dyn').[72] Elizabeth Johns of Abermarlais in Carmarthenshire, for example, was praised by Wiliam Llŷn essentially as a godly lady;[73] similarly, Catrin, wife of Gruffudd ap Siôn of Pen-y-berth was described as chaste and devotional ('Defosiynol foesol ferch'). Others were portrayed, largely in view of their hospitality and liberality, constantly maintaining the weak ('Yn dyfal gynnal gweiniaid').[74] The focus on godliness and good works, which increased with the emergence of the Puritan ethos, reinforced the view that gentlewomen were endowed with divine grace to perform specific duties which enhanced their own prestige as well as preserving the moral well-being of their community. Regardless of racial descent—whether of English, Norman or Welsh stock—the resident gentlewoman was considered worthy of adulation. It is a fact that marriage alliances with English families had increased during the course of the sixteenth century among aspiring families: the English connection was appreciably stronger in social relations and, under normal conditions, harmonious relations were established, a trend endorsed by the poets. Edwart ap Raff, for example, stressed that marital harmony exposed unity in the practice of virtue and preserved material resources.

> Cyd rannu, caid o rinwedd,
> Cyd euro gwlad, cyd roi gwledd;
> Cyd ddinydd cyd ddaioni,
> Cyd gynnal ein hardal ni.[75]

The element of sharing responsibilities and privileges is again exposed by this poet who makes a point of underlining the common goodness and inheritance which this couple were prepared to defend for the benefit of all. What was considered to be good and lasting in marriage was interpreted by the poets as being beneficial for the whole community. The activities of the virtuous housewife within the *plasty*, to them, corresponded to the peace, order and moral support given by the *uchelwr* in public life. Siôn Cain expressed this concept in an ode which compared the wife, who governed her household, to her husband who ruled his shire with a just hand.[76] The lady's function was essentially practical and her house was universally regarded as a citadel of charity. The image was flagrantly exaggerated but the basic notion of good housekeeping was the constant feature. The virtues of Ann, wife of Robert Wyn Bryncir, for example, were exhibited in the sumptuous banquets held in her new hall, where she became the focus of benevolence. In the court, the lines relate, twenty thousand are entertained at a splendid feast; there is abundance of wine for all and excellent company. These lines by Huw Pennant portray a situation which, realistically, lay beyond the material means of the Bryncir family, but the symbolic features of hospitality emerge as the most essential in the bardic tradition.[77]

Within the household strict control and supervision were exercised over children and servants. The eldest son and heir was constantly given attention because he symbolized the good name and fame of the family and preserved it. That would be accomplished chiefly through property inheritance, the holding of public offices and good breeding. The *corpus* of poetry in the post-Tudor settlement period placed greater emphasis on the forces of dynasticism which were fostered by the practice of primogeniture.[78] Eulogy of this nature, while giving an impression of grandeur, also drew attention to the heir's responsibilities to his family and community. No inheritance could be preserved, it was asserted, unless the successor had become aware of communal obligation. The mechanics of family relations are rarely considered as worthy of note except when counsel is given for specific reasons in cases of hostility which threatened to weaken the bonds of affinity. The intricate network of relations continued to function, though not in a legal capacity, and often undermined the harmony so highly valued by the poets. Salutary kindred relations served to buttress the power of the successor to property and to preserve his inheritance from extinction. Such views were normally associated with concepts of patriarchalism, authoritarianism and paternalism.[79] The poets consistently sought to preserve the *status quo*, to magnify order and degree and preserve the traditional virtues of *uchelwriaeth*. More time is devoted to the unity of the nuclear family and to the responses of immediate members of the household to the consequences of marriage, elevated status and death. To the poets social relations were, by definition, stable and unchanging. Political and social circumstances might vary but God's creation of hierarchy was immutable, suggesting that the solidarity of the organic family was never challenged. Thus the convention arose whereby the names of all the children were listed in *cywyddau* and *awdlau* and their singular qualities recorded. The kindred's affection, Siôn Phylip remarked, was essential to the well-being of the family ('Cariad sad . . . Ydyw cariad y ceraint').[80] Unsatisfactory kindred relations not only undermined but destroyed the integrity of the immediate family structure and also contributed towards creating unstable conditions in the realm. The patriarchal authority and patrilinear structure were the most conducive to good order, and the legitimate heir was regarded as the symbol of unity. His skills in mastering management techniques on his estate and extending his benevolent rule over all enabled him to establish his reputation and preserve his inheritance, both moral and material, to the future.[81]

The basis of gentility was legitimacy, which implied a natural succession to land and office and a common appeal for public acclamation. Honour, in this respect, stemmed from skill in management and governance. The essence of good inheritance was dynastic; the power and authority of the governor were entirely dependant on his ability to provide an heir to perpetuate what was essentially good, hence the crucial stress placed on the heir in successive elegies which mourn the past. Wiliam Llŷn had identified the heir to Robert ap Morus ap Siôn's estate at Parc in Merioneth as a worthy successor because he would maintain ancestral values which sprang from legitimate lineal descent.

> A duwoliaeth hyd elawr
> A wna'i blant, mewn meddiant mawr;
> Eu parch drwy gyfarch a gaf,
> A'u pen yw y mab hynaf;
> Lewys Anwyl sy uniawn,
> Piau'r llys a'r power llawn.[82]

His children, through their godliness, the poet maintains, are prosperous and they respected him each time he addressed them in verse. Their head is Lewys Anwyl, the eldest son, who is just and exercises his power in his own court, as he did, presumably, in a court of law.

The same poet eulogized the four sons of John Wyn ap Maredudd of Gwydir, principally because they had maintained the family and had respected their father through their individual reputations.[83] Elegies solemnly expressed the common lament of a whole family on the death of a notable patron and protector, revealing a sense of cohesiveness in social relations. Patriarchal control and primogenitural succession were identified as basic denominators in any examination of stability in the social order.

With the gradual decline of military service as a prime requirement of gentility during the course of the sixteenth century more emphasis was placed on education and office-holding, attributes which usually placed the eldest son in a favoured position. Younger sons, however, were not always as fortunate since property laws provided that the heir alone should succeed to the estate, and his younger brothers were obliged to seek their fortunes elsewhere in the church, the legal profession, trade and commerce, administration and the army. Those who did serve the Crown in a military capacity and who were acclaimed in verse, as well as in other official sources, for their exploits in Ireland or on the continent, were regarded as worthy descendants of men who had passed on to them the skills of leadership and valour.[84] The Renaissance concept of the perfect gentleman gave considerable prominence to military skills and attributes. 'You are a soldier like your grandfather', Siôn Mawddwy maintained, when addressing John Salusbury of Lleweni, 'but you are also reputed for your bounty at home, sagacity and learning'.[85] In other words, the warrior had been converted into the humane and enlightened figure who enjoyed the finer qualities of life and who prided himself on his lavish support for the art of learning. Twin portrayals of this kind abound in bardic eulogy in the sixteenth century. Dafydd Llwyd, second son of Thomas Wyn of Pen-y-berth, for example, fought at Boulogne in 1544 where, it was stated exaggeratedly, he drove a thousand Frenchmen from the battlefield with fiery gusto ('gyrraist fil o Ffrancod . . . trwy Fwlên . . . Egni tân y gwnait ti').[86] Conversely, in his house in Eifionydd, he behaved as the courteous and liberal provider for the destitute and needy. The two images are not entirely incompatible but they do indicate the two distinct modes of life to which the Welsh gentry were accustomed, even among the reputedly less well-endowed younger sons. Although circumstances did not always augur well for these members of the family bardic tributes to many of them did dwell on the material and moral qualities of heads of cadet families who had prospered in trade, the church and the legal profession and had set up smaller estates. They were well-respected men in their communities who normally kept close ties with the senior branch in matters regarding local politics and government. Like their superiors, they also maintained a sense of kindred solidarity; they were described as common inheritors of a historic past, the defenders of antiquated traditions based on regal status and custodians of virtue and honour in their spheres of governorship. For example, two sons of Robert ap Morus of Parc in Merioneth were London merchants in Cheapside but they also, in later years, assumed the duties of regional leaders in the same tradition as their ancestors, and it was this distinctive quality which appealed to Wiliam Llŷn.

Marsiandwyr mawr ras undeb,
A'u swydd yn Llundain a Siêb.
Na bo'n waeth yn benaethiaid
Trwy gariad, na'r tad, na'r taid.[87]

The couplets relate to the impact of younger sons beyond Offa's Dyke. They were notable merchants based at Cheapside, but owing to their affection for their native community in Merioneth they were still regarded by the poet as regional leaders. Their ancestry enabled them to claim and retain close ties with the native soil despite their involvement elsewhere, an interesting and equally intriguing sociological phenomenon.

Poets increasingly placed an emphasis on the learning ('dysg') of individual patrons and their expertise in the traditional twenty-four feats ('pedair camp ar hugain') and bardic craft.[88] In his praise for Dr Ellis Price of Plas Iolyn, Wiliam Llŷn commended him as a Hebrew and classical scholar ('Ebryw i'th fyw . . . Groeg a Lladin').[89] The same poet admired Simon Thelwall of Plas-y-ward, a notable lawyer and versatile scholar, because of his expert knowledge of the seven arts ('y saith gelfyddyd') studied at universities and his familiarity with bardic convention.[90] Wiliam Cynwal sang in a similar vein to Edward ap Roeser of Bodylling ('a pharod addysg a phrydyddiaeth . . . gyda cherddwriaeth')[91] and Lewys ab Edwart described fully the learning which characterized Humphrey Llwyd of Denbigh ('Gŵr oedd yn dwyn gwreiddyn dysg') who, like others, had mastered the seven arts.

Ar goll ar led ein gwledydd
Y saith gelfyddyd y sydd.
Gramer, Retrig, Miwsig maith,
Geiriau mesur grymuswaith,
Arthmetig, werth mwy ytoedd,
A dewis gwaith mewn dysg oedd;
Ni all gŵr o'n gwlad gymradwy
Hyder a stronimer mwy.
Loetsig heb gudd ufuddwaith,
Meddaf fi, Siometri saith.[92]

The involvement of the majority of the gentry in Wales in education and educational institutions also took them, for variable periods of time, over the borders to England where they were given instruction at Oxford and, to a lesser extent, at Cambridge. Many were given some legal knowledge as well at the Inns of Court where they familiarized themselves with the basic principles of property law and became proficient in matters regarding the management of estates and local courts of law as well as the prosecution of their own private suits against their rivals in landed affairs. Many had been instructed privately at home and in locally-endowed grammar schools, and the sons of eligible gentry were educated at English public schools, such as Eton, St. Albans, Winchester and Shrewsbury before embarking on an academic career at the two principal universities. There is no doubt that educational activity in this period increased at a rapid pace in England and Wales, and the poets duly referred in their eulogies to the achievements of their patrons in the institutions of higher learning. According to Phylip Siôn Phylip of Ardudwy, in his *cywydd* for Gruffudd Fychan of Corsygedol, education was considered to be an essential component in the career of the gentleman who wished to make the grade in public and private life.

Da ysgol o freiniol fri
I landdyn a ddeil ynddi;
Er cymaint ei fraint a'i fri
Bo dyn ym mhob daioni.
Hardda dim dan euraidd do
Dasg addas yw dysg iddo.[93]

Education, as Sir Thomas Elyot, Roger Ascham and other contemporary social commentators observed, was identified as one of the chief features in the character of the perfect governor. In an age when greater importance was placed on skills in government and administration it is hardly surprising that the Welsh poets attached considerable significance to fundamental academic training in the lives of *uchelwyr* of noble descent. It prepared them for a variety of professions, including the church and the law, and assisted in creating among them a sense of corporate responsibility in their dealings with family groupings and the community at large. Enlightenment among the ranks of gentry was usually interpreted in the context of a full and complete course of education, based on the classics and the law, two crucial elements in the formation of gentility in Tudor and Stuart Wales.

The respect shown for family ties in lineal descent was also manifested in the acknowledgement and exercise of regional responsibilities. 'Respect men', one poet retorted, 'and there will be respect for you'. These are the words of Rhisiart Cynwal.

> Ynillwch a cherwch wŷr
> Galon pawb, ŵr glân pybyr;
> Perchwch wŷr, mae parch i chwi,
> Parchus y cewch eich perchi.[94]

'Win the affection of men', he observed, 'and respect them as a valiant and virtuous gentleman.' The reference clearly cited the local lord as a person to whom respect was due only when he endeavoured to value others, high and low, in the community. Kindred animosities were the chief reason for expressing such a caution. Thus poets, when counselling *uchelwyr*, concentrated on the need to resolve their differences and to take concerted action in defence of their own honour. Many poems have survived which offer counsel of this kind, emphasizing the need for propriety in the handling of their affairs. In this context poets demonstrate a common concern to preserve organic entities based on lineal descent. Tudor Wales, regardless of political annexation and the further progress in racial interaction and integration, revealed tense family relations which arose principally over property disputes. The Salusburies, Herberts and Morgans, for example, were notorious for perpetuating kindred animosities chiefly because their collaterals were diverse and often created contention and strife. The very benefits which the Tudors brought to Wales, principally in the land settlement and parliamentary representation, had become sources of discord in many spheres by the mid-sixteenth century.[95] Such rivalries were often caused by a new social and economic climate which did lead to ruthless exploitation and a desire to profit at the expense of others, usually within the same kindred group. At a time when so much prominence was given to the need for unity and uniformity in political and religious affairs it is hardly surprising that any threats of disruption were utterly deplored. Often, as convention dictated, the bards considered that the demise of a powerful head of the household could create and perpetuate adverse circumstances, disturb kindred unity and deprive a region of its focal point ('gwlad heb pen').[96] Dafydd Benwyn even went as far as to state that the death of his mentor, Edmund Morgan of Bedwellte, a kinsman of the Morgans of Tredegyr, had symbolized the demise of true gentility('Pob gwaed aeth dan draed . . . Pan aeth hwn').[97] Meurig Dafydd of Llanisien mourned the extinction of regional unity as well as the family pride on one occasion ('Marw teulu a mur talaith') when the *uchelwr* died.[98] Poetic declaimers were constantly aware of the vast network of blood relations providing the functional bond of consanguinity which governed life among the gentle families. The exercise of talents in the service of the state for the common good was wholly dependent on attitudes and responses to immediate circumstances. Greed and aggression often deterred the effective control of affairs and usually led to disunity and discord. 'Not often is a son like his father', one poet maintained, suggesting that family fortunes could not at all times depend on the succession of a just and veritable heir.[99]

Factors beyond the gentry's control frequently disrupted their landed and other material interests. The impact of inflationary processes and the price rise, in addition to economic impoverishment in the Welsh countryside, had taken their toll. The economic *malaise* cut deeply into Welsh community life; gentry who were dependent on fixed rents and incomes found themselves often in debt and unable to maintain the efficient running of their estates and families.[100] Increased costs and higher expenses caused poets to comment on the reluctance of would-be patrons to honour their traditional duties as benevolent housekeepers. Household expenditure and the high costs of living ('drudaniaeth') placed patronage at greater risk than any change of heart among the *uchelwyr*. Another significant factor was the vulnerability of the native squire in his position as the cultural leader as well as his ability to command the support of his community. 'If riches increase', it was said by one leading landowner in a period of economic recession, 'they are increased that spend them, and what good have I thereof: none at all but a great care and cark to receive them and to lay them out again.'[101] Enlightened patrons were defined in eulogy as they who, regardless of financial stringency, endeavoured to meet their obligations. Edward Brwynllys, for example, sang to Hwmffre Huws of Gwerclas in Merioneth in 1609 admiring his hospitality in days of high prices: the portals of his houses were still open to the destitute, the poet maintained, and his heavy expenditure, which could, in periods of economic stress, undermine his landed power, did not deter him from keeping his reputation and performing his duties honourably.

> Pan aeth beth drudaniaeth dro
> A'r gweiniaid yn oer gwyno . . .
> Er cloi o swrn, Werclys oedd
> Yn agored iawn gaeroedd.[102]

These lines contain social comment in the sense that the poet identifies a specific economic reason for the decline in patronage at local level rather than denouncing vaguely the niggardly attitudes of the gentry in general. 'When prices were high and the weak in dire straits', the poet cheerfully maintains, 'Gwerclys was still open to me and my colleagues.' The increasing tendencies to borrow money and depend on the goodwill and forbearance of the London moneylenders created more difficulties than they solved and often hindered the landowners from honouring their debts. Tomas Brwynllys focused some of his lines on that very point when referring to the financial encumbrances which often lay heavily on the Welsh gentry. They were unable to maintain their estates, he explained, because of their increasing dependence on London moneylenders, and the dead times of the year when ready cash was extremely scarce in the Welsh countryside.

> Llawn travael yw r dyn haelwych
> Ar okrwr ydiw r gwr gwych
> Gwaed isel a godysent,
> A sy yn pryny pob rent.[103]

'The truly generous man is sorely troubled', the *cwndidwr* maintains, 'and the usurer is become the great man.' 'Low blood has been exalted', he continued, 'and is buying up every rent.' These bitter comments on the economic realities of late sixteenth-century Wales illustrate how serious a problem economic deficiencies and perils were to this antiquated bardic order. Such lines expressed the dangers which could stem from two major problems, the desire among modest gentry for a standard of living well beyond their reach and the crippling effects of a backward rural economy on progressive families who wished to improve their social status and prestige. The references to the niggardly and grudging attitudes of the gentry may represent a gross misunderstanding of the situation. It is a fact that the majority of the landed families in Wales were very modestly placed and that their material means were inferior to their counterparts elsewhere in other more prosperous areas of the realm. They were often on the breadline themselves and it is not surprising that patronage, in periods of financial stress, should consequently suffer.

> Cybydd ni rydd ddim o'i eiddo,
> Ef a gasgl aur rhudd i gael eu cuddio.[104]

The picture drawn of the miser who hoards properties and 'red gold' and who gives nothing away reveals a deep-seated disaffection on the part of poets, amateur and professional, towards the rapacious tendencies among grasping lay gentry, particularly moneylenders and borrowers and their clients in those days.

Such lines, of course, could be seriously misinterpreted since financial hardship did often handicap the most eligible among the gentry who battled to maintain their reputations as estate-owners. The accumulation of capital was needed as a backup in periods of stress but was not readily available. Several elegaic compositions set out to contrast the honourable bounty received from the deceased patron to the bleak outlook elsewhere in Wales. Wiliam Llŷn, in his poem for Siôn ap Huw ab Ifan of Bathafarn near Machynlleth, devoted several lines to describe the sorrow and despair experienced on the death of a munificent patron, but went on to extol the virtues which would sustain the family in times of adversity.[105] Such conventions are normal and reveal attempts to judge the individual responses of a variety of *uchelwyr* to the essential needs of society and to assess them on that basis. In another poem, the same poet compared his depressing position after the patron's death to the enjoyment which he had previously experienced. He was destitute and like a cripple without a stick ('Bardd wyf fi heb rodd i fyw . . . fel y crupl heb ffon'). Graphic words indeed but they do not necessarily describe hardship merely in a material sense.[106] The lines are best interpreted as a manifestation of the essential qualities displayed by the resident *uchelwr* in his court and the void which occurred on his departure. As a paragon of excellence he fulfilled an indispensable rôle in community life. That did not imply, of course, that financial stringency did not prevail. The poets are not always clear on that point, and several obscure the fact that very modest gentry struggled to maintain their households, and that those who did entertain in the remoter areas of Wales stretched their meagre resources for that purpose. The general impression given is that all houses, whatever their material means, were expected to offer hospitality.[107] Indeed, in view of the modest incomes of some houses the lavish testimony given by poets to their outlay in the provision of sustenance and entertainment is remarkable but equally questionable. The squire of Caethle in Merioneth is a case in point: Siôn Cain found Siôn Fychan to be an ideal provider, even in dire economic circumstances. His sustained financial aid to minstrels, according to the poet, was unashamedly extravagant and was explained principally by careful management and housekeeping.[108]

Owain Gwynedd, another much-travelled poet, discovered that patrons extended their hospitality as lavishly as their circumstances allowed. He attempted to explain the *malaise* by contrasting the niggardliness of the majority with the genuine humanity of the selected few.[109] Those who refused to perform acknowledged responsibilities, another poet maintained, were unnatural in that they abandoned one of the principal features of their birthright. Simwnt Fychan, whose active years covered periods of social distress in the late sixteenth century, composed odes which poignantly emphasized economic stress and impoverishment. He sang, for example, to Sir John Salusbury and described, in the most lavish manner, how he maintained expensive hospitality in his three mansions at Lleweni, Berain and in the town of Denbigh. He was more fortunate than others who were seriously hit by the economic blight and who were forced to abandon their houses and livings. Sir John, it was observed, unlike others who were mean and parsimonious, gave to poets and other dependants gold and silver at frequent intervals.

> Trwy gost . . . llawer sy'n waeth,
> A ordeiniodd ddrudaniaeth;

Ar gil aed ryw galedion
O'u tai y flwyddyn ddrud hon.[110]

The escalating costs of living, the poet remarked, had impoverished many, and he added that some had retreated elsewhere (probably to London) from their houses, chiefly in the depressed 1590s. 'It is better for a gentleman to become impoverished', Wiliam Llŷn explained, 'than for him to neglect his duties and responsibilities to those totally dependent upon him'. His epigrammatic style succinctly summarized the situation.

Gwell i ŵr golli arian
Na cholli gweddi'r dyn gwan.[111]

His plea signifies how crucial it was for the landlord to maintain the trust and support of his tenants and others who sought his protection. 'It is better for a man to lose his money', he commented, 'than lose the poor man's prayer'. There are echoes in some of Wiliam Llŷn's poems of the plight of peasant folk whose circumstances and prospects were even more gloomy, which suggests that he, more than other poets of his generation, excepting possibly Edwart ap Raff and others of his *milieu*, had valued this rare concept of organic social unity.

Gruffudd Phylip, again voicing a similar opinion, but in a different context, laid emphasis on family honour and the gentry's sense of vocation ('Mawr ei rym . . . Mawr ei dir a mwy'i air da').[112] Personal reputation counted for much, and the 'credit', so often referred to and revered by the gentry, was a prime feature in their studied assessments of others. It was inextricably bound to the concept of the inalienable birthright which they were instructed to respect and preserve. It formed the essence of the behavioural patterns which they so readily adopted and honoured in private and public life.

In spite of financial stringency, therefore, the period c. 1540-1640 saw significant visible changes in the Welsh countryside. The rise of some landed families to positions of economic power, however modest their estates might have been, is recounted, often in elaborate detail, in *awdl* and *cywydd* alike.[113] To the poets it symbolized a spirit of grandeur unsurpassed by anything of that nature that had gone before. Poems provide lengthy descriptions of ostentatious and sophisticated life in the halls of gentry, giving the impression that their material resources for this purpose were unlimited.

> Ni ochelud na chiliaw
> Arbed traul ar y byd draw,
> A hyn nid oedd o'r ran dau
> Yn yr oes un awr eisiau.[114]

In spite of economic stress this patron, the poet maintains, never eschews his responsibilities and is continually at hand to sustain all who are in need. An idealistic view of circumstances, perhaps, but nevertheless a pattern in poetic imagery which perpetuated the traditional concept of *uchelwriaeth* and doubtless presented an authentic portrayal of the remaining few among the smaller Welsh gentry who continued to foster good relations with existing poets.

The importance given to the status and maintenance of the goodly house where bounty was freely distributed to the poor implied that the quality of *perchentyaeth* was superior to any threatening attempts to dislodge the family's ascendancy. It is clear that a small band of Welsh gentry did use what resources they had available to buttress their standing in the community, and it is equally evident that the free use of ready money, to which several poets occasionally refer, in fact related to the charges involved in estate management. On the death of Gruffudd Fychan II of Corsygedol, Siôn Phylip excitingly sang his praises. He had served as sheriff of his shire in the years 1588 and 1603, had rebuilt most of his *plasty* in 1592-3 and had erected the family chapel as part of Llanddwywe parish church in 1615. The poet recalled that, in spite of all financial pressures, he did not practice coercion or extortion nor did he misappropriate public monies entrusted to him. On the contrary, he used them for the benefit of his community.[115] Whether or not this reputably worthy benefactor did in fact attend diligently to his duties there is no doubt that the marriage alliances, which were confidently arranged among the most substantial families, did ease the burdens of estate-management and augmented their landed power. Ann, daughter and heiress of Lewis Gwyn of Dolau Gwyn, married Gruffudd Nannau III, and her dowry added significantly to his estate and served to promote his interests. Siôn Cain was not slow in seizing the opportunity to stress these material benefits after Dolau Gwyn lands had been added to the Nannau inheritance.[116] In such a situation the opulent housewife or widow was generously disposed to deploy her financial resources to aid others. This was the testimony of all poets. Wiliam Cynwal, referring to Gaenor, wife of Huw Gwyn Bodfel of Llŷn, a leader among the anti-Leicester group in the Forest of Snowdon dispute (1575-8), applauded her sustenance ('lluniaeth') and her open-hearted generosity. The description is indeed delightful in the manner in which the poet depicts an efficient gentlewoman who was fully in charge of household affairs.[117]

Such a convention was broadly adopted by several other poets who magnified the firm partnership which exemplified gracious living. Deference and moral affluence ('golud', 'ffyniant') were reflected in gentry life and conduct. Its splendour and character radiated brilliantly in the area surrounding the mansion house.

> Ni werthai'r gŵr nerthwr gwan
> Ei gâr er aur ag arian;
> Caredig i'r câr ydoedd . . .
> Y goludog mewn gloywdeb.[118]

He was prosperous ('goludog'), principally because of his innate goodness ('daioni'), and luxurious as befitted a munificent gentleman ('Gŵr iraidd hael gorau ryw'); he was astute and richly-endowed ('goludog a glew') and the notable chief ox in the furrow ('ych bôn goludog').[119] Such a person, in bardic dimensions, projected a totally different kind of prosperity from that which characterized the avaricious and grasping dealer. He would rather enlighten and enrich his countryside by his exemplary character.

> Gŵr da rhwydd a geirda rhawg
> A wna'i wlad yn oludawg.[120]

Prosperity, the poet reminded the *uchelwr*, sprang chiefly from good stock, virtuous living and sustained communal service.

Economic affliction, however, did harass all sections of the community in varying degrees. Circumstances bore hard on landlords and tenants alike. In addition to estate management attention had to be given to matters relating to education, taxation, domestic needs as well as other incidental expenses. Furthermore, bad harvests and food shortages caused unease and destitution. It is not surprising that poets underlined the impoverishment of the needy ('gweiniaid'), the under-privileged, the innocent and uninitiated ('gwirion') as well as the capacity of the *bonheddig* to sustain them. The poets very rarely referred to the labouring ranks exclusively but they did support the close relationship which existed between landlord and tenant. The services rendered by dependants who were tied to the soil were regarded as indispensable in that they formed an essential component in the organic structure of communal life.

> Arddwr i hau'r ddaear hon
> Er daioni i'r dynion.[121]

The labourer who tilled the soil, it was observed, performed his task for the good of men. Whereas goodness was interpreted in an essentially different context for the *uchelwr*, nevertheless, a bond of unity is implied in the bardic exposition of the corporate features of the social entity. In this context, the *uchelwr* was described as the protector of the weak ('cadw'r gwan'). the provider for the poor ('A chadw'r gwŷr a chodi'r gwan') and the chief benefactor of his parish ('Da fu i'w blwy').[122] Relations between landlords and tenants varied and several poets became aware of the need for the privileged to respect the rights of those who served them. The portrayal of patrons as keepers of their communities, in this period of serious economic recession, stemmed largely from a strong sense of communal responsibility. The death of a leading landowner was interpreted essentially as the demise of controlled authority and sustenance. It was by God's will and the agreement of his peers, one poet maintained, that the individual prospered. God had given him grace to the exclusion of others and, with common consent, he was allowed to rule unchallenged over his region. It was basically this divine and social contract which assured him his hegemony.

> 'Wyllys daionus dynion
> A llaw Dduw sy'n llwydd i Siôn,
> Daeth gras, bo Duw i'th groesi,

Rhagor neb, yn d'wyneb di.
Rhuwlio'r wlad y bu'r tadau tau,
Rheol eich iaith, rhuwliwch chwithau.[123]

The goodwill of men and God's grace, more than anything else, the poet explains, enabled the *uchelwr* eulogized in this poem to rule the country as had his forefathers. Much of this kind of poetry was composed in the early or advanced stages of the withdrawal of patronage. It was evident to Morus Berwyn that Gruffudd Fychan II of Corsygedol was exemplary in his diligent attention to duty since he had resisted the temptation to change tenants or deprive them of their livings, to raise rents and practise extortion. Only the oppressive, it was said, would double the rent ('rhai cwmbrus barus . . . a ordria dyblu ardreth').[124] The perfect master was often compared favourably with Moses ('Moesen'), the giver of justice, and functioned in the common interest ('daioni cyffredinol'). The dangers of oppressive government alerted the poets to emphasize the virtues of regional custodianship. Aggressive and unprincipled tax-collectors, usurers and businessmen were attacked principally because of their inclinations to abuse their power and authority. Among these poets Edwart ap Raff, Edmwnd Prys, Siôn Tudur and Tomas Prys, Plas Iolyn, were the most outspoken.[125] Their social comment significantly focused on dire hardship and oppression, even subversive activity. They were evidently aware of the sharp practices of ambitious gentry, frequently in times of economic rigour. The years 1535, 1551, 1563, 1586-7, 1596-7 and 1623 were particularly harsh in purely economic terms. Edwart ap Raff's description of 1597—a critical year since three successive harvest failures had reached their climax at that time—drew attention to the increase in the price of wheat to sixty shillings a quarter. He provided a graphic picture of indigence among the lower orders in Welsh society. The ode is addressed to those 'churls' who had profited at the expense of the poor, and dwelt on the advantages given to the opulent and unscrupulous. 'For three months of this heavy summer season', the poet maintained, 'corn is expensive but oddly the rich are able to manipulate the situation' ('Tri mis haf trwm . . . Drud yw'r ŷd . . . Ond rhyfedd ... I gywaethog ei weithiaw').[126] References appear elsewhere to negligence, oppression, frequent absenteeism on the estates and malicious litigation at Ludlow, the seat of the Council in the Marches, and London.

> Llawer sy'n mynd yn lluoedd . . .
> Yn gecrus, gwmbrus eu gwaith;
> Yn gyfrwys yn y gyfraith . . .
> Ledled oedd i Lwydlo deg
> Ac i Lundain gu landeg.[127]

Such lines graphically describe the invidious activities of lawyers, administrators and litigants who enriched themselves by manipulating the law, in various ways, to suit their pockets. 'Many go in large groups to Ludlow and London', the poet scathingly remarks, 'and are devious and querulous in their dealings in legal matters.' This excellent satire on current trends, which followed social advance ment, does reflect significantly on the less attractive aspects of gentry life in the Tudor and early Stuart periods.

The consequences, according to bardic testimony, were devastating: economic recession, social deprivation, increased anglicization and the gradual alienation of the most eligible among the providers of sustenance from their native communities. The root cause of such a misfortune, it was considered, was miserliness, cupidity and extortion ('Cas unpwnc . . . Can bawddyn mewn cybyddieth').[128] An ardent plea was addressed to all virtuous gentlemen to lead and protect their tenants from the oppressions of others.

> Y cryf ar gwrs crafu'r gwan
> Ar drallod ordr âi allan;
> Dwyn cywoeth y dyn cywir,
> Trin dost, ac entrio'n ei dir.[129]

The poet deplores the oppression suffered by the needy and other victims of economic extortion among modest landed gentry. 'The tyrannous and overpowering', he says, 'scrape what they can from the destitute poor and, by entering upon his lands, deprive the true gentleman of his livelihood.'

Siôn Tudur was painfully aware of the dangers which might distort or even destroy the image of gentility. In his address to Siôn

Conwy of Botryddan he strongly counselled him to respect his breeding and to act accordingly, and further appealed to his good sense to maintain his loyalties to the Crown and his native dependants. It is a powerful composition which has, as its main theme, the oppressive tactics of slanderers ('athrodwyr') and moneylenders ('usurwyr'), and the poet counsels the young heir to act discreetly and consider the best interests of his people.[130] 'The poor man's prayer', it was said, 'has preserved your father's inheritance for you'. By divine sanction he had received innate skills to perform his duties commendably; it was his responsibility to nourish them for the common good. 'Nobility without virtue and wisdom', Roger Ascham maintained, 'is blood indeed, but blood truly without bones and sinews; and so of itself without the other very weak to bear the burden of weighty affairs.'[131] To act impetuously, the poet maintained, will not benefit the heir, and he is advised to crawl before walking ('cropio raid . . . Cyn cerdded'). Calmly, he will cultivate the art of good government. If wrath is justified then it should be directed towards passionate and irate oppressors ('cosba'r dig').[132] If men must suffer, the poet continued, he should not be among them because he deserves to enjoy his fortune. Siôn Conwy, he maintained further, should act rationally and equitably, oppose his enemies, support his kindred and perform his duties uprightly as a wise and chosen statesman ('Doeth wladwr detholedig').[133] This poem is a powerful attempt to attack the ills of the time, namely, greed, ill-will and wilful ambition. It is in such circumstances, Siôn Tudur observes, that the propitious governor should emerge as the champion of justice. This major theme appeared in several odes composed to congratulate new heirs on entering upon their inheritance and on attaining official rank in the shire.

> Na thrasom waith na thrais mawr,
> Nâd ar dy wlad o ledwg
> Dreth drom na gwladwriaeth drwg.[134]

'Do not allow oppressive, heavy taxation or inefficient government to lie heavily on your region', the poet requested: subversion of any kind will destroy communal unity and the integrity of those appointed to preserve it. The poet, in this instance, urged the heir not to act arrogantly; he should eschew covetousness, flattery and slander, and his demeanour should match his status. He should also be honourable in speech and action and resemble his forbears in all good things.

Nâd hiraeth yn y tiroedd
Am dy dad, pen dwywlad oedd;
Nâd trwy dyst a natur dau,
Un mis arnom ei eisiau.[135]

The emphasis on the rôle of prestigious *antecessores* is a cue to lines of this kind. 'Let us not long for your father in the land', the poet exclaims, 'and let us not feel need for him even for one month.' This ardent plea to the heir demands that he maintain the probity of his predecessor in his position as regional custodian.

Siôn Tudur, likewise, counselled Siôn Salusbury of Rug, charging him to shun all manner of unworthy practices in his legal dealings with others and to protect the weak. Exploitation for personal gain was doubtless a profitable avenue for many in public office and enabled them to rise unchallenged in their respective areas, not because they were virtuous but because they placed greed and ambition before all else. The distinct features of the kindred persisted, and the build-up of estates involved constant backbiting and intense rivalry. Hereditary rights were still claimed by proprietors in pasture and waste and there was also a fervent belief in the indestructibility of rights to land. Conflicts arose out of disputes concerning common rights and enclosure between Crown farmers and free tenants.[136] Over and above these territorial matters stood the principle of primogeniture which ousted younger sons from the inheritance and created more fractious dissension between kinsmen. Such fluid conditions in landed affairs led to legal wrangling inside and outside courts of law. Such discord, in bardic opinion, endangered the concepts which had been so fervently upheld in verse over many generations.[137] It is this picture of the immutable and sturdy protector of values, moulded in an image which Sir Thomas Elyot described in *The Governor*, which reflects his devotion to duty. On a higher plane emerged the social and moral values that set the seal of excellence on all who claimed legitimate *uchelwriaeth*. Sir John Salusbury of Lleweni was highly esteemed by Rhosier Cyffin because of four prime virtues ('doniau glân') which he cherished, namely wisdom, strength of purpose, power and justice, the attributes which facilitated the performance of essential obligations to the community and the body politic of the realm with equal dexterity.[138] It is he who, in the last resort, maintains justice at all levels, who ultimately comes to terms fully with his gentility and who masters the art of gracious living. Material gain doubtless assumed a significant rôle in the keeping up of appearances among the gentry, but the poets insisted that it be controlled; the essence of power, in their view, lay in the unchanging and steadfast character of the courteous and gracious gentleman ('Y gŵr aeddfed gwareiddfwyn'). Wisdom in speech, one poet remarked, was more honourable than the accumulation of gold ('Geiriau doeth gwell nag aur da').[139] Siôn Tudur, likewise, expressed similar sentiments when he advised a patron to cherish his kinsmen and not, like the miser, accumulate gold.[140] In an age when the threat to honourable *uchelwriaeth* lay essentially in the inability of an increasing number of gentry to attend to the basic moral and cultural needs of their people the concept of effective leadership was totally abandoned. It is in those circumstances that destructive materialism was at variance with the spirit of honour and moral integrity as conceived in the integrated social structure of Wales. It is this fundamental clash of interests which emerges in bardic eulogy from the late sixteenth-century onwards as a symbol of moral degeneration. Nostalgic excursions were often made into the past when *uchelwyr* were resident. To the poets moral propriety transcended all, as Owain Gwynedd showed in one of his *cywyddau mawl*.

> Gŵr oedd ef gwaraidd afael—
> Gair bery i hwn—gŵr brau hael;
> Gŵr a dyfai, gair difeth,
> Gair mwy parch, gŵr ym mhob peth.
> Gŵr da'i air, gŵr dierwin,
> Gŵr rhwydd draul, gŵr hawdd ei drin . . .
> Gŵr didwyll, gŵr da ydoedd,
> Gwir be byw, gŵr i bawb oedd.[141]

'He was a civilized person', it was observed, 'skilled, respected, honest and dependable in all matters.' This *uchelwr* was easily approachable, affable in his manner and a sincere person beloved by all. It is clearly a focus on the civil and urbane attributes of the sane and poised man of affairs. This extract concentrates on the essence of the good *uchelwr* and emphasizes the attributes of honour, status, probity, versatility and *sprezzatura* often sponsored by the Renaissance gentleman. He was a man who commanded total affection; sincere, flexible, amiable and innately good, indeed, a man for all seasons and for all men. It is in this context, primarily, that the true gentleman, despite significant social and economic trends, maintained his reputation. It was in such challenging circumstances that his endurance and perspicacity were highlighted. His sturdiness created a sense of cohesiveness in his shire ('Uniondeb dros wyneb sir')and incorporated the spirit of national political unity ('Synnwyr teyrnas ei hunan').[142] His actions, in other words, kept at bay the most menacing effects of social disintegration.

It was in these respects that *uchelwriaeth* was manifested and also exposed itself at its most vulnerable. The professional poets, in the last resort, were concerned about their own welfare and standard of living. Their constant appeals to patrons to heed the signs of the times and fortify themselves against the threats of material exploitation cast serious doubts on the abilities of the bardic fraternity to fulfil its traditional function in Welsh society. It is hardly surprising that some poets were prepared to betray their art and destroy their reputation by giving pedigrees to unworthy men. Dire economic conditions did endanger the survival of patronage; so also did the rise of the *nouveaux riches* who deprived the bardic order of its lifeblood.

This was largely indicative of current trends. New recruits to the ruling class had succeeded principally by advancing themselves in law, commerce, military life and administration. Older concepts of paternalism were gradually fading since they presupposed an inegalitarian, unchanging and rigidly hierarchical social order dominated by the *élite*. The *noblesse oblige* had governed English and Welsh life in the sixteenth century but potent economic factors had led to individuals infiltrating the towns to consolidate their fortunes and extend their social contacts. This was a feature which ultimately changed the structure of gentility, as Humphrey Llwyd and George Owen of Henllys had noticed in Wales, and Sir Thomas Smith and other commentators in England: 'a King of Heralds', Smith maintained, 'shall give him [i.e. an upstart] for money, arms newly made and invented, the title whereof shall pretend to have been found by the said Herald in perusing and viewing of old registers . . . Such men are called sometimes in scorn gentlemen of the first head'.[142] Smith did not deplore the practice but was, at the same time, well aware of the onerous obligations placed on such individuals to maintain their newly-acquired status. The older concepts failed to appeal chiefly because they did not flexibly accommodate themselves to the new forces with regard to conspicuous consumption and the methods of estate management in a new dynamic age. Likewise in Wales, on a more modest scale, the rise in status of legal and commercial families in the prospering towns added an extra dimension to *uchelwriaeth*, thus threatening the integrity of conservative notions which strictly adhered to the principle of deference to the privilege of birth.

The sixteenth-century treatise known as *Graduelys*, expounded the Great Chain of Being and concentrated on traditional values and virtues associated with *uchelwriaeth.*[144] It should be maintained, it was said, because of its dignified attachments and the magnanimity of mind and nobility of actions possessed by those who were considered worthy of it, qualities which 'upstarts of the first head', as Sir John Wynn of Gwydir described them, could never cultivate.[145] Siôn Tudur had perceived how trends were shaping, and expressed his fear that gentlemen in his days were in danger of losing a sense of vocation and prepared to apply and accept inferior standards in place of true gentility.

Pob taeog a'n cyflogai,
Peidiwn, gwybyddwn ein bai.
Onis trown ystryw ennyd
Ni chawn ni barch yn y byd.[146]

'Every churl would employ us', the poet commented bitterly: 'let us quit and perceive our crime for, unless we change our ways now, the world will not respect us.' It was a futile plea to prevent the tide of materialism from destroying all that was considered worthy in the ancient bardic lore.

In a similar vein Edmwnd Prys attacked Wiliam Cynwal and other professional poets of his generation for prostituting their craft.

A chanu a chloch weniaith
Iachau ar gam (och o'r gwaith!),
A rhoi arfau rhyw aurfainc
I frig coed afrywiog cainc,
A rhoi mawl i rhi' milwyr
I rai mân o ddirym wŷr.[147]

Prys's aim was to inspire the traditionalist poets to introduce humanist learning and godliness based on the Bible into their compositions. As a Christian scholar of the Renaissance Edmwnd Prys endeavoured in vain to appeal to a cultural order which considered it totally impracticable to modify its structure.

The 'beilchion' ('proud ones') and 'trawswyr' ('oppressors') referred to by Siôn Tudur and his fellow poets were those individuals who had, by means of their business acumen and good fortune, acquired offices which, at a time of rising prices and hardship, strengthened their positions to oppress the weak. This concept of possessive individualism and the shift which occurred in the *locus* of community life were concerns which caused Siôn Tudur, himself a man experienced in landed and administrative affairs, much anxiety since he was aware of the danger which transitions in society posed for the bardic order as well as for the image of *uchelwriaeth*. Who were the poets who transgressed by granting false pedigrees? They were, according to the petition submitted to the Council in the Marches in 1567 seeking permission to hold a second *eisteddfod* at Caerwys, 'vagrant and idle persons, naming themselves Minstrels, Rithmers and Bards' who discouraged 'expert minstrels and musicians in tongue' from practising their craft. The highest order of poets sang to individuals who had prospered in trade and commerce, asserting in their odes that a combination of good pedigree and tenacity in their private dealings had contributed immensely to their prestige as *uchelwyr*.[148] Siôn Tudur, among others, greeted entrepreneurs and soldiers such as Sir Richard Clough, Sergeant Pyrs and Siôn Gruffudd of Caerwys, and Richard Myddelton for that very reason. They were acclaimed as practical enterprising men, wise in the ways of the world, on condition that they conformed to the basic requirements of the medieval concept of *uchelwriaeth*. Nevertheless, in view of increasing tendencies to denigrate the bardic craft, a further—albeit unsuccessful—petition was submitted to the Council in the Marches in 1594 with a view to holding yet another assembly of bards. The poets and their mentors by then were clearly aware of the humiliation suffered at the hands of inferior rivals, and in that dire situation strict-metre composition had to compete with free-metre verse that was becoming more popular as a medium for social comment. Siôn Tudur himself used free-metre for satirical purposes but the professional poets generally deplored its growing popularity. Edwart ap Raff, in his ode for Wiliam Midleton, and Rhisiart Phylip of Ardudwy, in an *englyn*, dismissed this new trend as unworthy because it undermined all that was considered essential to safeguard bardic conventions. The poets feared that to lose their credibility in the community which had nurtured them and their predecessors over the centuries would be the most disastrous event in the history of the bardic system.

It was this loss of face which caused anxiety to the most highly respected exponents of eulogistic verse in late-sixteenth and early seventeenth-century Wales. Other threats as well caused concern among them, such as the danger posed by newer methods of practising genealogy and heraldry together with the forces of social and economic change.[149] Their endeavour to preserve what they considered to be the fundamental bond of unity within community life ('ein hiaith') was being wrecked more damagingly by internal factors in the bardic order itself as well as by modified concepts of *uchelwriaeth* in Wales than by other forces from outside. The poetic output of the earlier decades of the seventeenth century revealed succinctly how changing attitudes and responses among the *uchelwyr* themselves were to have permanent consequences for the nature and quality of eulogy.

NOTES

[1]W. O. Williams, 'Social Order in Tudor Wales', 167-78; T. Jones Pierce, 'Landlords in Wales', in J. Thirsk (ed.), *The Agrarian History of England and Wales,* IV, pp. 360-81.

[2]A. D. Carr, 'Historical Background', *Guide to Welsh Literature*, II, pp. 23-33; E. I. Rowlands, 'The Continuing Tradition', ibid. , pp. 308-20; G. Williams, *Recovery, Reorientation and Reformation,* pp. 149-55.

[3]*Gwaith Guto'r Glyn*, XX, p. 56.

[4]HGF, pp. 15-47, 54-7.

[5]'Awdurdod Cyfreithiol', 154-63. See also CSB, LXI, pp. 132-4; Gaianydd Williams, *Casgliad o Gywyddau Siôn Brwynog* (UCNW Gaianydd MS. 21); NBSF, I, lxxviii, II, CCXXI, p. 594, CCLXXII, pp. 596-7.

[6]E. I. Rowlands, *Gwaith Lewys Môn,* LXI, p. 199.

[7]*Gwaith Tudur Aled*, I, V, pp. 29-30; SLl, XXI, p. 176.

[8]*Gwaith Tudur Aled*, I, p. 134.

[9]Ibid., II, LIV, p. 220; J. Gwynfor Jones, 'The Wynn Estate of Gwydir: Aspects of its Growth and Development c. 1500-1580', NLWJ, XXII, 1981, 320-35.

[10]*Gwaith Tudur Aled*, II, LVII, p. 229.

[11]NBM, pp. 23, 82.

[12]*Statutes of Wales*, pp. 122-3.

[13]GWC(1), I, XLV, p. 157, XLIX, p. 171.

[14]Ibid., LXII, p. 217.

[15]CLl, p. 96.

[16]GEUGH, VII, p. 38.

[17]BWLl, XIV, pp. 32-3.

[18]GST, I, XXXVI, p. 151.

[19]W. O. Williams, *Cal. Caerns Quarter Sessions Records*, lix-lxiii.

[20]NBSF, II, CCCCVIII, p. 883.

[21]NBM, p. 87.

[22]NBSF, II, CCCI, p. 662.

[23]Ibid. , I, XLIII, pp. 98-100, II, CCC, p. 660; B. Jones, 'Beirdd yr Uchelwyr a'r Byd', *Ysgrifau Beirniadol*, VIII, pp. 29-42.

[24]NBM, p. 118.

[25]NBSF, II, CCII, p. 449.

[26]CLl, pp. 111-2.

[27]Cf GST, I, V, pp. 18-21; E. Roberts, 'Cywydd Cymod Hwmffre ap Hywel ap Siencyn a'i Geraint', *Journal of the Merioneth Historical and Record Society*, IV, 1964, 302-17.

[28]GST, I, XIV, p. 53; SLl, CIV, p. 440.

[29]NBSF, II, CCXXII, p. 488.

[30]GOG, I, XXVI, p. 92, LI, p. 171.

[31]SLl, XCIII, p. 413.

[32]Cardiff MS. 4. 101, 55b.

[33]Ibid., 51b.

[34]Cf. 'Iawn iddo . . . Lywio'i dir yn ôl ei dad. 'GWC(1), II, XIX, p. 598.

[35]NLW Brogyntyn MS. 8, 376.

[36]NLW MS. 9059E. 1088.

[37]UCNW Mostyn MS. 8, 22a.

[38]*Gwaith Tudur Aled*, I, LVII, p. 229.

[39]GWC (Mostyn III), II, CXI, p. 344, CXII, p. 348-9.

[40]A. H. Dodd, *Studies in Stuart Wales*, pp. 1-3, 10-13.

[41]GWC (Mostyn III), I, XV, p. 44; GWC(1), I, XXIII, p. 81.

[42]GST, I, XXVII, pp. 111-2.

[43]Kelso, op. cit. , p. 80.

[44]CLl, p. 99.

[45]CCM, p. 206; SLl, CLXXXVI, p. 615.

[46]'Brogyntyn Welsh Manuscripts', VI, 1949, 13, 37.

[47]GWC(1), II, XXVII, p. 634.

[48]*Penbrokshire*, III, p. 57.

[49]D. E. H. Roberts, 'Noddwyr Beirdd yn Sir Aberteifi', LlC, X, 1968-69, 96, 99.

[50]NBSF, I, XLIII, p. 99.

[51]L. Toulmin Smith (ed.), *The Itinerary in Wales* (London, 1906), e.g. pp. 12-13, 73, 84-5.
[52]GOG, II, XCII, p. 313.
[53]BWLl, XXXV, p. 88; CLI, p. 96.
[54]EP, XCI, p. 338.
[55]NBM, p. 65.
[56]NBSF, II, CCXC, p. 659.
[57]'Hanfodion Undod Gwladwriaethol', 78-82. See also J. Gwilym Jones, 'Cyfnod Olaf y Beirdd yng Ngwedir (1627-74)', pp. 121-30; BGHM, XXXIV, pp. 75-6, XXXV, pp. 76-9.
[58]GSM, XXIX, p. 102.
[59]SLl, LXXXI, p. 386.
[60]NBM, p. 118.
[61]GOG, I, XLVII, p. 155.
[62]'Brogyntyn Welsh Manuscripts', VI, 1949, 1-4; Kelso, *Doctrine for the Lady of the Renaissance*, loc. cit.
[63]CLl, p. 100.
[64]Stone. op. cit., pp. 21-4.
[65]NLW Llansteffan MS. 123, 194.
[66]Kelso, loc. cit.
[67]GWC (Mostyn III), I, XXXV, p. 109.
[68]GST, I, LXI, p. 251.
[69]NBSF, II, CCLXVI, p. 584, GSM, LXXI, p. 230.
[70]NBM. p. 81.
[71]Ibid. , p. 107. See also J. Ballinger, 'Katheryn of Berain', *Y Cymmrodor*, XL, 1929, 11-12, 34-7; E. Roberts, 'Priodasau Catrin o Ferain', *Trans. Denbs. Hist. Soc.*, XX, 1971, 31-56.
[72]GST, I, III, p. 11; NBM, p. 106.
[73]BWLl, XVII, pp. 39-40.
[74]NLW Llansteffan MS. 123, 60. See also ibid., MS. 125, 407.
[75]Cardiff MS. 4. 101, 61b.
[76]'Hanfodion Undod Gwladwriaethol', 95-7.
[77]'Brogyntyn Welsh Manuscripts', VI, 11, 36.
[78]T. Jones Pierce, 'Landlords in Wales', pp. 372-81.
[79]Stone, op. cit., pp. 21-36.
[80]NBSF, I, XIX, p. 39.
[81]'Hanfodion Undod Gwladwriaethol', 34-9.
[82]CLl, p. 112.
[83]Ibid., pp. 63, 65.
[84]J. Thirsk, 'Younger Sons in the Seventeenth Century', *History*, LIV, 1969, 358-77.
[85]GSM, XXXIV, p. 118.
[86]NLW Llansteffan MS. 125, 410.
[87]CLl., p. 112.
[88]SLI, LXXVI, p. 373, LXXVII, p. 376.
[89]BWLI, V, p. 12.
[90]Ibid., XXXIV, p. 85.
[91]GWC(1), II, XXVIII, p. 640.
[92]NLW Cw. MS. 5, 623; R. Geraint Gruffydd, 'Humphrey Llwyd of Denbigh: Some Documents and a Catalogue', *Trans. Denbs. Hist. Soc.*, XVII, 1968, 95; J. Gwynfor Jones, 'Patrymau Bonheddig Uchelwrol yn Sir Ddinbych c. 1540-1640: Dehongliad y Beirdd', ibid., XXIX, 1980, 77. See R. W. McDonald, 'Bywyd a Gwaith Lewis ab Edward' (unpublished M.A. dissertation, University of Liverpool, 1961), p. 117.
[93]Charlton, op. cit., p. 89 et seq.; J. Simon, *Education and Society in Tudor England* (Cambridge, 1967), pp. 333-69; W. P. Griffith, 'Beth oedd y Dyn Tuduraidd?', in D. G. Jones and J. E. Jones (ed.), *Bosworth a'r Tuduriaid* (Caernarfon, 1985), IV, pp. 31-9; idem, 'Schooling

and Society', in *Class, Community and Culture in Tudor Wales*, pp. 79-119. W. Ll. Davies, 'Phylipiaid Ardudwy—a Survey and a Summary', *Y Cymmrodor*, XLII, 1931, p. 208.

[94]'Brogyntyn Welsh Manuscripts', VI, 1949, 35.

[95]NLW MS. 9059E. 1188. See also GST, I, V, pp. 18-21; NBSF, II, CCCXCIII, pp. 852-3.

[96]CLl, p. 114.

[97]*Gwentian Poems of Dafydd Benwyn*, XLIX, p. 26.

[98]MDLlS, II, XVII, p. 513.

[99]BWLl, II, p. 4.

[100]G. D. Owen, *Elizabethan Wales*, pp. 74-89; J. Gwynfor Jones, 'Sir John Wynn and his Tenants: the Dolwyddelan and Llysfaen Land Disputes', WHR, XI, 1982, 1-30.

[101]NLW MS. 9053E. 439.

[102]NBM, p. 100.

[103]L. J. Hopkin-James and T. C. Evans (ed.), *Hen Gwndidau, Carolau a Chywyddau* (Bangor, 1910), C, p. 170.

[104]Ibid., XLII, pp. 59-60, LIX, pp. 97-8, LXI, pp. 99-100, C, pp. 170-2. Cf GST, I, CXLVII, pp. 589-91; CLII, pp. 612-5.

[105]CLl, p. 113-4.

[106]Ibid., p. 111.

[107]E.g. NBM, pp. 11, 23, 62.

[108]Ibid., p. 23.

[109]Ibid., p. 62.

[110]SLl, LXXXVIII, p. 400.

[111]BWLl, XXXVII, p. 93.

[112]NBM, p. 14.

[113]E. Wiliam, "Let Use be Preferred to Uniformity'; Domestic Architecture' in *Class, Community and Culture in Tudor Wales*, pp. 159-93; P. Smith, 'Architecture in Wales during the Renaissance', *Celts and the Renaissance*, VI, pp. 101-13.

[114]BWLl, XXXVI, p. 90.

[115]NBSF, I, XLI, p. 92.

[116]Ibid., I, CXXXII, p. 299.

[117]GWC (Mostyn III), II, III, pp. 344-5. Among the poets who supported the anti Leicester group in north Wales at that time were Cadwaladr Cesail, Edmwnd Prys, Morus Dwyfech, Huw Llŷn and Huw ap Rhisiart of Cefnllanfair, CLl, pp. 154, 182-3; *Council in the Marches of Wales*, pp. 237-9.

[118]CLI, p. 124.

[119]Ibid., p. 171; CCM, p. 288, NBSF, II, CCCIII, p. 666; CCM, p. 288.

[120]NBSF, II, CCLXIII, p. 578.

[121]GOG, II, LXXXIII, p. 280.

[122]GWC (Mostyn III), I, IX, p. 28; II, CI, p. 313.

[123]SLl, LXXXIII, p. 389.

[124]NBSF, I, XXXI, p. 67.

[125]Cf. GST, I, CV, pp. 602-5; *Oxford Book of Welsh Verse*, CXX, pp. 244-8; *Hen Gwndidau*, C, pp. 170-2.

[126]D. J. Bowen, 'Y Cywyddwyr a'r Dirywiad', 453-62; J. G. Jones, 'Beirdd yr Uchelwyr a'u Cymdeithas, 1540-1640', in G. H. Jenkins (ed.), *Cof Cenedl; Ysgrifau ar Hanes Cymru*, II, pp. 29-60.

[127]'Brogyntyn Welsh Manuscripts', VI, 225-6, 242; *Studies in Stuart Wales*, pp. 7-9.

[128]D. H. E. Roberts and R. A. Charles, 'Raff ap Robert ac Edwart ap Raff', BBCS, XXIV, 1971, 295.

[129]Ibid., NLW, R. A. Charles, 'Gwaith Edwart ap Raff'' (Casgliad Teipiedig, 1970), pp. 89-90, 201.

[130]GST, I, V, p. 19.
[131]Charlton, op. cit., p. 79.
[132]GST, I, V, pp. 19-20.
[133]Ibid., p. 20.
[134]NBSF, I, XIX, p. 39.
[135]Ibid.
[136]T. I. Jeffreys Jones (ed.), *Exchequer Proceedings concerning Wales in Tempore James I* (Cardiff, 1955), xv-xviii; T. Jones Pierce, 'Notes on the History of Rural Caernarvonshire in the Reign of Elizabeth', *Medieval Welsh Society*, pp. 61-85.
[137]GST, I, V, pp. 18-21.
[138]SLl, CXXXIII, p. 513.
[139]GEUGH, XV, p. 76.
[140]GST, I, V, p. 21.
[141]GOG, I, LXIV, pp. 213-4.
[142]NBSF, I, XLI, p. 92.
[143]Smith, *De Republica Anglorum,* p. 28.
[144]*Gramadegau'r Penceirddiaid*, pp 198-9; *Guide to Welsh Literature*, II, p. 90.
[145]HGF, p. 34.
[146]GST, I, CLI, p. 608.
[147]*Ymryson Edmwnd Prys a Wiliam Cynwal,* XXVI, pp. 197-8; Lewis, *Braslun o Hanes Llenyddiaeth Gymraeg,* pp. 105-8; G. E. Ruddock, 'Siôn Cent', in *Guide to Welsh Literature*, II, pp. 183-7; R. M. Jones, 'Pwnc Mawr Beirniadaeth Lenyddol Cymraeg', in *Llên Cymru a Chrefydd*, V, pp. 211-21.
[148]D. J. Bowen, *Gruffudd Hiraethog a'i Oes,* pp. 63-4; J. G. Evans, *Reports on Manuscripts in the Welsh Language* (London, 1898), I, pp. 291-2.
[149]F. Jones, 'An Approach to Welsh Genealogy', *Trans. Cymmr.*, 1948, 365 et seq.

Conclusion

In 1587, Robert ab Ifan, a modest gentleman from Brynsiencyn in Anglesey, commented sadly on the declining standards of the bardic order. 'The thief is far better off', he remarked, 'because he is able to mix freely with prominent burgesses and has money to spend': 'a'r gŵr wrth gerdd', he maintained further, 'a gaiff rodio yma a thraw heb un yn cynnig cwmpnïaeth iddo rhag ofn talu trosto achos mae pawb yn cilio rhagddo ac yn tynnu o'r neilltu rhag ennill gair da y gŵr wrth gerdd.'[1] 'The poet', it is said, 'is allowed to wander here and there and no one offers him company in case they have to remunerate him.' 'Everyone hides away from him', it is further said, 'to avoid having to accept his eulogy.' This comment contains two significant truths relating to the social structure of Wales as it affected the poets at the close of the sixteenth and opening decades of the following century. In the first instance, attention is drawn to the greater respect enjoyed by lawbreakers than by honest declaimers of song struggling to earn an honest living, which is indeed a scathing comment on adverse economic conditions in the late Elizabethan period. Also, it is claimed, there was a total disregard for those who had endeavoured to maintain concepts of society considered by then to be wholly anachronistic. So much had occurred in Tudor society during the half century between the Acts of Union and the outbreak of war with Spain—underlying changes in religion, the economy, government and administrative development—each deeply affecting Wales in its relations with the English state. In Wales itself the bardic order was looked upon increasingly with derision and contempt. Writing in 1595, in his preface to his translation of Bishop John Jewel's *Apologia Ecclesiae Anglicanae*, Morus Kyffin remarked scornfully on their lack of learning and initiative in saving the language.[2] Siôn Dafydd Rhys, that renowned Roman Catholic grammarian, endeavoured to save some of their reputation by appealing to them in an open letter to revive classical traditions in their verse and become re-acquainted with ancient learning.[3]

The proposed reform of the order, as envisaged by the humanist scholars, which entailed recasting eulogy in the same mould as the English concept of gentility and creating a new type of advanced urbane Renaissance poet had, alas, been projected too late. Bardic commentary in *awdl* and *cywydd* alike increasingly referred to a spent tradition no longer viable in a mobile and aggressively materialistic society. Dissolute life, the Anglesey *uchelwr* asserted, was more rewarding at a time when new forces were emerging which rendered formal eulogy irrelevant. One major threat which endangered the integrity of the poetic interpretation of *uchelwriaeth* was the identification of a one-time prestigious institution with poverty and vagrancy. One chief reason for convening the two *eisteddfodau* at Caerwys in 1523 and 1567 was to distinguish between poets who were considered worthy of achieving bardic orders and the imposters who, according to the royal commission which legalized the 1567 *eisteddfod*, were forced to seek employment 'upon pain to be taken as sturdy and idle vagabonds'.[4] It was, in fact, to be the last official attempt to impose some order on the bardic system and to grade practitioners of the craft according to their skills.

The following half century revealed a cultural heritage which was receding further into the background in the Welsh social structure than it had in the formative years following the Acts of Union. The fact that Gruffudd Hiraethog, doubtless the most prominent poet of his generation and the Chief of Song who had left a deep influence on the bardic and heraldic craft, had died three years before this *eisteddfod* was held, is, in itself, a significant milestone in the history of the declining tradition. Excepting his best disciples who attained the highest grade within their order there were no other bardic declaimers who maintained high standards in the early seventeenth century. The renowned Phylip family of Ardudwy in Merioneth, particularly Siôn Phylip, were indeed remarkable for the quality of their output and so were Rhys and Siôn Cain, father and son, from Oswestry. Siôn Cain was the last herald-poet in Wales, but his standards of accomplishment were appreciably lower than those of his father. Their poetry was characterized by a marked degree of insecurity and despair. Siôn Phylip was constantly an acute and percipient observer of his age. If he had lived earlier in the sixteenth century his reputation as a poet doubtless would have matched that of the most prestigious in his profession. Social conditions militated against him and often blunted the appeal of his eulogistic compositions.

This *malaise* also affected other bardic practitioners of Siôn Phylip's generation, and the quality of composition had become increasingly trite and uninspiring. Not only had fundamental changes in attitudes among the more prosperous *uchelwyr* created serious consequences for the bardic order but also lack of initiative among the poets themselves in the early seventeenth century and their inability or ineptitude to put their own house in order had doomed their fragile organization. The *cwrs clera* had lost most of its appeal and, with some notable exceptions, eulogists mechanically regurgitated largely outmoded concepts. Siôn Dafydd Rhys lamented the inability of the poets to reverse the trends which endangered their profession and regrettably recorded that they had been deprived of *eisteddfodau*, privileges and degrees.[5] In his ode to Wiliam Midleton, the famous Welsh Renaissance figure, Edwart ap Raff, a poet of considerable skill and a discerning social commentator, deplored the popularity of carols and verses in free metres which some of the acknowledged professional poets were prepared to compose from the latter half of the sixteenth century onwards.[6] The oft-quoted letter by Wiliam Bodwrda, the copyist of manuscripts, to Siôn Cain in 1647—a critical year in the history of the monarchy and its institutions—focused directly on this central problem.

> Yr ych chwi yn cael y gair (yr hwn nid wyf i yn amau nas haeddech) o fod yn un o'r arwyddfeirdd gorau a mwyaf cyfarwydd. Aml oedd prydyddion gynt a wyddai wir achau ac arfau a gwych weithredoedd boneddigion Cymru. Eithr yn awr, pallu a myned ar goll a wnaeth y gelfyddyd ganmoladwy hon. Heb eich llaw chwi yn unig, ni chlywaf sôn am un arall yn holl Wynedd â gwybodaeth gymedrol ganddo.[7]

The comment is remarkable in that it draws attention to the *malaise* which had plagued cultured society in Wales by that time. 'You have the reputation (which I doubt not that you deserve)', it is said, 'of being one of the best and most accomplished herald poets.' 'Often in the past', Wiliam Bodwrda continues, ' there were poets who knew pedigrees and arms and the excellent deeds of Welsh gentlemen. But now, this worthy craft has failed and disappeared. Excepting your part I do not hear of any other in the whole of Gwynedd who has moderate knowledge of it.' He laments the serious decline in heraldry, and identifies *uchelwyr* of repute with worthy ancestors. Indeed, the letter symbolizes the detachment of the bardic order from its vital rôle in civilized society and underlines the divorce that rapidly was becoming a fact of life in relations between native gentry and the poets. It was indicative of the times that Robert Vaughan, the celebrated antiquary of Hengwrt, had to instruct Siôn Cain in 1632 precisely how he should compose an elegy for Sir Siôn Llwyd of Ceiswyn in Merioneth, a stalwart maintainer of poets and a person of high rank in the legal and administrative world.

> yr ydwyf yn dwyn ar ddallt i chwi mae dvwsvlynyd yr apwyntiwyd i ddyfod a barnadav Sr. Sion llwyd i Aber llwyfeni, mi a ddisyfaf arnoch gymeryd peth gofal yn ych gwaith. och rhann ych hvn, ag o rann y gwr yr ydych yn koffa am danaw, yr hwnn (mi ai gwnn yn dda iawn) a haeddai ar ych llaw chwi, a chwbloll or prydyddion ewyllysgar vyfyrdod a choffadwriaeth am danaw.[8]

'I understand that shrove Sunday has been appointed to compose elegies for Sir John Lloyd at Aberllefenni', Vaughan maintained, 'and I request that you take some care with your work, for your part and in consideration of the gentleman whom you commemorate'. 'He (I know well)', he continued, 'deserves it from you and other willing declaimers who meditate in his memory'. It is clear that the squire of Hengwrt had little confidence in poets, even Siôn Cain, and expressed doubts whether he could compose a genuinely worthy poem to a reputable figure without his assistance. The letter seems to imply that the poets, by that time, had not the resources necessary to do justice to their craft but that eulogy, if well presented, would doubtless mark the event in the most fitting manner. Even in the twilight days of Welsh poetic tradition the grandiloquent bardic tribute was still considered to be the worthiest means of commemorating *uchelwriaeth*.

What had the bardic tradition achieved during this period of transition? Regardless of the changing face of society and the increasing rôle of its leaders in the national sovereign state it firmly remained the mainstay of conservatism. The large *corpus* of composition spanning the century between the Acts of Union and the outbreak of the Civil Wars had concentrated principally on preserving cultural heritage, social harmony and distinctive virtues. It was a period when Renaissance traditions demanded that more attention be given to the positively urbane and sophisticated facets of life in the *plastai* of the Tudor *uchelwyr*. Conscious efforts were made by individual poets, however, to identify the patron as a pattern of excellence within the context of the native community although well-defined elements of the New Learning had subtly crept into their interpretation, thereby offering a more contemporary version of the complete gentleman. The emphasis on the learning ('dysg') of patrons, their association with centres of civilized life and conduct and their endeavour to maintain a standard of living commensurate with others of their *milieu* in the more prosperous areas of the realm emerges prominently in the better quality eulogies which appeared before c. 1600.

Four principal elements characterize the bardic heritage relative to the individual *uchelwr*: intellectual perceptiveness focusing on concepts of the ideal gentleman, the qualities of civility, humanity and grace; notions of Tudor statehood which gave the *uchelwr*, in the broadest sense, the opportunity to emerge progressively as a gentleman of action; the impact of social and economic forces on the quality of life, and the nature and status of gentility as applied to Wales in transition; the cultural *malaise* and the hiatus which emerged between the gentry, as protectors of a communal identity, and self-seeking landed adventurers. All four factors, in varying degrees, highlight the advantages of learning, public function, economic progress and cultural obligation—the four major principles which governed the exercise of regional responsibility and control in Tudor Wales. The main achievement of Welsh poetry in this period was to emphasize what were considered to be the norms of a progressive, acquisitive and competitive society which still retained its distinct identity with native *uchelwriaeth* stemming from the ancient British heritage.

> Coed Brutys dywys Deau—a Gwynedd,
>   O ganol prif lwythau;
> Cael moroedd a'r tiroedd tau,
> Cynnyddfawr yw'r cynneddfau.[9]

The salient features are predictable in this *englyn* by Wiliam Llŷn in his *awdl* for Eliza ab Wiliam Llwyd of Rhiwedog: 'The stock of Brutus leads the chief tribes of Deheubarth and Gwynedd', it maintains, 'and the attributes of lineage and virtue are abundantly increased . . .' The lines again dictate the chief avenues of thought which constituted the essence of the doctrine of gentility in the *corpus* of poetic tribute.

The patron's innate faculties enhanced his prestige as custodian of the prime qualities of justice and moral probity. The bardic dilemma in the early seventeenth century is exposed in the pessimistic outbursts lamenting the forsaken qualities of the tradition, the loss of aristocratic independence in status and function, the lack of initiative to serve the national interests of Wales, and the failure to preserve traditional community values of leadership and justice. It was incumbent upon him, who had assumed the ascendancy in his native region, to employ his skills specifically in community service, to act charitably and offer universal protection. The integrity normally ascribed to the versatile *uchelwr* revealed his sense of public morality and his innate talents in maintaining that lasting bond of unity between ranks and degrees focused on the *plasty*.

It is often considered contradictory that such a well-founded and conservative social institution should have embraced two seemingly divergent standpoints, namely the preservation of pure Welsh gentility and the qualities of the Renaissance governor. The explanation emanates from various strands of thought and social attitudes. In spite of their often antiquated and restricted vision the Welsh poets upheld some well-defined ideals concerned with common moral values. Their experiences of the world about them taught them how to come to terms with those features which were to have indelible effects on the social structure of England and Wales. Furthermore, it was accepted that the principles of eulogy stood apart from other mundane considerations: they were universal and shared by all civilized communities. Justice was paramount, a quality which transcended all other values and hailed by the poets as the most distinctive feature of honourable life. The forces of law and order were also highly regarded, and in eulogistic verse it was expressly desired that the exercise of responsibility, security and good order should be considered a priority in local and regional government. The increasing incidence of intermarriage between gentry families on both sides of Offa's Dyke also inspired the bardic tradition, basically because it underlined yet again the universality of *uchelwriaeth*. Wiliam Llŷn, for example, when addressing John Conwy of Botryddan in Flintshire, whose ancestry stemmed from Anglo-Norman stock, considered his lineage to be exemplary.

> Ni ddiwraidd pren gwyrenig,
> Ni chrina ni freua'i frig.[10]

'Your thriving stock will never be uprooted nor will it erode or wither', the poet maintained when referring to the mixed strata of ancestral forbears which his patron represented, thus exposing how *uchelwriaeth* shared the rare qualities of a common inheritance. The situation as it affected the poets, however, drew attention to different and less hopeful circumstances a generation or so later.

In any examination of the bardic order in its last century it is appropriate to consider aspects which clarify its central rôle in Welsh society. There is a danger, of course, of accepting too readily at face value the responses of the poets to their patrons and applying too rapidly their idealism to the routine daily life of modest gentry often struggling in a harsh and unsympathetic world. In spite of the rigid rules which governed their craft, in days of economic hardship and social reorientation several of the poets did endeavour to present a more realistic portrait of the situation in Wales. They were more prepared to defy convention at a time when the concept of the archetypal *uchelwr* had become blurred. They became more aware of the crisis which had deeply affected them as well as their patrons and cast a more sceptical eye on status, behaviour and attitudes. It is evident that the overall picture portrayed by the poets of heroic qualities and moral rectitude was not realistic nor was it meant to be. The recipients of eulogy doubtless accepted such accolades as being merely the manifestation of convention which they had respected and preserved as an essential part of their inheritance. They were, after all, men of the world with estates to administer, official positions to maintain, families to care for and their own social standing to protect. Doubtless the acclamations were at odds with their normal practices, and to that extent the actions of the unworthy were the norm. It cannot be said, however, that the poets had betrayed their craft because the virtues attributed to individual gentlemen represented the potential which lay in those who possessed the basic features of *uchelwriaeth*. In purely material terms the gentry did act obtrusively and oppressively as the records of courts of law amply prove, and it is evident that some poets were compelled to warn patrons of the dangers to themselves and their dependents of being over-indulgent and high-handed. To that extent poetic evidence needs to be treated discerningly. The historian will find much that is valuable when attempting to broaden perspectives on social and cultural life in Tudor and early Stuart Wales. Nevertheless, impressive *awdlau* and *cywyddau* fall short of being concrete evidence of gentry life in its entirety. Indeed, it had not been the poets' intention to provide such a comprehensive picture; their contribution lies chiefly in demonstrating how convention had survived and had been adapted to the new social environment, how attitudes and reactions among the traditionally 'worthy' had been transformed and how older medieval concepts of *uchelwriaeth* had fared in an age governed by new dynamic pressures. It is possible to extract from this kind of evidence individual strands of development in Welsh cultural society which reveal parallel features in a broader European context and, in that respect, its contribution is positive and constructive.

In all, however, the picture which emerges is gloomy. The rivalries between poets such as Siôn Mawddwy and Meurig Dafydd and Edmwnd Prys and Wiliam Cynwal did not reveal a vibrant and inspired group of bards seeking favour in a wide range of gentry houses but rather a depressing state of anxiety among those who grasped at any opportunity to maintain their livelihood. Whereas in previous generations they had obtained support and sustenance in *plastai* where congenial owners resided permanently and often revealed an expert knowledge of bardic lore, the early decades of the seventeenth century saw a marked degree of absenteeism, changing social attitudes and apathy among an increasing number of Welsh *uchelwyr*. Poets clung desperately to their diminishing resources and, in combat with each other, launched bitter and destructive attacks on their colleagues and the system, thus losing the sympathy of existing patrons and irreparably harming their own and their profession's reputation. Bardic debate, when conducted from a position of strength, was revitalizing and rewarding but, when conducted from a position of weakness, did nothing but totally undermine their credibility.

Although Gruffudd Phylip continued to practice the conventions in his elegy, composed in 1624, for Ffowc Prys, son of Edmwnd Prys, of Tyddyn Du, Maentwrog, much of the zest and exuberance which had characterized his predecessors in the craft was barely recognizable in his *cywydd.* Both father and son, the poet lamented, had contributed overwhelmingly to sustaining the cultural traditions of their province, and their demise had created a void in Maentwrog and the surrounding areas. The couplets are sombre and full of foreboding, contrasting the days of fullness and privilege ('braint') with the vacuous circumstances of the time.

> Hwn a'i dad hynod odiaith
> Oedd yn help i naddu'n hiaith;
> Am ein hiaith, o'u marw weithion,
> Amddifad yw'r hollwlad hon.
> Na bo o'r gri mewn bro Gred
> Fyth gellwair y fath golled . . .[11]

How circumstances had changed. 'He and his remarkable father', the poet observed, 'helped to preserve the language and its culture, which is now orphaned as is the countryside in which they lived.' 'Let us not take this loss lightly in our land', he ominously continued, thus revealing a sense of betrayal as well as bereavement in the land of Merioneth. Then came the anticipated rhetorical question.

> Mae'n lle enwog? mae'n lluniaeth?
> Mae'n rhoddion mawrion a'n maeth?

'Where is the famed residence', he despairingly asked, 'where is our sustenance? Where are our bounteous gifts and where is our nourishment?' The reverberating hollow expressions of gloom and despondency forebodingly sounded the death knell of the medieval bardic structure as well as the fundamental concepts of the Welsh nobility.

NOTES

[1]D. J. Bowen, *Gruffudd Hiraethog a'i Oes*, p. 63. See also by the same author 'Y Cywyddwyr a'r Dirywiad', loc. cit., for an advanced study of bardic decline in this period. See also R. Geraint Gruffydd, 'The Renaissance and Welsh Literature', in *Celts and the Renaissance,* pp. 35-6; Glanmor Williams, 'Dadeni, Diwygiad a Diwylliant Cymru', repr. in *Grym Tafodau Tân*, pp. 63-86.

[2]W. P. Williams (ed.), *Deffynniad Ffydd Eglwys Loegr* (Bangor, 1908), viii-x.

[3]B. Jarvis, 'Llythyr Siôn Dafydd Rhys at y Beirdd', LlC., XII, 1972-3, 45-56.

[4]Gwyn Thomas, *Eisteddfodau Caerwys*, pp. 41, 101-9.

[5]*Gruffudd Hiraethog a'i Oes,* pp. 64-5; Thomas Jones (ed.), *Rhyddiaith Gymraeg,* II, *Llawysgrifau a Llyfrau, 1547-1618* (Cardiff, 1956), pp. 155-60.

[6]*Gruffudd Hiraethog a'i Oes*, pp. 63-5.

[7]Ibid., p. 66.

[8]NBM, p. 35.

[9]CLI, p. 10; D. J. Bowen, 'Canrif Olaf y Cywyddwyr', loc. cit.; 'Welsh Poets and their Patrons', 268-77. J. Gwilym Jones, 'Cyfnod Olaf y Beirdd yng Ngwedir (1627-74)', pp. 121-41.

[10]CLl, p. 62.

[11]NBM, pp. 209-10.

Select Bibliography

This bibliography is restricted to those works which the author considered to be of particular relevance when compiling this volume. Several valuable contributions cited in the notes should also be consulted. For more extensive bibliographical details and further information on original sources readers should consult the following. A. E. Davies (ed.), *Traethodau Ymchwil Cymraeg a Chymreig 1887-1971: Welsh Language and Welsh Dissertations* (Cardiff, 1973); J. Gwenogvryn Evans (ed.), *Reports on Manuscripts in the Welsh Language* (London, 1898-1910); T. Parry and M. Morgan (ed.), *Llyfryddiaeth Llenyddiaeth Gymraeg* (Cardiff, 1976) [and Appendix I]; *Mynegai i Farddoniaeth Gaeth y Llawysgrifau* (Board of Celtic Studies, 1978); J. E. Lloyd and R. T. Jenkins (ed.), *Dictionary of Welsh Biography down to 1940* (London, 1959) [and *Y Bywgraffiadur Cymreig 1941-1950* (London, 1970)]; *A Bibliography of the History of Wales* (Board of Celtic Studies, 1962) [and Supplements 1963, 1966 and 1969)]; P. H. Jones (ed.), *A Bibliography of the History of Wales* (Board of Celtic Studies, 1989); M. Stephens (ed.), *The Oxford Companion to the Literature of Wales* (Cardiff, 1986).

A. Sources

1. Manuscript Sources

NLW.

Brogyntyn MSS. 3, 8.
Cwrtmawr MSS. 12; 27; 204.
Llansteffan MSS. 35; 122; 123; 124; 125.
Mostyn MSS. 96; 145.
NLW MSS. 12731; 13062; 13066.
Peniarth MSS. 68; 69; 72; 96; 117; 124.
Wynn (of Gwydir) MSS. 9052E; 9053E; 9055E; 9059E.

UCNW

Mostyn MS. 8.

South Glamorgan County Library, Cardiff.

MS. 4. 101 (old reference MS. 83).
MS. 8.
MS. 19.

2. Printed Sources

B. Castiglione, *The Book of the Courtier*, ed. J. H. Whitfield (London, 1975)
A. Conran (trans.), *The Penguin Book of Welsh Verse* (London, 1967)
D. J. Bowen, *Gwaith Gruffudd Hiraethog* (Cardiff, 1990)
R. A. Charles, *'Gwaith Edwart ap Raff'* (typed copy NLW 1970)
C. Davies (ed.), *Rhagymadroddion a Chyflwyniadau Lladin, 1551-1632* (Cardiff, 1980)
I. ab O. Edwards (ed.), *A Catalogue of Star Chamber Proceedings relating to Wales* (Cardiff, 1929)

J. Fisher (ed.), *The Cefn Coch MSS* (Bangor, 1899)
J. Kyrle Fletcher (ed.), *The Gwentian Poems of Dafydd Benwyn* (Cardiff, 1909)
W. Harrison, *The Description of England,* ed. G. Ebelen (New York, 1968)
L. J. Hopkin-James and T. C. Evans (ed.), *Hen Gwndidau, Carolau a Chywyddau* (Bangor, 1910)
G. H. Hughes (ed.), *Rhagymadroddion, 1546-1659* (Cardiff, 1951)
J. Jones (ed.), *Cynfeirdd Lleyn, 1500-1800* (Pwllheli, 1905)
T. Jones (ed.), *Rhyddiaith Gymraeg,* II, *Llawysgrifau a Llyfrau 1547-1618* (Cardiff 1956)
T. Gwynn Jones (ed.), *Gwaith Tudur Aled,* 2 vols. (Cardiff, 1926)
T. I. Jeffreys Jones (ed.), *Exchequer Proceedings concerning Wales in Tempore James I* (Cardiff, 1955)
J. Leland, *The Itinerary in Wales,* ed. L. Toulmin Smith (London, 1906)
J. C. Morrice (ed.), *Barddoniaeth Wiliam Llŷn* (Bangor, 1908)
Thomas Parry (ed.), *The Oxford Book of Welsh Verse* (Oxford, 1962)
C. Read (ed.), *William Lambarde and Local Government* (New York, 1962)
E. Roberts (ed.), *Gwaith Siôn Tudur,* 2 vols. (Bangor, 1976)
T. R. Roberts (ed.), *Edmwnd Prys: Archddiacon Meirionydd* (Caernarfon, 1899)
E. I. Rowlands (ed.), *Gwaith Lewys Môn* (Cardiff, 1975)
E. I. Rowlands (ed,), *Gwaith Iorwerth Fynglwyd* (Cardiff, 1975)
T. Smith, *De Republica Anglorum* (Menston, 1970)
W. J. Smith (ed.), *Calendar of Salusbury Correspondence, 1553—c.1700* (Cardiff, 1954)
G. Aled Williams (ed.), *Ymryson Edmwnd Prys a Wiliam Cynwal* (Cardiff, 1986)
G. J. Williams and E. J. Jones (ed.), *Gramadegau'r Penceirddiaid* (Cardiff, 1934)
I. Williams and J. Ll. Williams (ed.), *Gwaith Guto'r Glyn* (Cardiff, 1939)
O. Gaianydd Williams, *Casgliad o Gywyddau Siôn Brwynog* (UCNW Gaianydd MS. 21)

3. Unpublished Dissertations

D. J. Bowen, 'Y Gymdeithas Gymreig yn Niwedd yr Oesoedd Canol fel yr adlewyrchir hi yn y Farddoniaeth Uchelwrol' (M.A. Wales, 1952)
R. A. Charles, 'Noddwyr y Beirdd yn Sir y Fflint' (M.A. Wales, 1967)
E. R. Ll. Davies, 'Noddwyr y Beirdd yn Sir Gaerfyrddin' (M.A. Wales, 1977)
J. D. Davies, 'Astudiaeth Destunol o Waith Siôn Mawddwy' (M.A. Wales, 1965)
E. E. Edwards, 'Noddwyr y Beirdd yn Siroedd Morgannwg a Mynwy' (M.A. Wales, 1970)
A. Griffiths, 'Rhai Agweddau ar y Syniad o Genedl yng Nghyfnod y Cywyddwyr, 1320-1603' (Ph.D. Wales, 1988)
A. Ll. Hughes, 'Noddwyr y Beirdd yn Sir Feirionnydd: Casgliad o'r Cerddi i Deuluoedd Corsygedol, Dolau-gwyn, Llwyn, Nannau, Y Rug, Rhiwedog, Rhiw-goch, Rhiwlas ac Ynysymaengwyn' (M.A. Wales, 1969)
D. L. James, 'Bywyd a Gwaith Huw Machno' (M.A. Wales, 1960)
D. A. Jones, 'Gwaith Wiliam Llŷn' (M.A. Wales, 1975)
G. P. Jones, 'Astudiaeth Destunol o Ganu Wiliam Cynwal yn Llawysgrif (Bangor) Mostyn 4' (M.A. Wales, 1969)
J. Gwilym Jones, 'Teulu Gwedir fel Noddwyr Beirdd' (M.A. Wales, 1975)
R. L. Jones, 'Astudiaeth Destunol o Awdlau, Cywyddau ac Englynion gan Wiliam Cynwal' (M.A. Wales, 1969)
R. Ll. P. Jones, 'Arolwg ar y Farddoniaeth Nawdd yn Sir Fôn' (M.A. Wales, 1975)
T. T. Jones, 'Testun Beirniadol o Farddoniaeth Edward Urien a Gruffudd Hafren gyda Rhagymadrodd, Nodiadau a Geirfa' (M.A. Wales, 1966)
R. M. Kerr, 'Cywyddau Siôn Brwynog' (M.A. Wales, 1960)
T. Llwyd, 'Noddwyr Beirdd yn Siroedd Brycheiniog a Maesyfed' (M.A. Wales, 1988)
R. W. McDonald, 'Bywyd a Gwaith Lewis ab Edward' (M.A. Liverpool, 1961)
O. Owens, 'Gweithiau Barddonol Morus Dwyfech' (M.A. Wales, 1944)

M. Phillips, 'Noddwyr y Beirdd yn Llŷn' (M.A. Wales, 1973)
T. O. Phillips, 'Bywyd a Gwaith Meurig Dafydd (Llanisien) a Llywelyn Siôn (Llangewydd)' (M.A. Wales, 1937)
D. H. E. Roberts, 'Noddwyr y Beirdd yn Sir Aberteifi' (M.A. Wales, 1969)
J. W. Roberts, 'Edmwnd Prys: ei Fywyd a Chasgliad o'i Weithiau' (M.A. Wales, 1938)
R. L. Roberts, 'Noddwyr y Beirdd yn Sir Drefaldwyn' (M.A. Wales, 1980)
J. Rowlands, 'A Critical Edition and Study of the Welsh Poems written in Praise of the Salusburies of Lleweni' (D. Phil. Oxford, 1967-68)
W. Rowlands, 'Barddoniaeth Tomos Prys o Blas Iolyn' (M.A. Wales, 1912).
J. Rhys, 'Bywyd a Gwaith Edward Dafydd o Fargam a Dafydd o'r Nant, a Hanes Dirywiad y Gyfundrefn Farddol ym Morgannwg' (M.A. Wales, 1953)
D. R. Saer, 'Testun Beirniadol o Waith Owain Gwynedd ynghyd â Rhagymadrodd, Nodiadau a Geirfa' (M.A. Wales, 1961)
E. J. Saunders, 'Gweithiau Lewys Morgannwg' (M.A. Wales, 1922)
R. Stephens, 'Gwaith Wiliam Llŷn' (Ph.D. Wales, 1983)
G. Thomas, 'A Study of the Changes in the Tradition of Welsh Poetry in North Wales in the Seventeenth Century' (D. Phil., Oxford, 1964-65)
D. W. Wiliam, 'Y Traddodiad Barddol ym Modedern, Môn, hyd at 1900' (M.A. Wales, 1970).
I. Ll. Williams, 'Noddwyr y Beirdd yn Sir Gaernarfon' (M.A. Wales, 1987)
I. W. Williams, 'Testun Beirniadol ac Astudiaeth o Gerddi Wiliam Llŷn yn Llaw'r Bardd ei hun' (M.A. Wales, 1957)
S. Rh. Williams, 'Testun Beirniadol o Gasgliad Llawysgrif Mostyn III o Waith Wiliam Cynwal ynghyd â Rhagymadrodd, Nodiadau a Geirfa' (M.A. Wales, 1965)

B. Secondary Sources

1. Volumes

E. Barker, *Principles of Social and Political Theory* (Oxford, 1962)
D. J. Bowen, *Gruffudd Hiraethog a'i Oes* (Cardiff, 1958)
F. Caspari, *Humanism in the Social Order in Tudor England* (Chicago, 1954)
K. Charlton, *Education in Renaissance England* (London, 1965)
C. Davies, *Latin Writers of the Renaissance* (Cardiff, 1981)
G. Davies, *Noddwyr Beirdd ym Meirion* (Dolgellau, 1974)
R. R. Davies, *Lordship and Society in the March of Wales, 1282-1400* (Oxford, 1978)
R. R. Davies, *Conquest, Coexistence and Change: Wales 1063-1415* (Oxford/Cardiff, 1987)
G. R. Elton, *England under the Tudors* (London, 1955)
W. H. Greenleaf, *Order, Empiricism and Politics, 1500-1700* (Oxford, 1964)
J. Huizinga, *The Waning of the Middle Ages* (London, 1955)
A. O. H. Jarman and G. R. Hughes (ed.), *A Guide to Welsh Literature, II* (Swansea, 1979)
D. Jenkins, *Cyfraith Hywel* (Llandysul, 1976)
G. H. Jenkins, *Hanes Cymru yn y Cyfnod Modern Cynnar, 1530-1760* (Cardiff, 1983)
G. E. Jones, *The Gentry and the Elizabethan State* (Swansea, 1977)
J. G. Jones, *Wales and the Tudor State, 1534-1603* (Cardiff, 1989)
J. G. Jones (ed.), *Class, Community and Culture in Tudor Wales* (Cardiff, 1989)
J. G. Jones, *Patrymau Diwylliant a Moes yn Nheulu'r Wyniaid o Wedir* (Gwasanaeth Llyfrgell Gwynedd, 1989)
R. M. Jones, *Llên Cymru a Chrefydd: Diben y Llenor* (Swansea, 1977)
R. Kelso, *Doctrine for the Lady of the Renaissance* (Illinois, 1956)
R. Kelso, *The Doctrine of the English Gentleman in the Sixteenth Century* (Massachusetts, 1964)

J. R. Lander, *English Justices of the Peace, 1461-1509* (Gloucester, 1989)
P. Laslett, *The World we have Lost* (London 1971)
S. Lewis, *Braslun o Hanes Llenyddiaeth Gymraeg hyd at 1535* (Caerdydd, 1935)
S. Lewis, *Gramadegau'r Penceirddiaid* (Cardiff, 1967)
S. Lewis, *Meistri'r Canrifoedd,* ed. R. G. Gruffydd (Cardiff, 1973)
H. A. Lloyd, *The Gentry of South-West Wales 1540-1640* (Cardiff, 1968)
A. O. Lovejoy, *The Great Chain of Being* (Massachusetts, 1936)
J. E. Mason, *Gentlefolk in the Making* (Philadelphia, 1935)
J. A. Mazzeo, *Renaissance and Revolution: the Remaking of European Thought* (London, 1967)
G. D. Owen, *Wales in the Reign of James I* (London, 1988)
T. Parry, *Hanes Llenyddiaeth Gymraeg hyd 1900* (Cardiff, 1953)
[Trans. by H. I. Bell, *A History of Welsh Literature* (Oxford, 1959)]
T. Jones Pierce, *Medieval Welsh Society,* ed. J. B. Smith (Cardiff, 1972)
E. Roberts, *Braslun o Hanes Llên Powys* (Denbigh, 1965)
E. Roberts, *Bwyd y Beirdd 1400-1600* (Bangor, 1976)
E. Roberts, *Y Beirdd a'u Noddwyr ym Maelor* (Wrexham, 1977)
G. Roberts, *Aspects of Welsh History,* ed. J. G. Williams (Cardiff, 1969)
A. L. Rowse, *The Elizabethan Renaissance: the Life of the Society* (London, 1971)
J. Samaha, *Law and Order in Historical Perspective* (London, 1974)
J. Schochet, *Patriarchalism in Political Thought* (Oxford, 1975)
J. Simon, *Education and Society in Tudor England* (Cambridge, 1967)
R. Stephens, *Gwynedd, 1528-1547; Economy and Society in Tudor Wales* (Ann Arbor, Michigan, 1979)
L. Stone, *The Crisis of the Aristocracy, 1558-1641* (Oxford, 1965)
L. Stone and J. C. Fawtier Stone, *An Open Elite? England 1540-1880* (Oxford, 1986)
J. Thirsk (ed.), *The Agrarian History of England and Wales: IV 1500-1640* (Cambridge, 1967)
G. Thomas, *Eisteddfodau Caerwys* (Cardiff, 1967)
G. Thomas, *Y Traddodiad Barddol* (Cardiff, 1976)
E. M. W. Tillyard, *The Elizabethan World Picture* (London, 1960)
A. R. Wagner, *English Genealogy* (Oxford, 1960)
G. Williams, *The Welsh Church from Conquest to Reformation* (Cardiff, 1962)
G. Williams, *Dadeni, Diwygiad a Diwylliant Cymru* (Cardiff, 1964)
G. Williams, *Welsh Reformation Essays* (Cardiff, 1967)
G. Williams (ed.), *Glamorgan County History: Early Modern Glamorgan,* IV (Cardiff, 1974)
G. Williams, *Religion, Language and Nationality in Wales* (Cardiff, 1979)
G. Williams, *Grym Tafodau Tân: Ysgrifau Hanesyddol ar Grefydd a Diwylliant* (Llandysul, 1984)
G. Williams, *Recovery, Reorientation and Reformation: Wales c. 1415-1642* (Oxford/Cardiff, 1987)
G. Williams and R. O. Jones (ed.), *The Celts and the Renaissance: Tradition and Innovation* (Cardiff, 1990)
G. Aled Williams, *Dyffryn Conwy a'r Dadeni* (Llanrwst, 1989)
G. J. Williams, *Traddodiad Llenyddol Morgannwg* (Cardiff, 1948)
G. J. Williams, *Agweddau ar Hanes Dysg Gymraeg,* ed. A. Lewis (Cardiff, 1969)
J. E. Caerwyn Williams, *Geiriadurwyr y Gymraeg yng Nghyfnod y Dadeni* (Cardiff, 1983).
P. Williams, *The Council in the Marches of Wales under Elizabeth I* (Cardiff, 1958)
W. O. Williams (ed.), *Calendar of the Caernarvonshire Quarter Sessions Records: I, 1541-1558* (Caernarfon, 1956) [also *Tudor Gwynedd* (Caernarfon, 1958)]
W. G. Zeeveld, *Foundations of Tudor Policy* (Massachusetts, 1948)

2. Articles

D. J. Bowen, 'Gruffudd Hiraethog ac Argyfwng Cerdd Dafod', LlC, II, 1952-53
D. J. Bowen, 'Ail Eisteddfod Caerwys a Chais 1594', LlC, III, 1954-55
D. J. Bowen, 'Agweddau ar Ganu'r Unfed Ganrif ar Bymtheg' *Trans. Cymmr.*, 1969 (Pt. ii)
D. J. Bowen, 'Rhai o'r Beirdd a Ganai rhwng Dwy Eisteddfod Caerwys', BBCS, XXIV, 1970
D. J. Bowen, 'Cywyddau Gruffudd Hiraethog i Dri o Awduron y Dadeni', *Trans. Cymmr.*, 1974-5
D. J. Bowen, 'Canu Gruffudd Hiraethog i Degeingl', BBCS, XXVI, 1975
D. J. Bowen, 'Awdl Ddychan gan Ruffudd Hiraethog', BBCS, XXVI, 1976
D. J. Bowen, 'Y Cywyddau a fu rhwng Gruffudd Hiraethog a Beirdd Eraill', BBCS, XXVII, 1977
D. J. Bowen, 'Y Cywyddwyr a'r Noddwyr Cynnar', in J. E. Caerwyn Williams (ed.), *Ysgrifau Beirniadol*, XI (Denbigh, 1979)
D. J. Bowen, 'Y Cywyddwyr a'r Dirywiad', BBCS, XXIX, 1981
D. J. Bowen, 'Canrif Olaf y Cywyddwyr', LlC, XIV, 1981-82
A. D. Carr, 'An Aristocracy in Decline: the Native Welsh Lords after the Edwardian Conquest', WHR, V, 1970
R. A. Charles, 'Teulu Mostyn fel Noddwyr y Beirdd', LlC, IX, 1966-67
R. A. Charles, 'Noddwyr y Beirdd yn Sir y Fflint', LlC, XII, 1972-73
C. Davies, 'Erasmus and Welsh Renaissance Learning', *Trans. Cymmr.,* 1983
D. Davies, 'Siôn Mawddwy', LlC, VIII, 1964-65
E. R. Ll. Davies and E. E. Edwards, 'Teulu Ifor Hael a'r Traddodiad Mawl', in *Ysgrifau Beirniadol,* XII, 1982
R. R. Davies, 'Owain Glyndŵr and the Welsh Squirearchy', *Trans. Cymmr.,* 1968 (Pt. ii)
W. Ll. Davies, 'Phylipiaid Ardudwy—a Survey and a Summary', *Y Cymmrodor*, XLII, 1931
E. E. Edwards, 'Cartrefi Noddwyr y Beirdd yn Siroedd Morgannwg a Mynwy', LlC, XIII, 1974-81
E. J. Evans, 'Noddwyr y Beirdd yn Sir Benfro', *Trans. Cymmr.,* 1972-73
F. J. Fisher, 'The Development of London as a Centre of Conspicuous Consumption in the Sixteenth and Seventeenth Centuries', *Transactions of the Royal Historical Society,* XXX, 1948
C. Fychan, 'Y Canu i Wŷr Eglwysig Gorllewin Sir Ddinbych', *Transactions of the Denbighshire Historical Society,* XXVIII, 1979
W. P. Griffith, 'Beth oedd y Dyn Tuduraidd?', in D. G. Jones and J. E. Jones (ed.), *Bosworth a'r Tuduriaid* (Caernarfon 1985)
W. P. Griffith, 'Anglicaniaid a Phiwritaniaid: Myfyrwyr a Diwinyddion Prifysgolion Lloegr, 1560-1640', LlC, XVI, 1989
R. G. Gruffydd, 'Humphrey Llwyd: dyneiddiwr', *Efrydiau Athronyddol,* XXXIII, 1970
R. G. Gruffydd, 'The Life of Dr. John Davies of Brecon (Siôn Dafydd Rhys)', *Trans. Cymmr.*, 1971
R. Gwyndaf, 'Sir Richard Clough of Denbigh c. 1530-1570', ibid., XIX, 1970; XX, 1971
R. Gwyndaf, 'References in Welsh Poetry to 16th and 17th Century Houses in North-East Wales', ibid., XXII, 1973
G. Harries, 'Ail Eisteddfod Caerwys', LlC, III, 1954-55
A. Ll. Hughes, 'Rhai o Noddwyr y Beirdd yn Sir Feirionnydd', LlC, X, 1968-69
G. H. Hughes 'Ffasiynau'r Dadeni', in *Ysgrifau Beirniadol*, V (Denbigh, 1970)
B. Jarvis, 'Llythyr Siôn Dafydd Rhys at y Beirdd', LlC, XII, 1972-3
B. Jones, 'Beirdd yr Uchelwyr a'r Byd: Wiliam Llŷn ac Awdurdod Dinesig', in *Ysgrifau Beirniadol,* VIII, (Denbigh, 1974)
E. D. Jones, 'The Brogyntyn Welsh Manuscripts', NLWJ, V, 1948, VI, 1949-50
F. Jones, 'An Approach to Welsh Genealogy', *Trans. Cymmr.,* 1948
Gwendraeth Jones, 'Siôn Conwy III a'i Waith', BBCS, XXII, 1966-8

G. E. Jones, 'Local Administration and Justice in Sixteenth-Century Glamorgan', *Morgannwg*, IX, 1965
G. E. Jones, 'A Case of Corruption', in S. Williams (ed.), *Glamorgan Historian,* V (Barry, 1968)
G. P. Jones and R. L. Jones, 'Wiliam Cynwal', LlC, XI, 1970-71
J. Gwilym Jones, 'Cyfnod Olaf y Beirdd yng Ngwedir (1627-74)', in *Ysgrifau Beirniadol*, XV (Denbigh 1988)
J. G. Jones, 'Awdurdod Cyfreithiol a Gweinyddol Lleol yng Ngogledd Cymru yn y Cyfnod 1540-1640 yn ôl Tystiolaeth y Beirdd', LlC, XII, 1972-73
J. G. Jones, 'Priodoleddau Bonheddig yn Nheulu'r Wynniaid o Wedir', *Trans. Cymmr.*, 1978
J. G. Jones, 'Y Bardd a'r Uchelwr, 1540-1640: Rhai Argraffiadau', *Taliesin,* XXXIX, 1979
J. G. Jones, 'The Welsh Poets and their Patrons c. 1550-1640', WHR, IX, 1979
J. G. Jones, 'Patrymau Bonheddig Uchelwrol yn Sir Ddinbych c. 1540-1640: Dehongliad y Beirdd', *Transactions of the Denbighshire Historical Society,* XXIX, 1980
J. G. Jones, 'Reflections on Concepts of Nobility in Glamorgan 1540-1640', *Morgannwg*, XXV, 1981
J. G. Jones, 'Rhai Agweddau ar y Consept o Uchelwriaeth yn Nheuluoedd Bonheddig Cymru yn yr Unfed a'r Ail Ganrif ar Bymtheg', in *Ysgrifau Beirniadol*, XII, (Denbigh, 1982)
J. G. Jones, 'Governance, Order and Stability in Caernarfonshire c. 1540-1640', *Transactions of the Caernarfonshire Historical Society*, XCIV, 1983
J. G. Jones, 'The Merioneth Gentry in the Social Order: Bardic Evidence c. 1540-1640', *Journal of the Merioneth Historical and Record Society,* IX (Pt. iii and iv), 1984
J. G. Jones, 'Hanfodion Undod Gwladwriaethol, Cyfraith a Threfn yng Nghymru Cyfnod y Tuduriaid: Tystiolaeth Beirdd yr Uchelwyr', LlC, XV. 1984-86
J. G. Jones, 'Cyfraith a Threfn yn Sir Gaernarfon c. 1600-1640: yr Uchelwyr a'r Byd Gweinyddol', *Transactions of the Caernarfonshire Historical Society*, XCVII, 1986
J. G. Jones, 'Beirdd yr Uchelwyr a'u Cymdeithas, 1540-1640', in G. H. Jenkins (ed.), *Cof Cenedl: Ysgrifau ar Hanes Cymru*, III (Llandysul, 1987)
J. G. Jones, 'Ymateb y Beirdd i'r Cyfnewidiadau Crefyddol c 1536-1640', LlC, XVI, 1989
R. L. Jones, 'Huw Pennant', LlC, XII, 1972-73
T. Jones, 'Edward Urien a Gruffudd Hafren', LlC, IX, 1966-67
C. W. Lewis, 'The Literary History of Glamorgan from 1550 to 1770', GCH, IV (Cardiff, 1974)
S. Lewis, 'The Essence of Welsh Poetry', *Wales*, VII (27), 1947
H. G. Owen,'Family Politics in Elizabethan Merionethshire', BBCS, XVIII, 1959.
F. G. Payne, 'Cwysau o Foliant Cyson', *Y Llenor*, XXVI, 1947
D. H. E. Roberts, 'Noddwyr y Beirdd yn Sir Aberteifi', LlC, X, 1968-69
D. H. E. Roberts and R. A. Charles, 'Raff ap Robert ac Edwart ap Raff', BBCS, XXIV, 1971
E. Roberts, 'Siôn Tudur', LlC, II, 1952-3
E. Roberts, 'Wiliam Cynwal', *Transactions of the Denbighshire Historical Society,* XII, 1963
E. Roberts, 'Teulu Plas Iolyn', ibid., XIII, 1964
E. Roberts, 'Cywydd Cymod Hwmffre ap Hywel ap Siencyn a'i Geraint', *Journal of the Merioneth Historical and Record Society,* IV, 1964
E. Roberts, 'Canu Wiliam Cynwal i Glerigwyr', *Transactions of the Denbighshire Historical Society*, XIV, 1965
E. Roberts, 'Ymrysonau y Salsbriaid 1593', ibid., XVII, 1968
E. Roberts, 'Siôn Tudur yn Llundain', ibid., XVIII, 1969
E. Roberts, 'Rhagor am Siôn Tudur yn Llundain', ibid., XIX, 1970
E. Roberts, 'Priodasau Catrin o Ferain', ibid., XX, 1970
E. Roberts, 'Uchelwyr y Beirdd', ibid., XXIV, 1975
P. R. Roberts, 'The Union with England and the Identity of 'Anglican' Wales', *Transactions of the Royal Historical Society,* XXII, 1972
P. R. Roberts, 'The Act of Union in Welsh History', *Trans. Cymmr.*, 1972-73
Rh. F. Roberts, 'Y Dr. John Davies o Fallwyd', LlC, II, 1952-53

W. R. B. Robinson, 'The Tudor Revolution in Welsh Government, 1536-1543: its Effects on Gentry Participation', *English Historical Review*, CCCCVI, 1988

G. E. Ruddock 'Siôn Cent', in A. O. H. Jarman and G. R. Hughes (ed.), *A Guide to Welsh Literature*, II (Swansea 1979)

D. R. Saer, 'Owain Gwynedd', LlC, VI, 1970-71

G. J. Schochet, 'Patriarchalism, Politics and Mass Attitudes in Stuart England', *The Historical Journal*, XII (iii), 1969

K. Sharpe, 'Crown, Parliament and Locality: Government and Communities in Early Stuart England', *English Historical Review*, CCCXCIX, 1986

W. J. Smith, 'The Salusburies as Maintainers of Murderers—a Chirk Castle View 1599', NLWJ, VII, 1951-2

J. Thirsk, 'Younger Sons in the Seventeenth Century', *History*, LIV, 1969

G. Thomas, 'Y Portread o Uchelwr ym Marddoniaeth Gaeth yr Ail Ganrif ar Bymtheg', in *Ysgrifau Beirniadol*, VIII, (Denbigh, 1974)

G. Thomas, 'Golwg ar Gyfundrefn y Beirdd yn yr Ail Ganrif ar Bymtheg', in *Bardos: Penodau ar y Traddodiad Barddol Cymreig a Cheltaidd*, ed. R. G. Gruffydd (Cardiff, 1982)

D. G. Williams, 'Syr Owain ap Gwilym', LlC, VI, 1960-61

E. N. Williams, 'Sir William Maurice of Clenennau', *Transactions of the Caernarfonshire Historical Society*, XXIV, 1963

G. Williams, 'Religion and Welsh Literature in the Age of the Reformation', *Proceedings of the British Academy*, LXIX, 1983

G. A. Williams, 'Twf Hanesyddol y Syniad o Genedl yng Nghymru', *Efrydiau Athronyddol*, XXIV, 1961

G. Aled Williams, 'Edmwnd Prys (1543/4-1623): Dyneiddiwr Protestannaidd', *Journal of the Merioneth Historical and Record Society*, VIII, 1977-80

G. Aled Williams, 'Golwg ar Ymryson Edmwnd Prys a Wiliam Cynwal', in *Ysgrifau Beirniadol*, VIII, 1974

G. Aled Williams, 'William Salesbury a 'Blaendorri'r Iâ' ', *Cof Cenedl IV*, 1989

J. E. Caerwyn Williams, 'Thomas Wiliems, Y Geiriadurwr', *Studia Celtica*, XVI—XVII, 1981

G. J. Williams, 'Traddodiad Llenyddol Dyffryn Clwyd a'r Cyffiniau', *Transactions of the Denbighshire Historical Society*, I, 1952

G. J. Williams, 'Llythyr Siôn Dafydd Rhys at y Beirdd', in T. Jones (ed.), *Rhyddiaith Gymraeg*, II (Cardiff, 1956)

I. M. Williams, 'Ysgolheictod Hanesyddol yr Unfed Ganrif ar Bymtheg', LlC, II, 1952-3

J. G. Williams, 'Rhai Agweddau ar y Gymdeithas Gymreig yn yr Ail Ganrif ar Bymtheg', *Efrydiau Athronyddol*, XXX, 1968

P. Williams, 'Controversy in Elizabethan Glamorgan: the Rebuilding of Cardiff Bridge', *Morgannwg*, II, 1958.

Rh. Williams 'Wiliam Cynwal', LlC, VIII, 1964-65

W. O. Williams, 'The Survival of the Welsh Language after the Union of England and Wales: the First Phase, 1536-1642', WHR, II, 1964

W. O. Williams, 'The Social Order in Tudor Wales', *Trans. Cymmr.*, 1967 (Pt. ii)

INDEX